ART Takeshi Obata

STORY Tsugumi Ohba

Platinum End

PLATINVM END

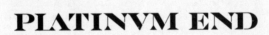

11

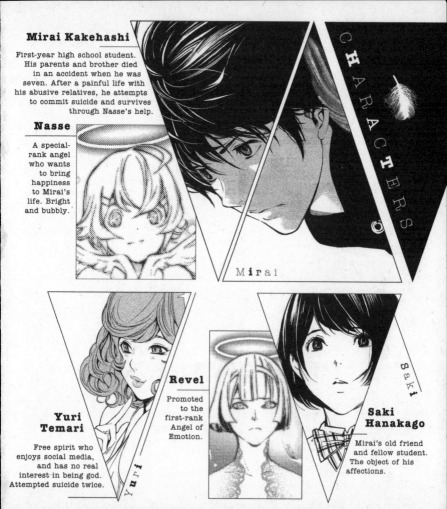

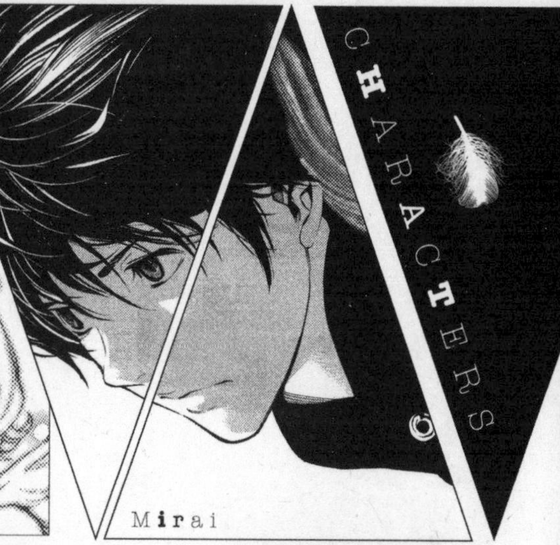
CHARACTERS
Mirai

Mirai Kakehashi

First-year high school student. His parents and brother died in an accident when he was seven. After a painful life with his abusive relatives, he attempts to commit suicide and survives through Nasse's help.

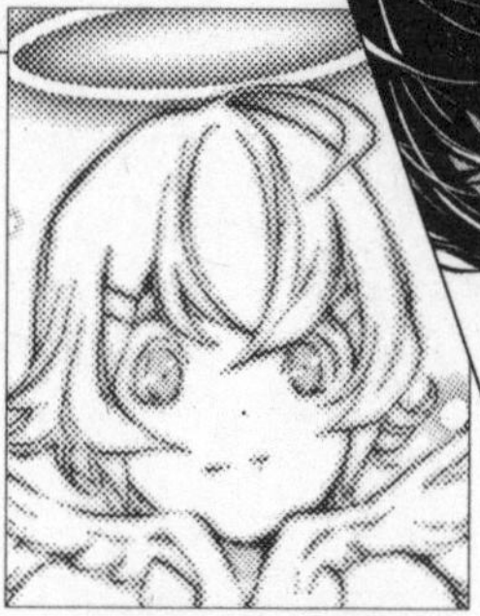

Nasse

A special-rank angel who wants to bring happiness to Mirai's life. Bright and bubbly.

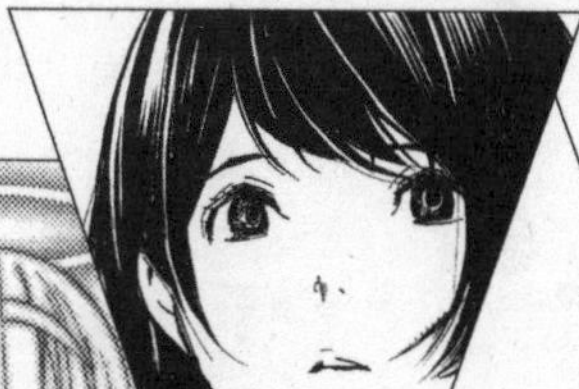
Saki

Saki Hanakago

Mirai's old friend and fellow student. The object of his affections.

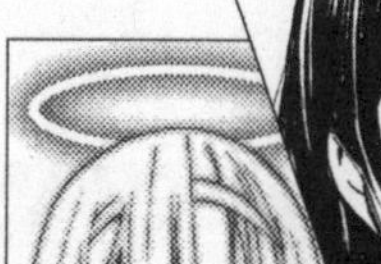

Revel

Promoted to the first-rank Angel of Emotion.

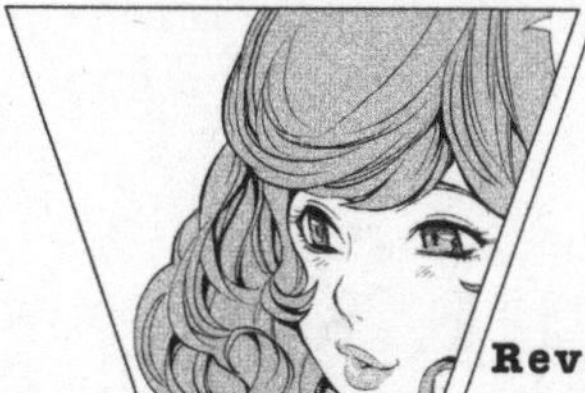
Yuri

Yuri Temari

Free spirit who enjoys social media, and has no real interest in being god. Attempted suicide twice.

Story

"My time has come. I leave the seat of god to the next human. To a younger, fresher power.

The next god shall be chosen from the 13 humans chosen by you 13 angels.When the chosen human is made the next god, your angelic duty is finished, and you may live beside that god in peace.

You have 999 days remaining..."

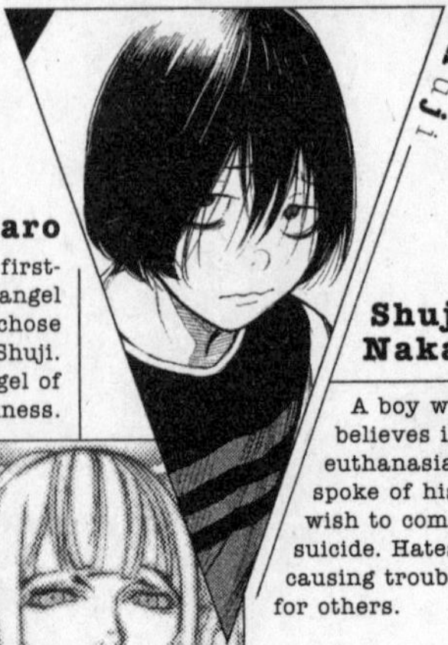
Shuji

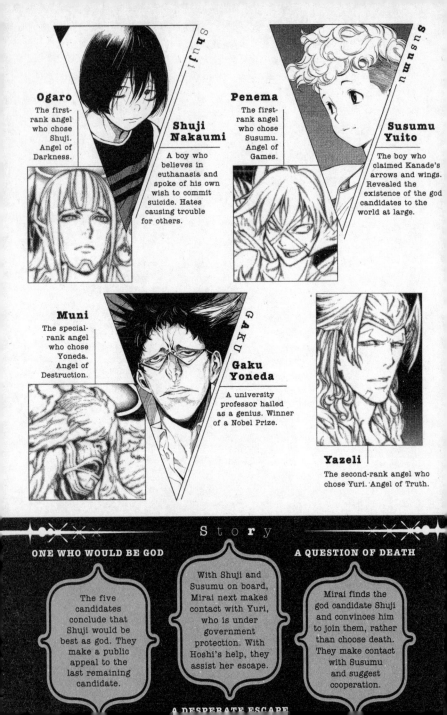

Ogaro

The first-rank angel who chose Shuji. Angel of Darkness.

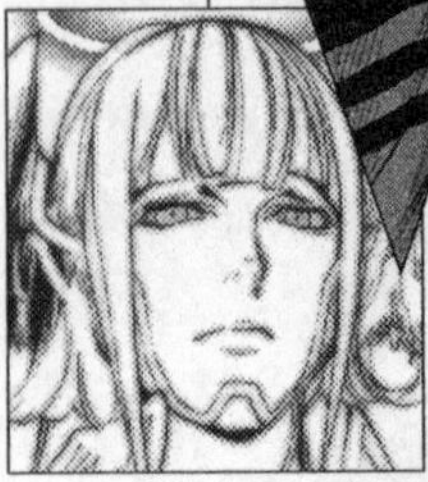

Shuji Nakaumi

A boy who believes in euthanasia and spoke of his own wish to commit suicide. Hates causing trouble for others.

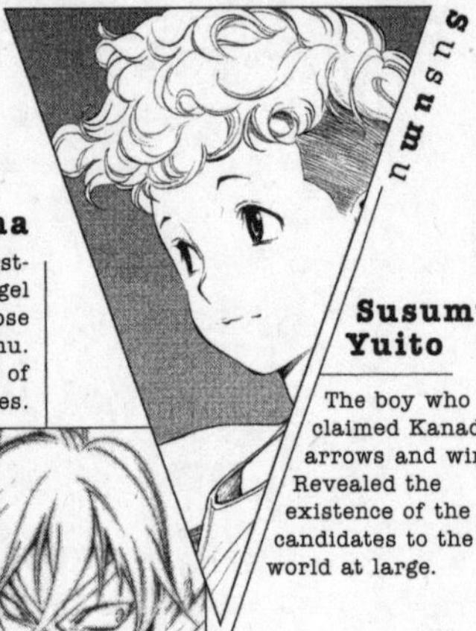
Susumu

Penema

The first-rank angel who chose Susumu. Angel of Games.

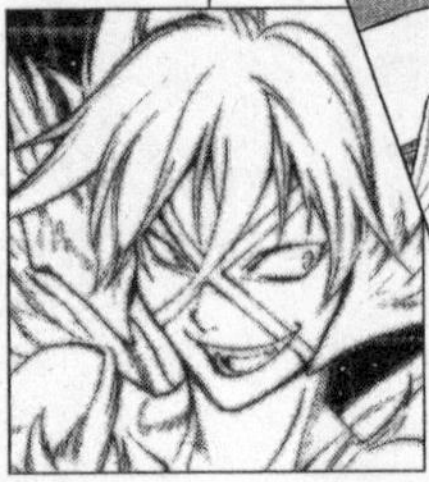

Susumu Yuito

The boy who claimed Kanade's arrows and wings. Revealed the existence of the god candidates to the world at large.

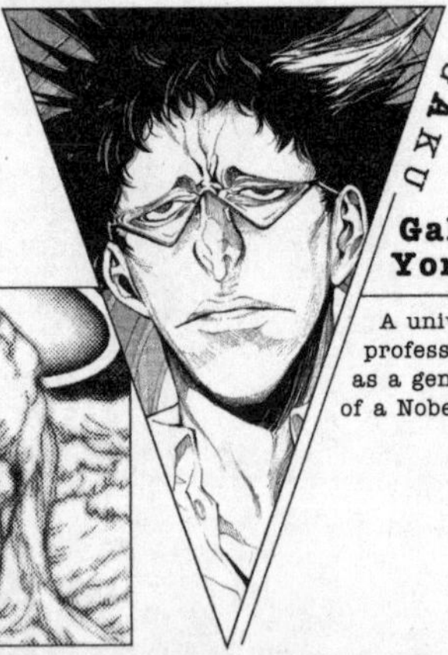
GAKU

Muni

The special-rank angel who chose Yoneda. Angel of Destruction.

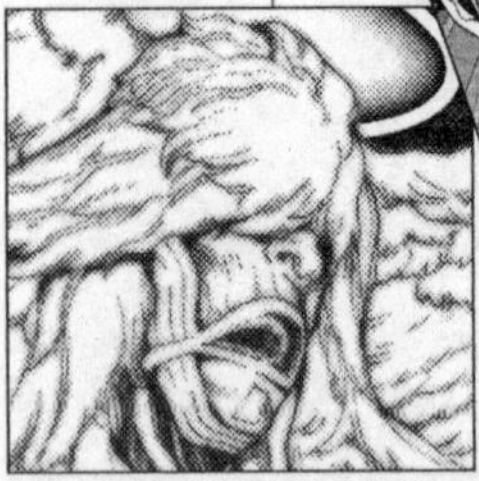

Gaku Yoneda

A university professor hailed as a genius. Winner of a Nobel Prize.

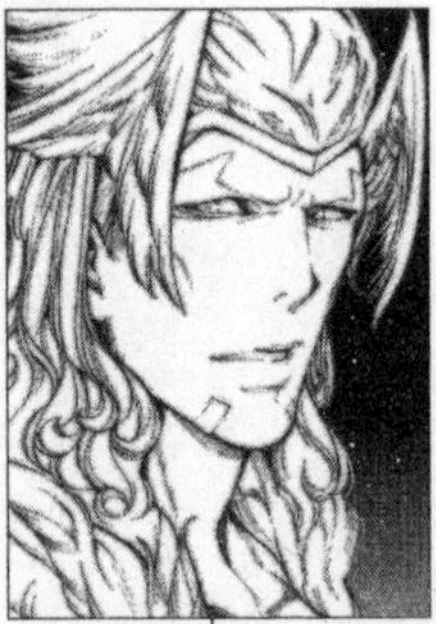

Yazeli

The second-rank angel who chose Yuri. Angel of Truth.

Story

A QUESTION OF DEATH

Mirai finds the god candidate Shuji and convinces him to join them, rather than choose death. They make contact with Susumu and suggest cooperation.

A DESPERATE ESCAPE

With Shuji and Susumu on board, Mirai next makes contact with Yuri, who is under government protection. With Hoshi's help, they assist her escape.

ONE WHO WOULD BE GOD

The five candidates conclude that Shuji would be best as god. They make a public appeal to the last remaining candidate.

CONTENTS

11

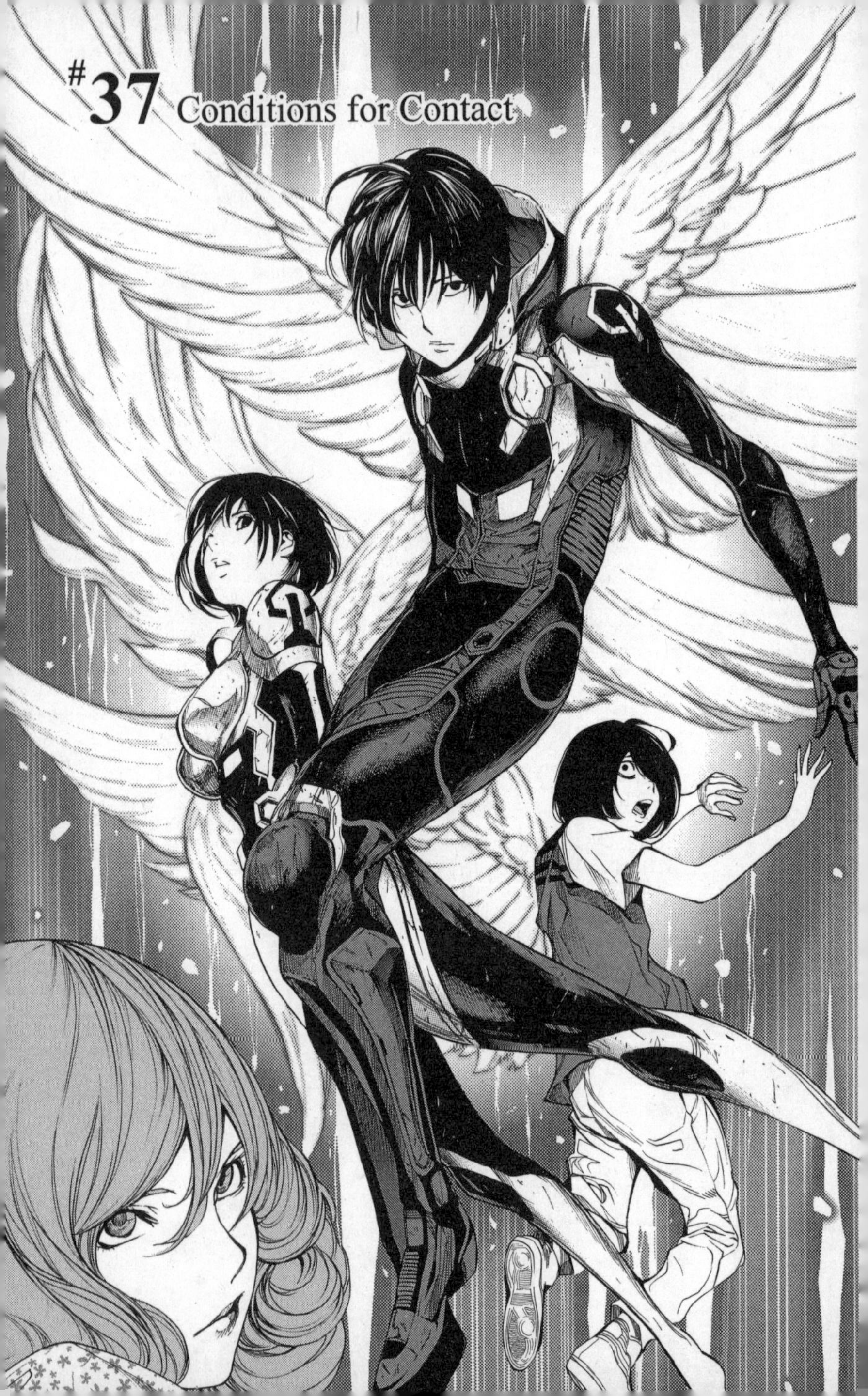
#37 Conditions for Contact

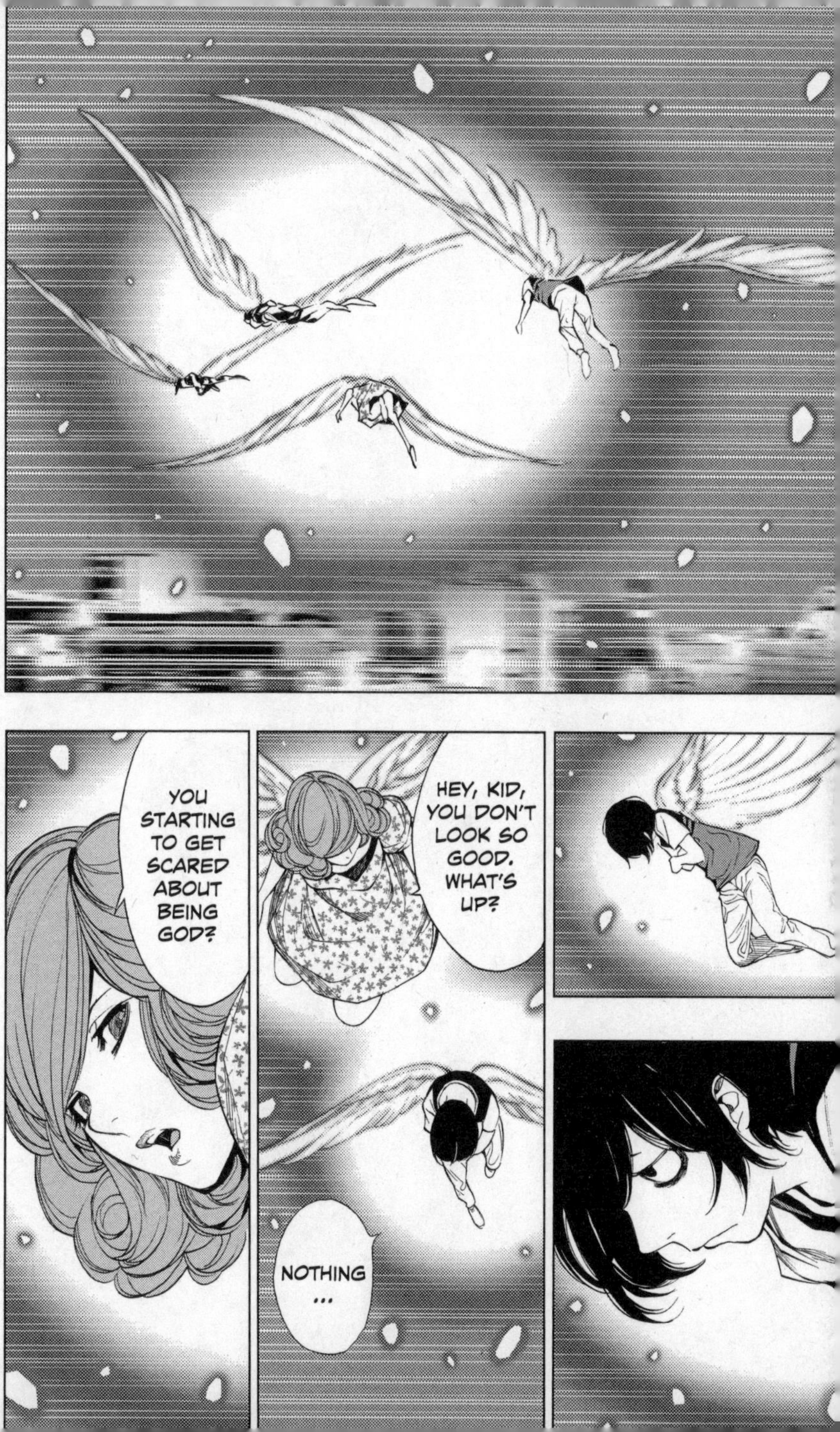
HEY, KID, YOU DON'T LOOK SO GOOD. WHAT'S UP?
NOTHING ...
YOU STARTING TO GET SCARED ABOUT BEING GOD?

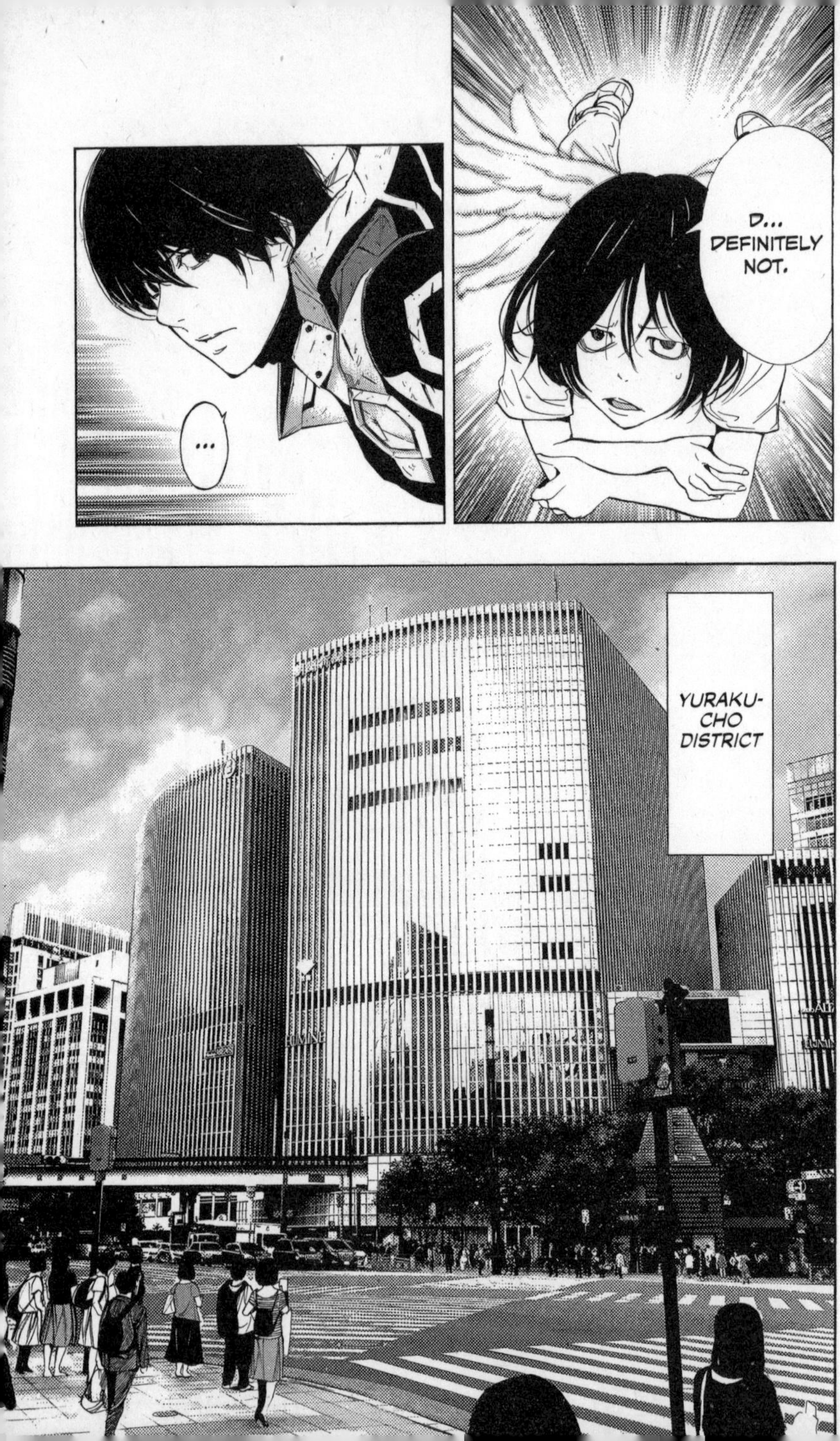
D... DEFINITELY NOT.
...
YURAKU-CHO DISTRICT

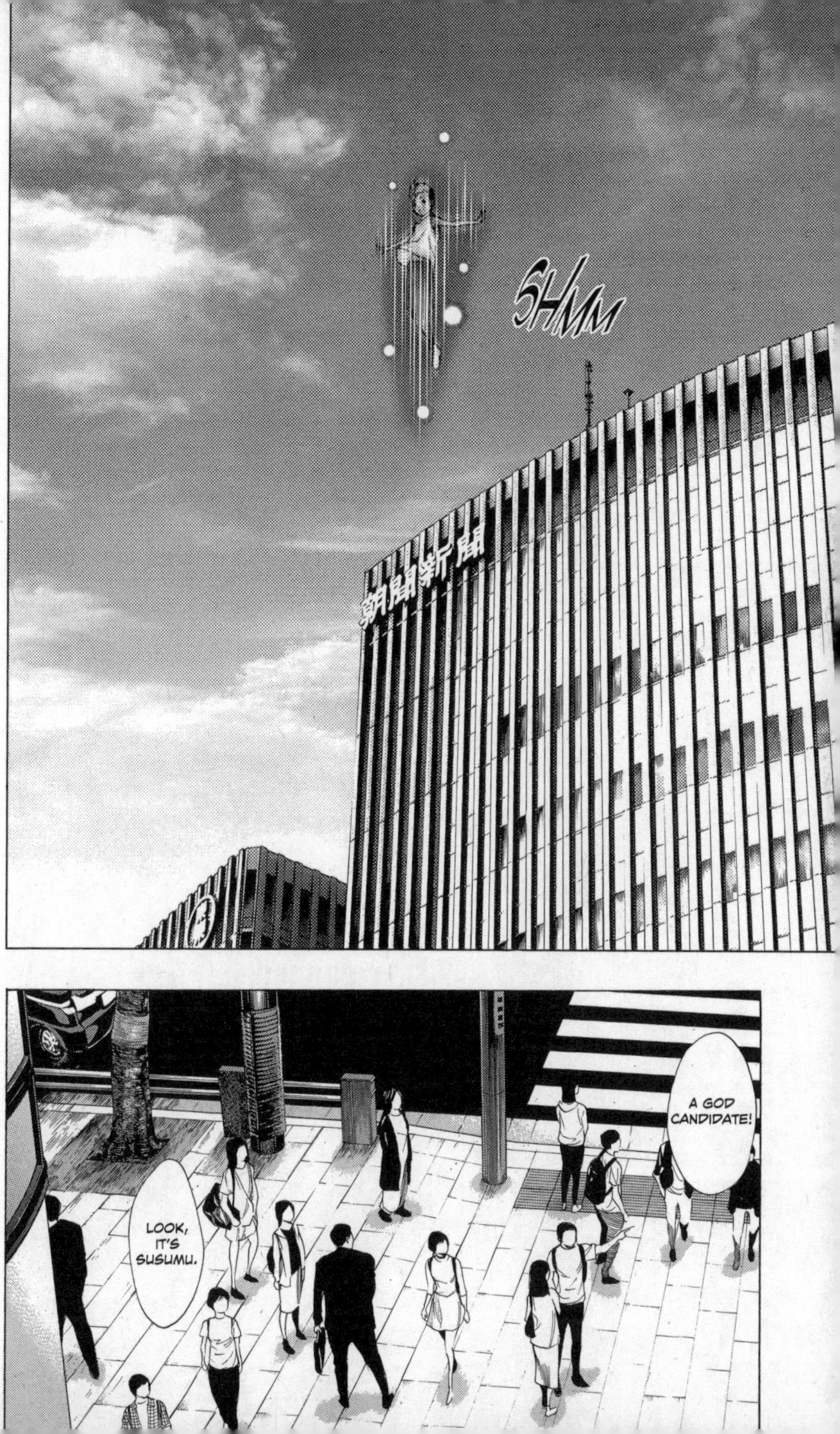
SHMM
A GOD CANDIDATE!
LOOK, IT'S SUSUMU.

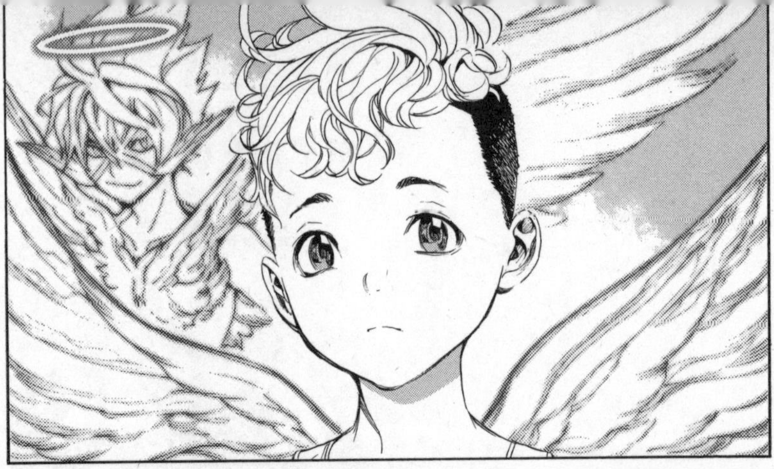

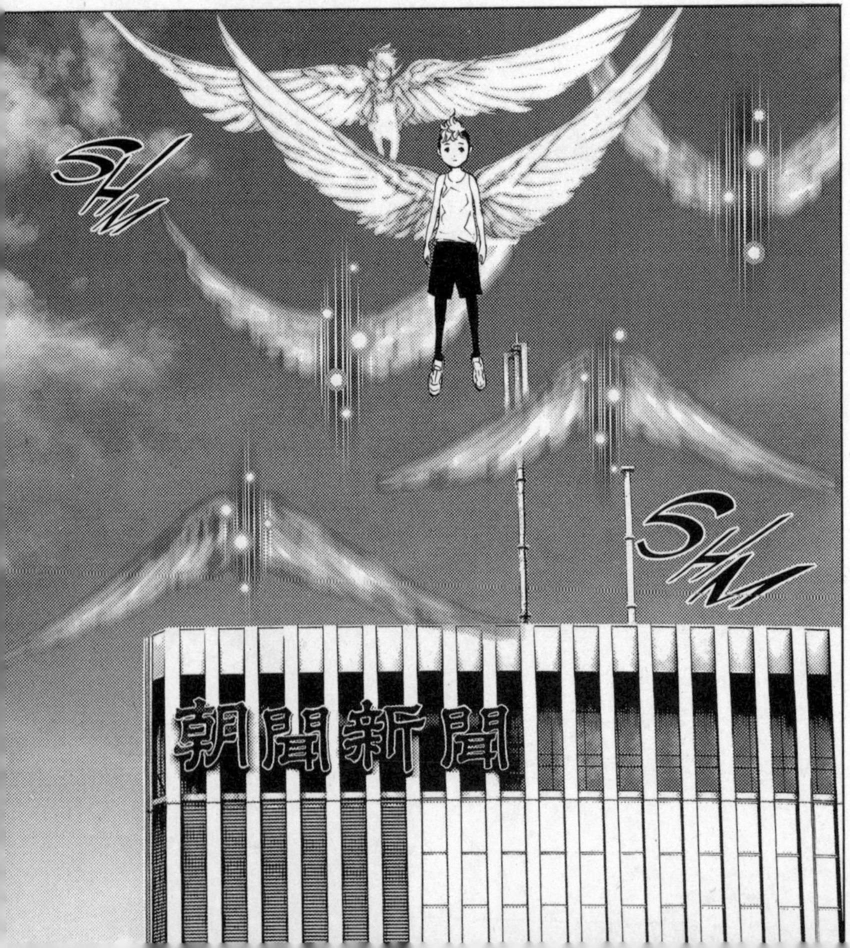
SHM
SHM
朝聞新聞

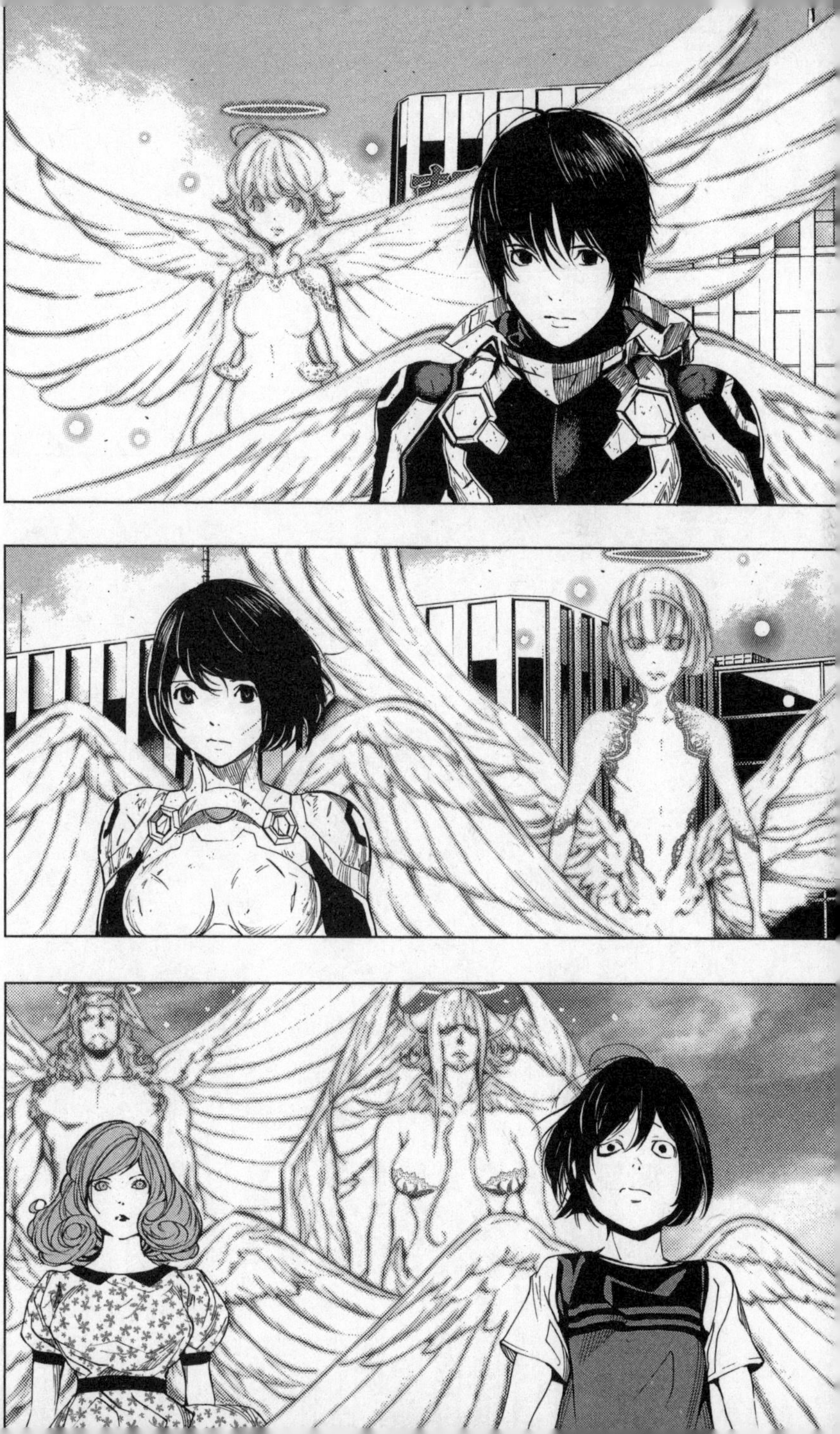

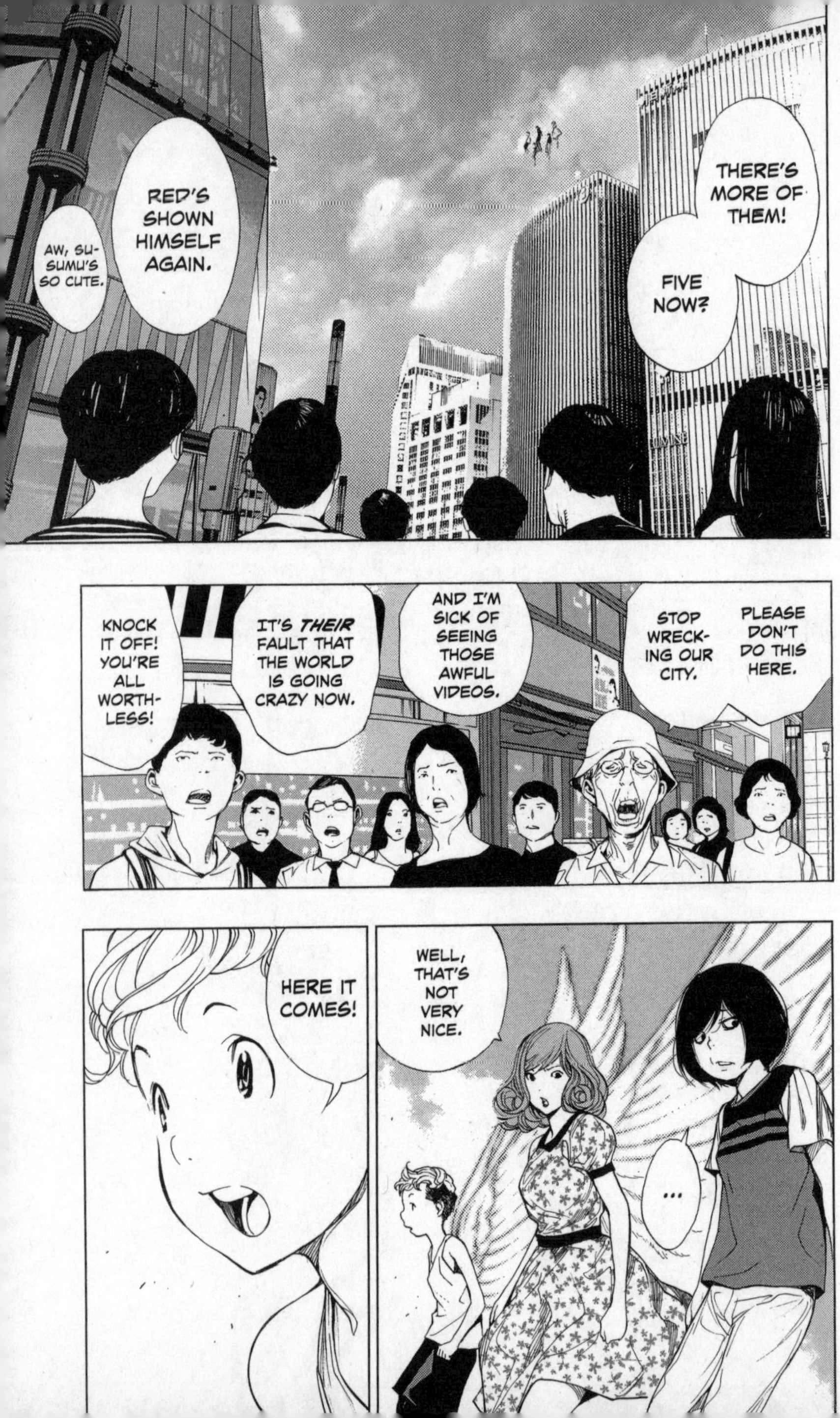
THERE'S MORE OF THEM!
FIVE NOW?
RED'S SHOWN HIMSELF AGAIN.
AW, SU-SUMU'S SO CUTE.
PLEASE DON'T DO THIS HERE.
STOP WRECK-ING OUR CITY.
AND I'M SICK OF SEEING THOSE AWFUL VIDEOS.
IT'S *THEIR* FAULT THAT THE WORLD IS GOING CRAZY NOW.
KNOCK IT OFF! YOU'RE ALL WORTH-LESS!
WELL, THAT'S NOT VERY NICE.
...
HERE IT COMES!

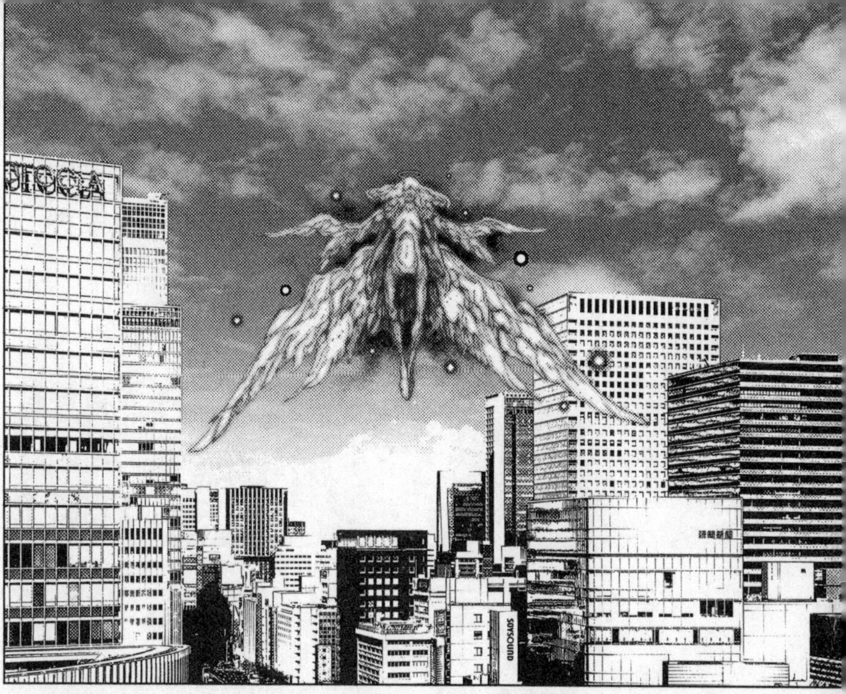

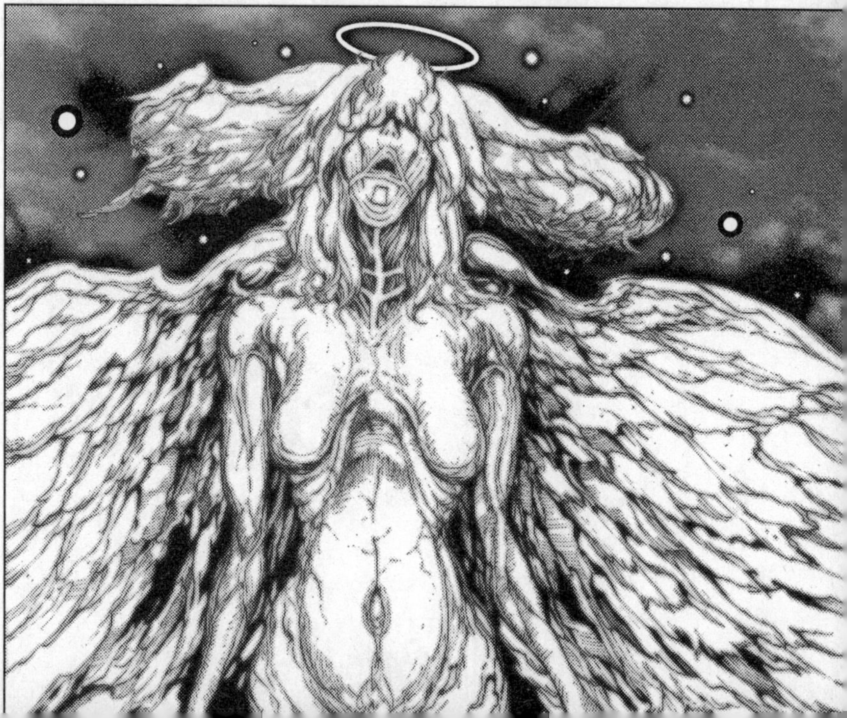

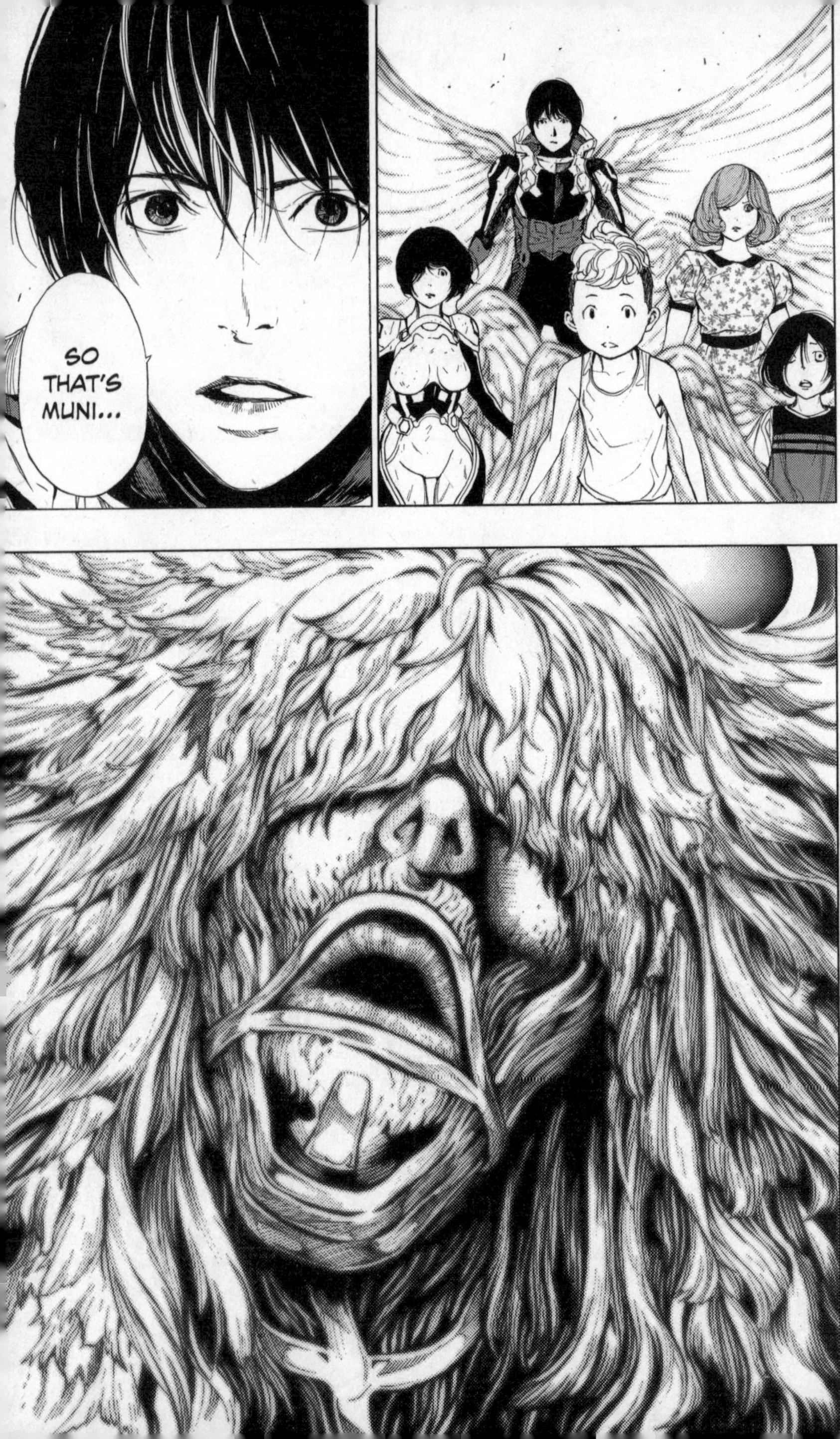
SO THAT'S MUNI...

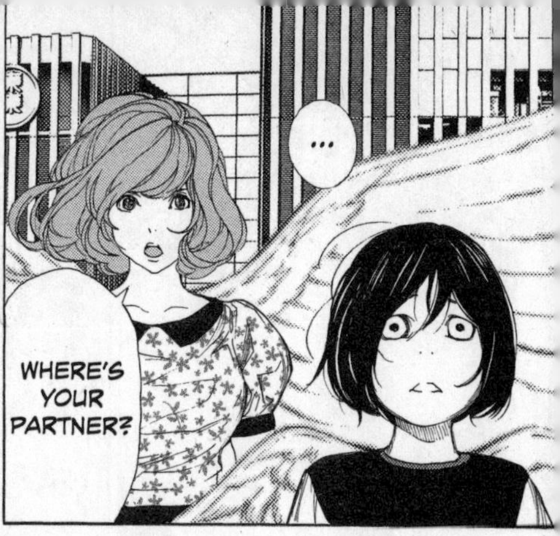
...
WHERE'S YOUR PARTNER?
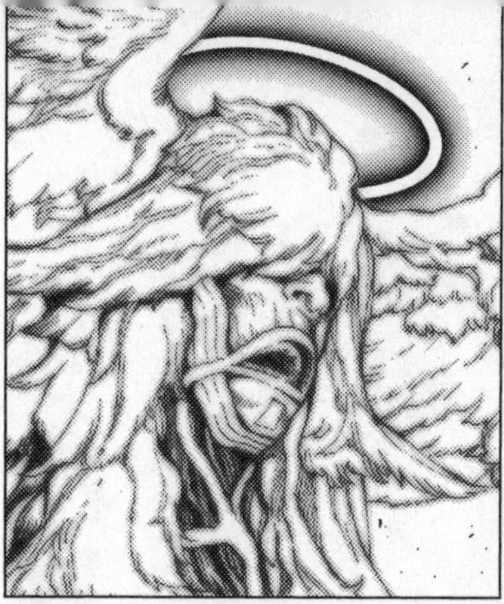
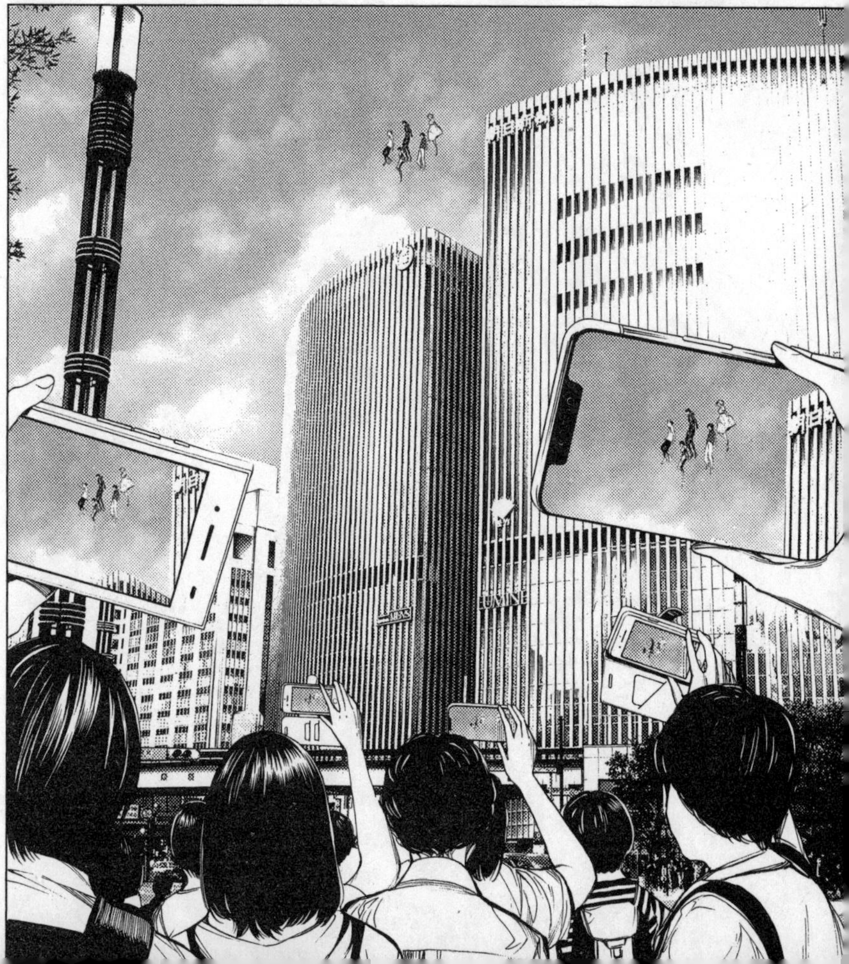

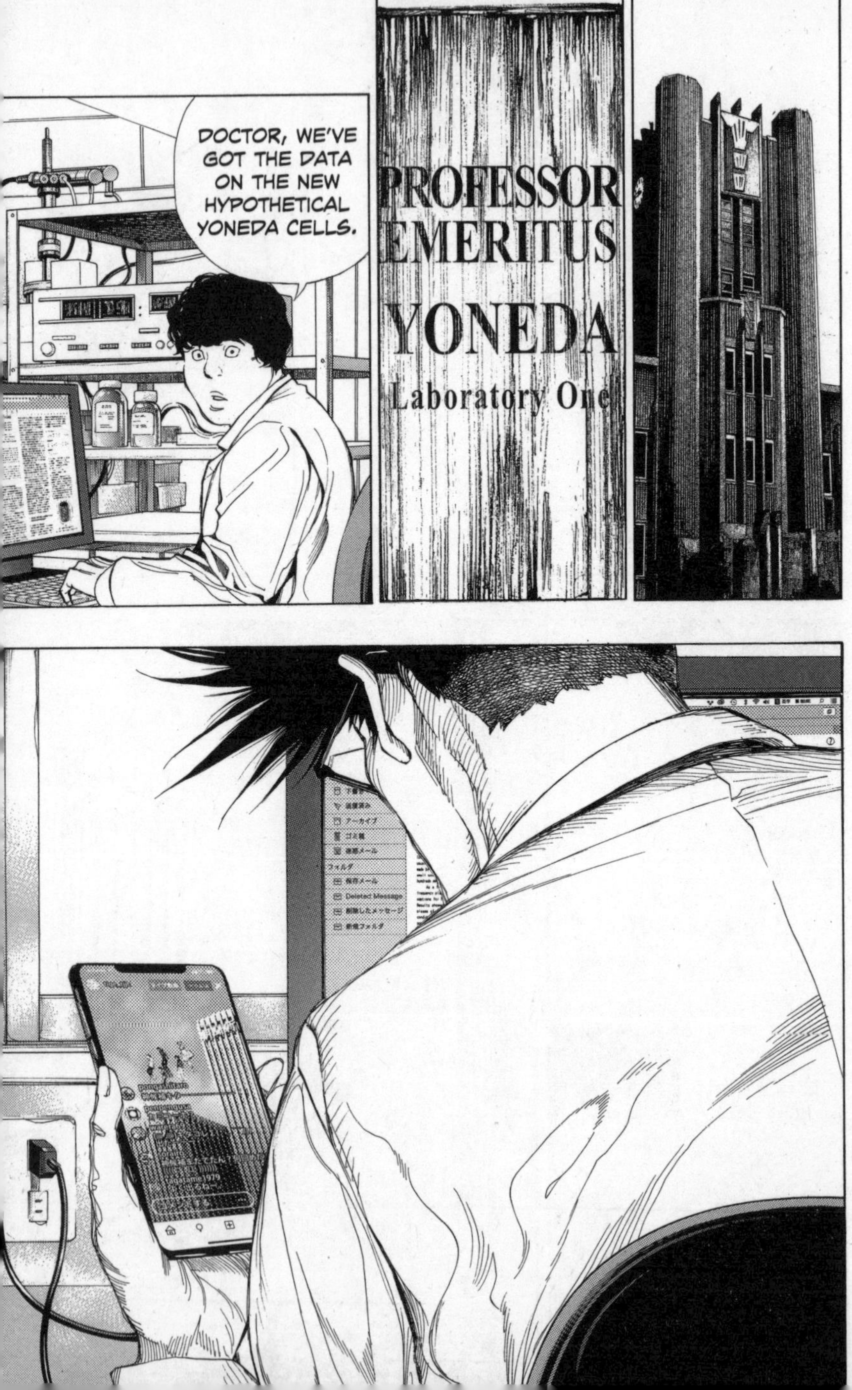
PROFESSOR EMERITUS YONEDA
Laboratory One
DOCTOR, WE'VE GOT THE DATA ON THE NEW HYPOTHETICAL YONEDA CELLS.

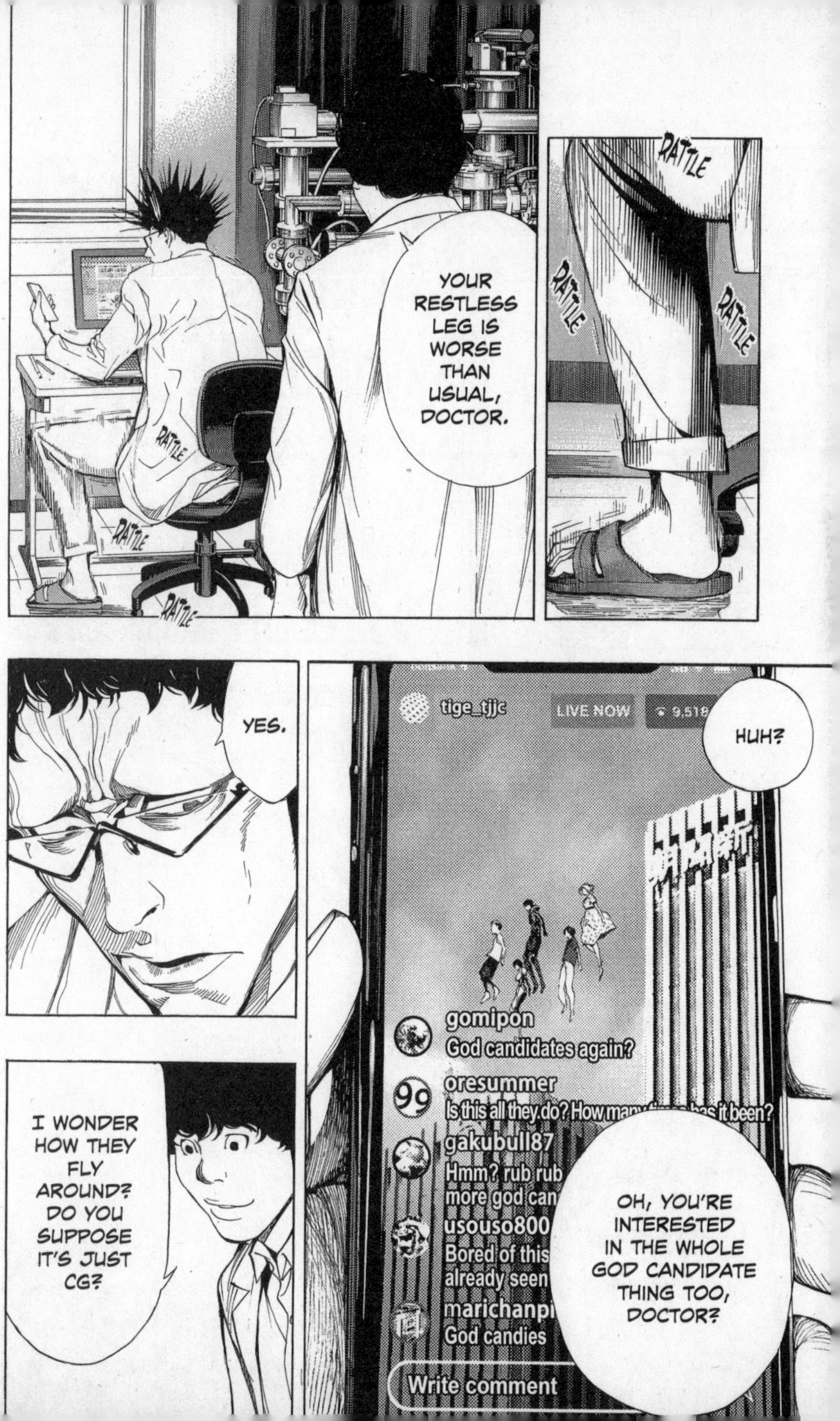
RATTLE
RATTLE
RATTLE
YOUR RESTLESS LEG IS WORSE THAN USUAL, DOCTOR.
RATTLE
RATTLE
RATTLE
tige_tjc
LIVE NOW
9,518
HUH?
gomipon
God candidates again?
oresummer
Is this all they do? How many times has it been?
gakubull87
Hmm? rub rub
more god can
usouso800
Bored of this
already seen
marichanpi
God candies
Write comment
OH, YOU'RE INTERESTED IN THE WHOLE GOD CANDIDATE THING TOO, DOCTOR?
YES.
I WONDER HOW THEY FLY AROUND? DO YOU SUPPOSE IT'S JUST CG?

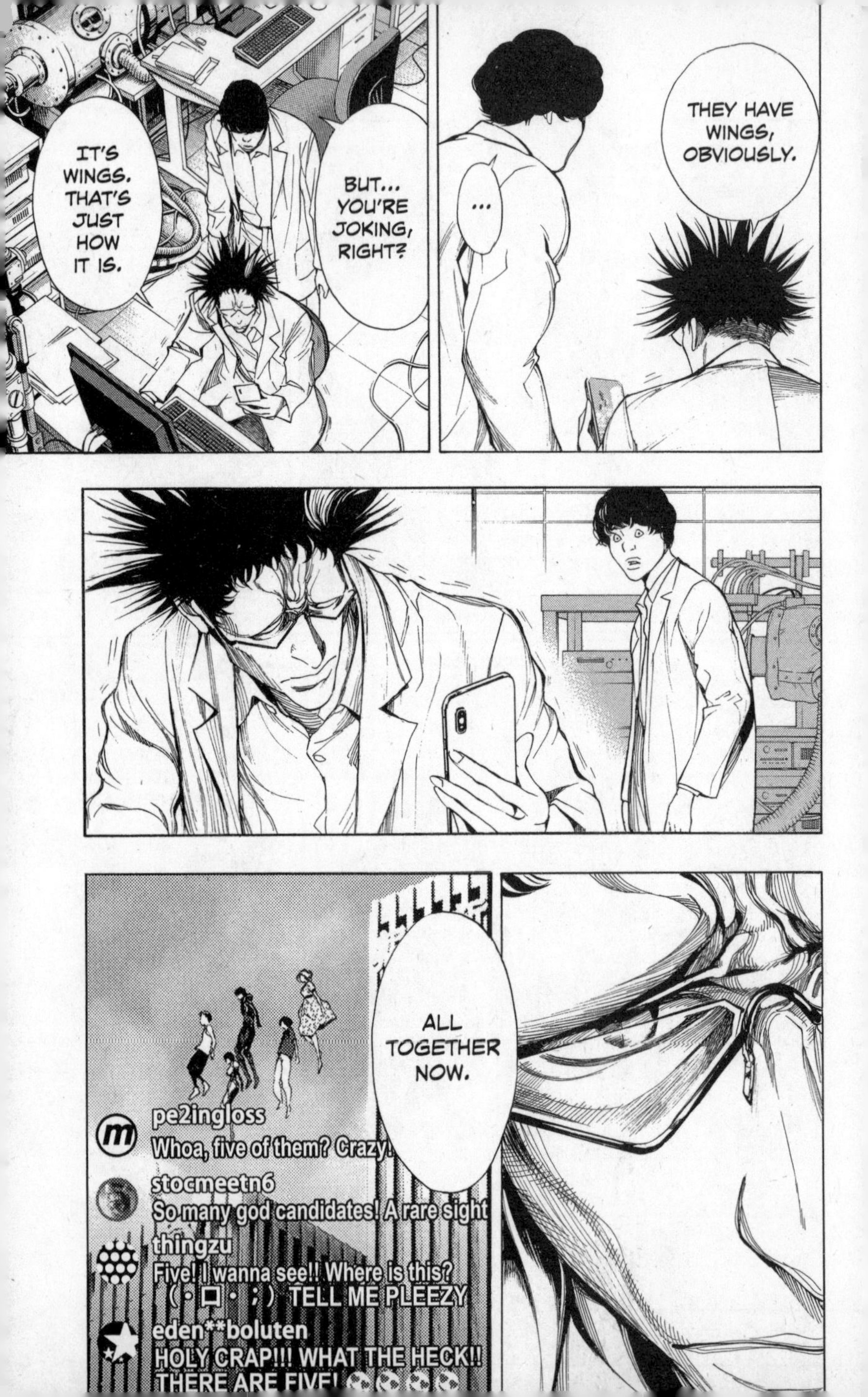
THEY HAVE WINGS, OBVIOUSLY.
...
BUT... YOU'RE JOKING, RIGHT?
IT'S WINGS. THAT'S JUST HOW IT IS.
ALL TOGETHER NOW.
pe2ingloss
Whoa, five of them? Crazy!
stocmeetn6
So many god candidates! A rare sight
thingzu
Five! I wanna see!! Where is this?
(•口•;) TELL ME PLEEZY
eden**boluten
HOLY CRAP!!! WHAT THE HECK!!
THERE ARE FIVE!

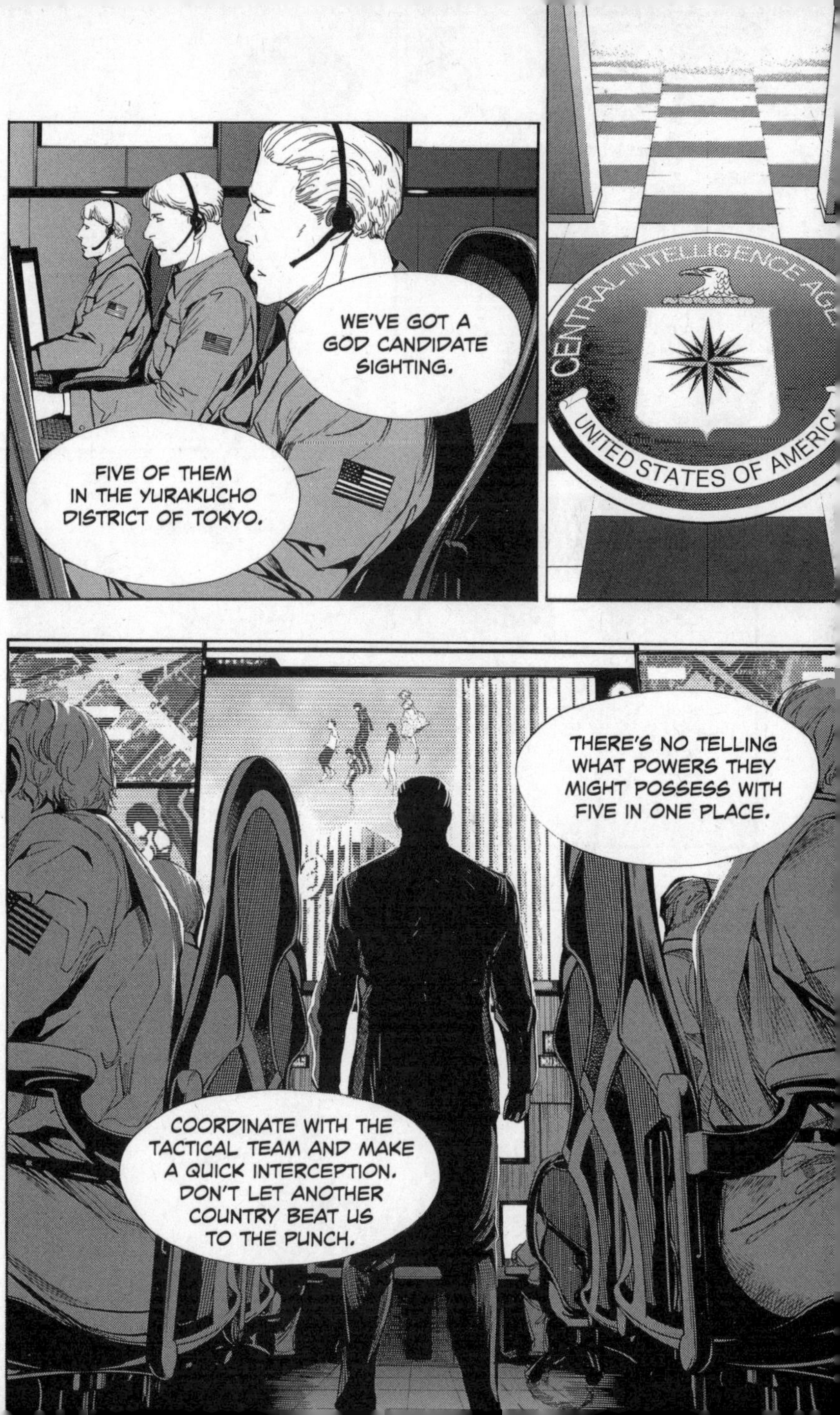
CENTRAL INTELLIGENCE AGE
UNITED STATES OF AMERIC
WE'VE GOT A GOD CANDIDATE SIGHTING.
FIVE OF THEM IN THE YURAKUCHO DISTRICT OF TOKYO.
THERE'S NO TELLING WHAT POWERS THEY MIGHT POSSESS WITH FIVE IN ONE PLACE.
COORDINATE WITH THE TACTICAL TEAM AND MAKE A QUICK INTERCEPTION. DON'T LET ANOTHER COUNTRY BEAT US TO THE PUNCH.

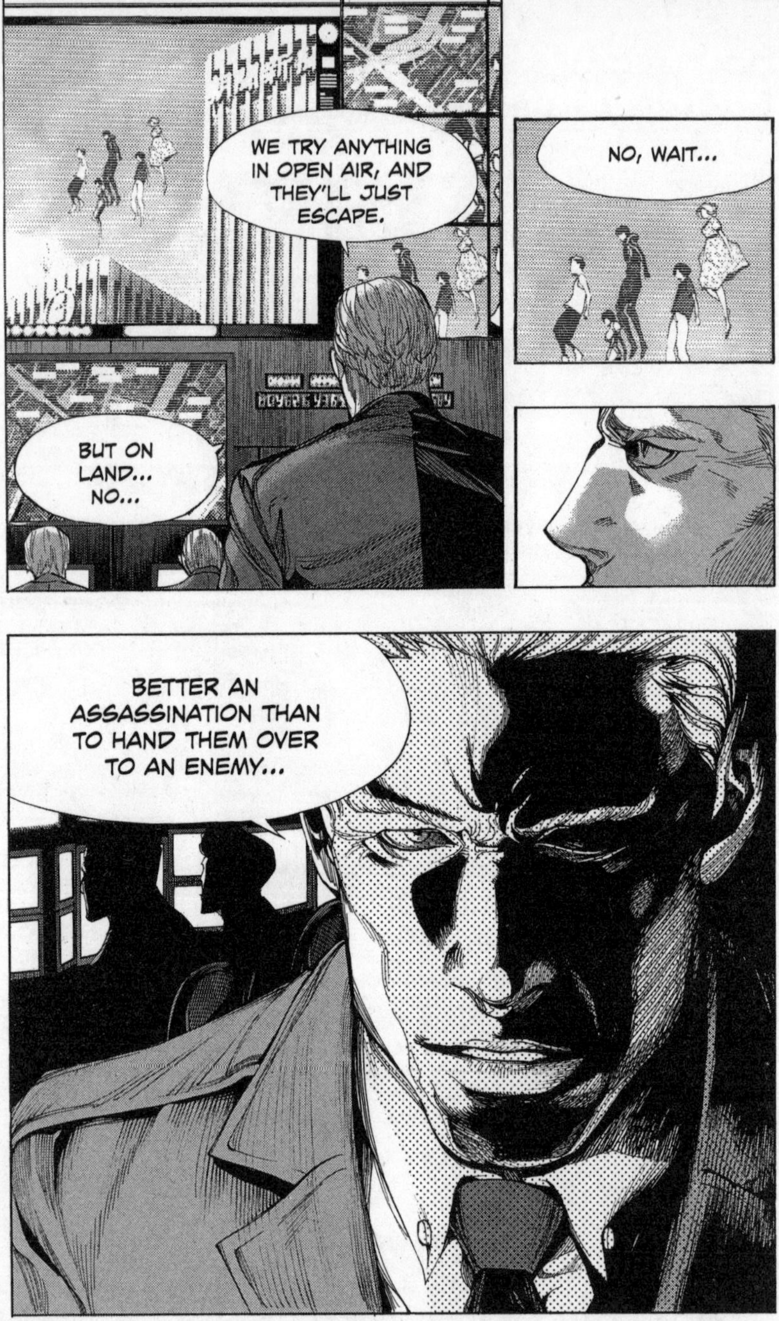
NO, WAIT...
WE TRY ANYTHING IN OPEN AIR, AND THEY'LL JUST ESCAPE.
BUT ON LAND... NO...
BETTER AN ASSASSINATION THAN TO HAND THEM OVER TO AN ENEMY...

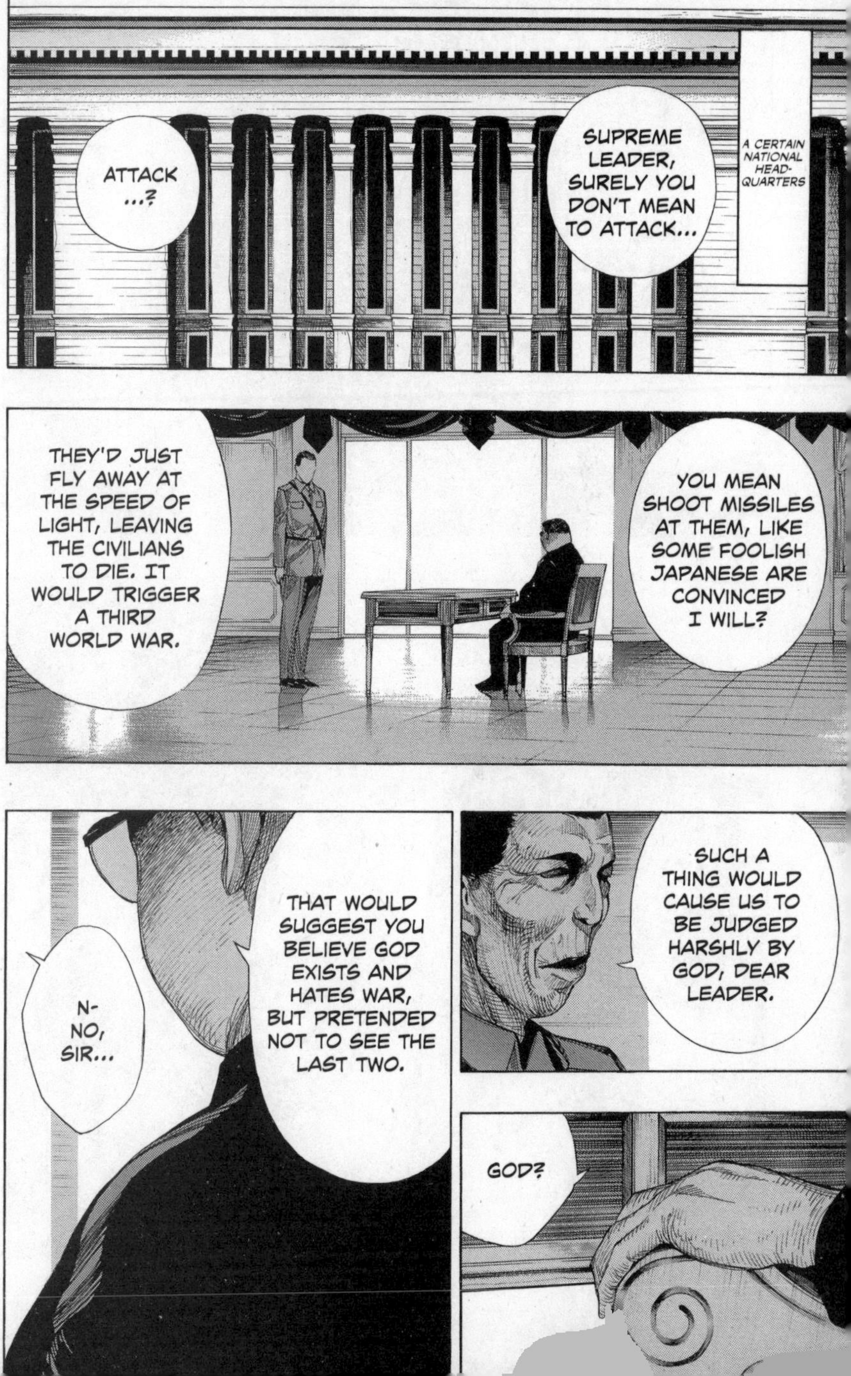
A CERTAIN NATIONAL HEAD-QUARTERS
SUPREME LEADER, SURELY YOU DON'T MEAN TO ATTACK...
ATTACK ...?
YOU MEAN SHOOT MISSILES AT THEM, LIKE SOME FOOLISH JAPANESE ARE CONVINCED I WILL?
THEY'D JUST FLY AWAY AT THE SPEED OF LIGHT, LEAVING THE CIVILIANS TO DIE. IT WOULD TRIGGER A THIRD WORLD WAR.
SUCH A THING WOULD CAUSE US TO BE JUDGED HARSHLY BY GOD, DEAR LEADER.
GOD?
THAT WOULD SUGGEST YOU BELIEVE GOD EXISTS AND HATES WAR, BUT PRETENDED NOT TO SEE THE LAST TWO.
N- NO, SIR...

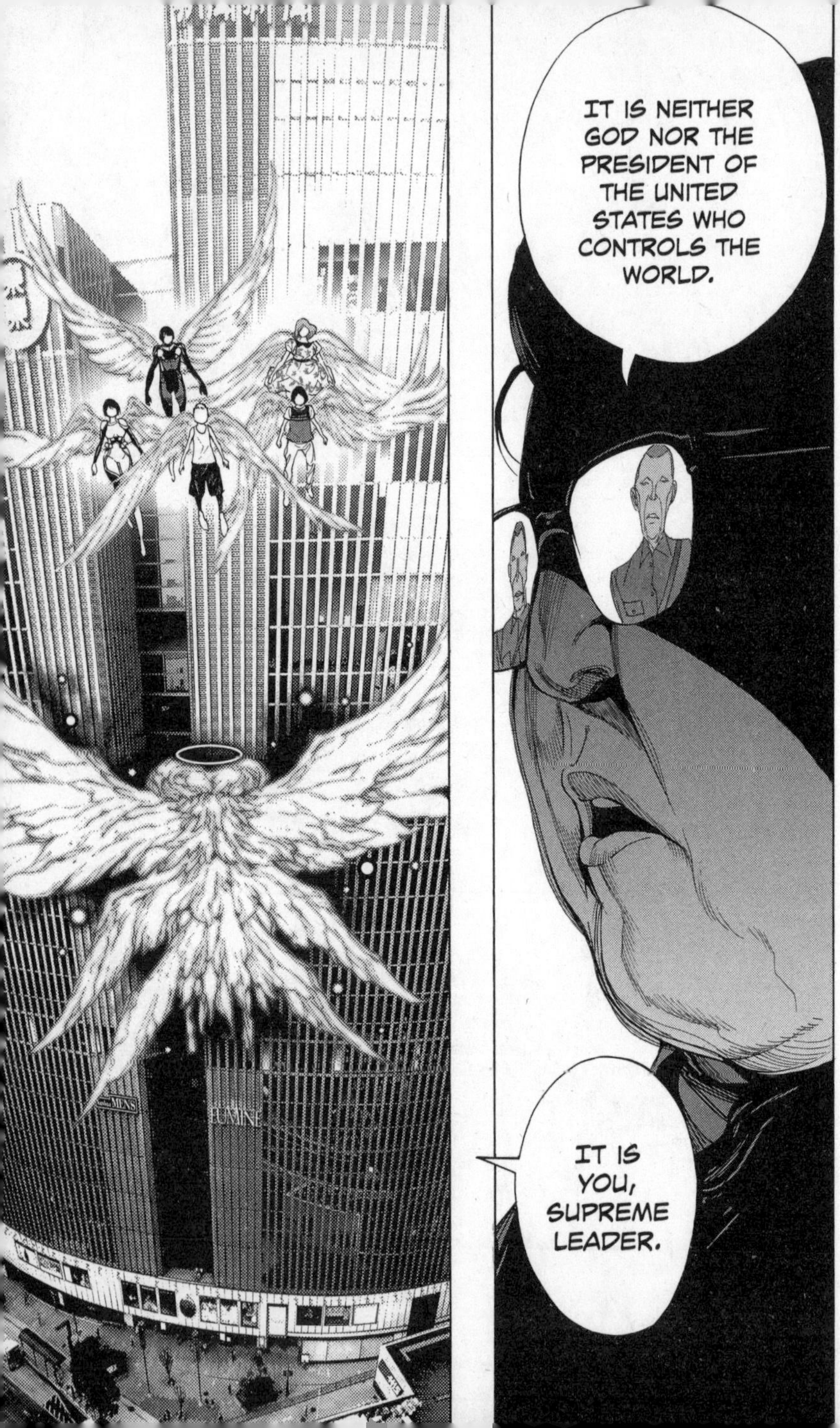
IT IS NEITHER GOD NOR THE PRESIDENT OF THE UNITED STATES WHO CONTROLS THE WORLD.
IT IS YOU, SUPREME LEADER.

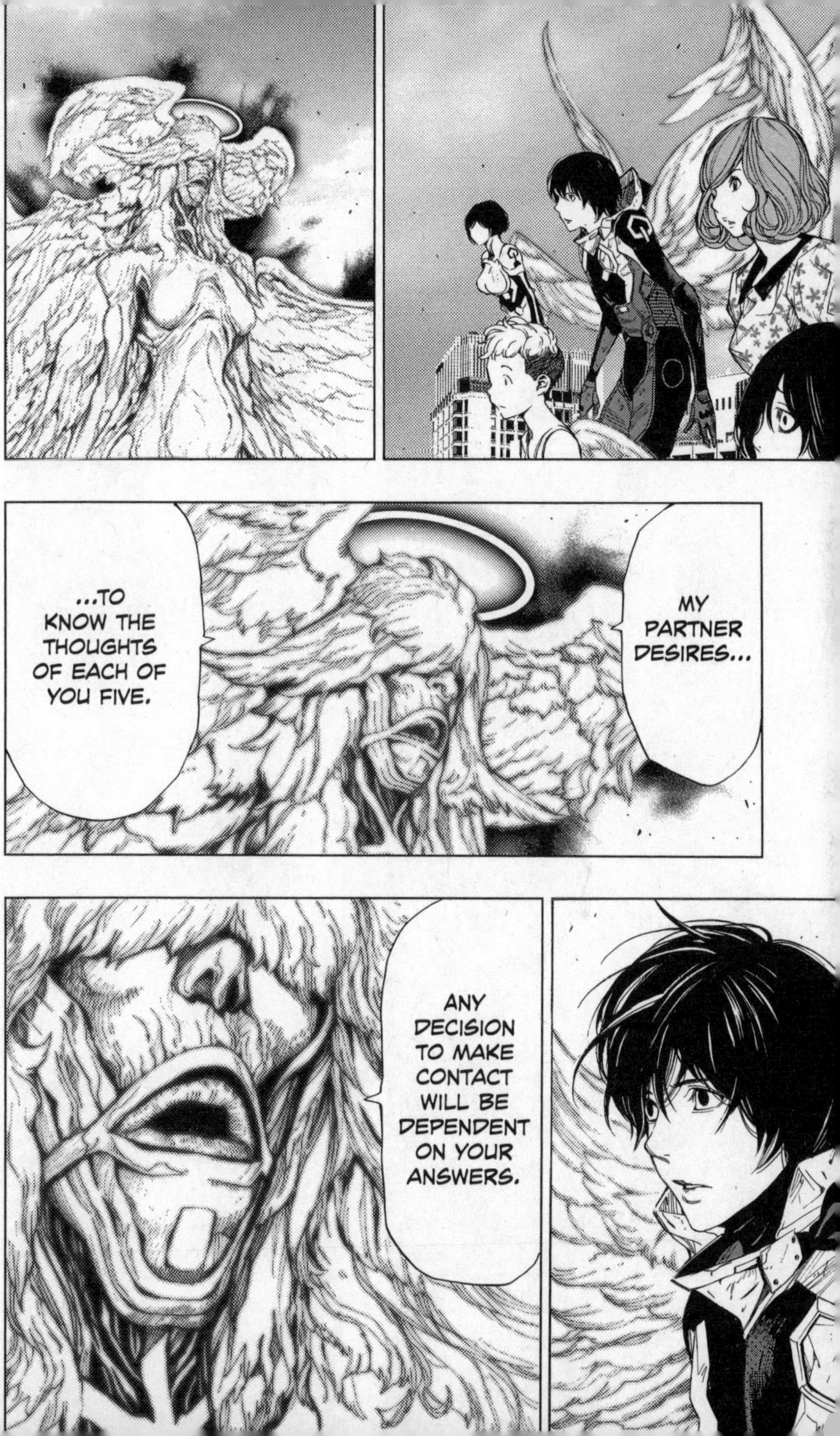
MY PARTNER DESIRES...
...TO KNOW THE THOUGHTS OF EACH OF YOU FIVE.
ANY DECISION TO MAKE CONTACT WILL BE DEPENDENT ON YOUR ANSWERS.

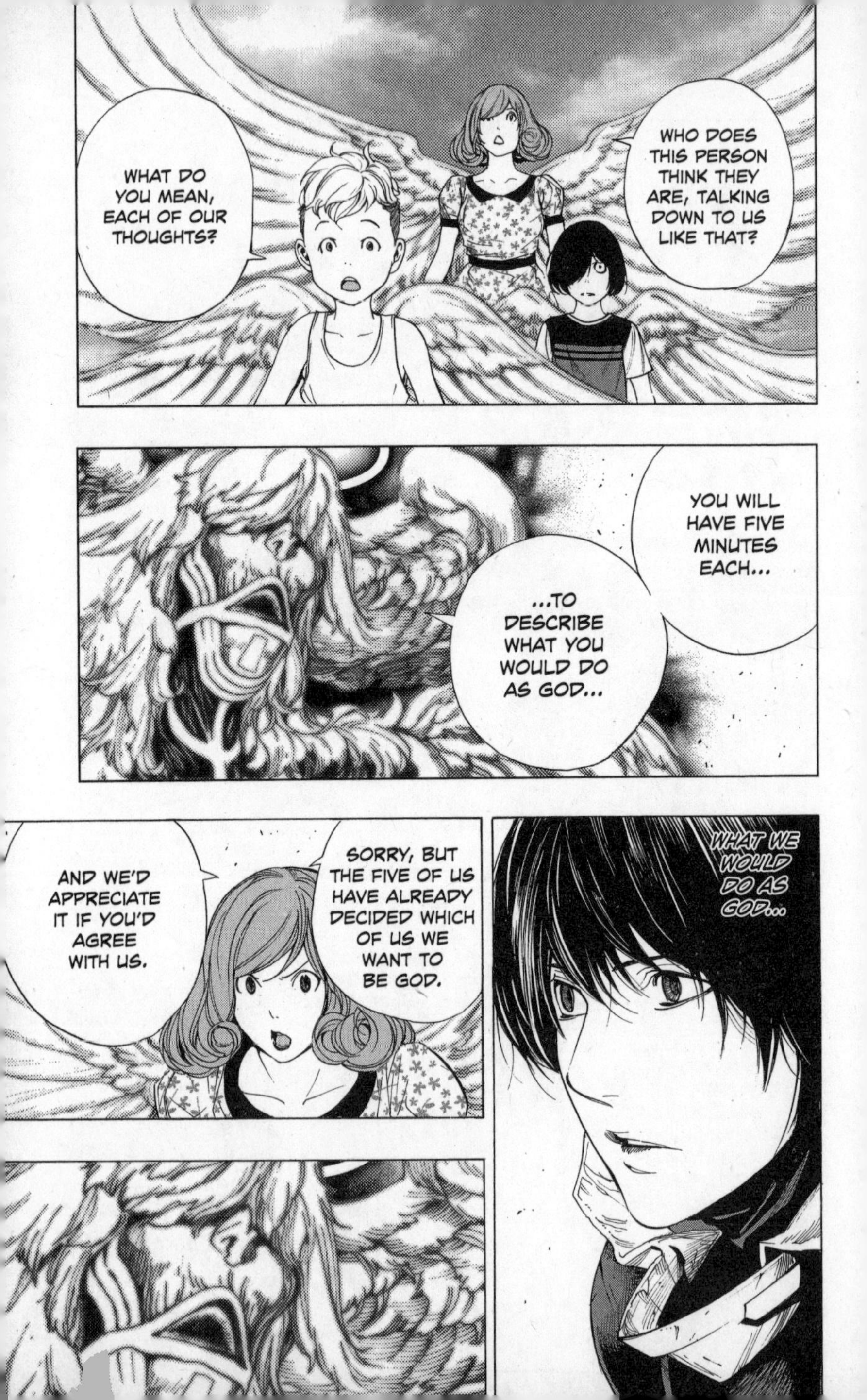
WHO DOES THIS PERSON THINK THEY ARE, TALKING DOWN TO US LIKE THAT?
WHAT DO YOU MEAN, EACH OF OUR THOUGHTS?
YOU WILL HAVE FIVE MINUTES EACH...
...TO DESCRIBE WHAT YOU WOULD DO AS GOD...
WHAT WE WOULD DO AS GOD...
SORRY, BUT THE FIVE OF US HAVE ALREADY DECIDED WHICH OF US WE WANT TO BE GOD.
AND WE'D APPRECIATE IT IF YOU'D AGREE WITH US.

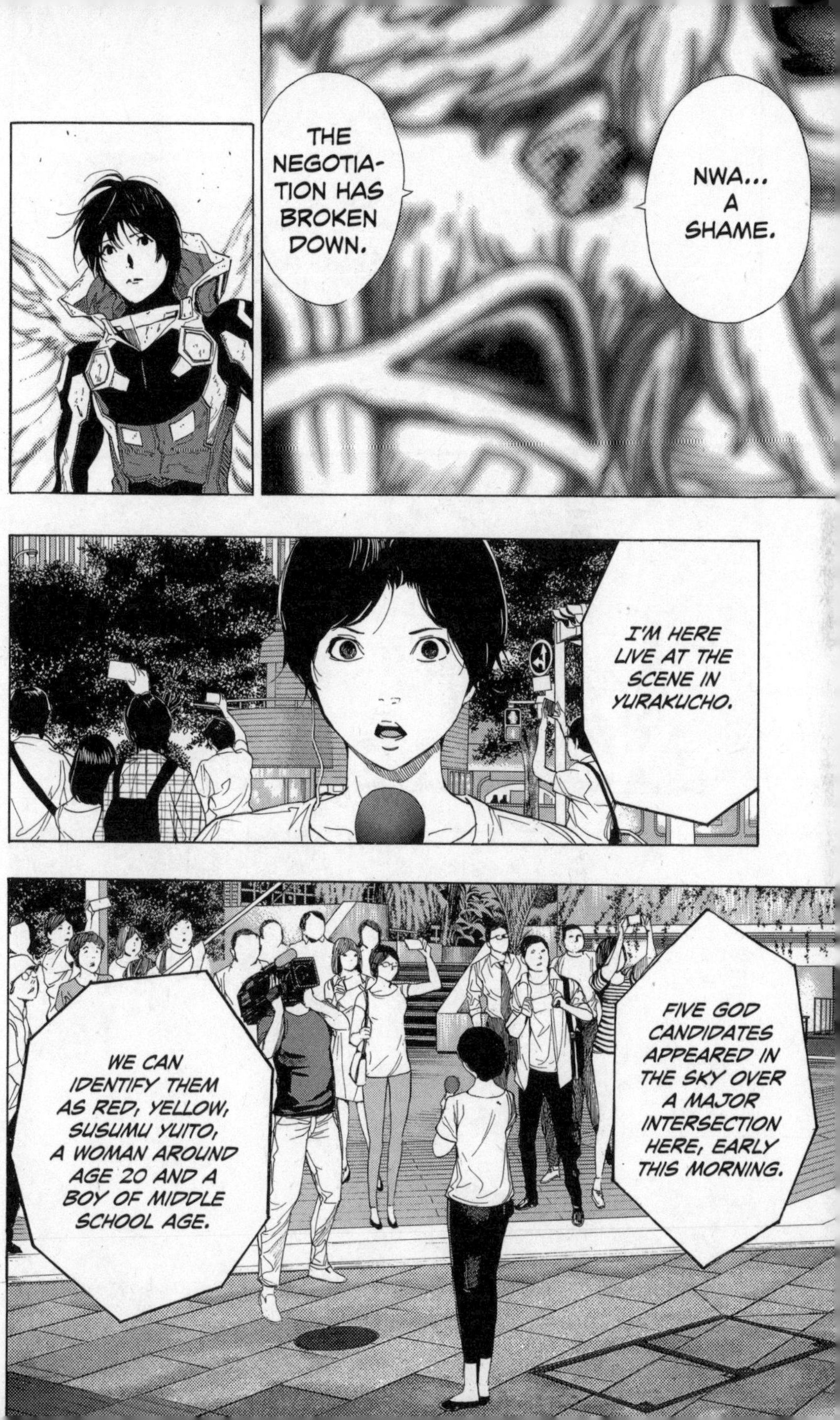
NWA... A SHAME.
THE NEGOTIATION HAS BROKEN DOWN.
I'M HERE LIVE AT THE SCENE IN YURAKUCHO.
FIVE GOD CANDIDATES APPEARED IN THE SKY OVER A MAJOR INTERSECTION HERE, EARLY THIS MORNING.
WE CAN IDENTIFY THEM AS RED, YELLOW, SUSUMU YUITO, A WOMAN AROUND AGE 20 AND A BOY OF MIDDLE SCHOOL AGE.

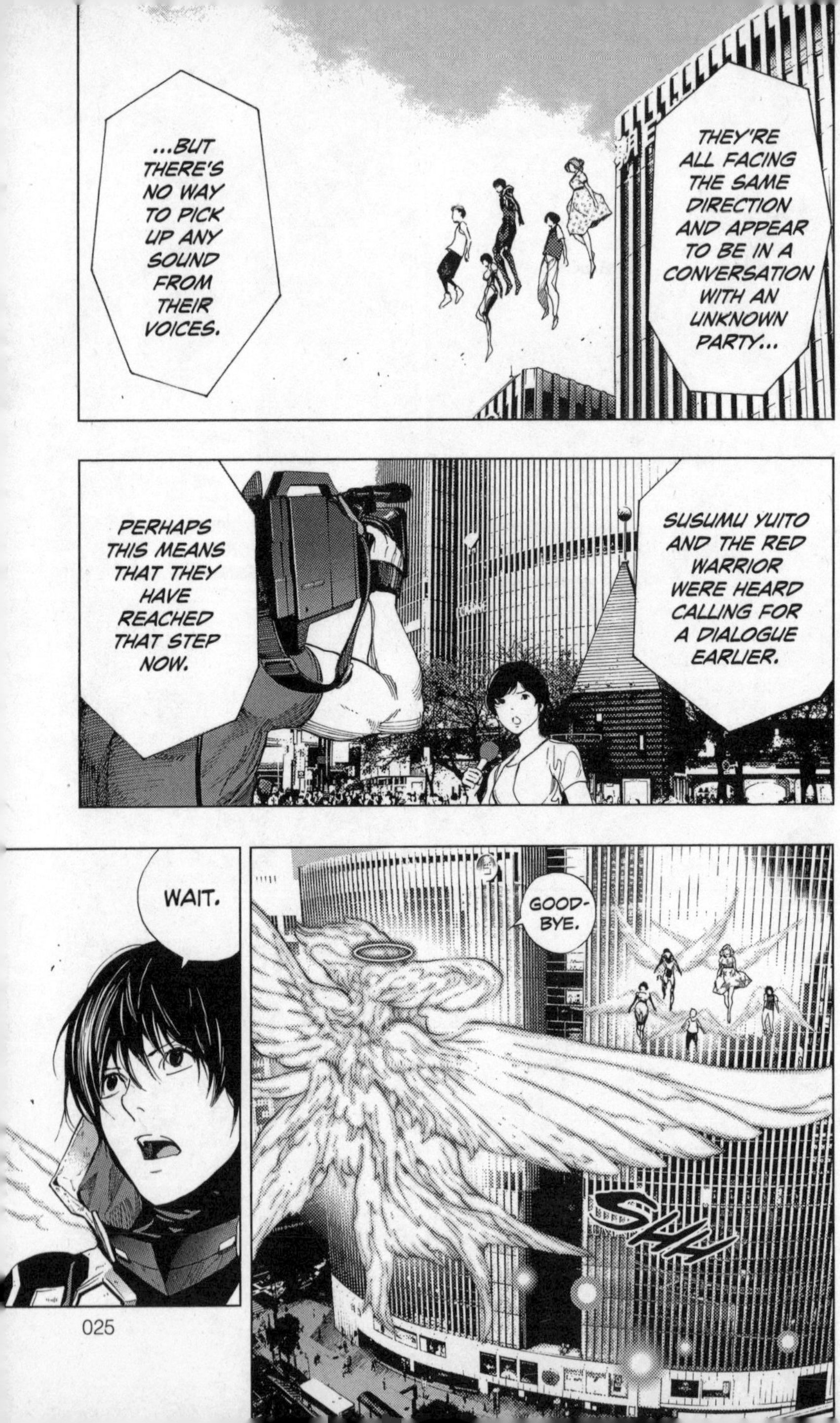
THEY'RE ALL FACING THE SAME DIRECTION AND APPEAR TO BE IN A CONVERSATION WITH AN UNKNOWN PARTY...
...BUT THERE'S NO WAY TO PICK UP ANY SOUND FROM THEIR VOICES.
SUSUMU YUITO AND THE RED WARRIOR WERE HEARD CALLING FOR A DIALOGUE EARLIER.
PERHAPS THIS MEANS THAT THEY HAVE REACHED THAT STEP NOW.
GOOD-BYE.
WAIT.

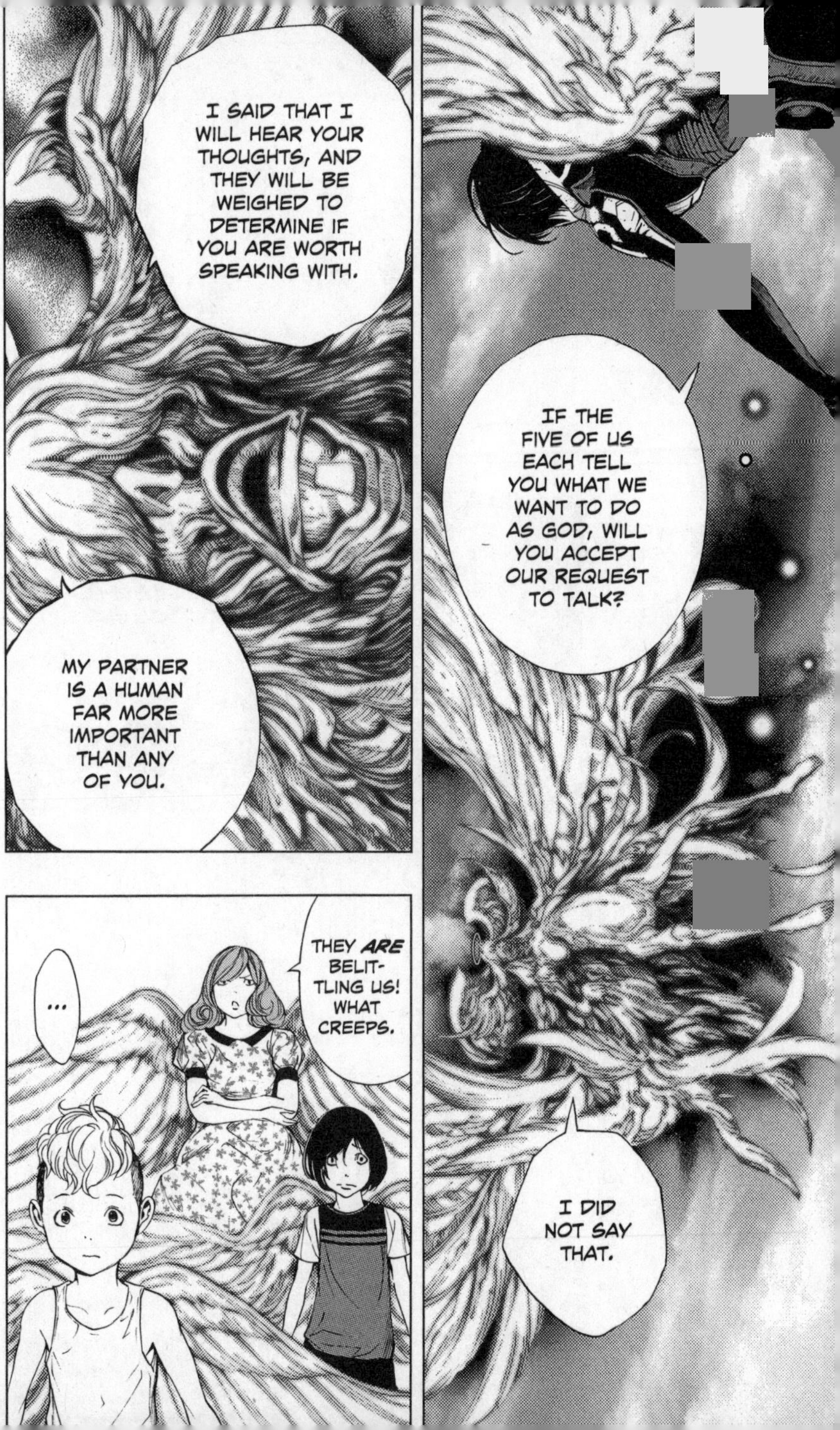
IF THE FIVE OF US EACH TELL YOU WHAT WE WANT TO DO AS GOD, WILL YOU ACCEPT OUR REQUEST TO TALK?
I DID NOT SAY THAT.
I SAID THAT I WILL HEAR YOUR THOUGHTS, AND THEY WILL BE WEIGHED TO DETERMINE IF YOU ARE WORTH SPEAKING WITH.
MY PARTNER IS A HUMAN FAR MORE IMPORTANT THAN ANY OF YOU.
THEY *ARE* BELIT-TLING US! WHAT CREEPS.
...

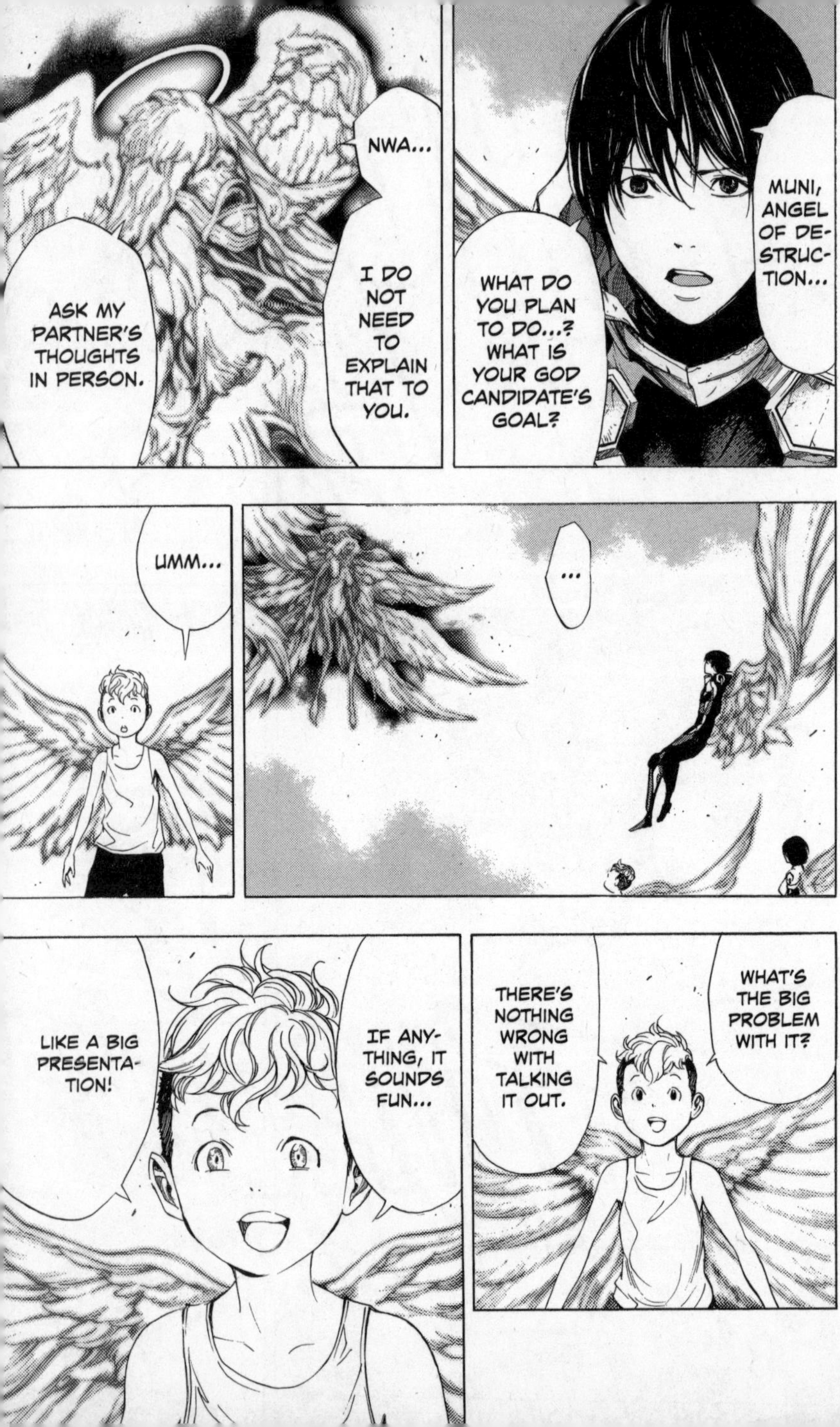
MUNI, ANGEL OF DESTRUCTION...
WHAT DO YOU PLAN TO DO...? WHAT IS YOUR GOD CANDIDATE'S GOAL?
NWA...
I DO NOT NEED TO EXPLAIN THAT TO YOU.
ASK MY PARTNER'S THOUGHTS IN PERSON.
...
UMM...
WHAT'S THE BIG PROBLEM WITH IT?
THERE'S NOTHING WRONG WITH TALKING IT OUT.
IF ANYTHING, IT SOUNDS FUN...
LIKE A BIG PRESENTATION!

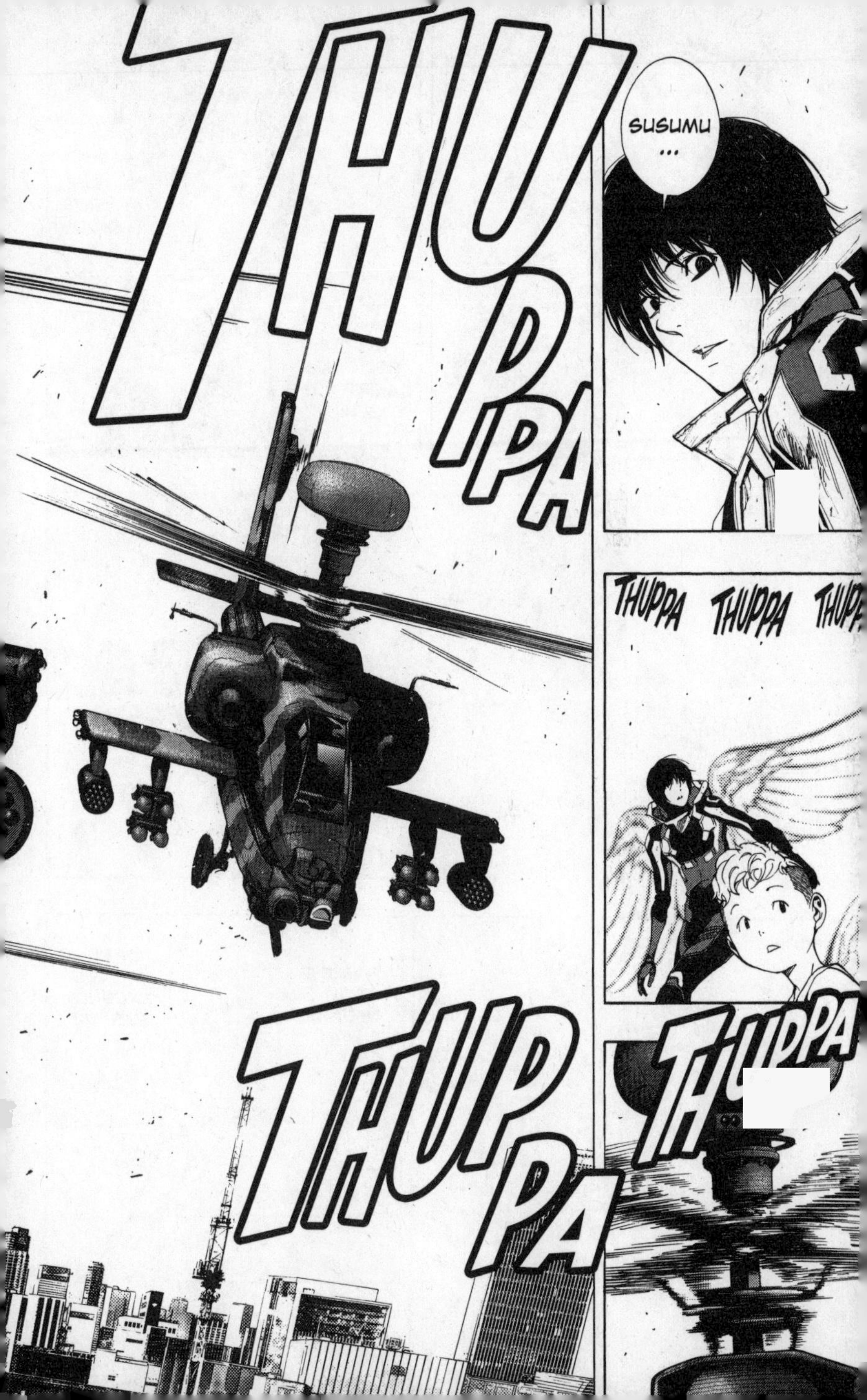
SUSUMU ...
THUPPA THUPPA THUPP
THUPPA
THUPPA
THUPPA

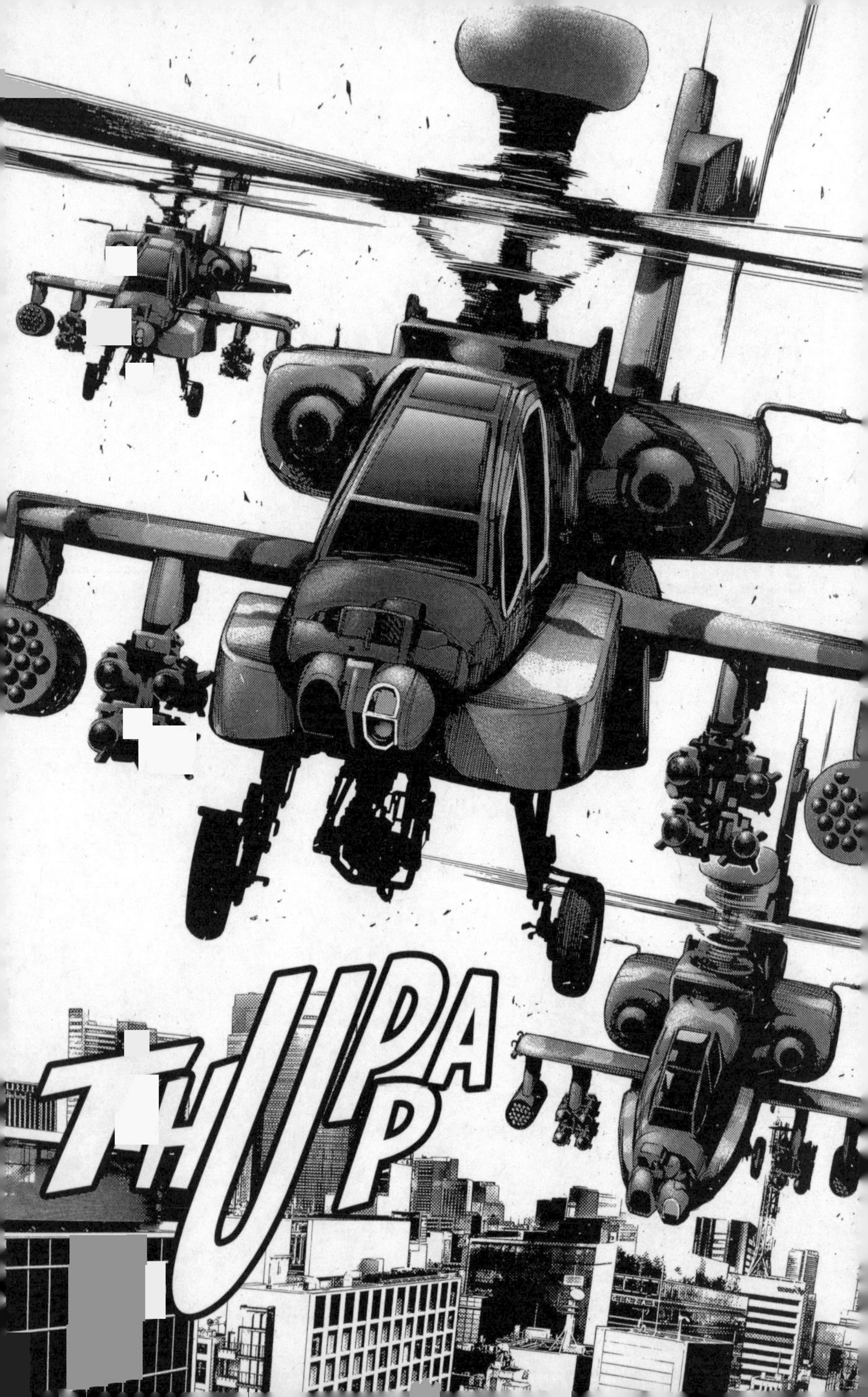
THUPAP

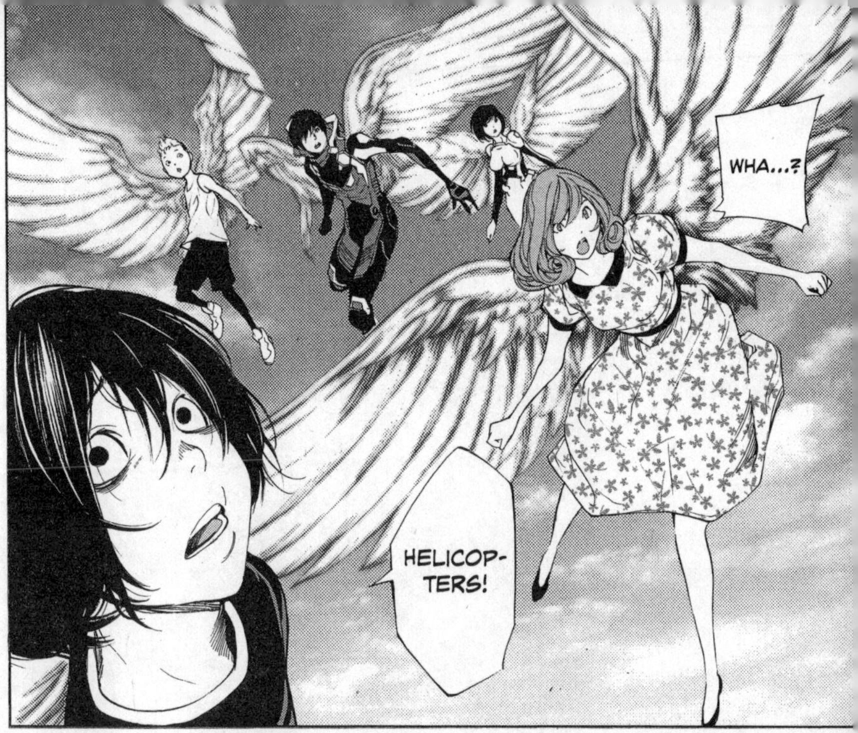
WHA...?
HELICOP-
TERS!
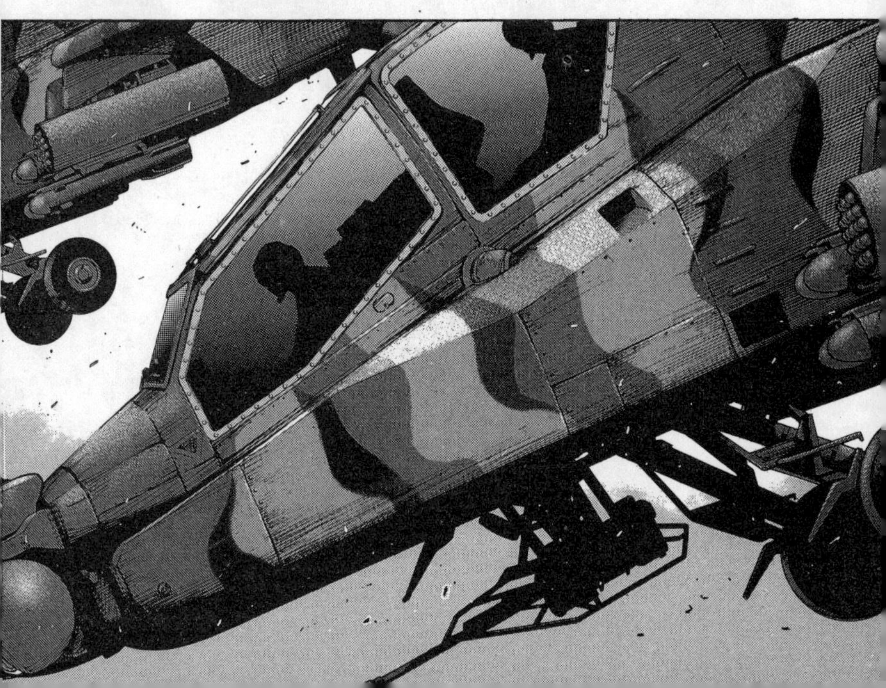

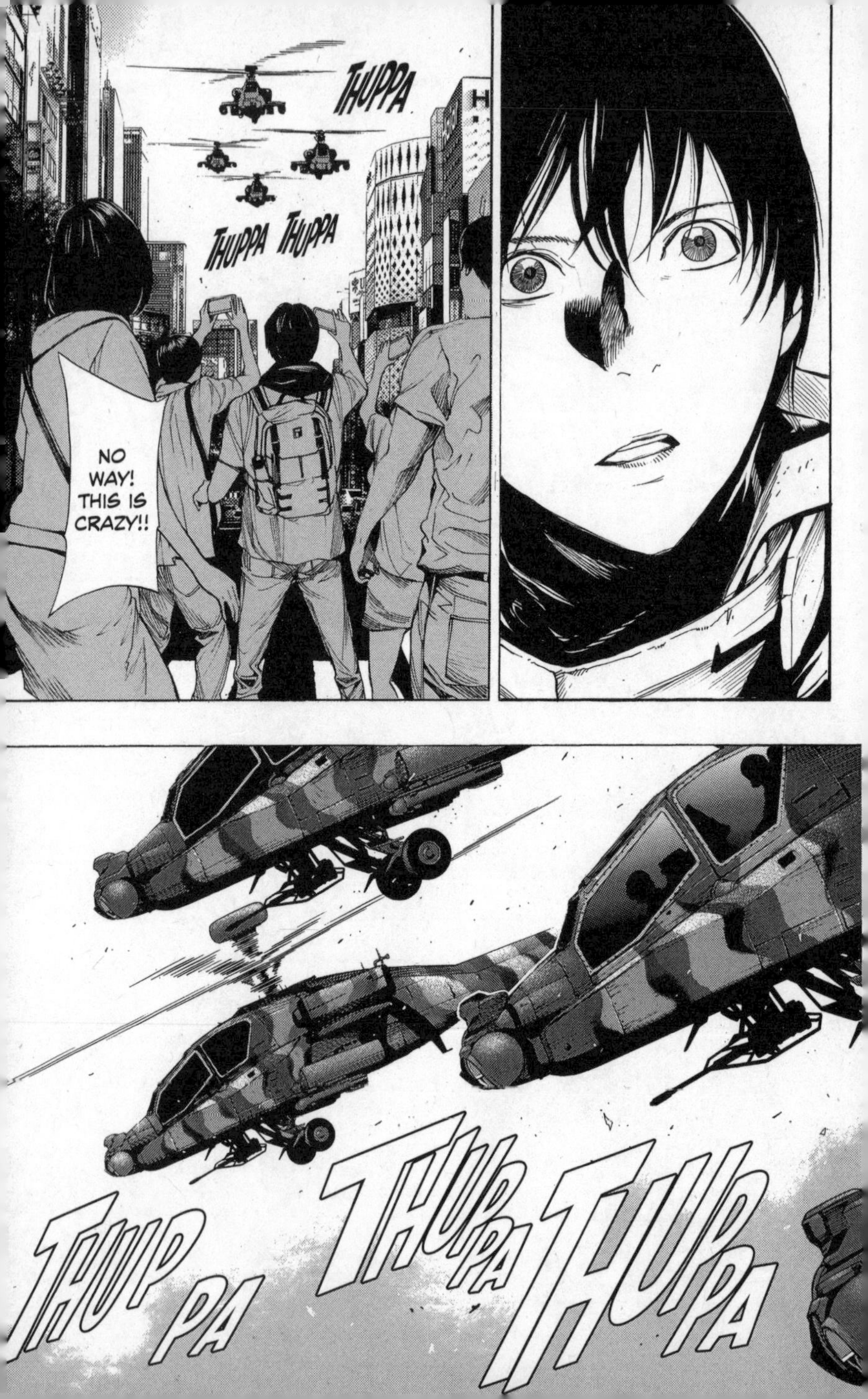
THUPPA
THUPPA THUPPA
NO WAY! THIS IS CRAZY!!
THUPPA
THUPPA
THUPPA

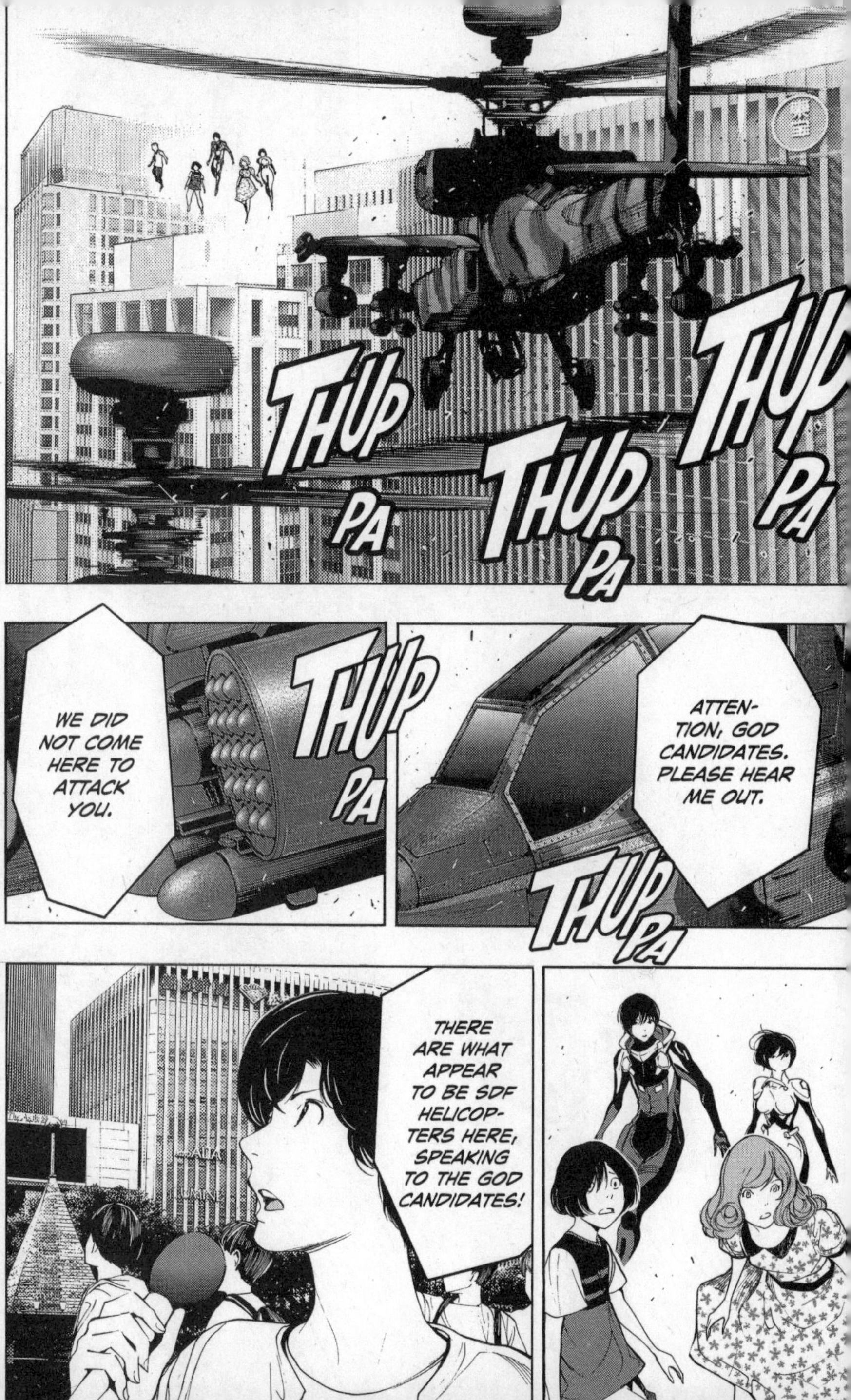
THUP PA
THUP PA
THUP PA
ATTEN-TION, GOD CANDIDATES. PLEASE HEAR ME OUT.
THUP PA
WE DID NOT COME HERE TO ATTACK YOU.
THUP PA
THERE ARE WHAT APPEAR TO BE SDF HELICOP-TERS HERE, SPEAKING TO THE GOD CANDIDATES!

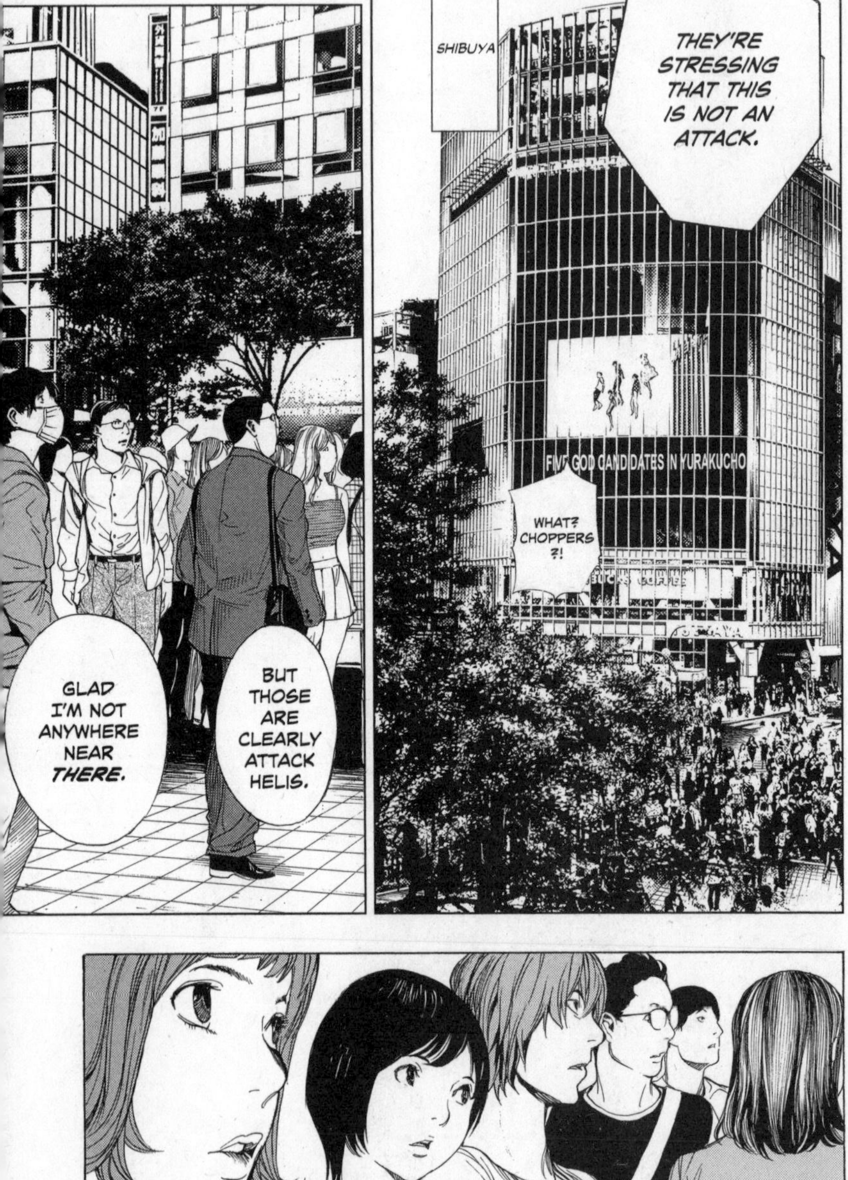
SHIBUYA
THEY'RE STRESSING THAT THIS IS NOT AN ATTACK.
FIVE GOD CANDIDATES IN YURAKUCHO
WHAT? CHOPPERS ?!
BUT THOSE ARE CLEARLY ATTACK HELIS.
GLAD I'M NOT ANYWHERE NEAR *THERE.*

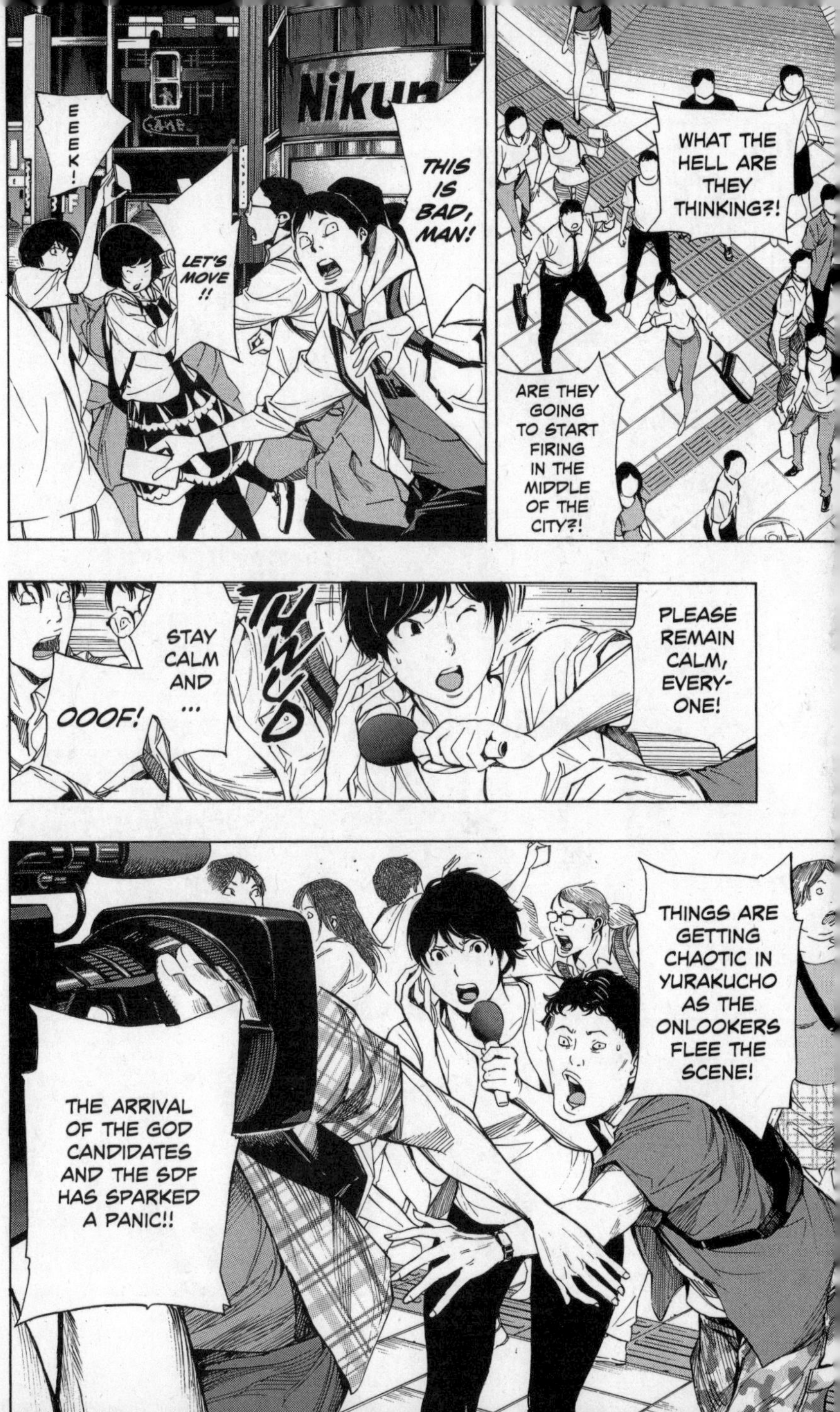
WHAT THE HELL ARE THEY THINKING?!
ARE THEY GOING TO START FIRING IN THE MIDDLE OF THE CITY?!
THIS IS BAD, MAN!
LET'S MOVE !!
EEEK!
PLEASE REMAIN CALM, EVERYONE!
THWUD
STAY CALM AND ...
OOOF!
THINGS ARE GETTING CHAOTIC IN YURAKUCHO AS THE ONLOOKERS FLEE THE SCENE!
THE ARRIVAL OF THE GOD CANDIDATES AND THE SDF HAS SPARKED A PANIC!!

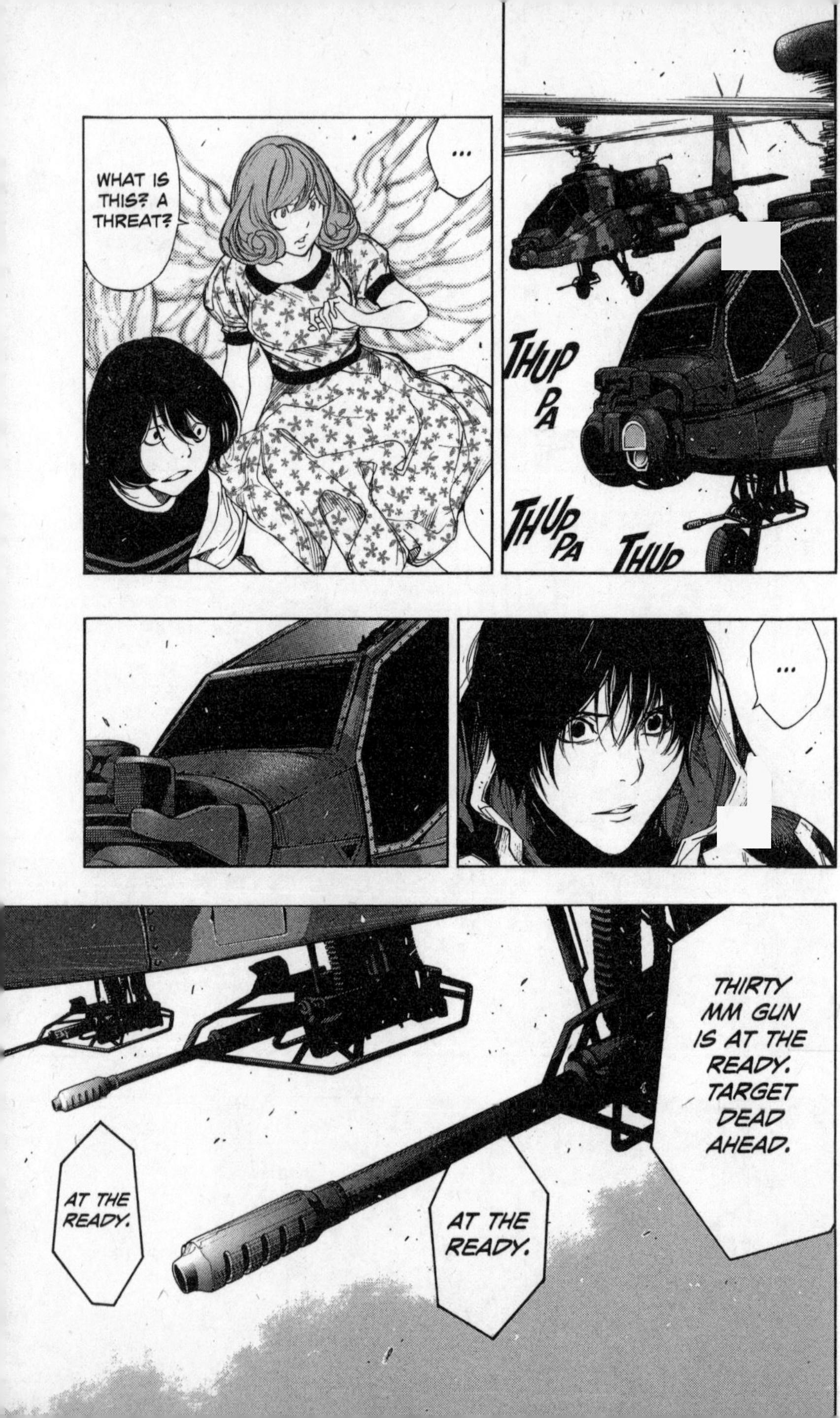
THUP PA
THUP PA
THUP
...
WHAT IS THIS? A THREAT?
...
THIRTY MM GUN IS AT THE READY. TARGET DEAD AHEAD.
AT THE READY.
AT THE READY.

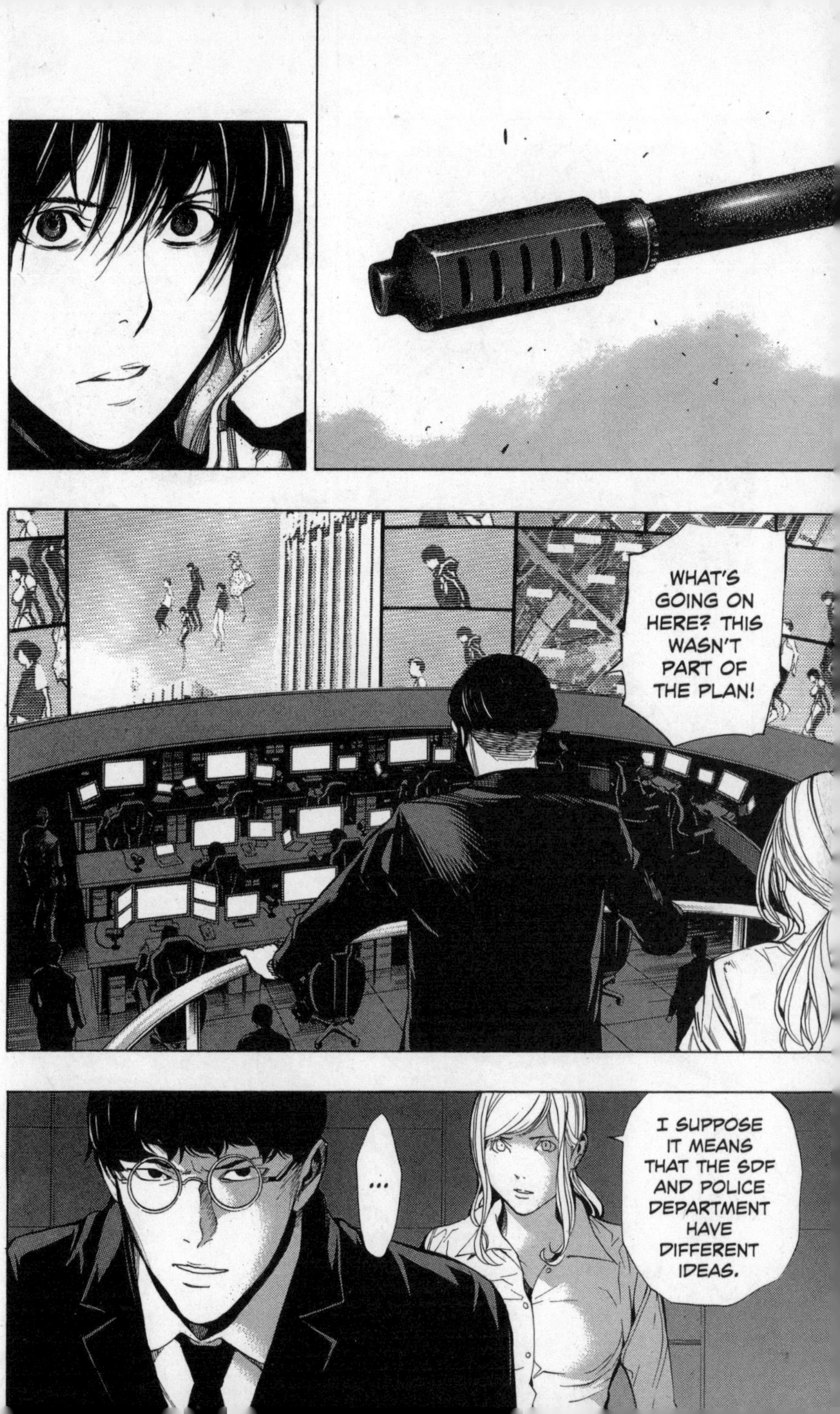
WHAT'S GOING ON HERE? THIS WASN'T PART OF THE PLAN!
I SUPPOSE IT MEANS THAT THE SDF AND POLICE DEPARTMENT HAVE DIFFERENT IDEAS.
...

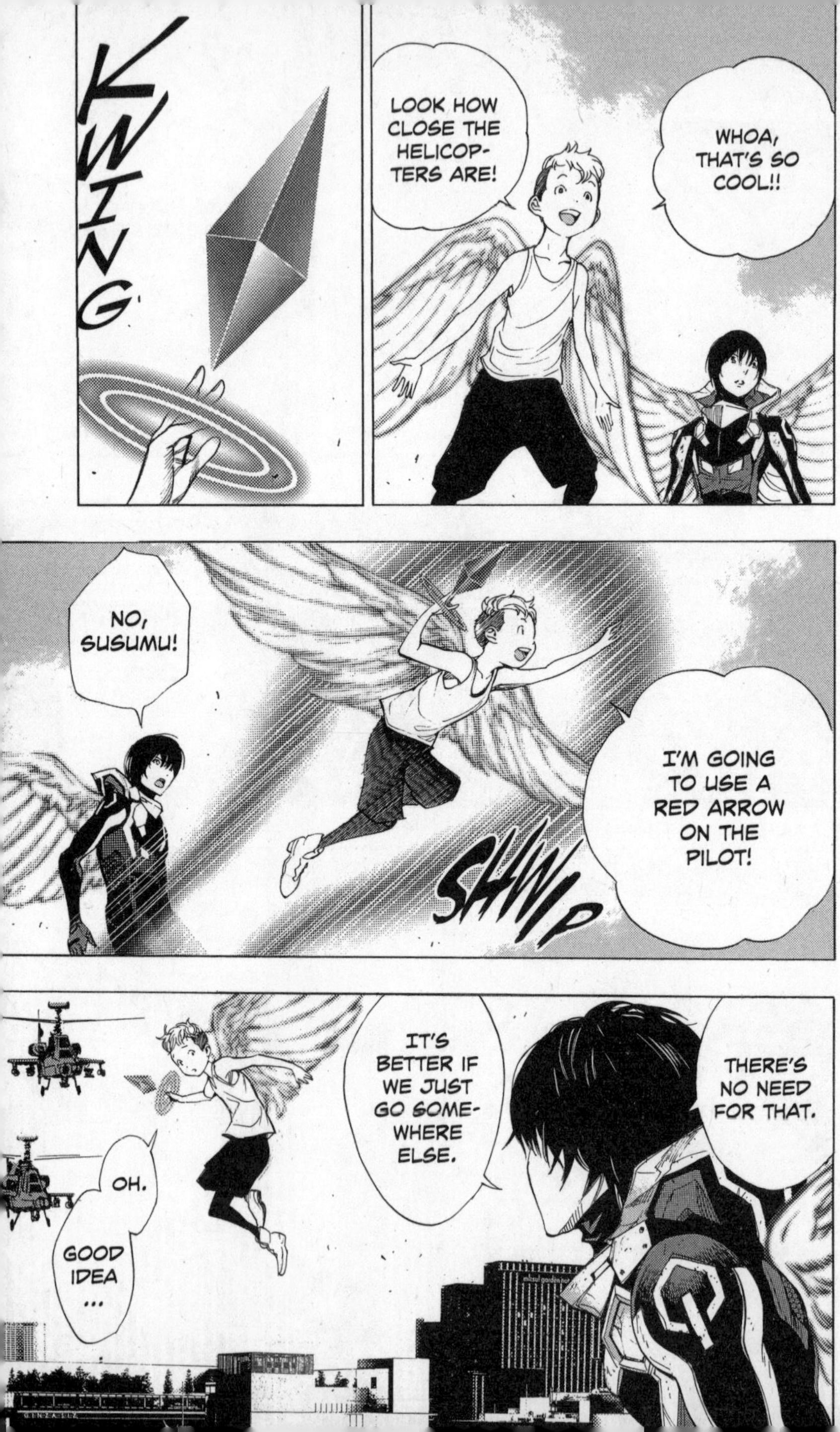
WHOA, THAT'S SO COOL!!
LOOK HOW CLOSE THE HELICOP-TERS ARE!
KWING
I'M GOING TO USE A RED ARROW ON THE PILOT!
SHWIP
NO, SUSUMU!
THERE'S NO NEED FOR THAT.
IT'S BETTER IF WE JUST GO SOME-WHERE ELSE.
OH.
GOOD IDEA ...

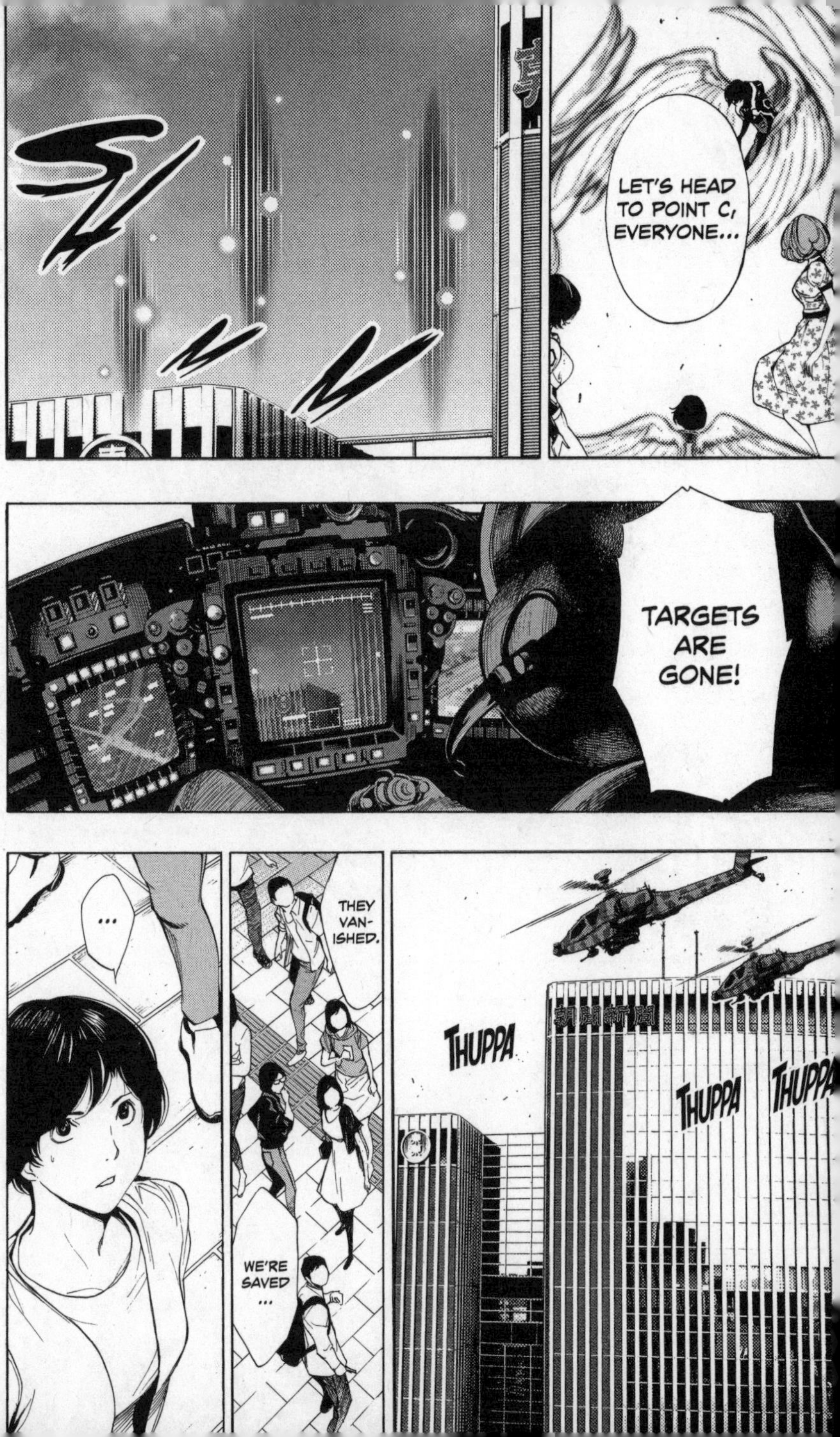
LET'S HEAD TO POINT C, EVERYONE...
TARGETS ARE GONE!
THUPPA
THUPPA
THUPPA
THEY VAN-ISHED.
WE'RE SAVED ...
...

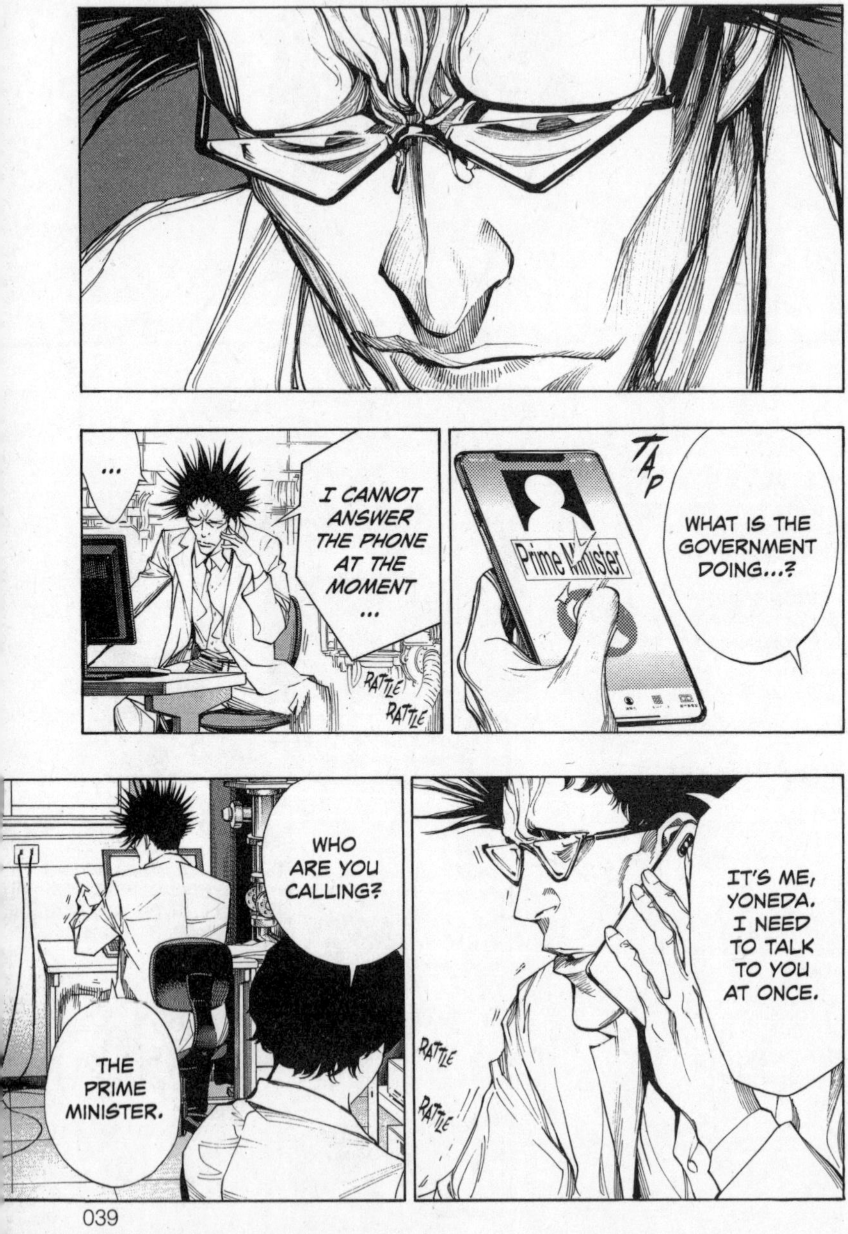
WHAT IS THE GOVERNMENT DOING...?
TAP
Prime Minister
I CANNOT ANSWER THE PHONE AT THE MOMENT ...
...
RATTLE
RATTLE
IT'S ME, YONEDA. I NEED TO TALK TO YOU AT ONCE.
RATTLE
RATTLE
WHO ARE YOU CALLING?
THE PRIME MINISTER.

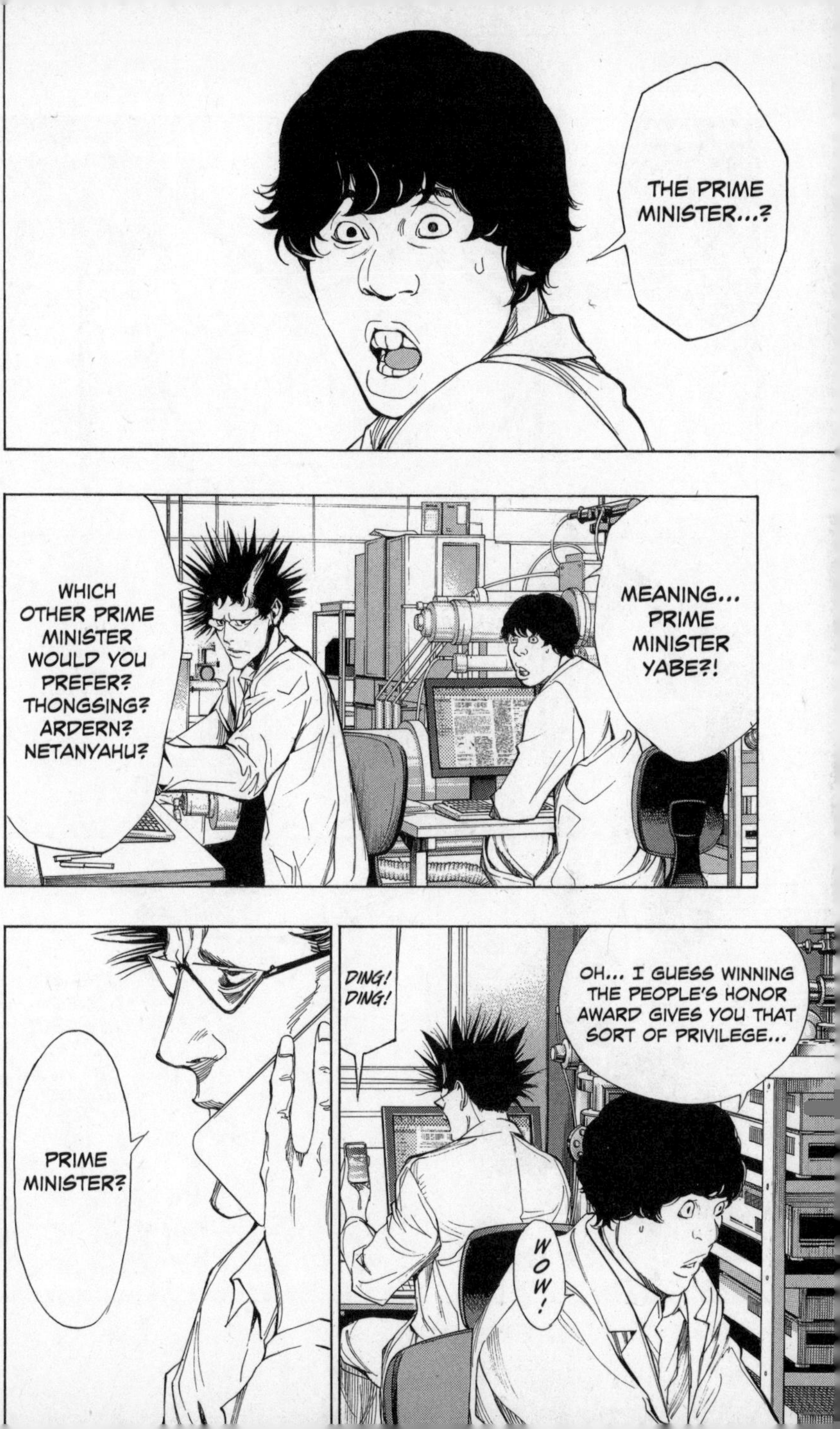

THE PRIME MINISTER...?
MEANING... PRIME MINISTER YABE?!
WHICH OTHER PRIME MINISTER WOULD YOU PREFER? THONGSING? ARDERN? NETANYAHU?
OH... I GUESS WINNING THE PEOPLE'S HONOR AWARD GIVES YOU THAT SORT OF PRIVILEGE...
DING! DING!
WOW!
PRIME MINISTER?

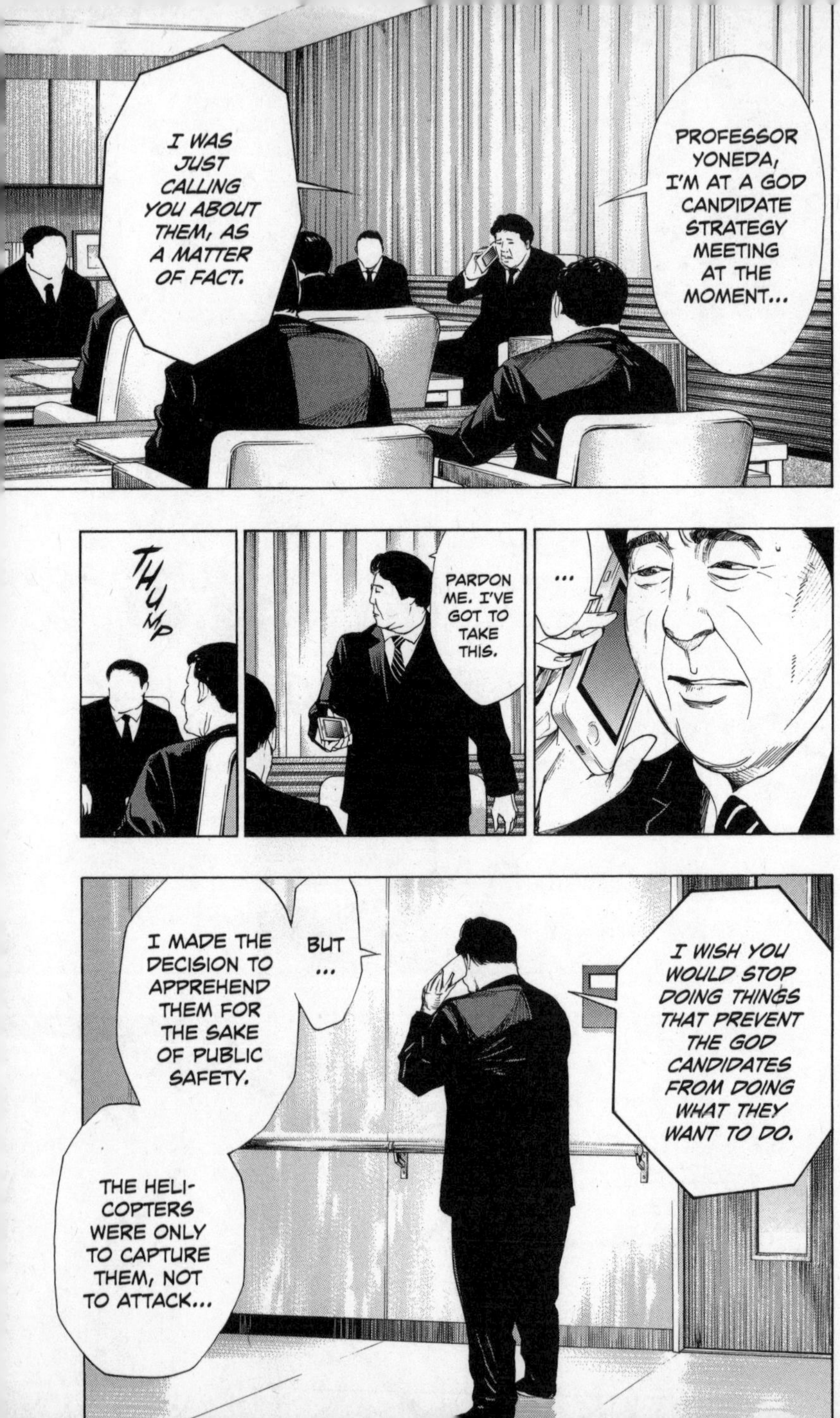
PROFESSOR YONEDA, I'M AT A GOD CANDIDATE STRATEGY MEETING AT THE MOMENT...
I WAS JUST CALLING YOU ABOUT THEM, AS A MATTER OF FACT.
...
PARDON ME. I'VE GOT TO TAKE THIS.
THUMP
I WISH YOU WOULD STOP DOING THINGS THAT PREVENT THE GOD CANDIDATES FROM DOING WHAT THEY WANT TO DO.
BUT ...
I MADE THE DECISION TO APPREHEND THEM FOR THE SAKE OF PUBLIC SAFETY.
THE HELI-COPTERS WERE ONLY TO CAPTURE THEM, NOT TO ATTACK...

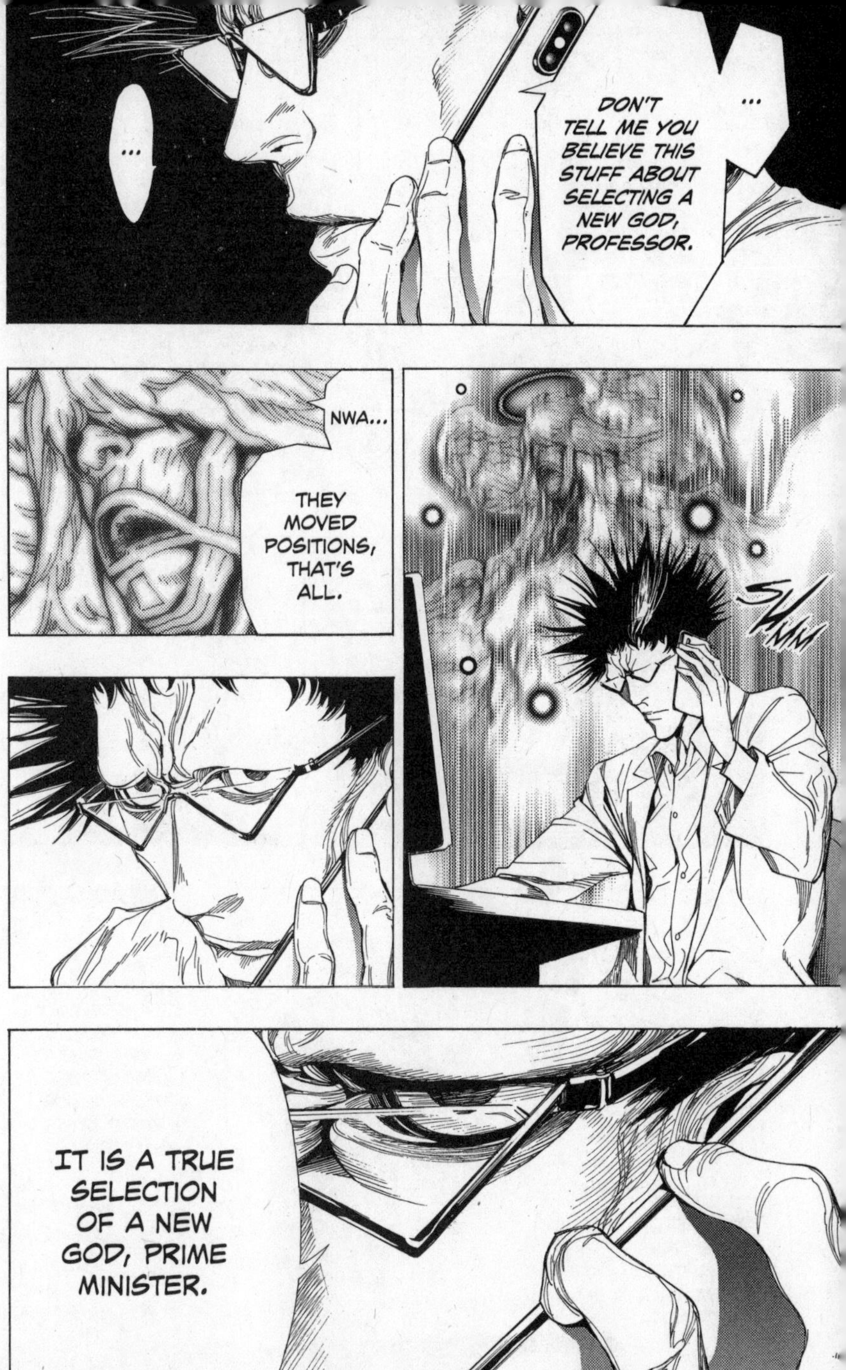
...
DON'T TELL ME YOU BELIEVE THIS STUFF ABOUT SELECTING A NEW GOD, PROFESSOR.
...
SHMM
NWA...
THEY MOVED POSITIONS, THAT'S ALL.
IT IS A TRUE SELECTION OF A NEW GOD, PRIME MINISTER.

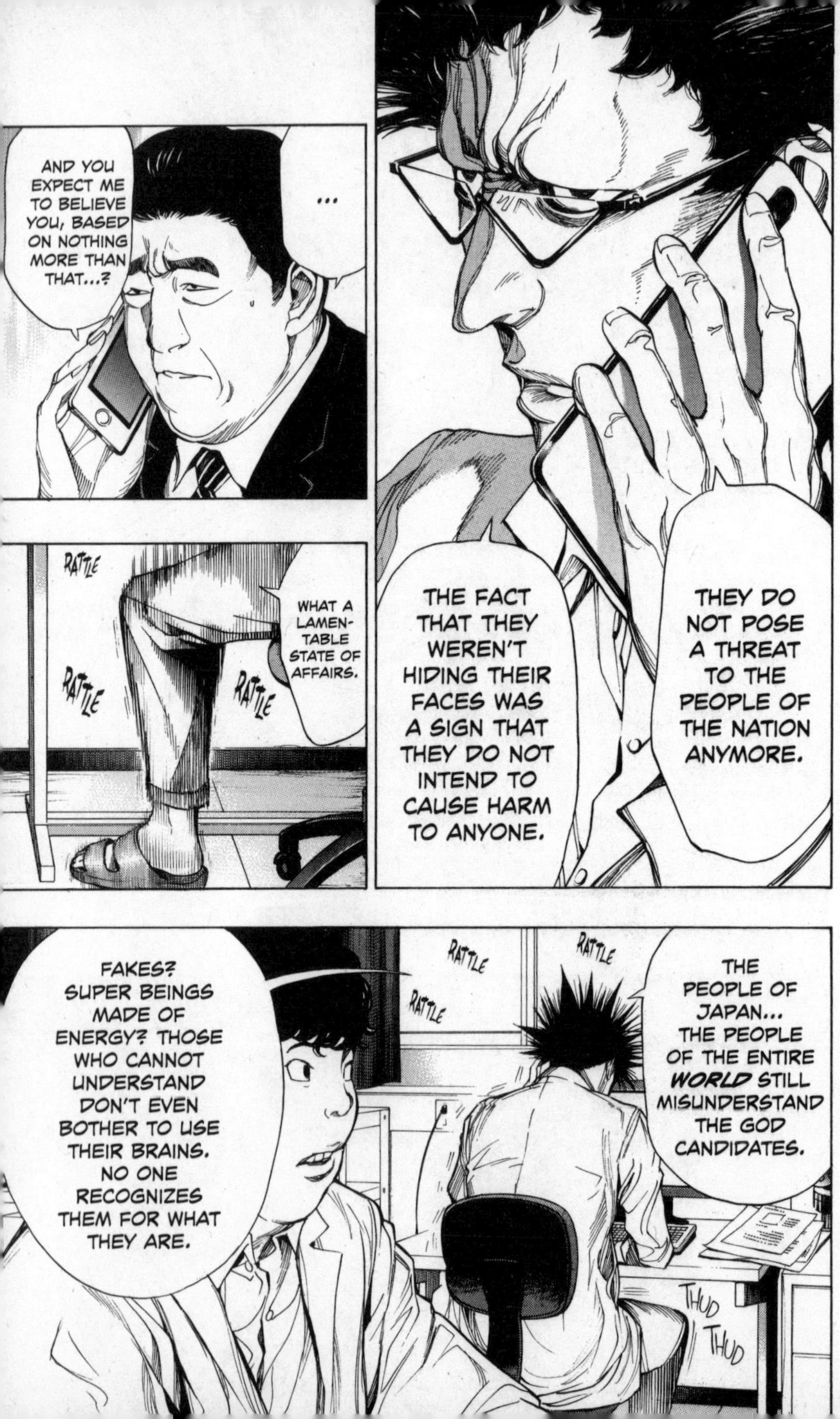
THEY DO NOT POSE A THREAT TO THE PEOPLE OF THE NATION ANYMORE.
THE FACT THAT THEY WEREN'T HIDING THEIR FACES WAS A SIGN THAT THEY DO NOT INTEND TO CAUSE HARM TO ANYONE.
...
AND YOU EXPECT ME TO BELIEVE YOU, BASED ON NOTHING MORE THAN THAT...?
RATTLE
RATTLE
RATTLE
WHAT A LAMENTABLE STATE OF AFFAIRS.
RATTLE
RATTLE
RATTLE
THE PEOPLE OF JAPAN... THE PEOPLE OF THE ENTIRE *WORLD* STILL MISUNDERSTAND THE GOD CANDIDATES.
THUD THUD
FAKES? SUPER BEINGS MADE OF ENERGY? THOSE WHO CANNOT UNDERSTAND DON'T EVEN BOTHER TO USE THEIR BRAINS. NO ONE RECOGNIZES THEM FOR WHAT THEY ARE.

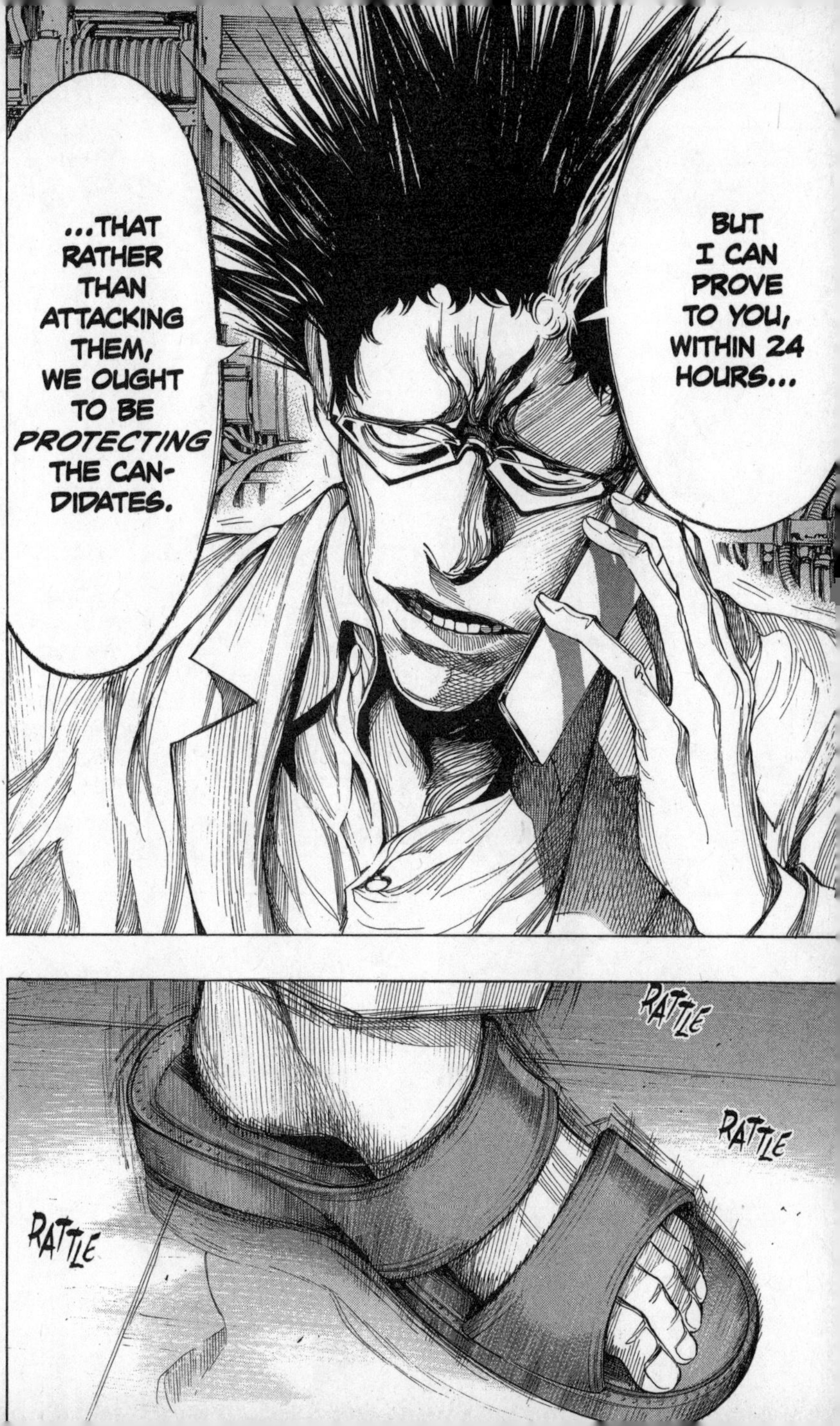
BUT I CAN PROVE TO YOU, WITHIN 24 HOURS...
...THAT RATHER THAN ATTACKING THEM, WE OUGHT TO BE *PROTECTING* THE CAN-DIDATES.
RATTLE
RATTLE
RATTLE

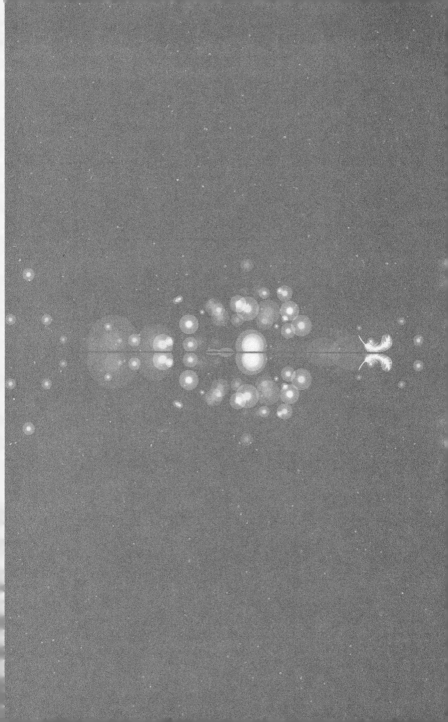

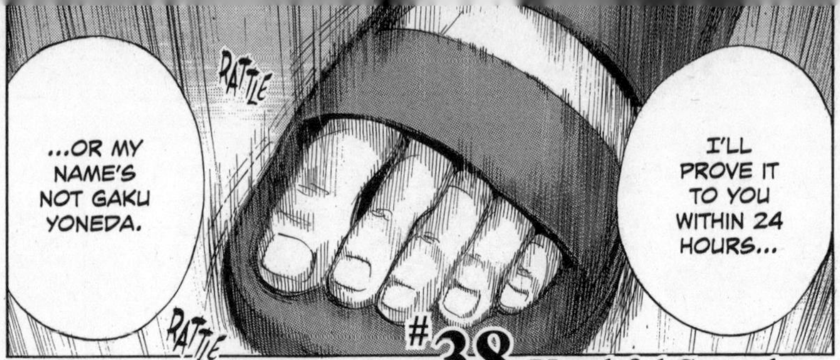
I'LL PROVE IT TO YOU WITHIN 24 HOURS...
RATTLE
...OR MY NAME'S NOT GAKU YONEDA.
RATTLE

#38 Youthful Speeches

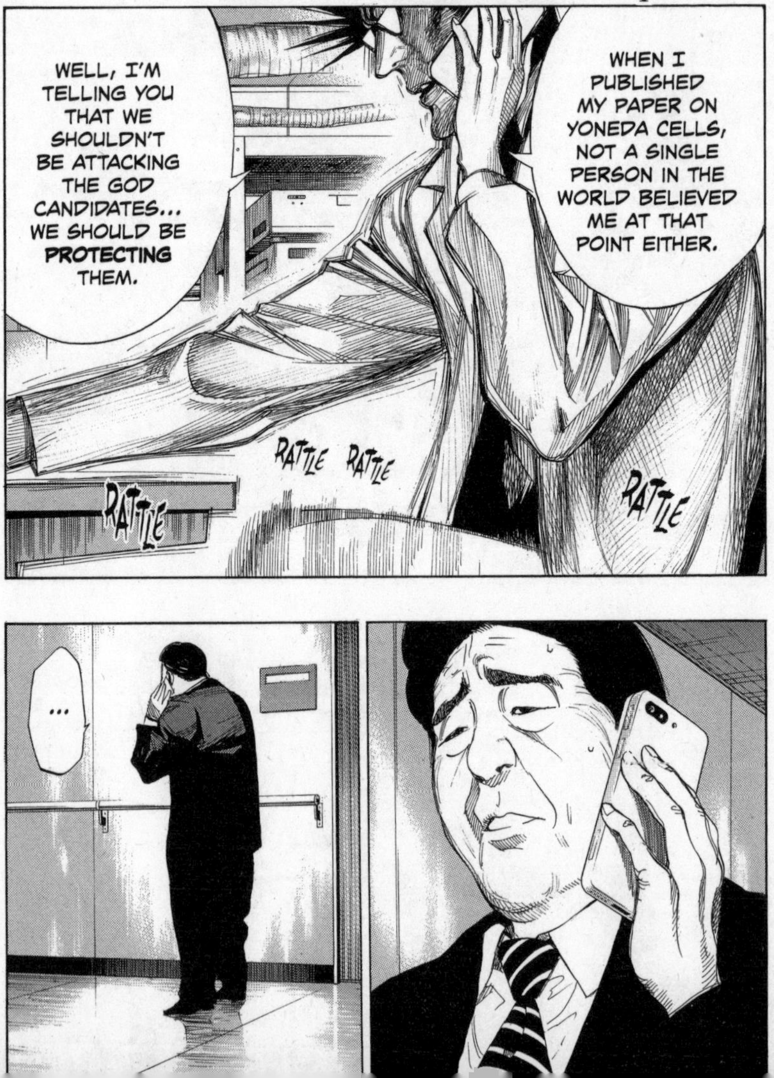
WHEN I PUBLISHED MY PAPER ON YONEDA CELLS, NOT A SINGLE PERSON IN THE WORLD BELIEVED ME AT THAT POINT EITHER.
WELL, I'M TELLING YOU THAT WE SHOULDN'T BE ATTACKING THE GOD CANDIDATES... WE SHOULD BE **PROTECTING** THEM.
RATTLE
RATTLE RATTLE
RATTLE
...

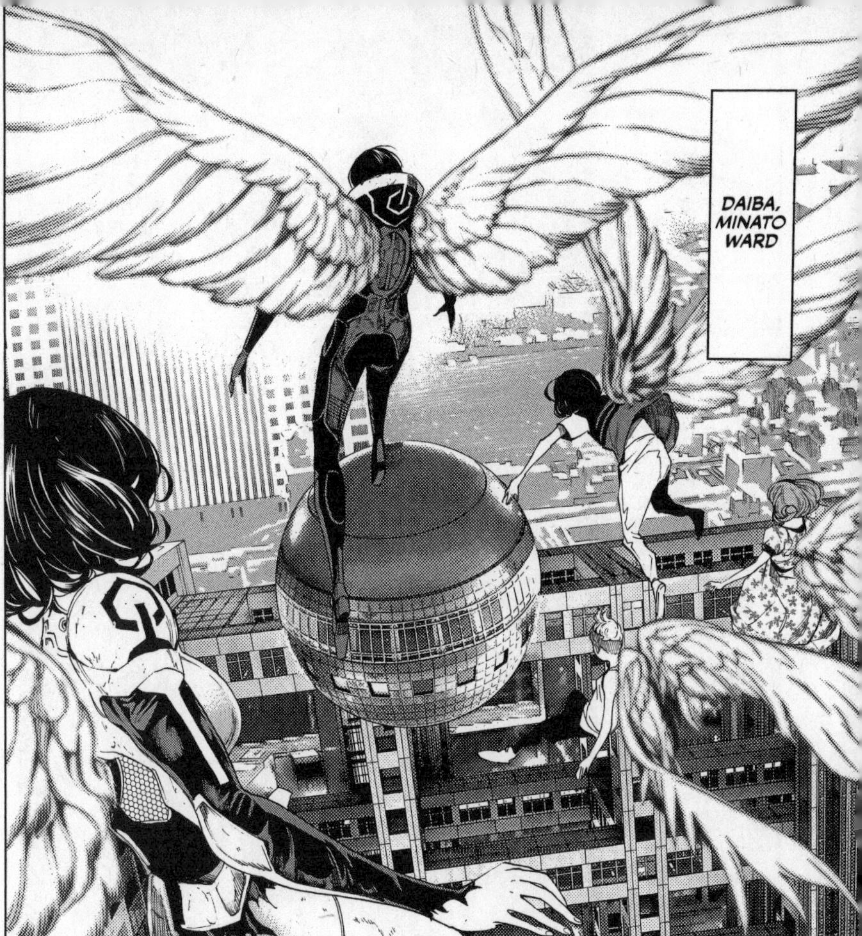
DAIBA, MINATO WARD

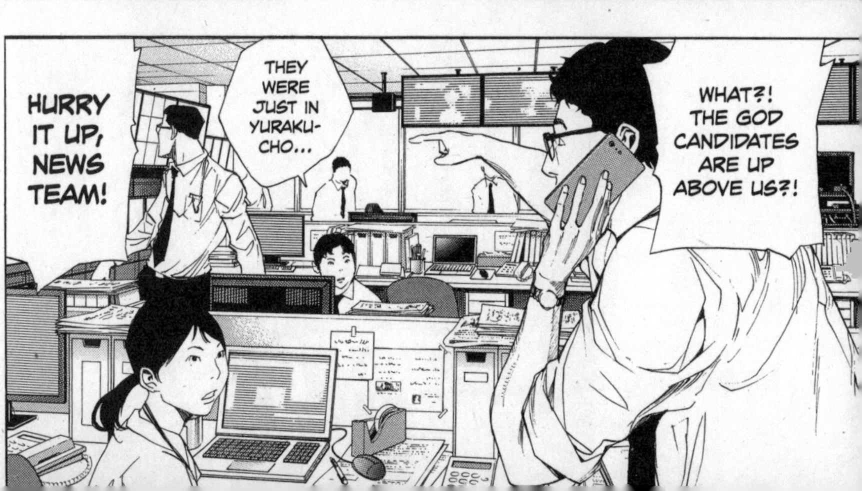
WHAT?! THE GOD CANDIDATES ARE UP ABOVE US?!
THEY WERE JUST IN YURAKU-CHO...
HURRY IT UP, NEWS TEAM!

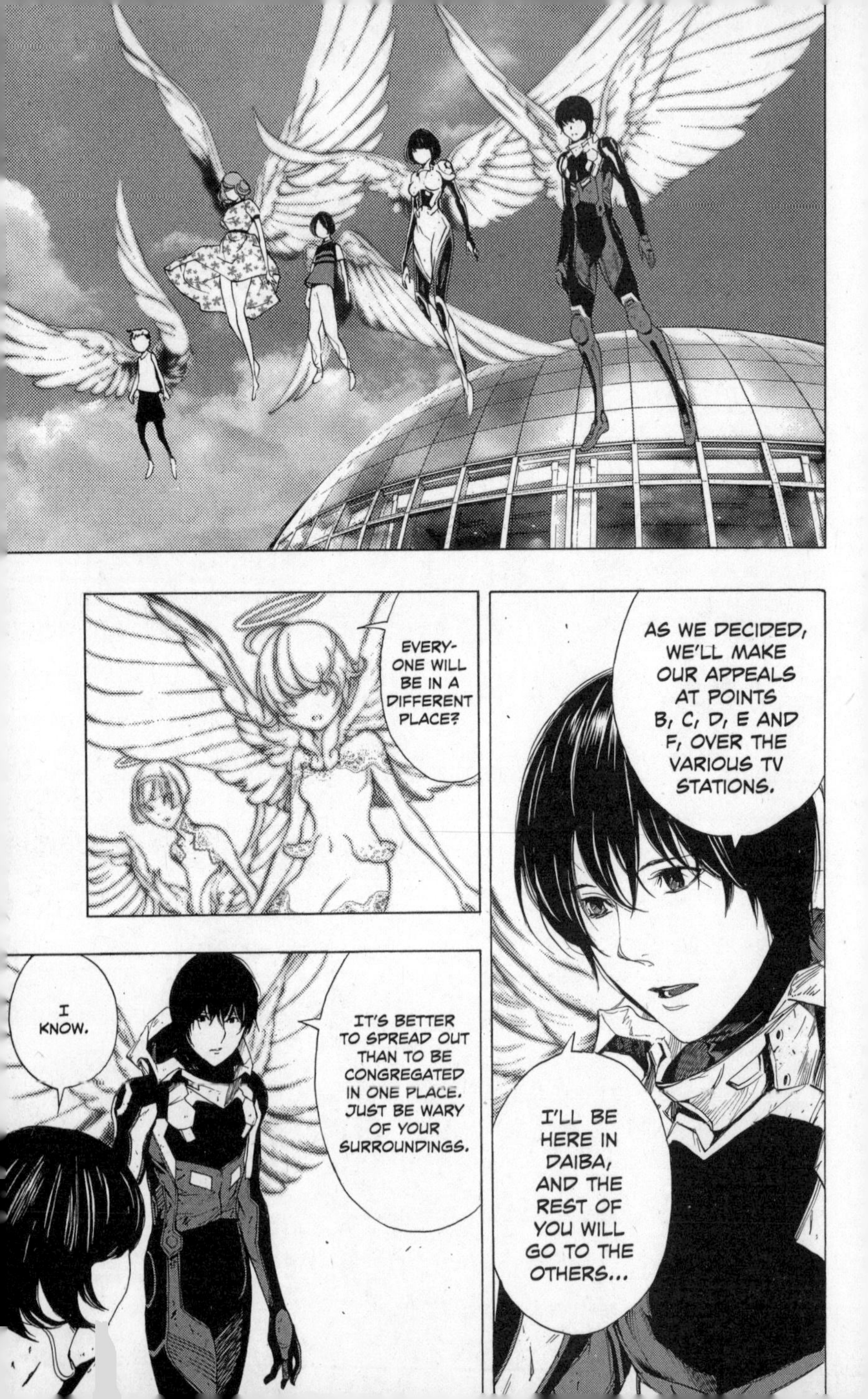
AS WE DECIDED, WE'LL MAKE OUR APPEALS AT POINTS B, C, D, E AND F, OVER THE VARIOUS TV STATIONS.
I'LL BE HERE IN DAIBA, AND THE REST OF YOU WILL GO TO THE OTHERS...
EVERY-ONE WILL BE IN A DIFFERENT PLACE?
IT'S BETTER TO SPREAD OUT THAN TO BE CONGREGATED IN ONE PLACE. JUST BE WARY OF YOUR SURROUNDINGS.
I KNOW.

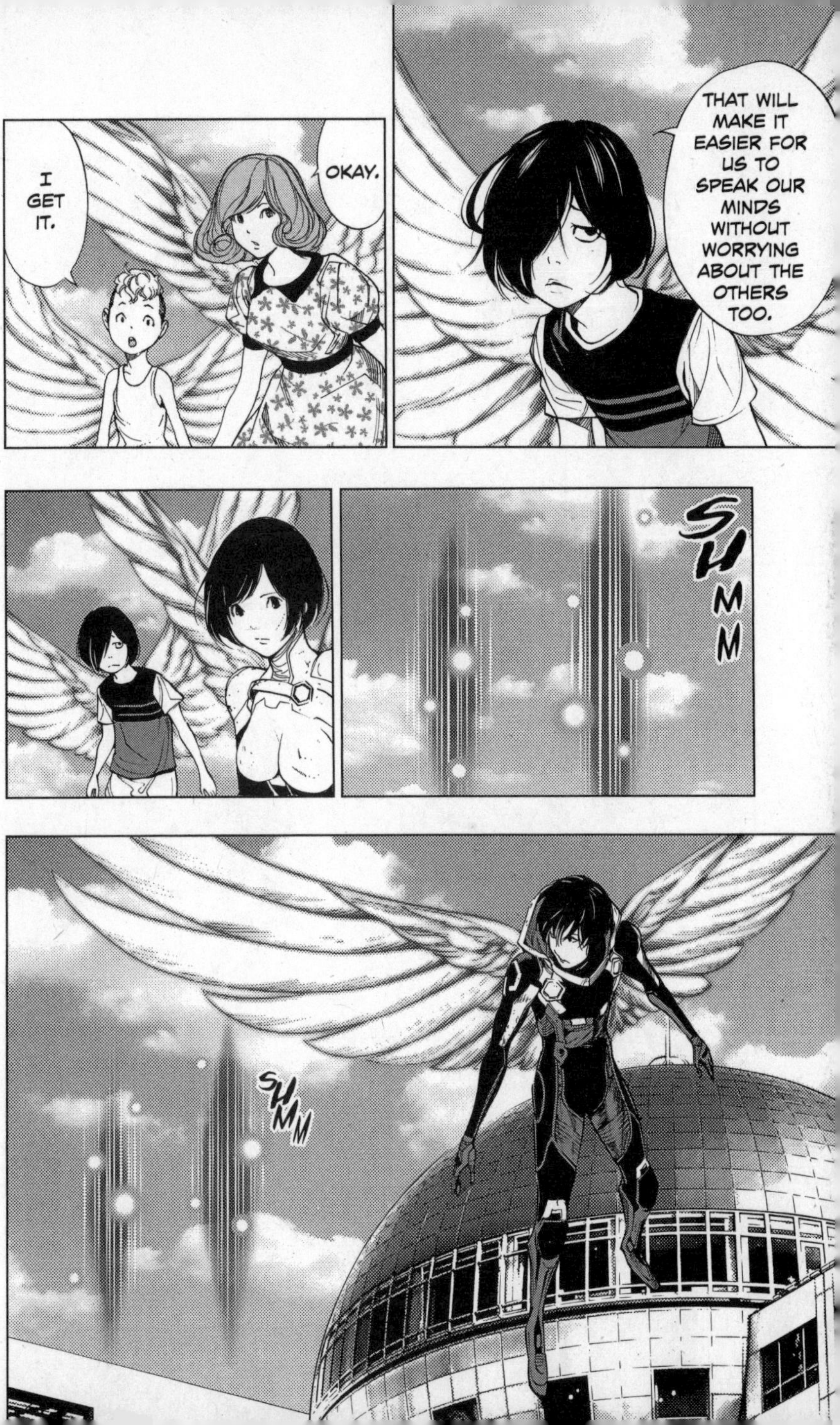
THAT WILL MAKE IT EASIER FOR US TO SPEAK OUR MINDS WITHOUT WORRYING ABOUT THE OTHERS TOO.
OKAY.
I GET IT.
SHMM
SHMM

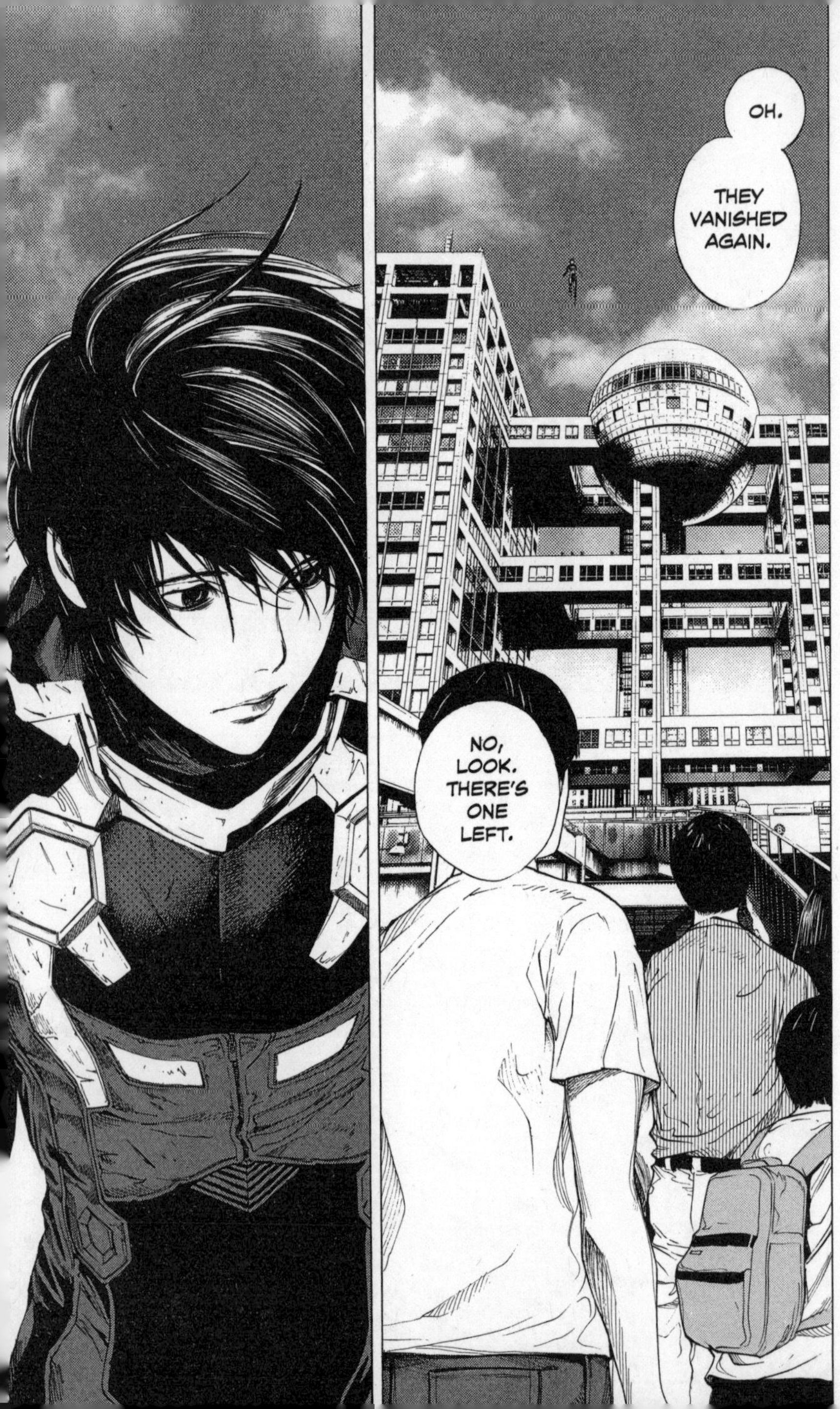
OH.
THEY VANISHED AGAIN.
NO, LOOK. THERE'S ONE LEFT.

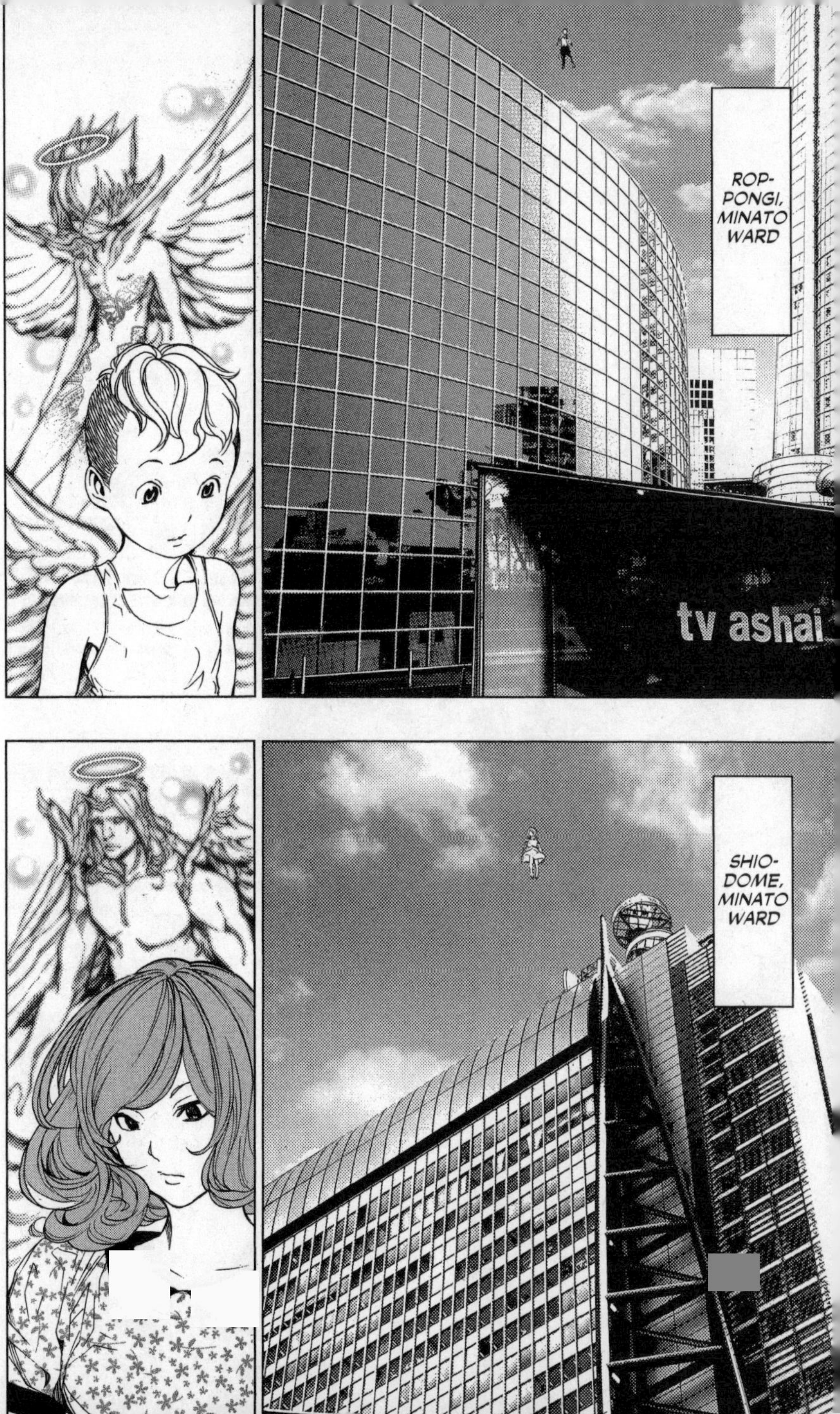
ROP-PONGI, MINATO WARD
tv ashai
SHIO-DOME, MINATO WARD

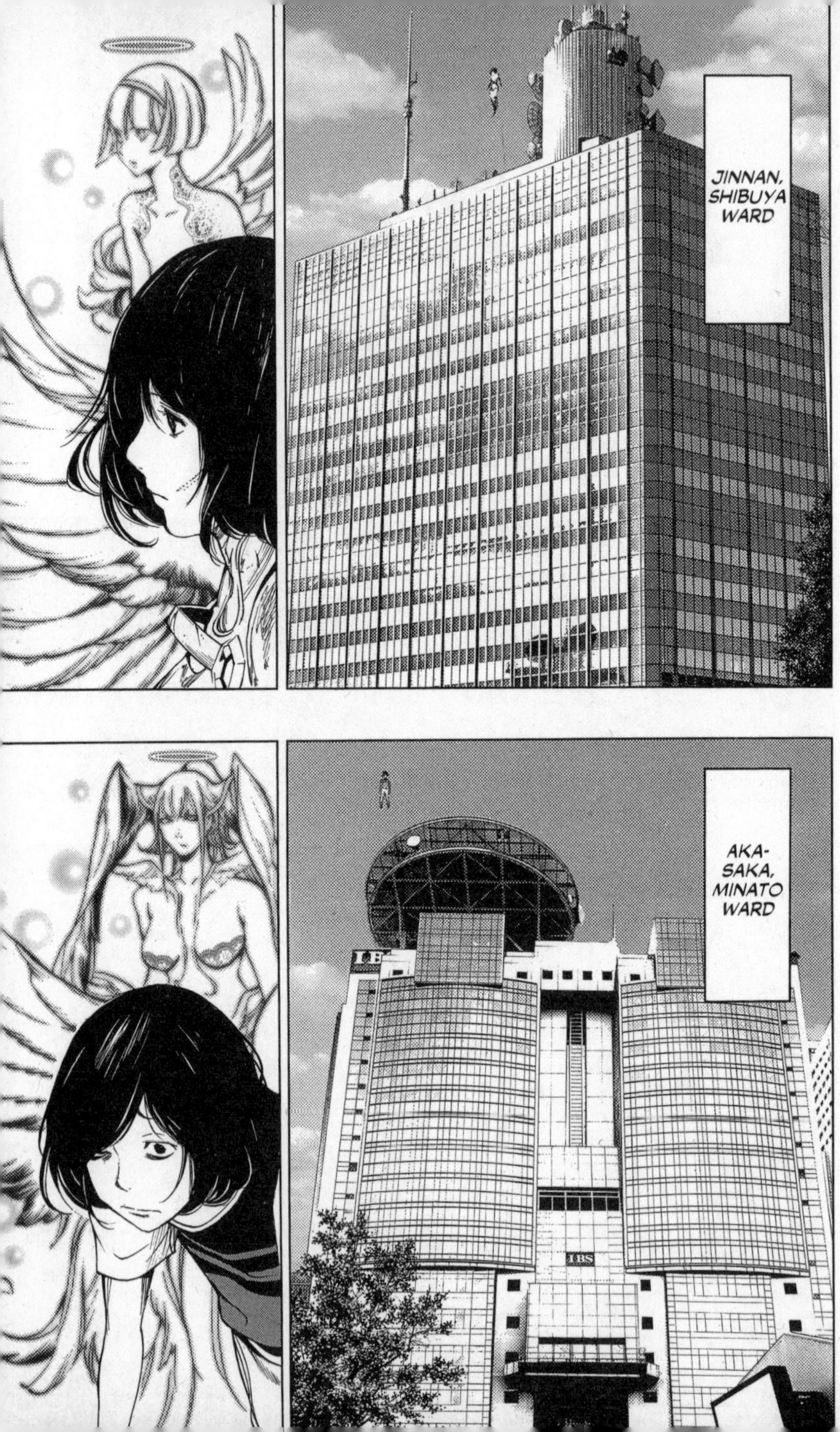
JINNAN, SHIBUYA WARD
AKA-SAKA, MINATO WARD

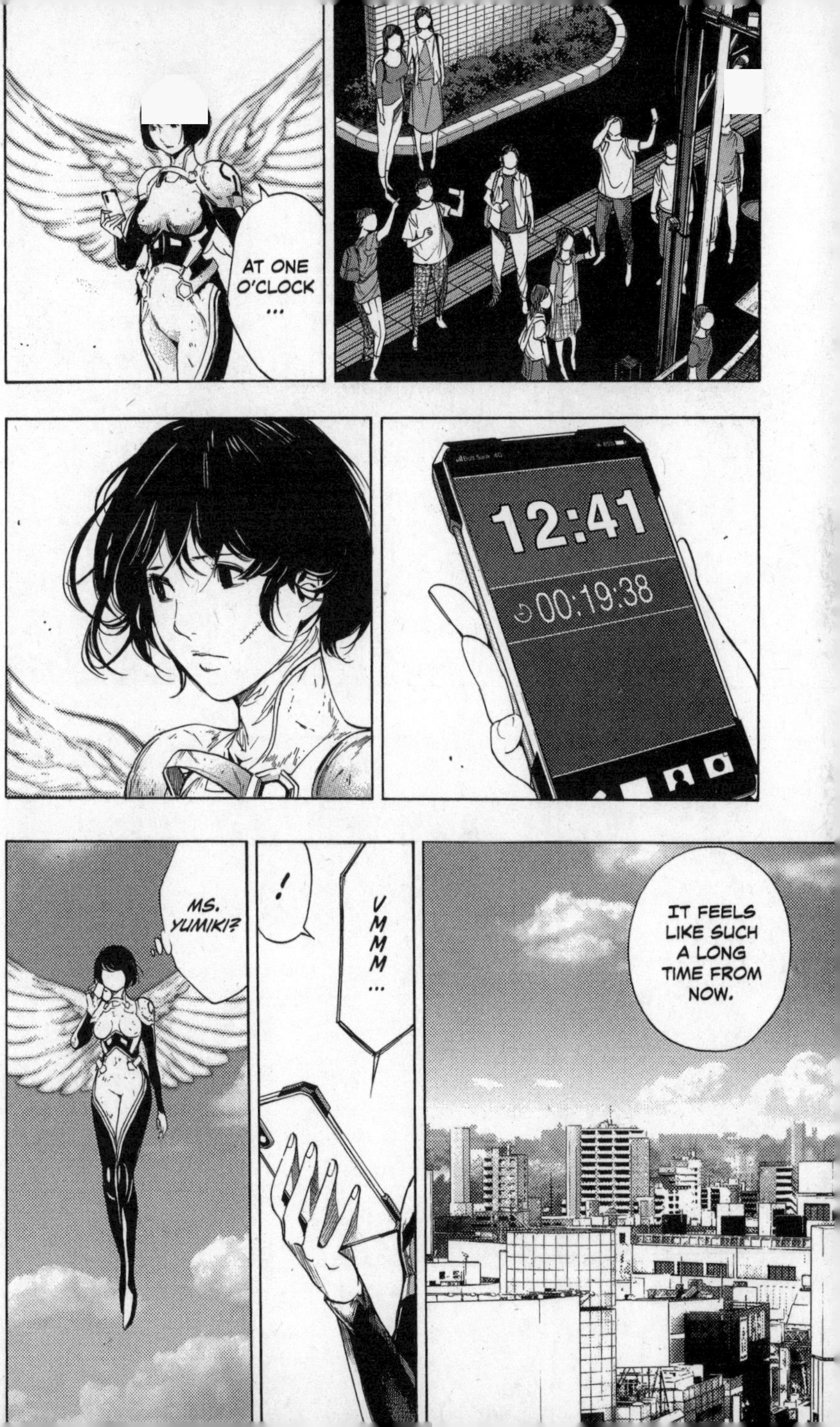
AT ONE O'CLOCK ...
12:41
00:19:38
IT FEELS LIKE SUCH A LONG TIME FROM NOW.
!
VMMM ...
MS. YUMIKI?

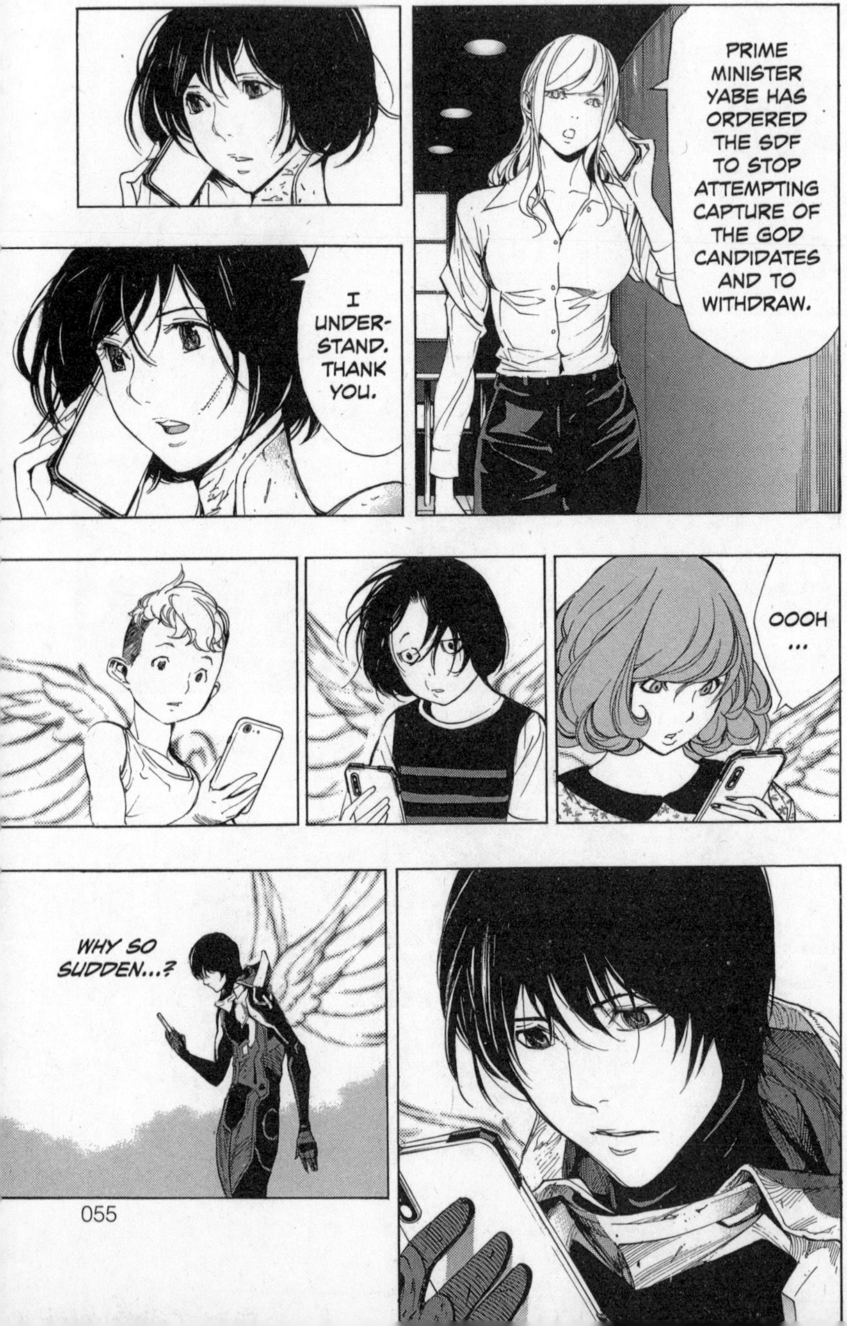
PRIME MINISTER YABE HAS ORDERED THE SDF TO STOP ATTEMPTING CAPTURE OF THE GOD CANDIDATES AND TO WITHDRAW.
I UNDER-STAND. THANK YOU.
OOOH ...
WHY SO SUDDEN...?

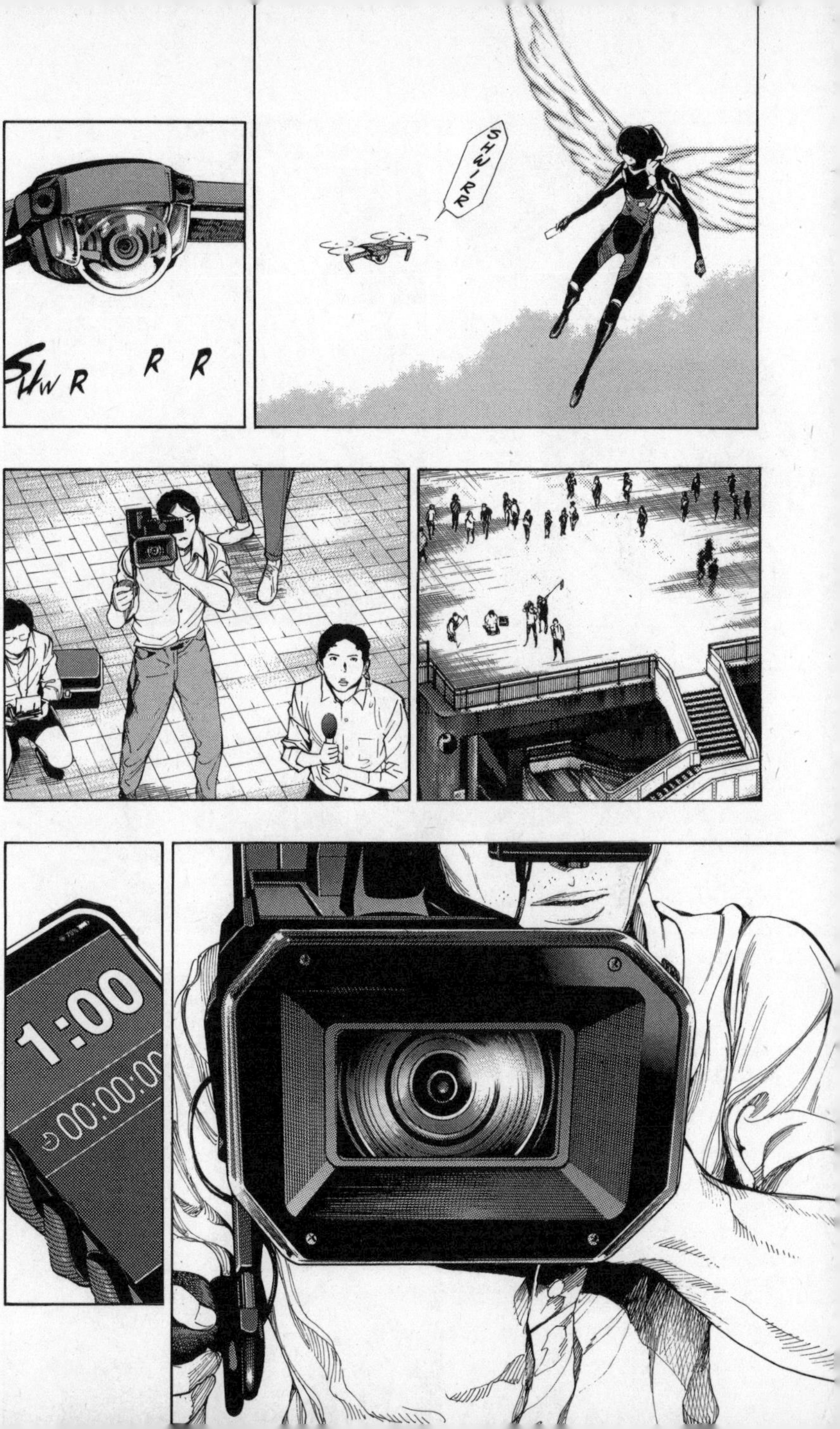
SHWIRR
SHWR R R
1:00
00:00:0

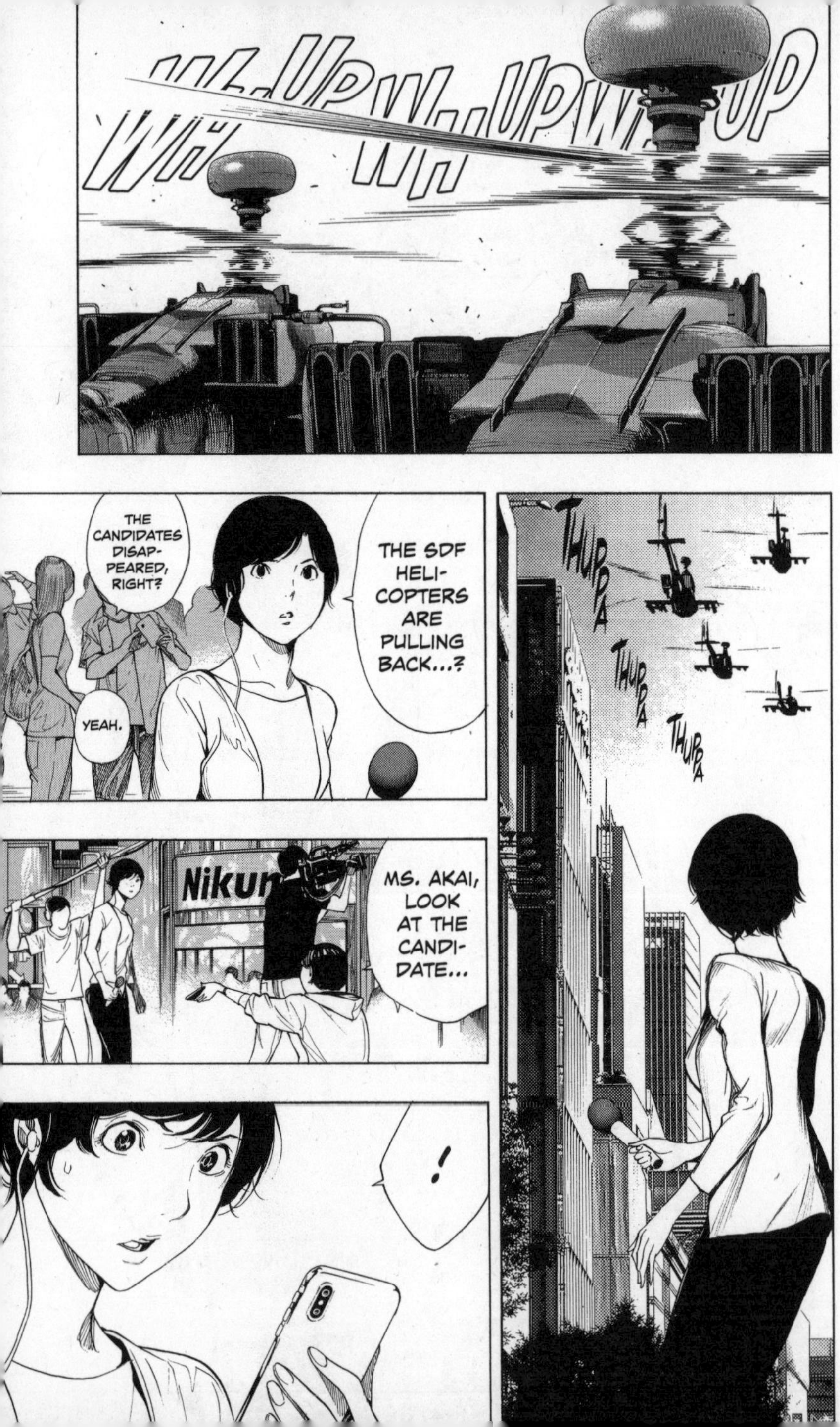
WHUPWHUPWHUP
THUPPA
THUPPA
THUPPA
THE SDF HELICOPTERS ARE PULLING BACK...?
THE CANDIDATES DISAPPEARED, RIGHT?
YEAH.
MS. AKAI, LOOK AT THE CANDIDATE...
!

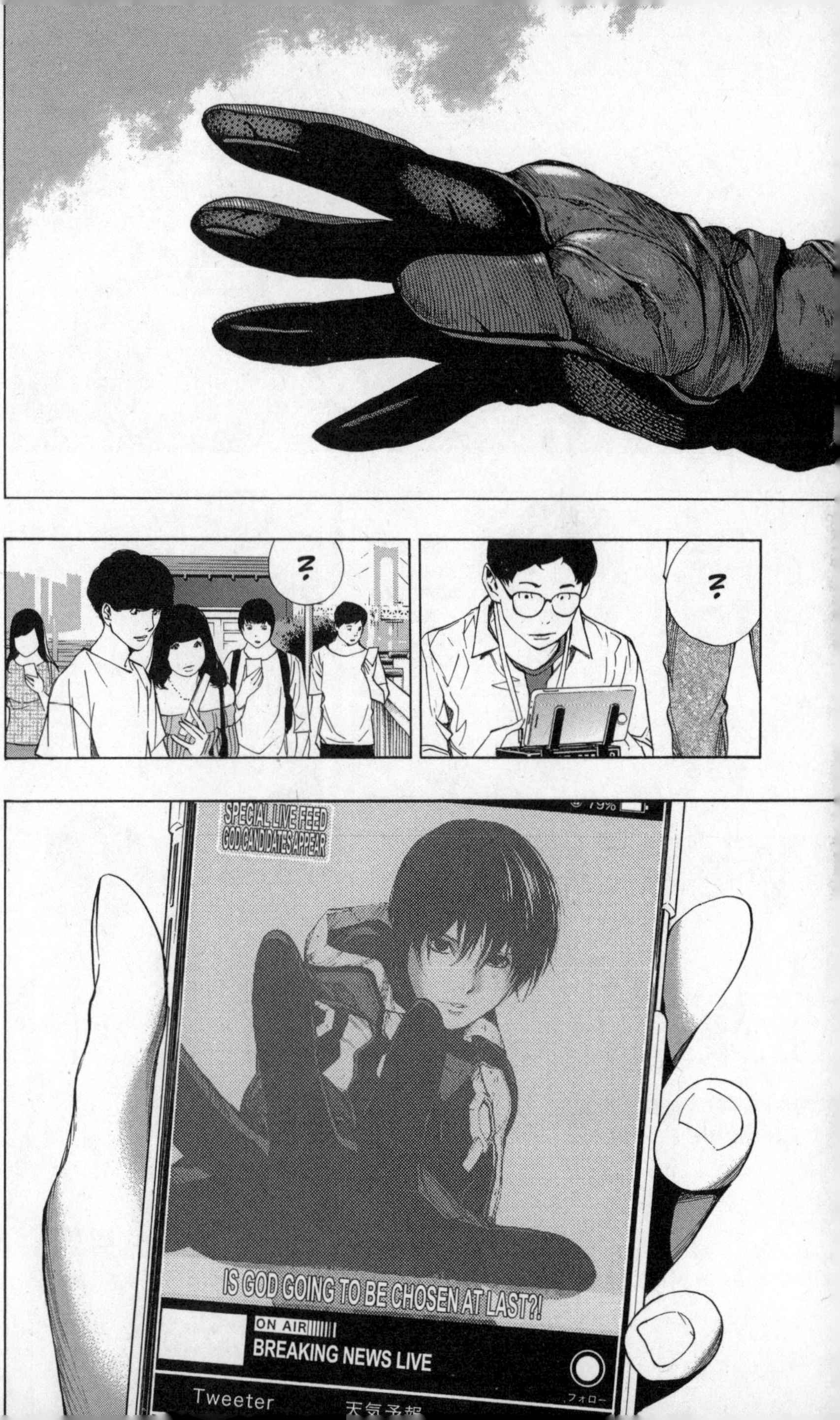
?
?
79%
SPECIAL LIVE FEED
GOD CANDIDATES APPEAR
IS GOD GOING TO BE CHOSEN AT LAST?!
ON AIR
BREAKING NEWS LIVE
Tweeter
フォロー

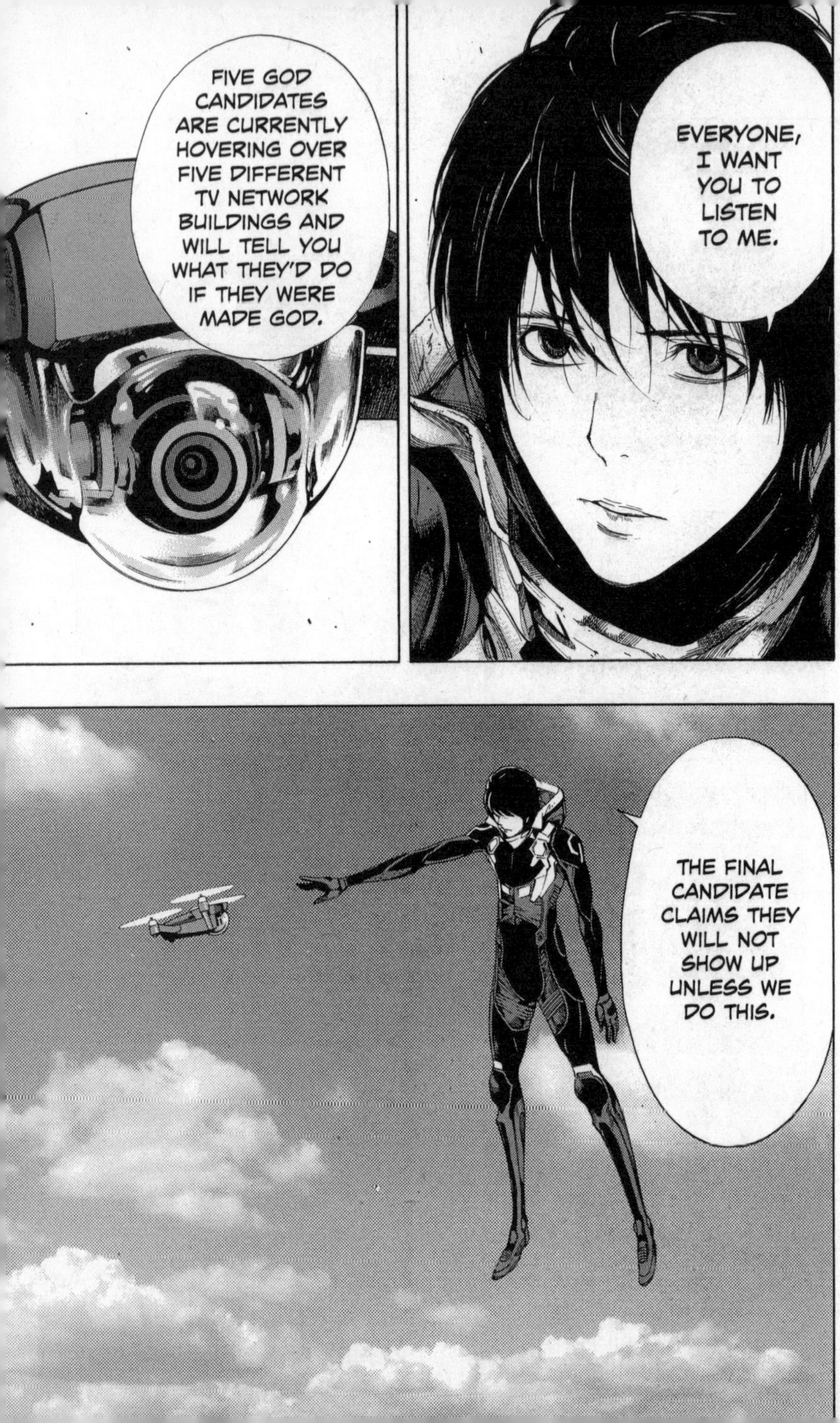
EVERYONE, I WANT YOU TO LISTEN TO ME.
FIVE GOD CANDIDATES ARE CURRENTLY HOVERING OVER FIVE DIFFERENT TV NETWORK BUILDINGS AND WILL TELL YOU WHAT THEY'D DO IF THEY WERE MADE GOD.
THE FINAL CANDIDATE CLAIMS THEY WILL NOT SHOW UP UNLESS WE DO THIS.

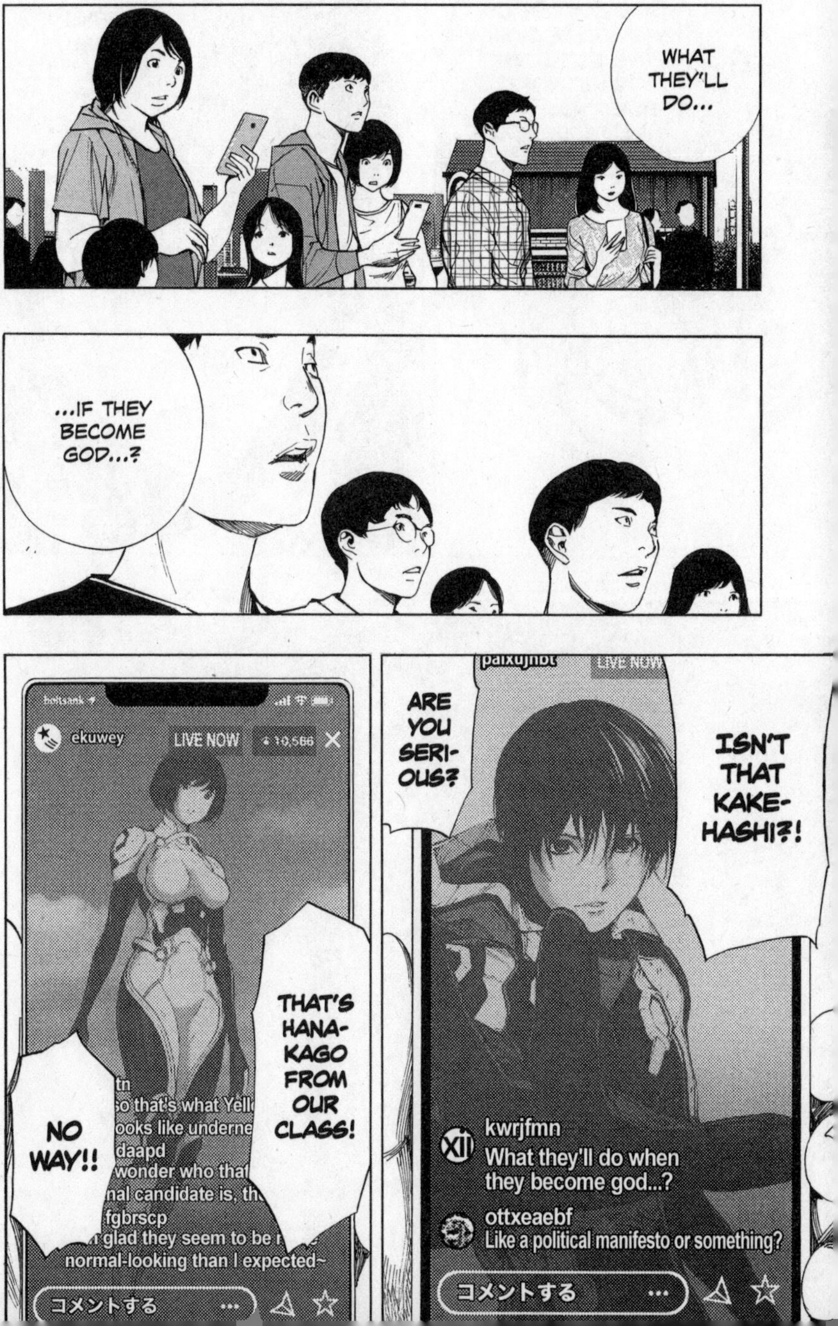
WHAT THEY'LL DO...
...IF THEY BECOME GOD...?
paixujnbt
LIVE NOW
ISN'T THAT KAKE-HASHI?!
ARE YOU SERI-OUS?
kwrjfmn
What they'll do when they become god...?
ottxeaebf
Like a political manifesto or something?
コメントする
ekuwey
LIVE NOW
THAT'S HANA-KAGO FROM OUR CLASS!
NO WAY!!
daapd
fgbrscp
normal-looking than I expected~
コメントする

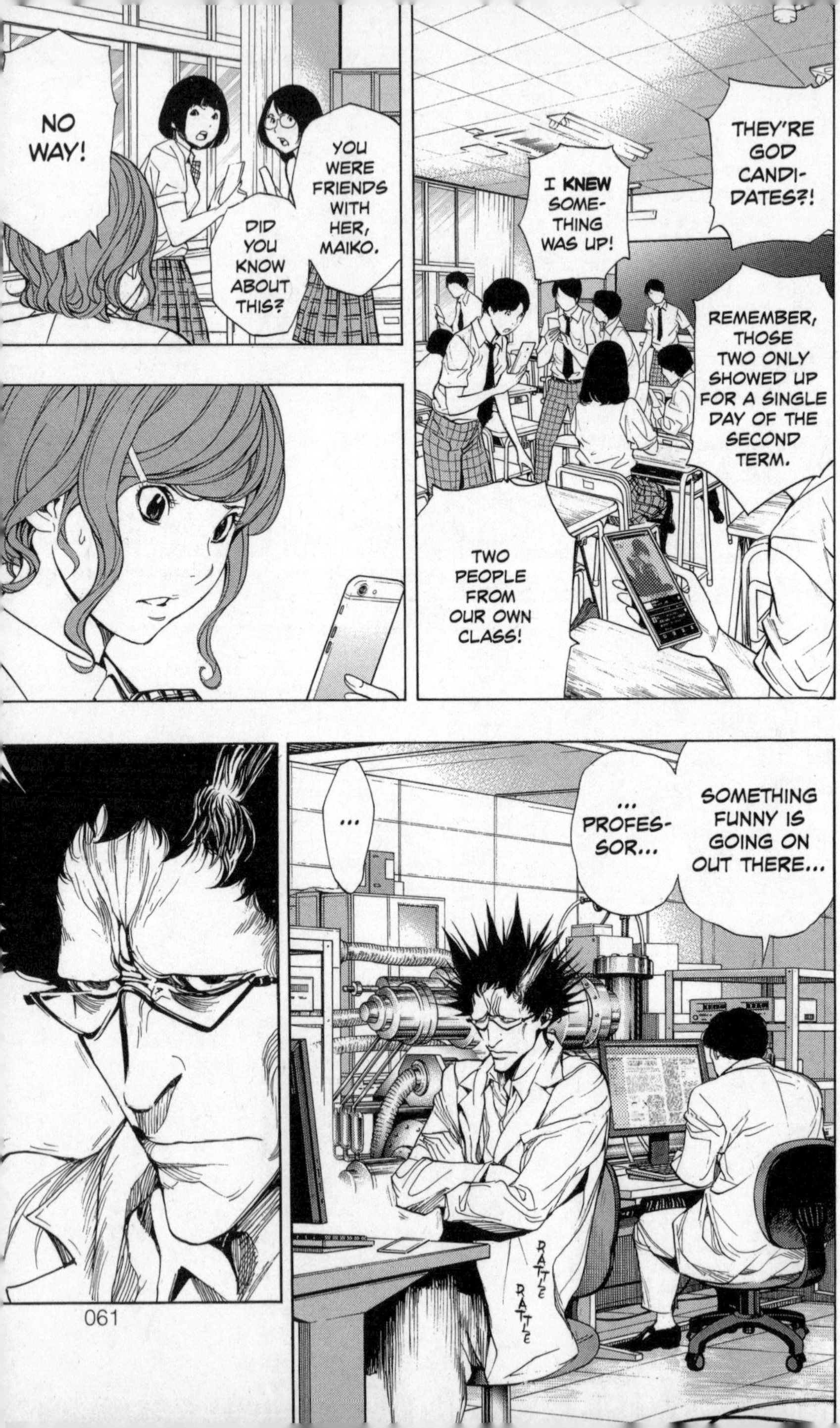
THEY'RE GOD CANDIDATES?!
I KNEW SOMETHING WAS UP!
REMEMBER, THOSE TWO ONLY SHOWED UP FOR A SINGLE DAY OF THE SECOND TERM.
TWO PEOPLE FROM OUR OWN CLASS!
YOU WERE FRIENDS WITH HER, MAIKO.
DID YOU KNOW ABOUT THIS?
NO WAY!
SOMETHING FUNNY IS GOING ON OUT THERE...
... PROFESSOR...
...
RATTLE
RATTLE

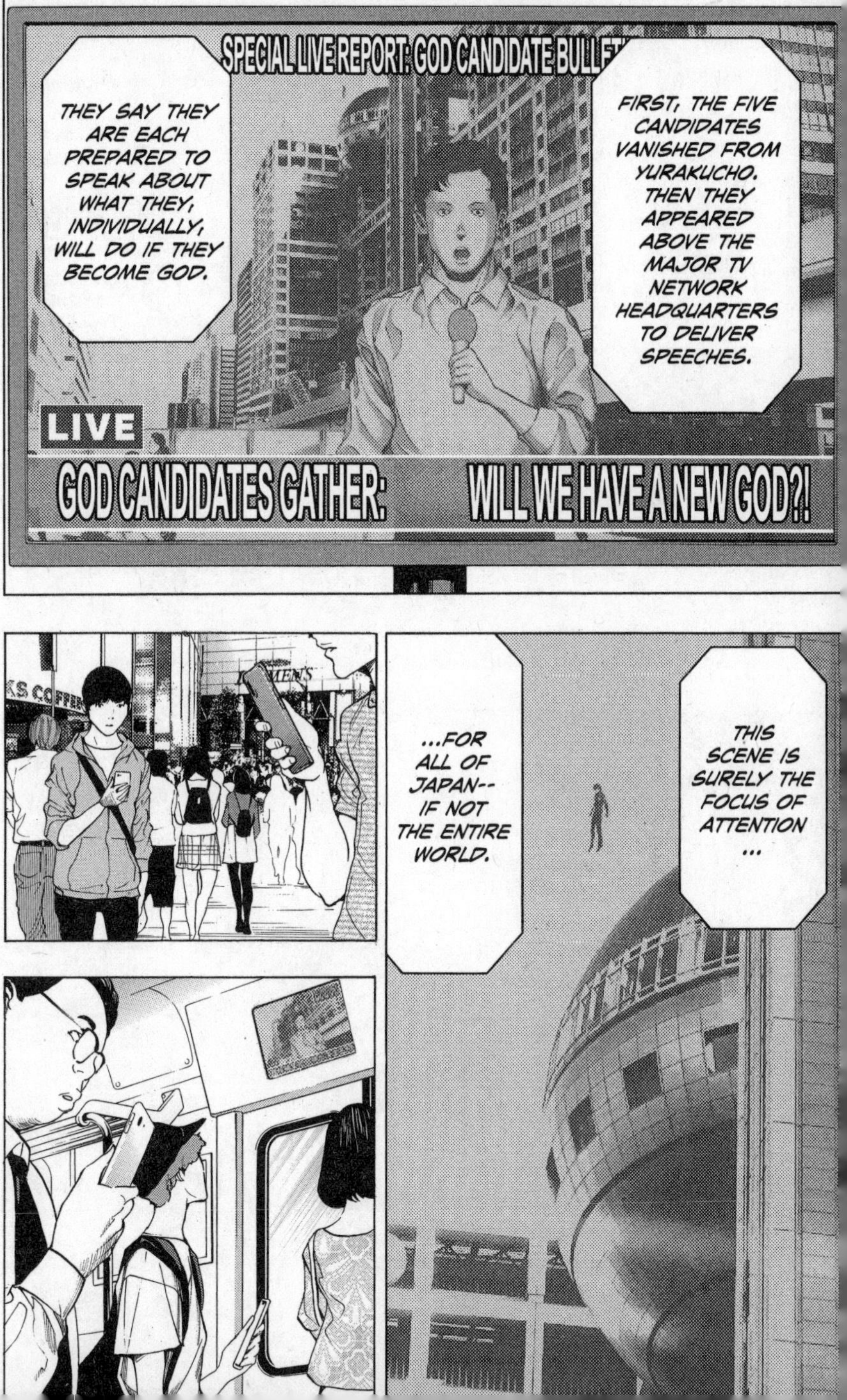
SPECIAL LIVE REPORT: GOD CANDIDATE BULL
FIRST, THE FIVE CANDIDATES VANISHED FROM YURAKUCHO. THEN THEY APPEARED ABOVE THE MAJOR TV NETWORK HEADQUARTERS TO DELIVER SPEECHES.
THEY SAY THEY ARE EACH PREPARED TO SPEAK ABOUT WHAT THEY, INDIVIDUALLY, WILL DO IF THEY BECOME GOD.
LIVE
GOD CANDIDATES GATHER: WILL WE HAVE A NEW GOD?!
THIS SCENE IS SURELY THE FOCUS OF ATTENTION ...
...FOR ALL OF JAPAN-- IF NOT THE ENTIRE WORLD.

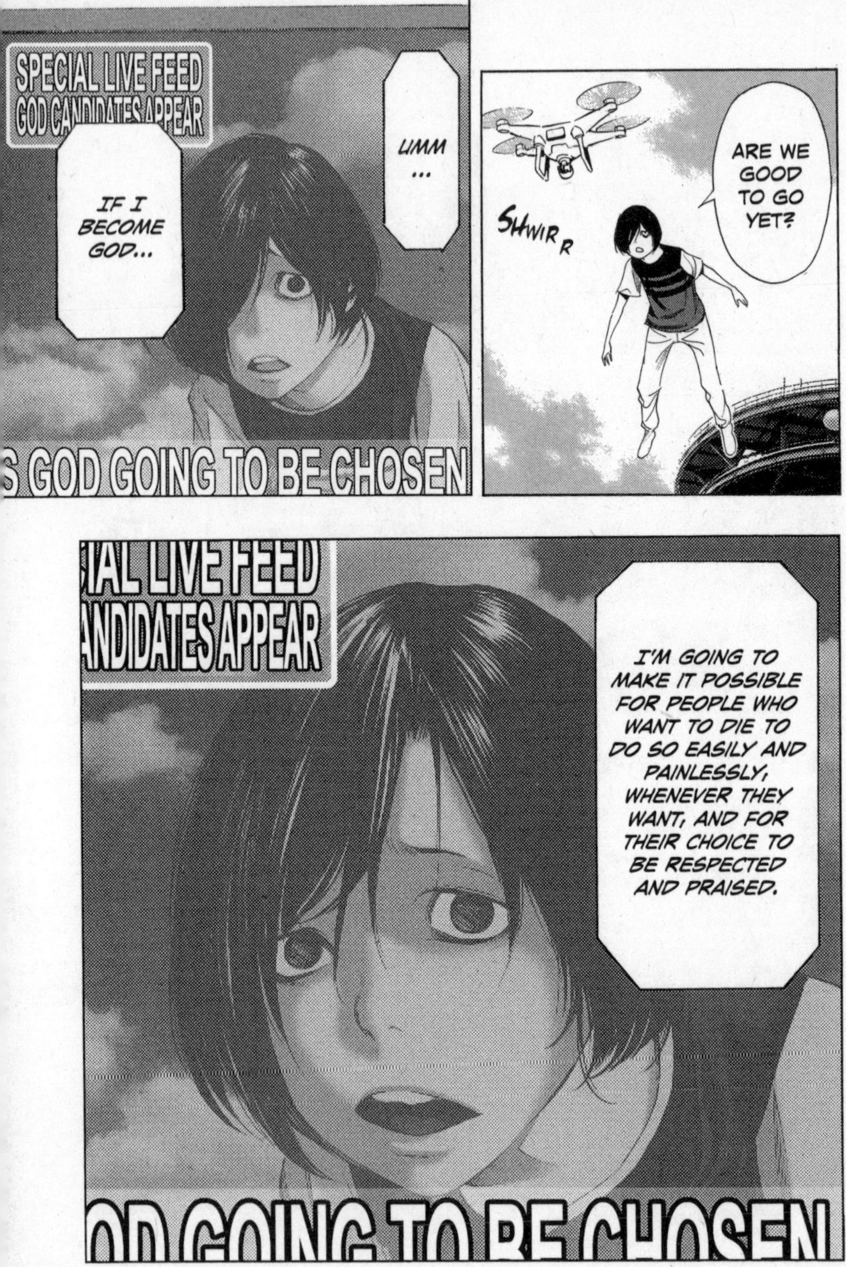
ARE WE GOOD TO GO YET?
SHWIRR
UMM ...
SPECIAL LIVE FEED
GOD CANDIDATES APPEAR
IF I BECOME GOD...
S GOD GOING TO BE CHOSEN
IAL LIVE FEED
ANDIDATES APPEAR
I'M GOING TO MAKE IT POSSIBLE FOR PEOPLE WHO WANT TO DIE TO DO SO EASILY AND PAINLESSLY, WHENEVER THEY WANT, AND FOR THEIR CHOICE TO BE RESPECTED AND PRAISED.
OD GOING TO BE CHOSEN

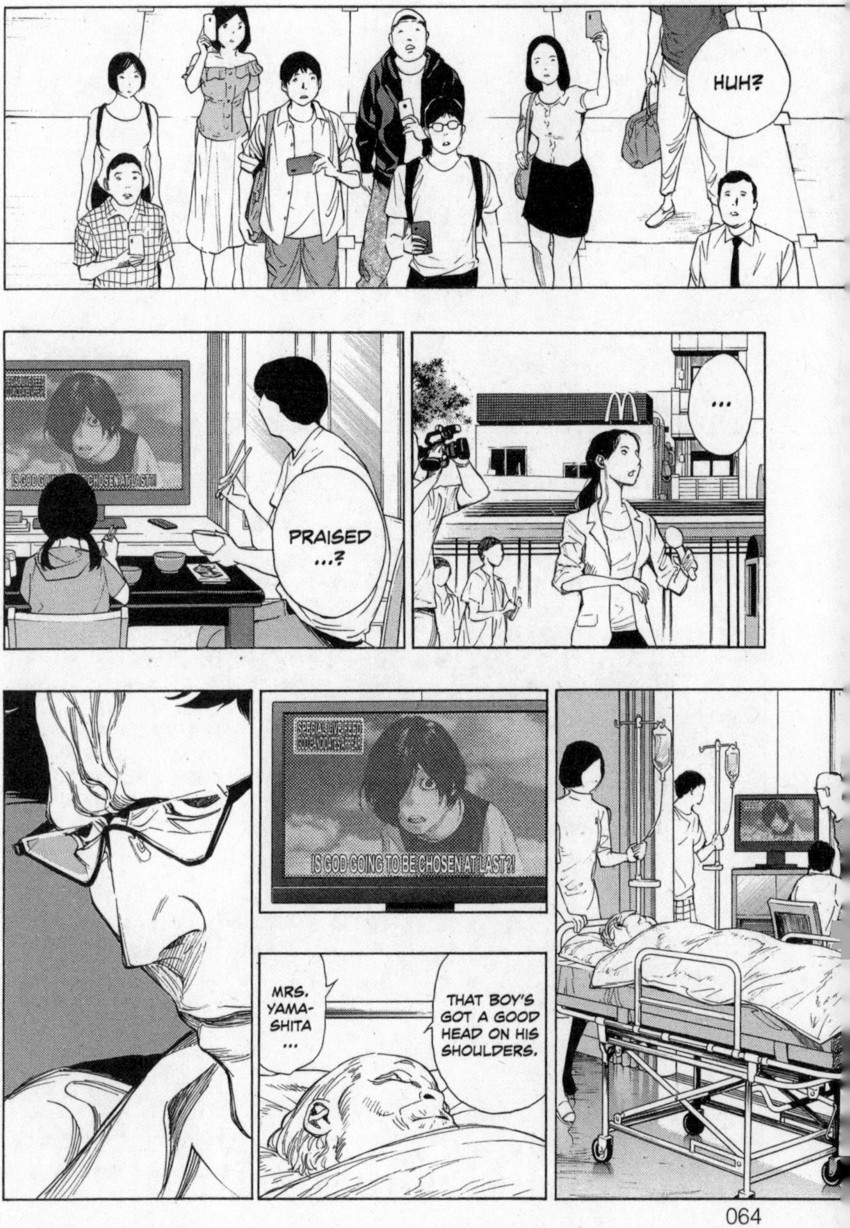
HUH?
...
PRAISED ...?
SPECIAL LIVE FEED
GOD CANDIDATES APPEAR
IS GOD GOING TO BE CHOSEN AT LAST?!
THAT BOY'S GOT A GOOD HEAD ON HIS SHOULDERS.
MRS. YAMA-SHITA ...

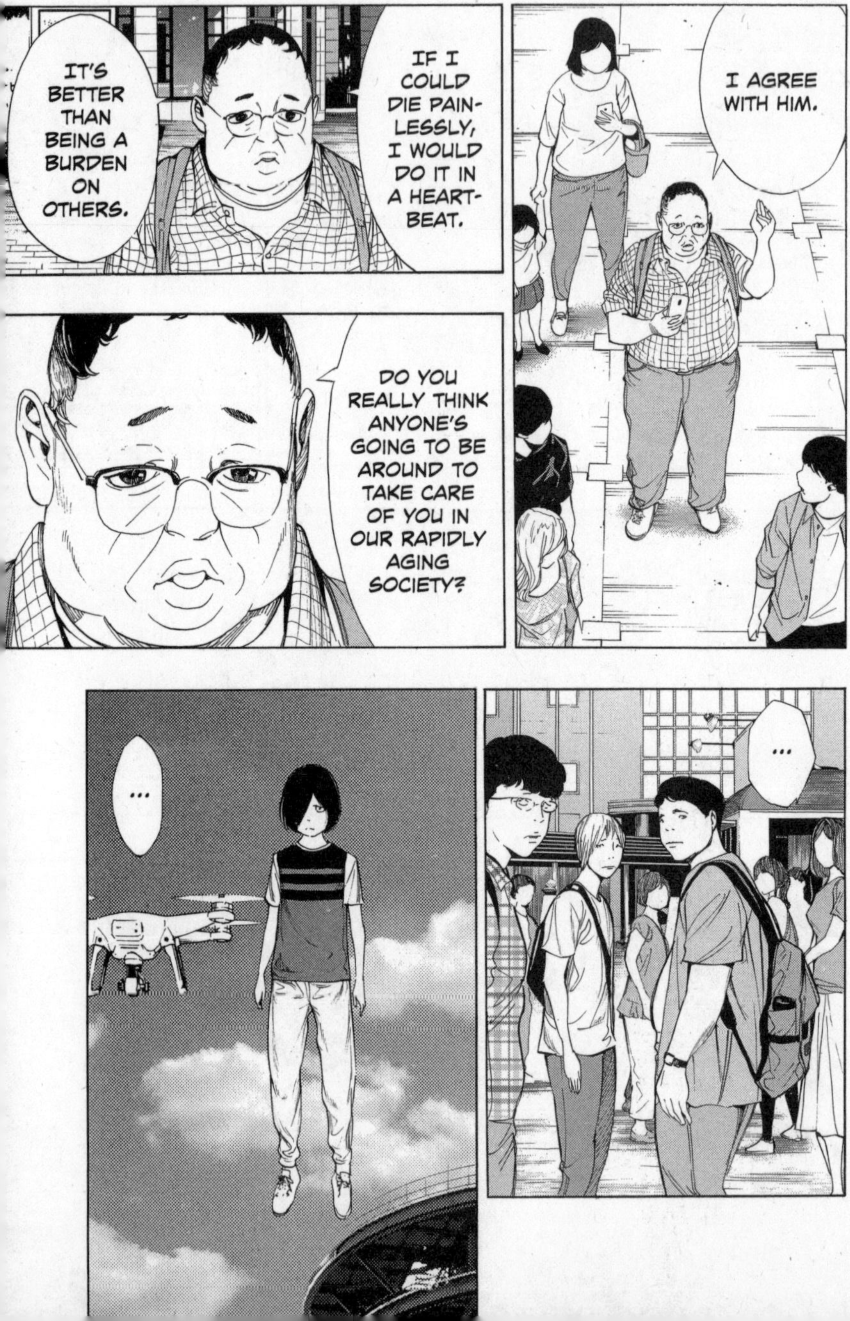
I AGREE WITH HIM.
IF I COULD DIE PAINLESSLY, I WOULD DO IT IN A HEARTBEAT.
IT'S BETTER THAN BEING A BURDEN ON OTHERS.
DO YOU REALLY THINK ANYONE'S GOING TO BE AROUND TO TAKE CARE OF YOU IN OUR RAPIDLY AGING SOCIETY?
...
...

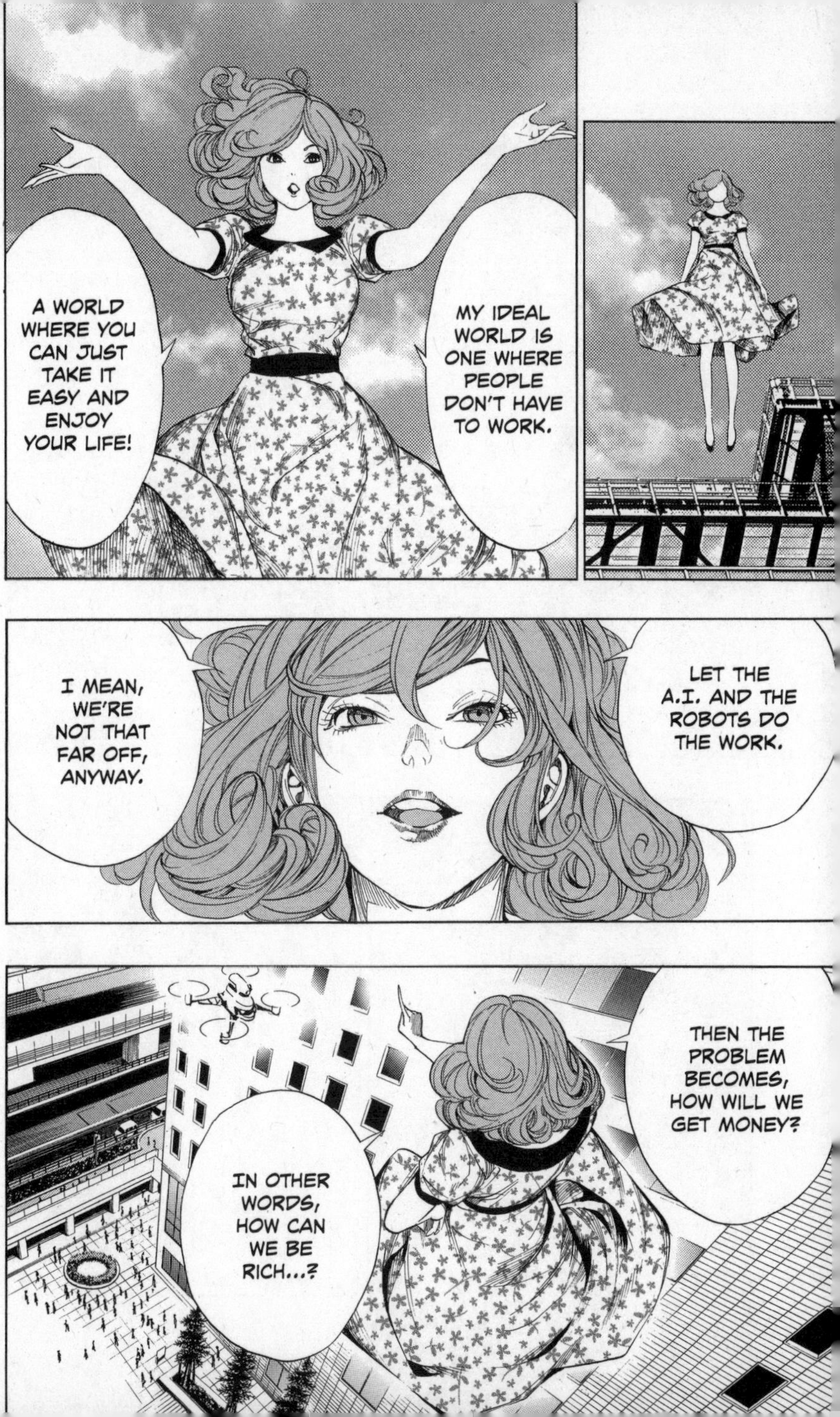
MY IDEAL WORLD IS ONE WHERE PEOPLE DON'T HAVE TO WORK.
A WORLD WHERE YOU CAN JUST TAKE IT EASY AND ENJOY YOUR LIFE!
LET THE A.I. AND THE ROBOTS DO THE WORK.
I MEAN, WE'RE NOT THAT FAR OFF, ANYWAY.
THEN THE PROBLEM BECOMES, HOW WILL WE GET MONEY?
IN OTHER WORDS, HOW CAN WE BE RICH...?

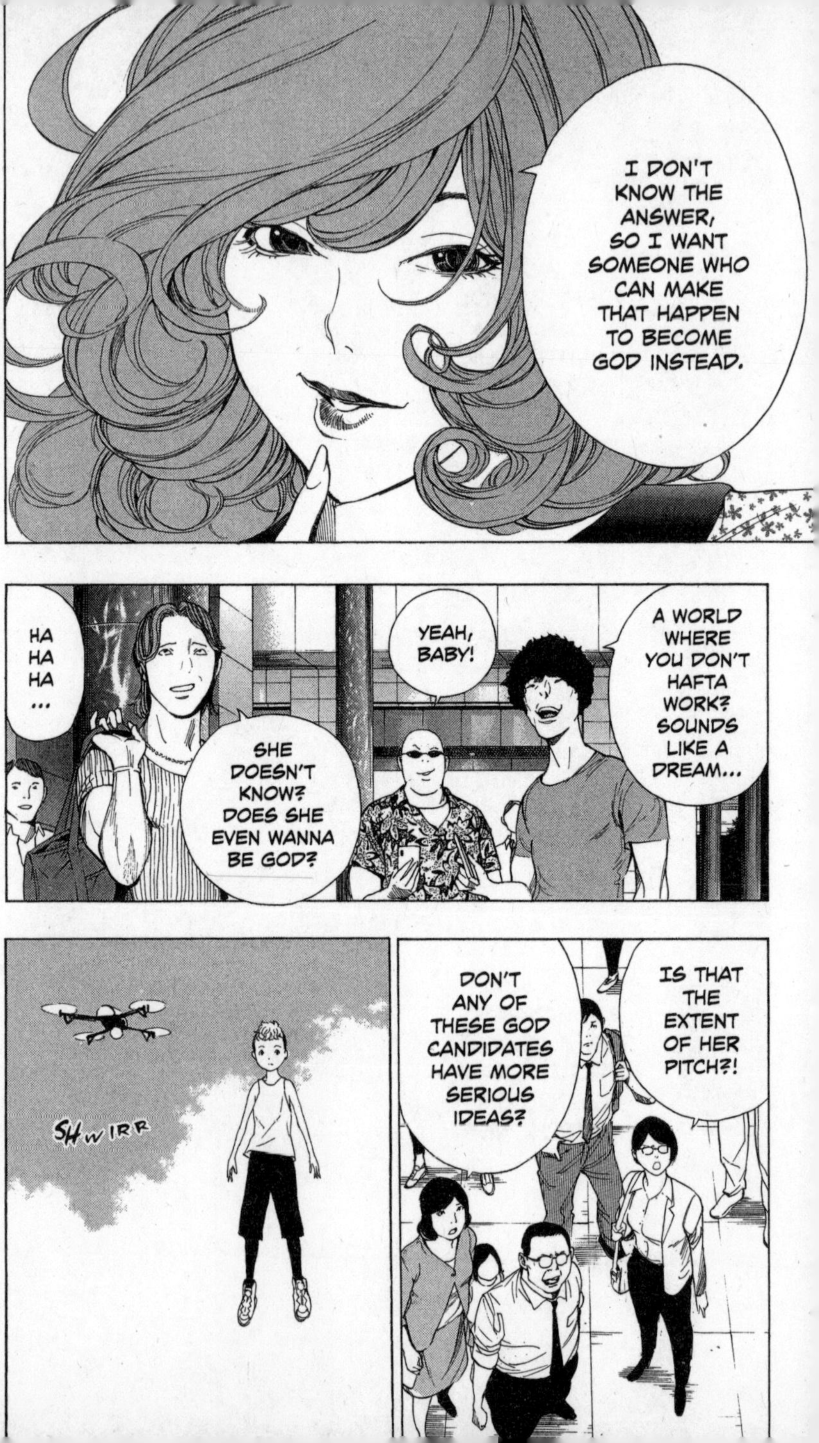
I DON'T KNOW THE ANSWER, SO I WANT SOMEONE WHO CAN MAKE THAT HAPPEN TO BECOME GOD INSTEAD.
A WORLD WHERE YOU DON'T HAFTA WORK? SOUNDS LIKE A DREAM...
YEAH, BABY!
SHE DOESN'T KNOW? DOES SHE EVEN WANNA BE GOD?
HA HA HA ...
IS THAT THE EXTENT OF HER PITCH?!
DON'T ANY OF THESE GOD CANDIDATES HAVE MORE SERIOUS IDEAS?
SHWIRR

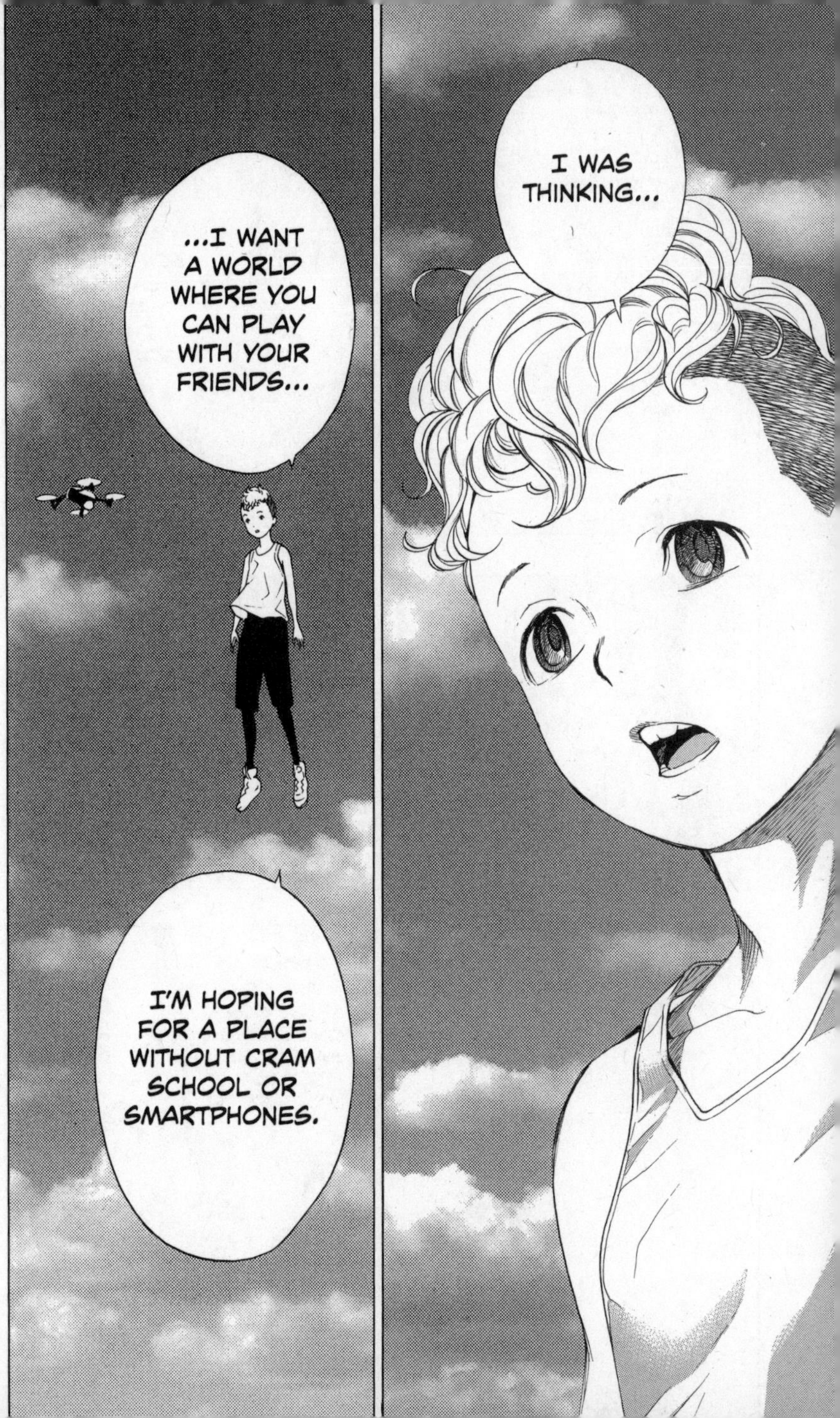
I WAS THINKING...
...I WANT A WORLD WHERE YOU CAN PLAY WITH YOUR FRIENDS...
I'M HOPING FOR A PLACE WITHOUT CRAM SCHOOL OR SMARTPHONES.

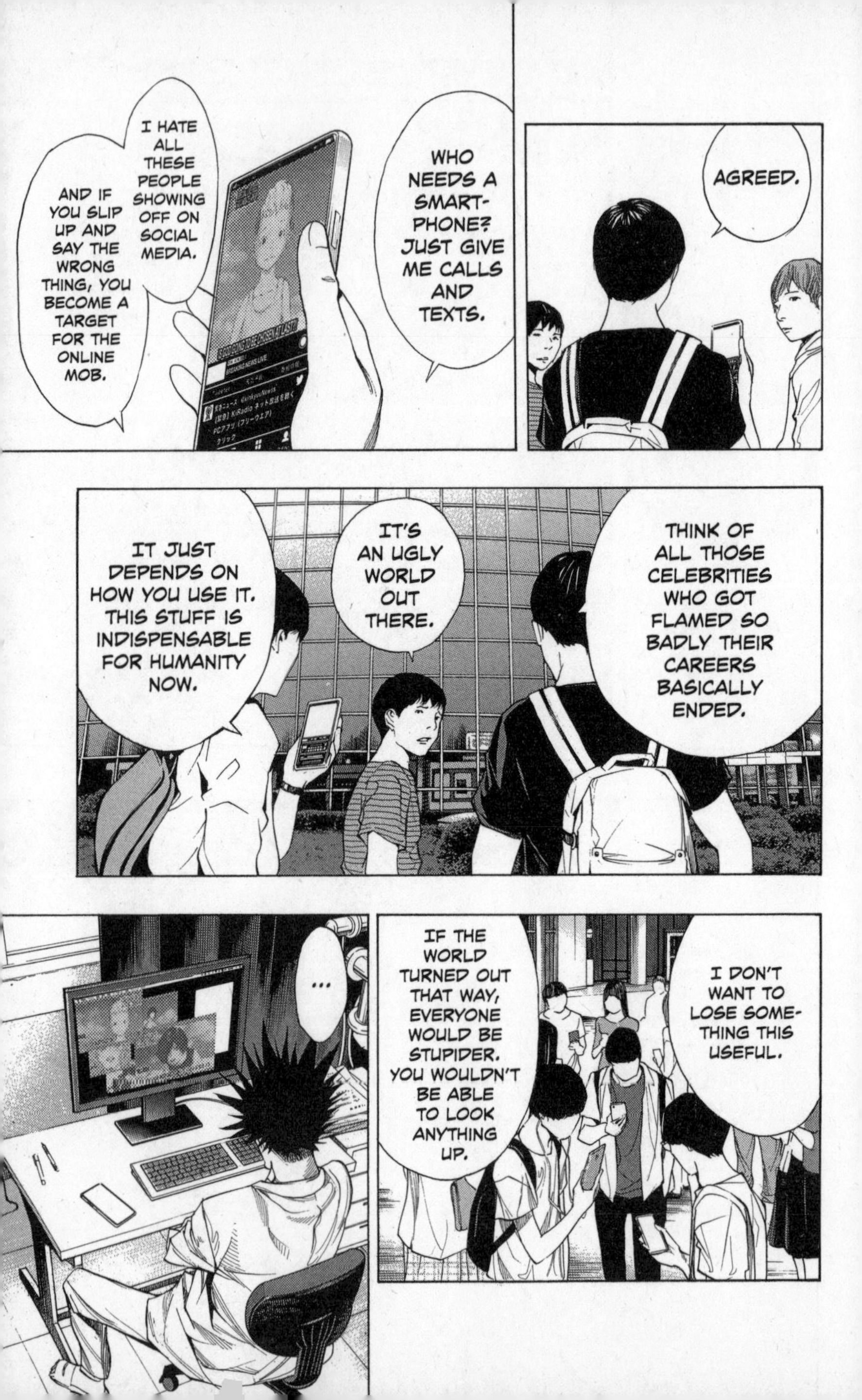
AGREED.
WHO NEEDS A SMART-PHONE? JUST GIVE ME CALLS AND TEXTS.
I HATE ALL THESE PEOPLE SHOWING OFF ON SOCIAL MEDIA.
AND IF YOU SLIP UP AND SAY THE WRONG THING, YOU BECOME A TARGET FOR THE ONLINE MOB.
THINK OF ALL THOSE CELEBRITIES WHO GOT FLAMED SO BADLY THEIR CAREERS BASICALLY ENDED.
IT'S AN UGLY WORLD OUT THERE.
IT JUST DEPENDS ON HOW YOU USE IT. THIS STUFF IS INDISPENSABLE FOR HUMANITY NOW.
I DON'T WANT TO LOSE SOME-THING THIS USEFUL.
IF THE WORLD TURNED OUT THAT WAY, EVERYONE WOULD BE STUPIDER. YOU WOULDN'T BE ABLE TO LOOK ANYTHING UP.
...

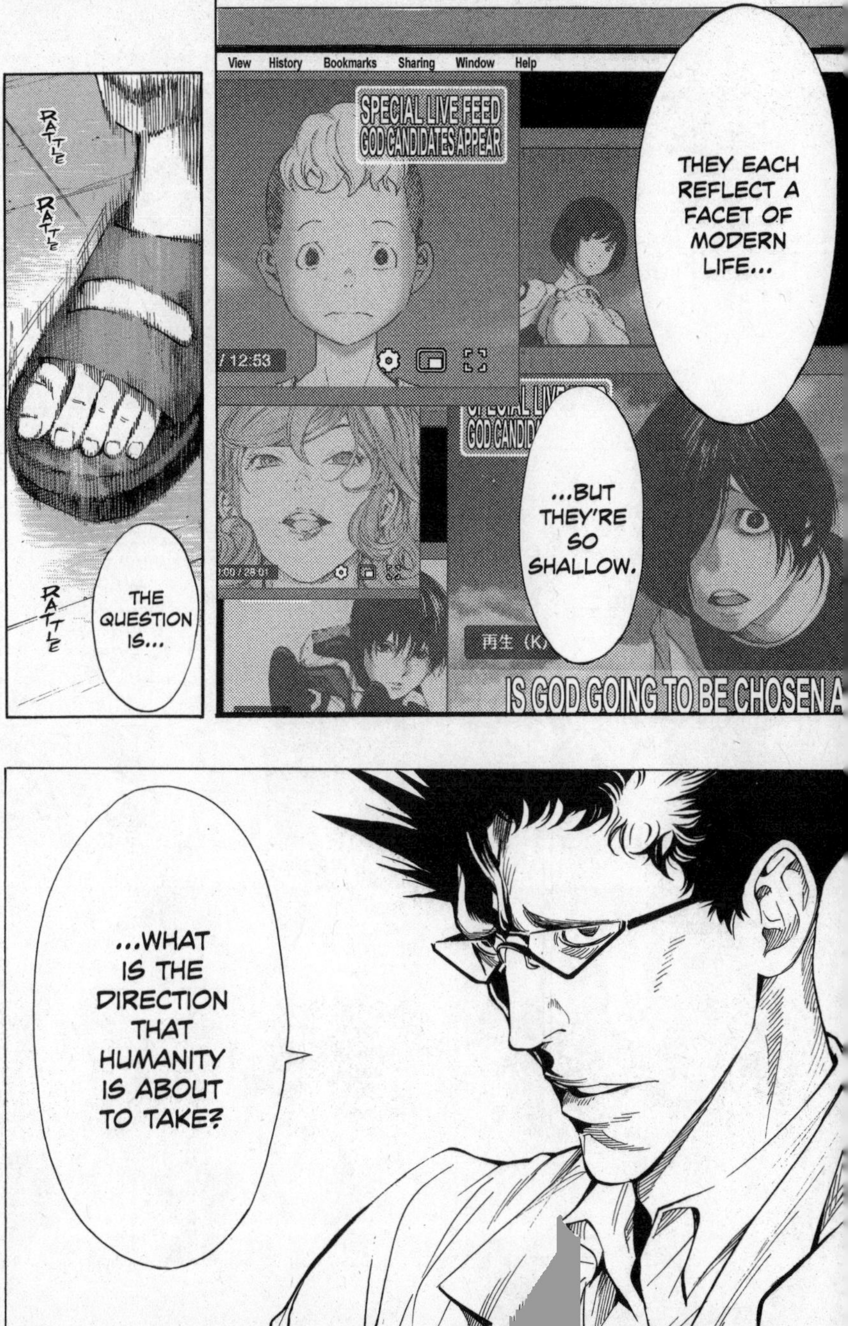

View History Bookmarks Sharing Window Help
SPECIAL LIVE FEED
GOD CANDIDATES APPEAR
THEY EACH REFLECT A FACET OF MODERN LIFE...
...BUT THEY'RE SO SHALLOW.
再生 (K)
IS GOD GOING TO BE CHOSEN A
RATTLE
RATTLE
THE QUESTION IS...
RATTLE
...WHAT IS THE DIRECTION THAT HUMANITY IS ABOUT TO TAKE?

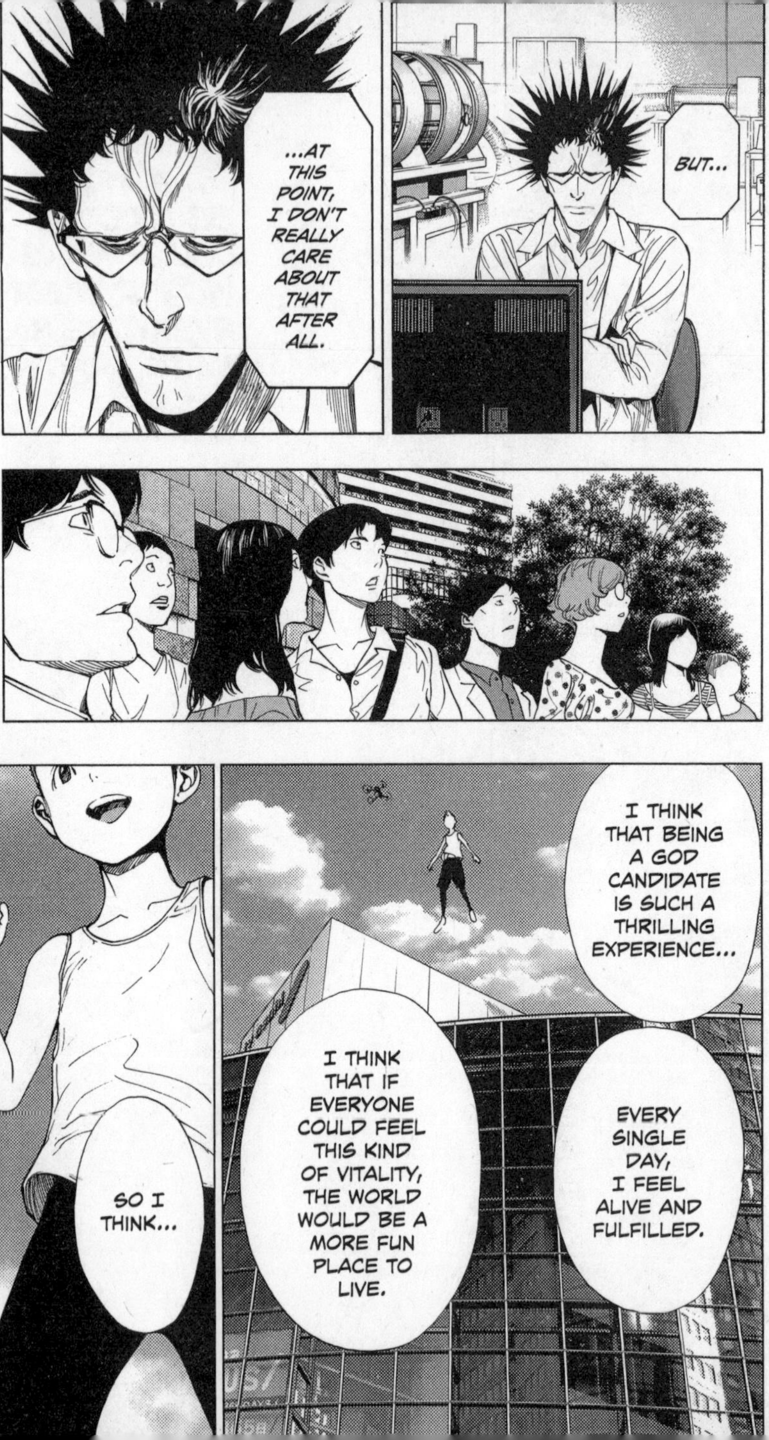
BUT...
...AT THIS POINT, I DON'T REALLY CARE ABOUT THAT AFTER ALL.
I THINK THAT BEING A GOD CANDIDATE IS SUCH A THRILLING EXPERIENCE...
EVERY SINGLE DAY, I FEEL ALIVE AND FULFILLED.
I THINK THAT IF EVERYONE COULD FEEL THIS KIND OF VITALITY, THE WORLD WOULD BE A MORE FUN PLACE TO LIVE.
SO I THINK...

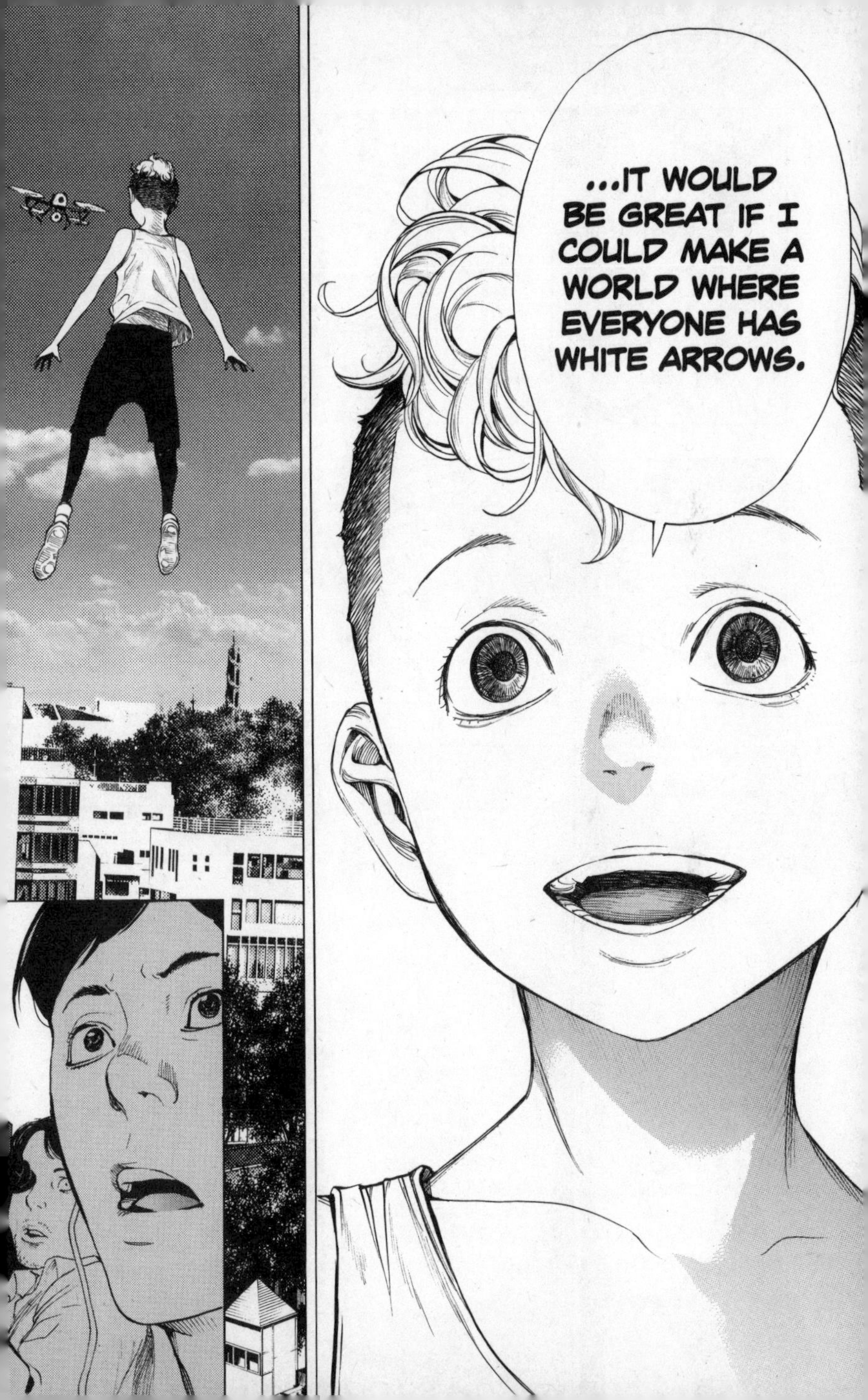
...IT WOULD BE GREAT IF I COULD MAKE A WORLD WHERE EVERYONE HAS WHITE ARROWS.

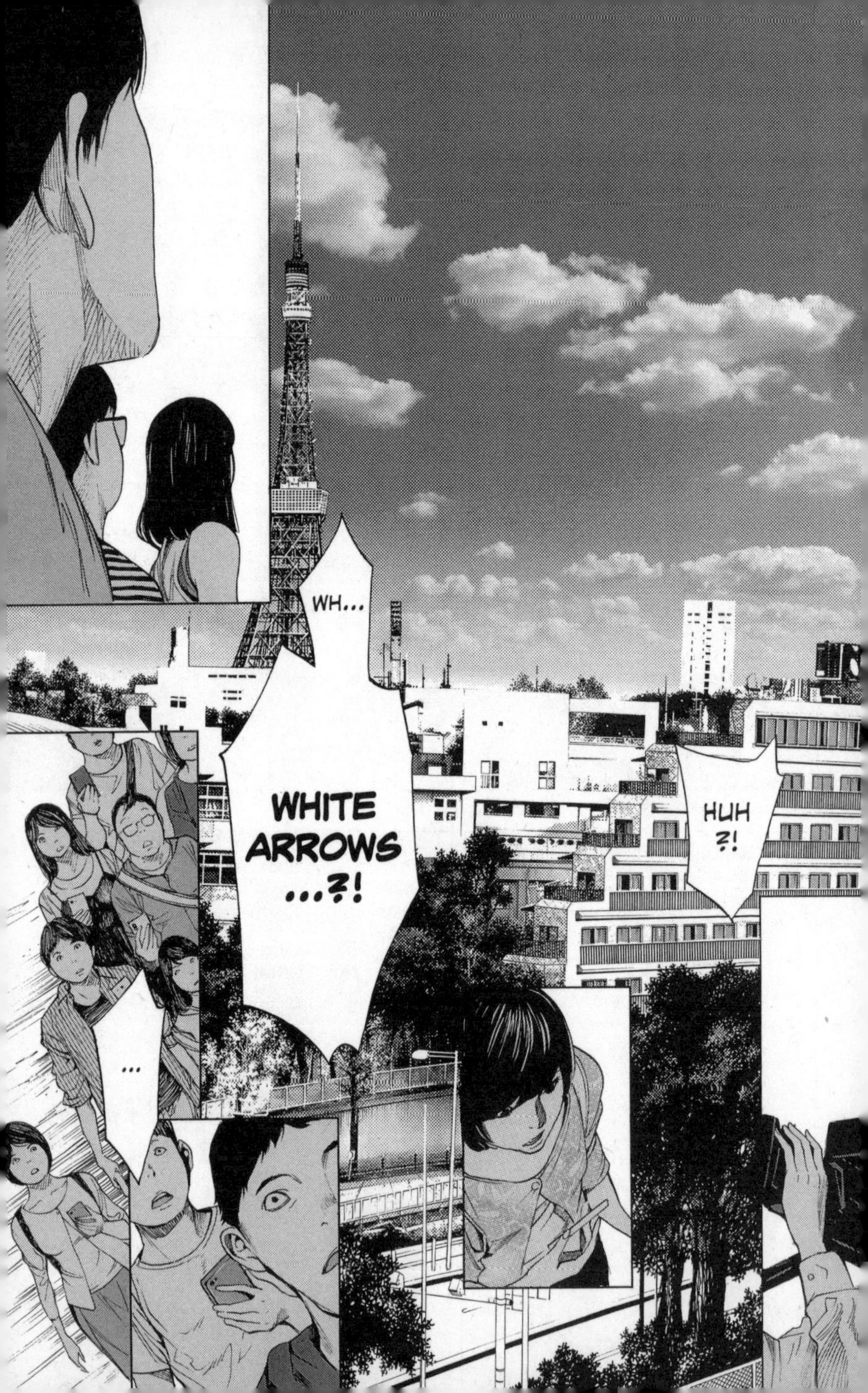
WH...
WHITE ARROWS ...?!
HUH ?!
...

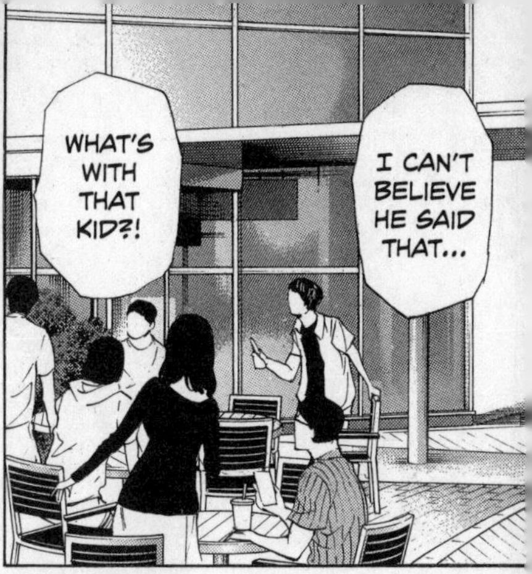
I CAN'T BELIEVE HE SAID THAT...
WHAT'S WITH THAT KID?!
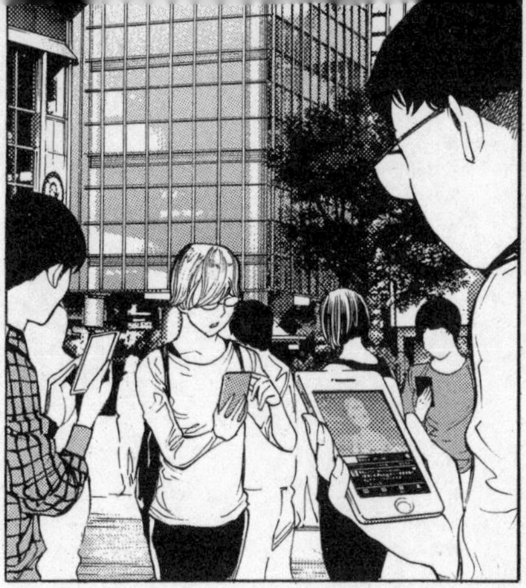
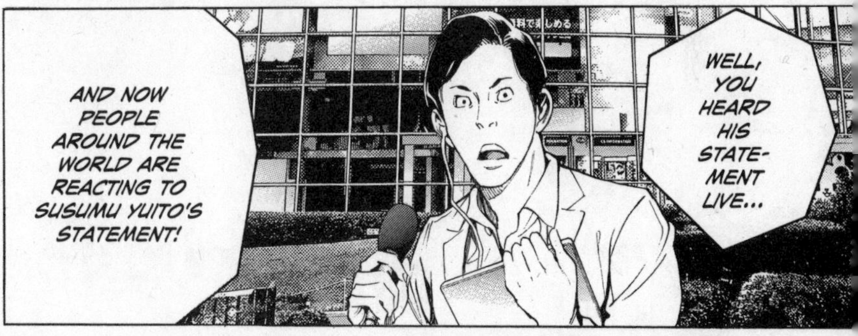
WELL, YOU HEARD HIS STATEMENT LIVE...
AND NOW PEOPLE AROUND THE WORLD ARE REACTING TO SUSUMU YUITO'S STATEMENT!
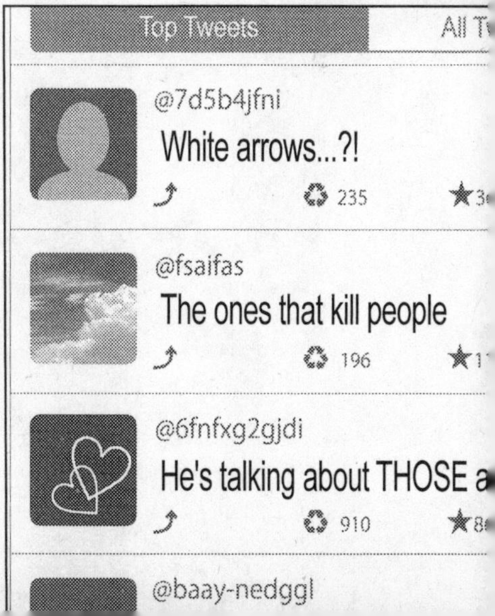
Top Tweets
@7d5b4jfni
White arrows...?!
235
@fsaifas
The ones that kill people
196
@6fnfxg2gjdi
He's talking about THOSE
910
@baay-nedggl
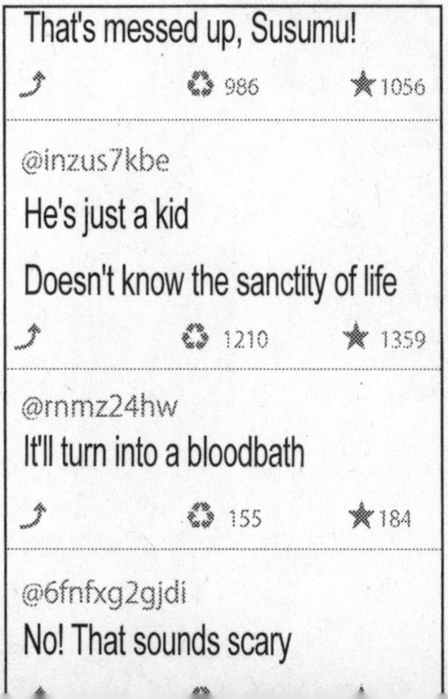
That's messed up, Susumu!
986 1056
@inzus7kbe
He's just a kid
Doesn't know the sanctity of life
1210 1359
@rnmz24hw
It'll turn into a bloodbath
155 184
@6fnfxg2gjdi
No! That sounds scary

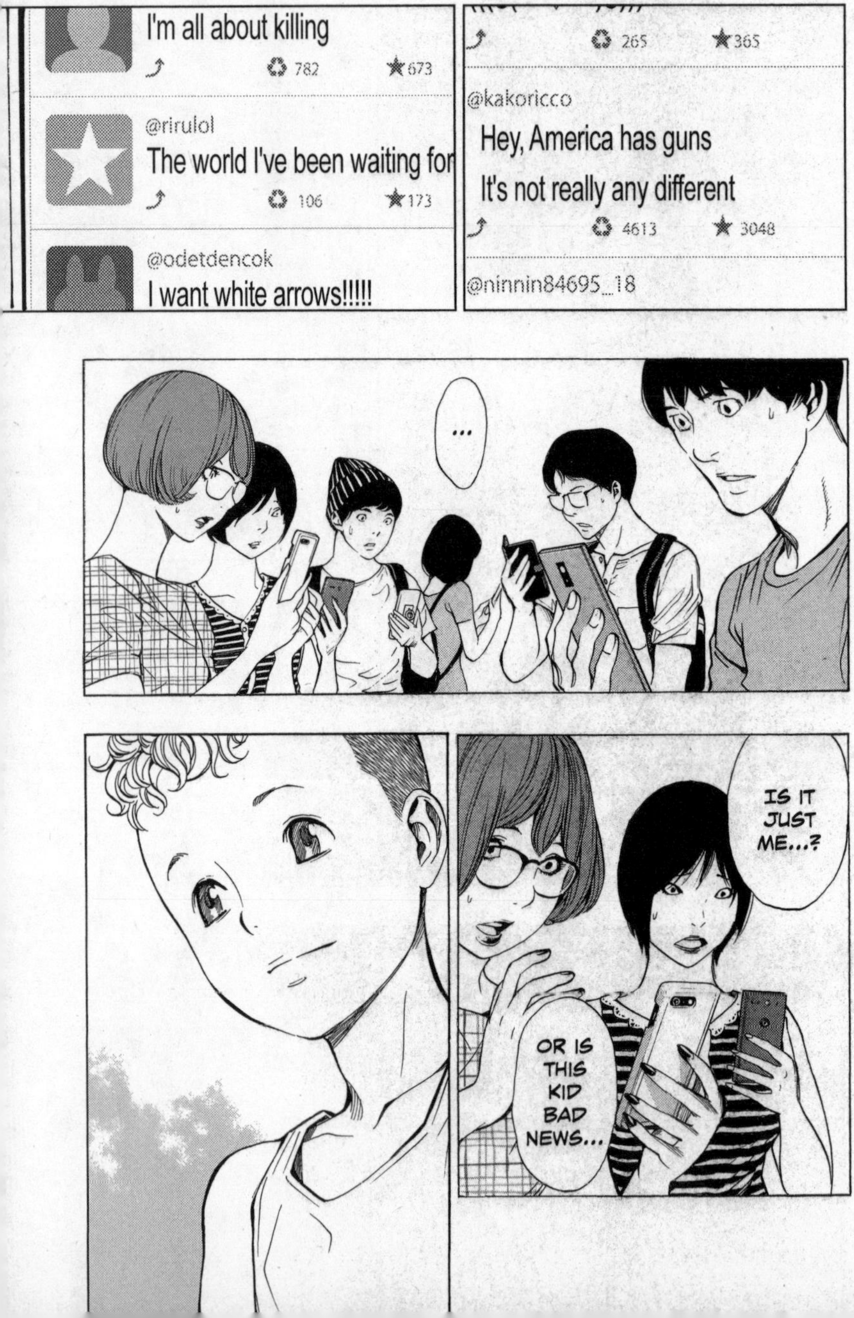
265 365
@kakoricco
Hey, America has guns
It's not really any different
4613 3048
@ninnin84695_18
I'm all about killing
782 673
@rirulol
The world I've been waiting for
106 173
@odetdencok
I want white arrows!!!!!
...
IS IT JUST ME...?
OR IS THIS KID BAD NEWS...

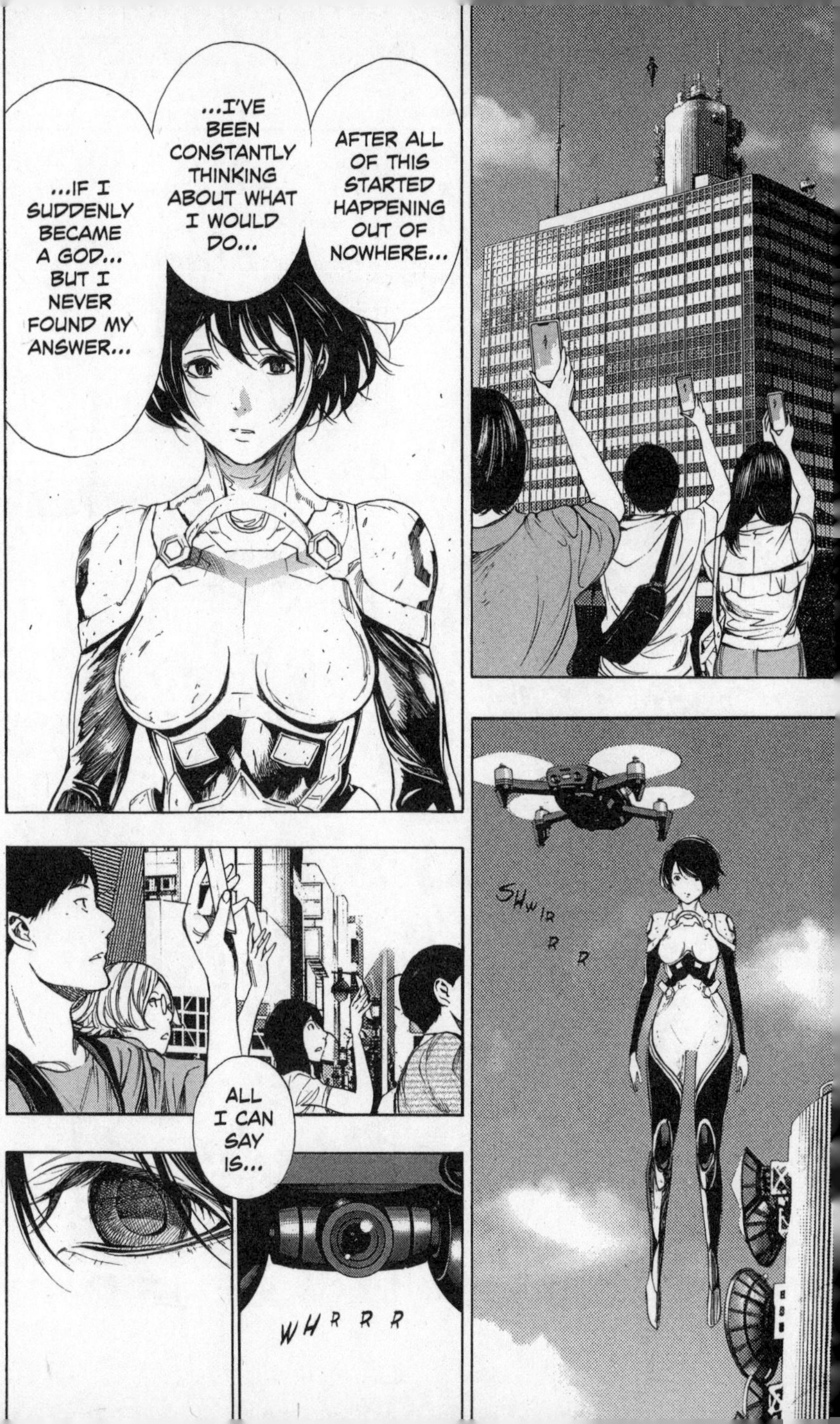
AFTER ALL OF THIS STARTED HAPPENING OUT OF NOWHERE...
...I'VE BEEN CONSTANTLY THINKING ABOUT WHAT I WOULD DO...
...IF I SUDDENLY BECAME A GOD... BUT I NEVER FOUND MY ANSWER...
SHWIRR R R
ALL I CAN SAY IS...
WHRRR

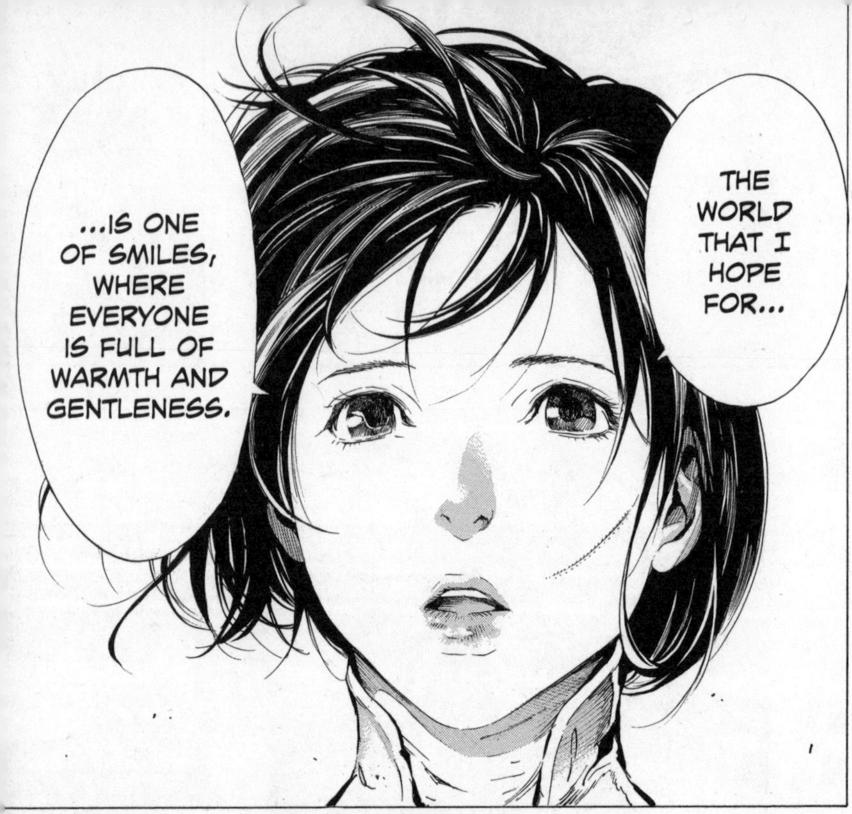
THE WORLD THAT I HOPE FOR...
...IS ONE OF SMILES, WHERE EVERYONE IS FULL OF WARMTH AND GENTLENESS.

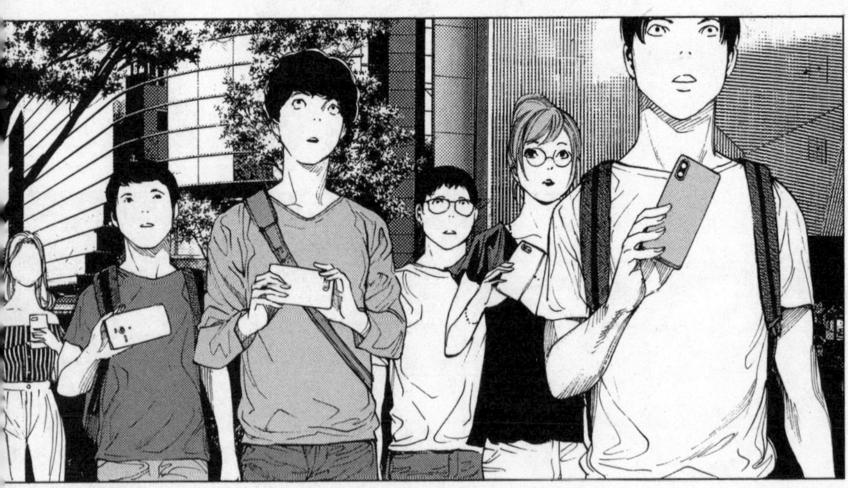

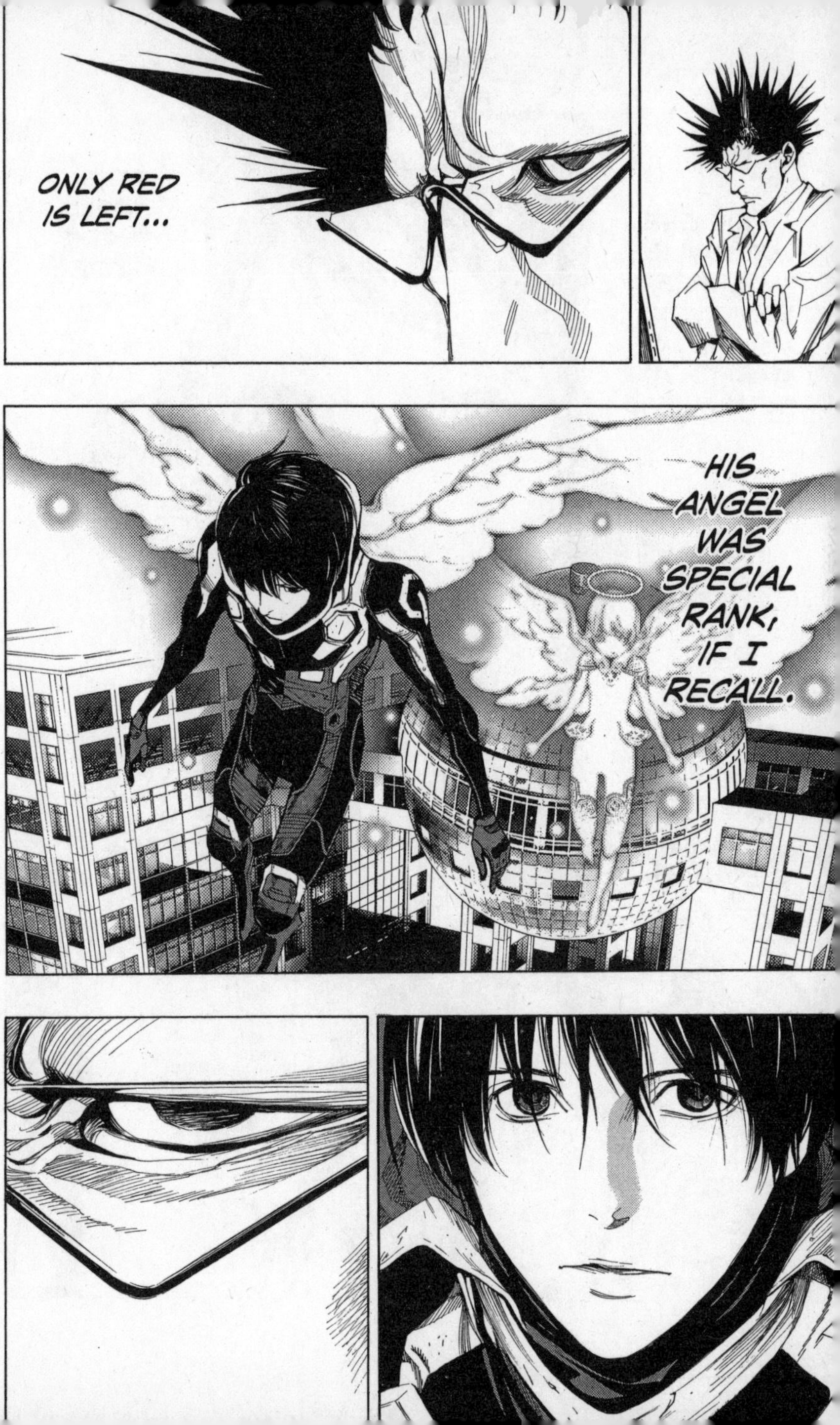
ONLY RED IS LEFT...
HIS ANGEL WAS SPECIAL RANK, IF I RECALL.

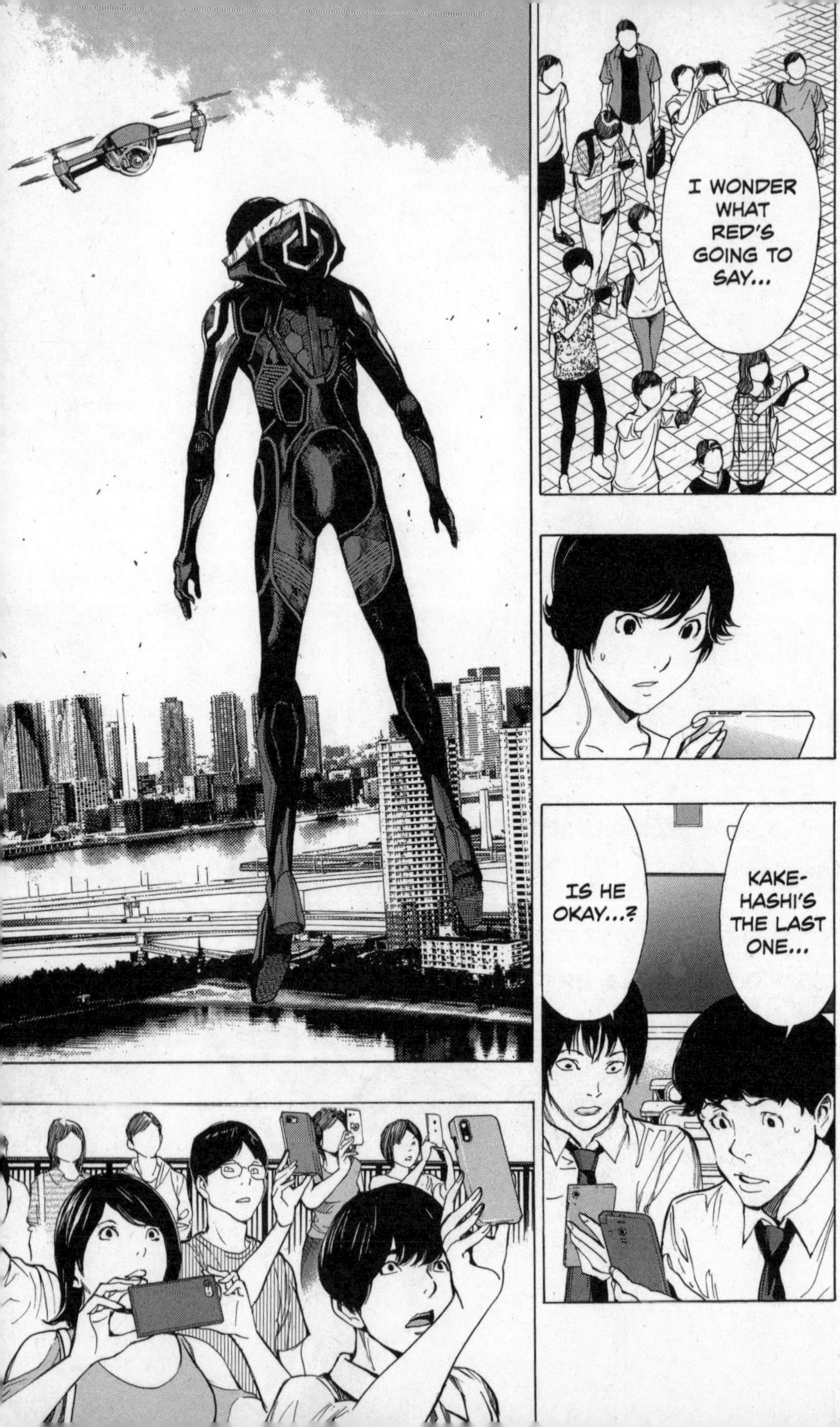
I WONDER WHAT RED'S GOING TO SAY...
KAKE-HASHI'S THE LAST ONE...
IS HE OKAY...?

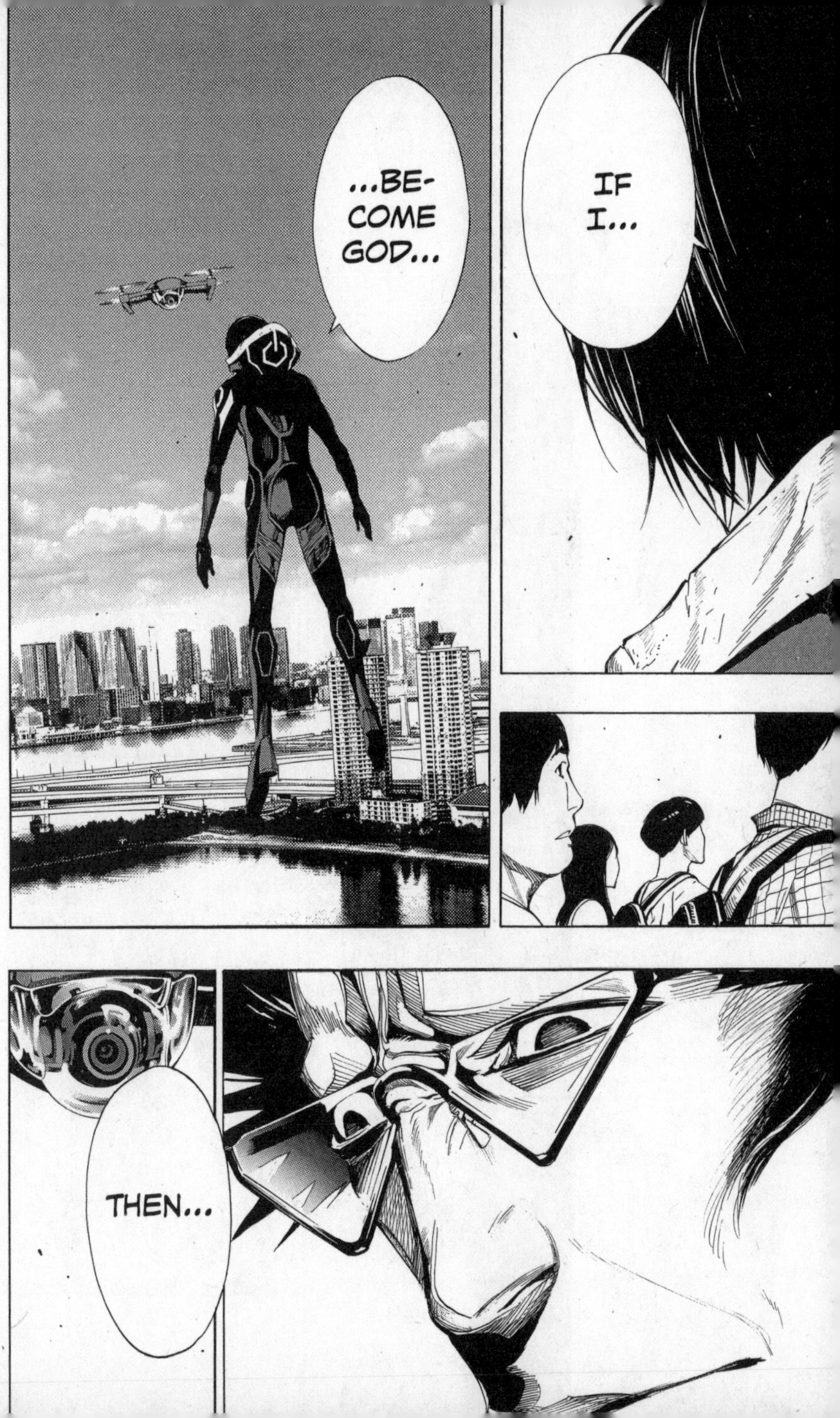
IF I...
...BE-COME GOD...
THEN...

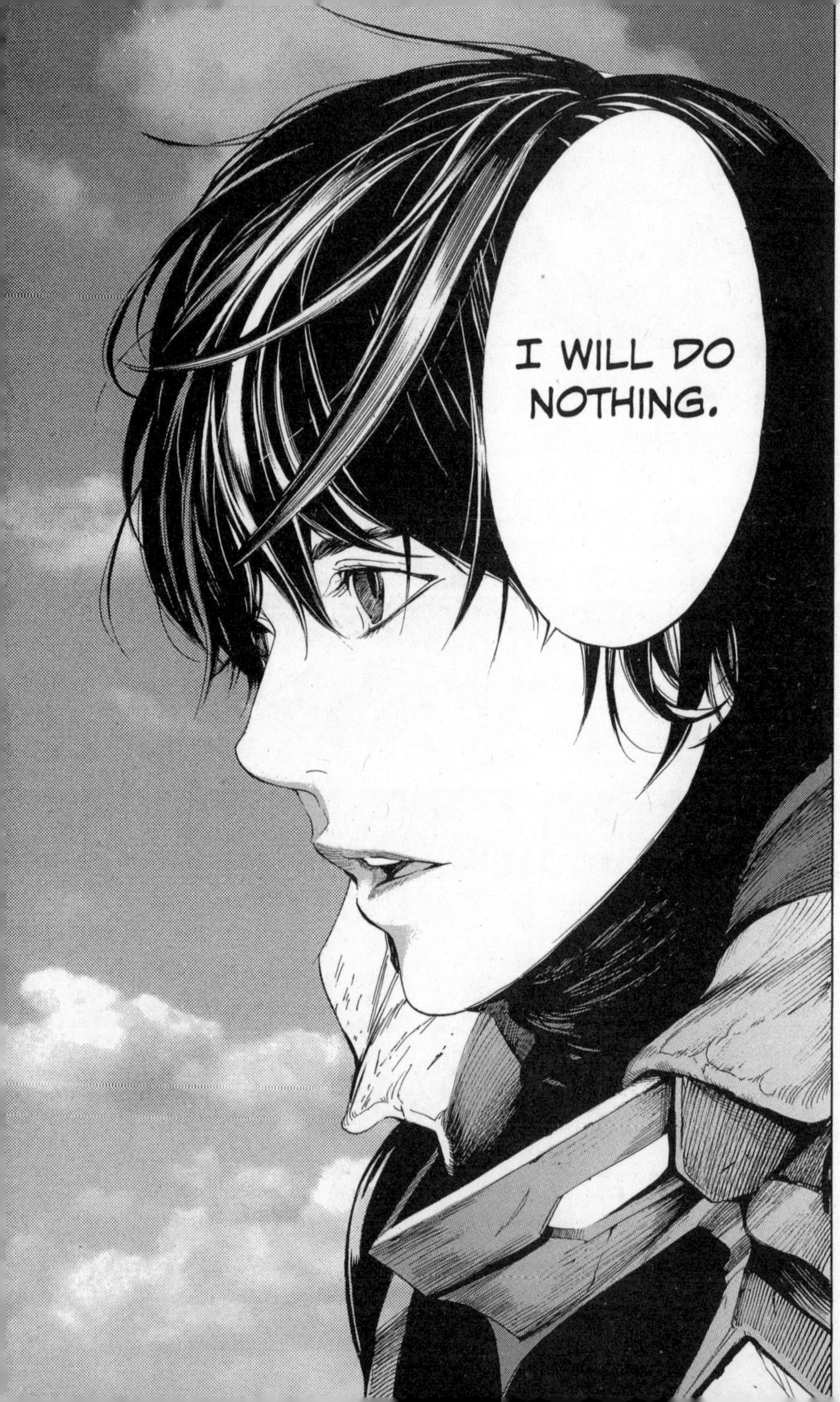
I WILL DO NOTHING.

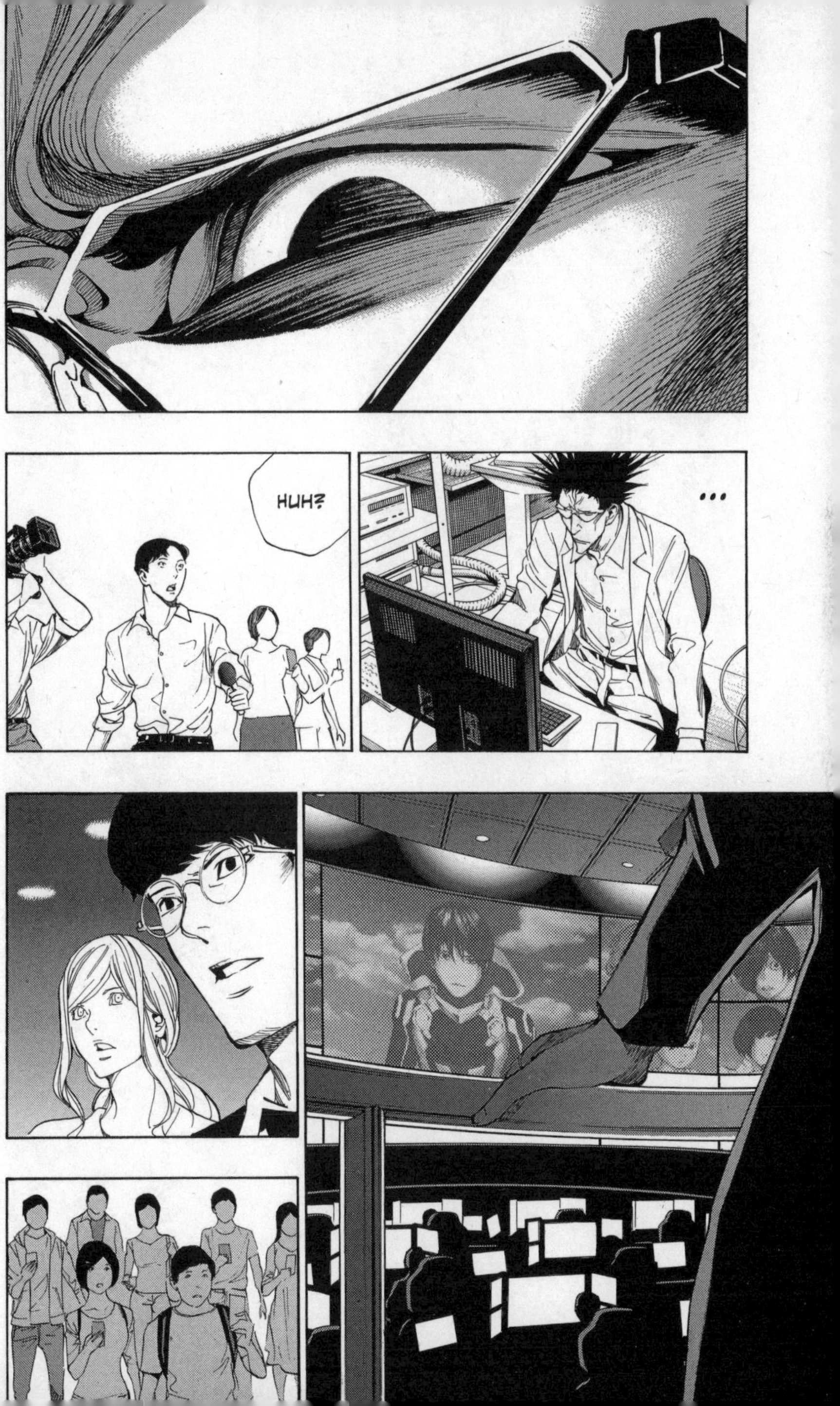
...
HUH?

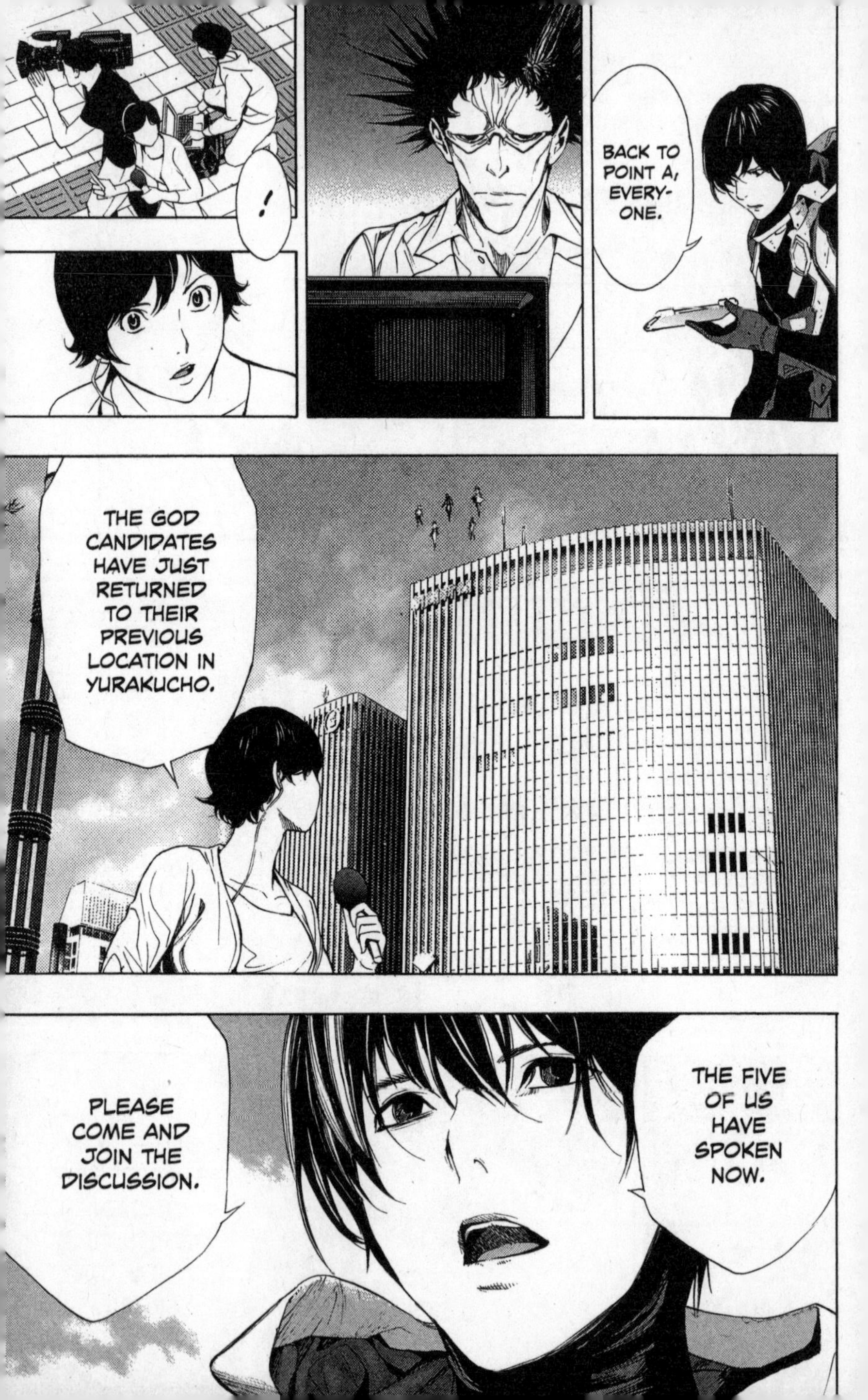
BACK TO POINT A, EVERY-ONE.
!
THE GOD CANDIDATES HAVE JUST RETURNED TO THEIR PREVIOUS LOCATION IN YURAKUCHO.
THE FIVE OF US HAVE SPOKEN NOW.
PLEASE COME AND JOIN THE DISCUSSION.

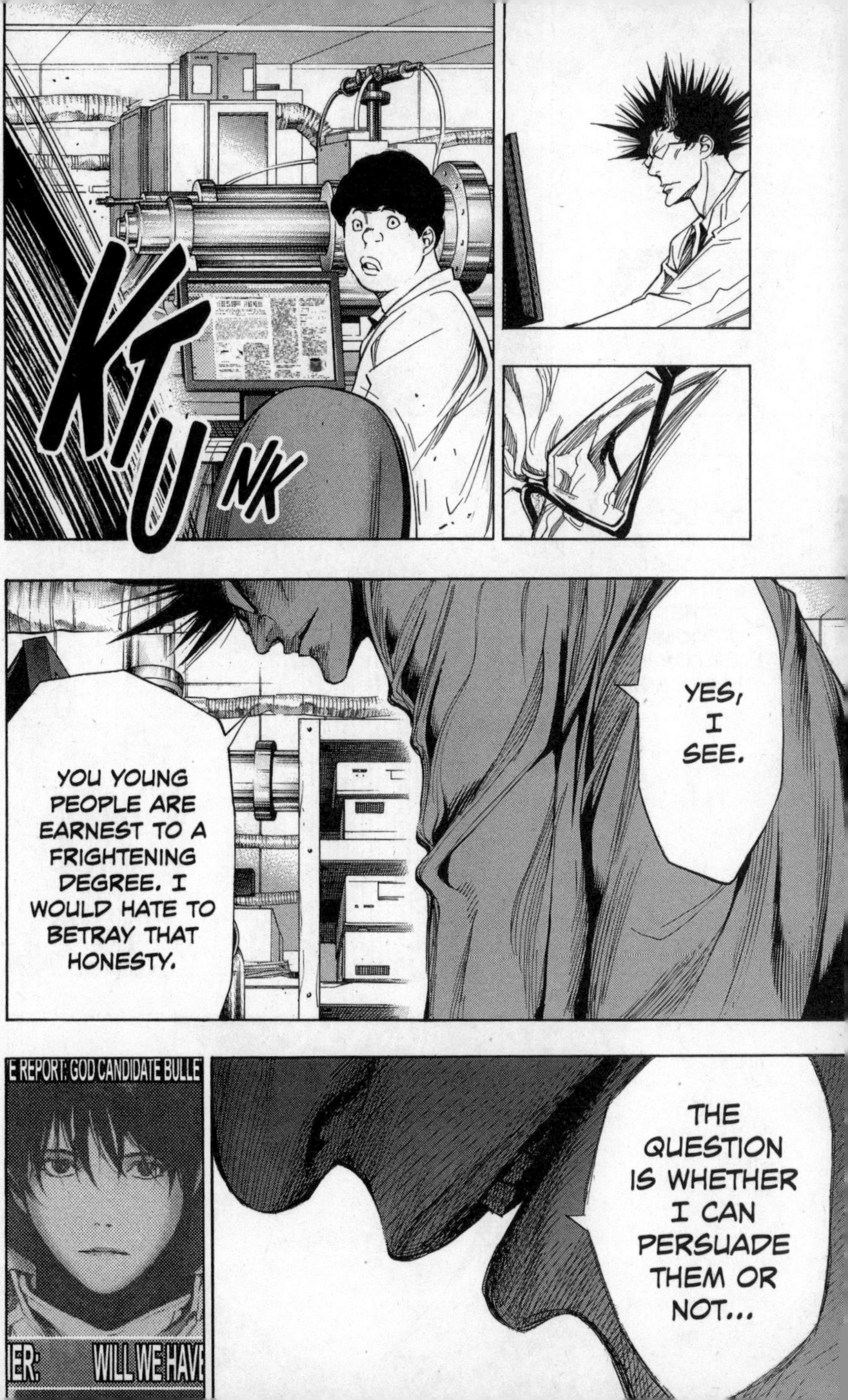
KTUNK
YES, I SEE.
YOU YOUNG PEOPLE ARE EARNEST TO A FRIGHTENING DEGREE. I WOULD HATE TO BETRAY THAT HONESTY.
THE QUESTION IS WHETHER I CAN PERSUADE THEM OR NOT...
E REPORT: GOD CANDIDATE BULLE
ER: WILL WE HAVE

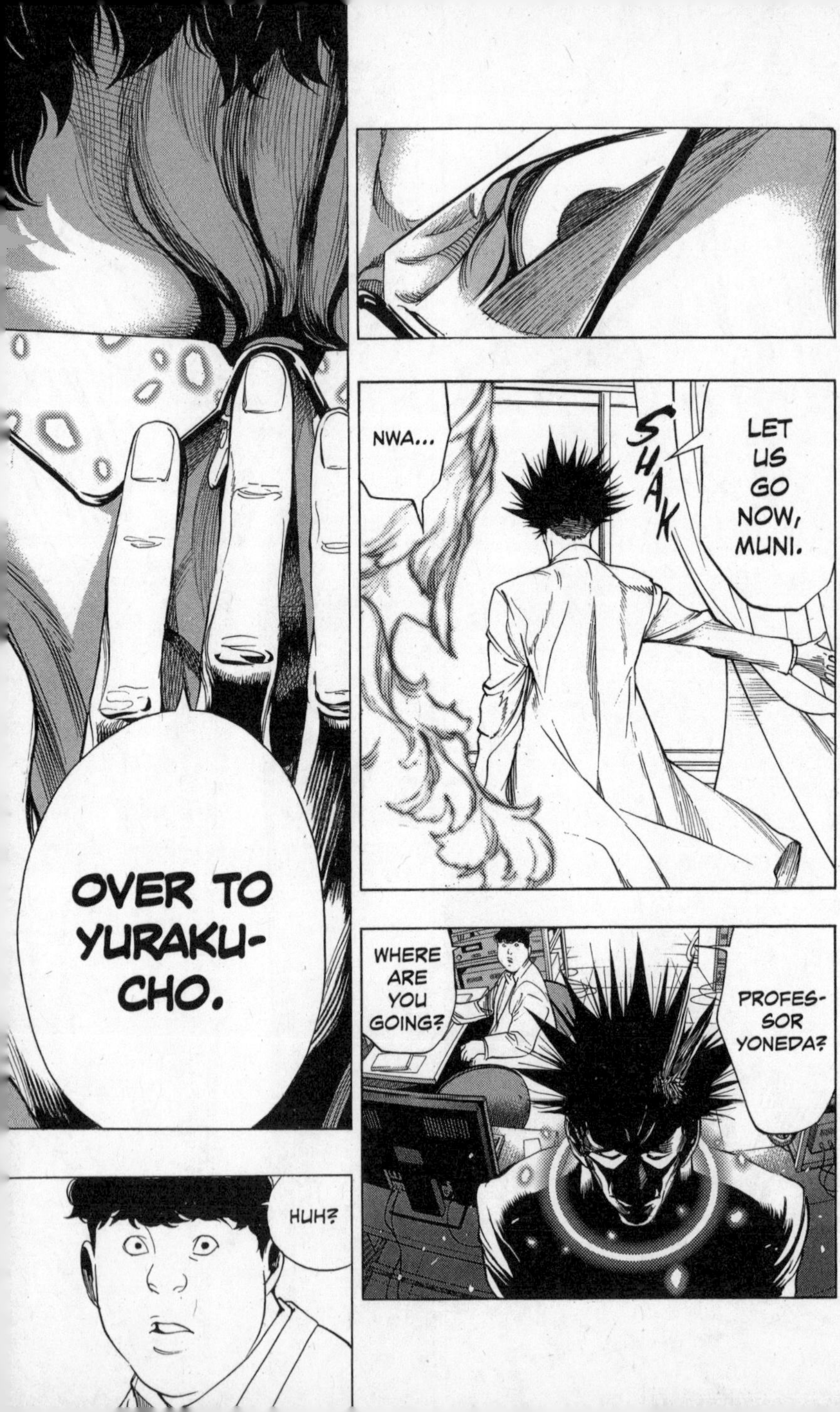
LET US GO NOW, MUNI.
SHAK
NWA...
PROFES-SOR YONEDA?
WHERE ARE YOU GOING?
OVER TO YURAKU-CHO.
HUH?

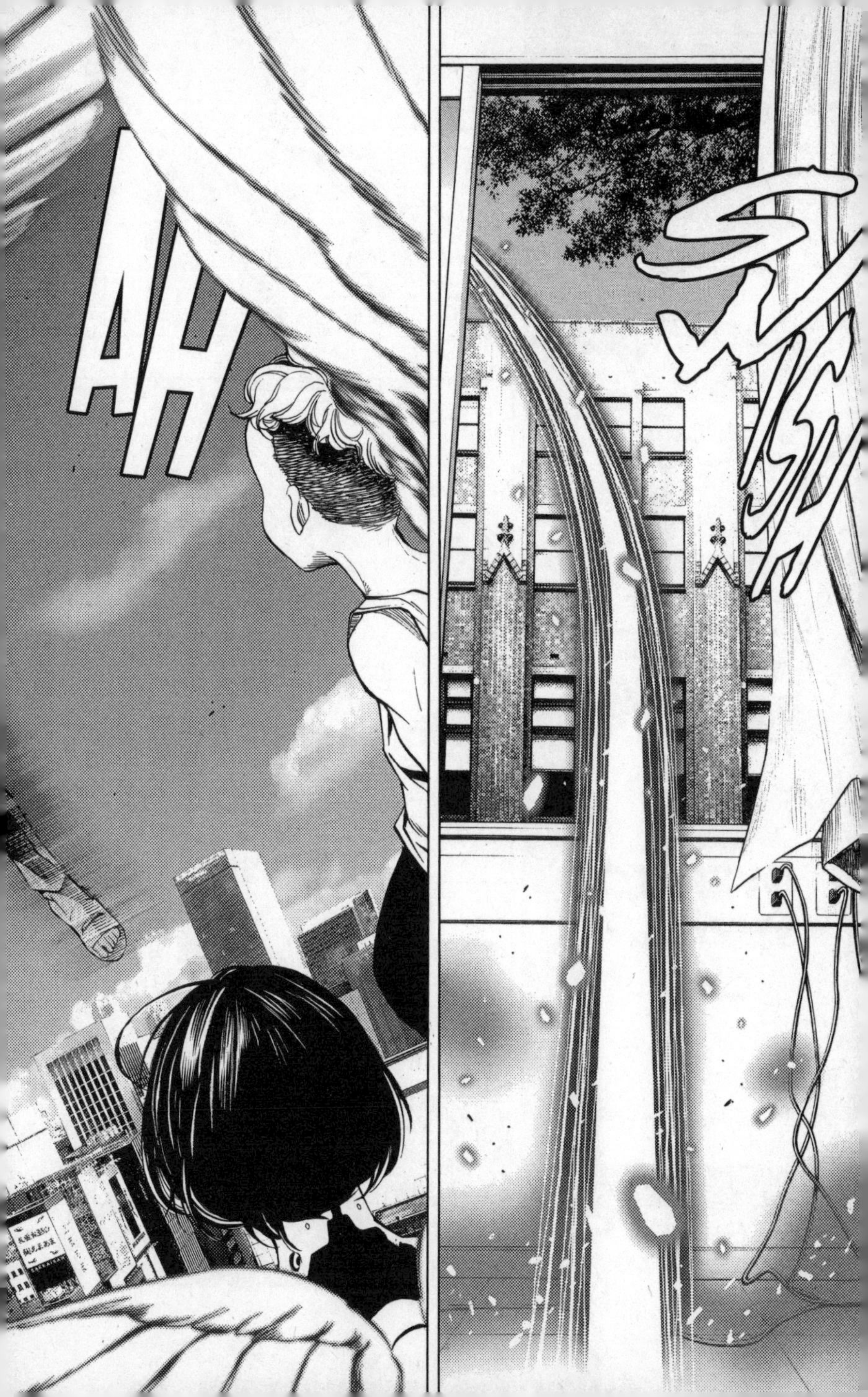
SWISH
AH

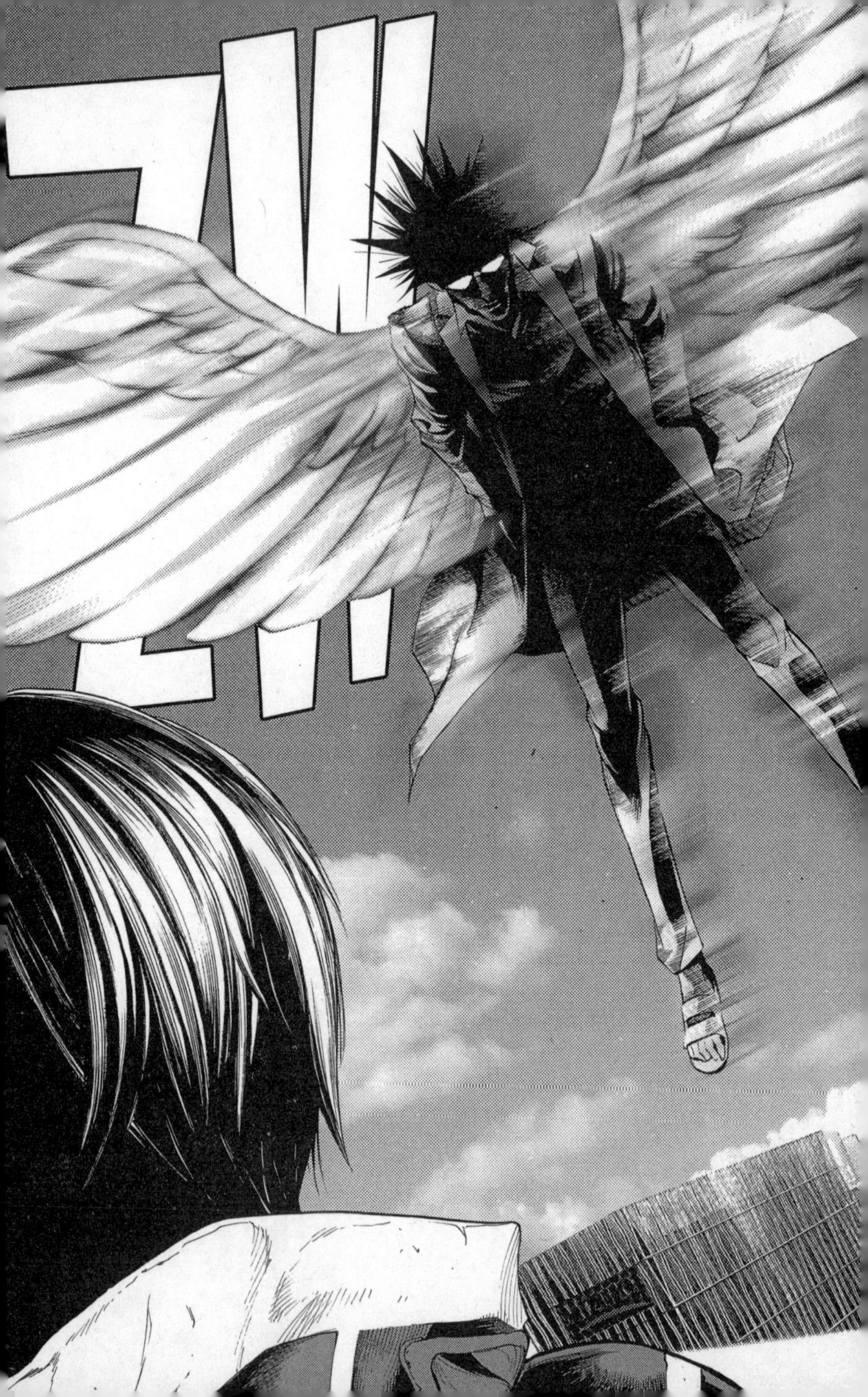

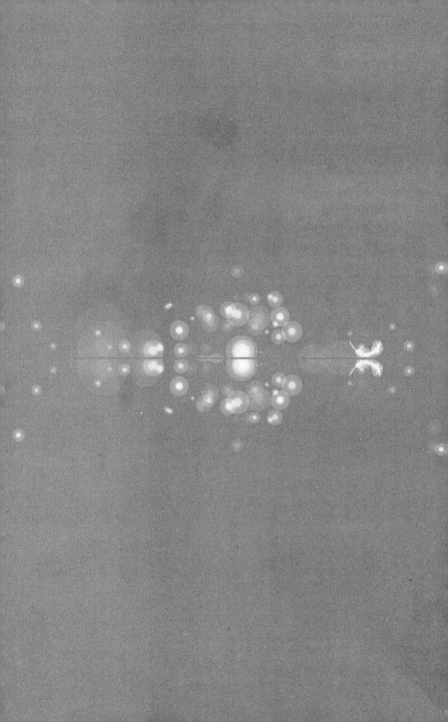

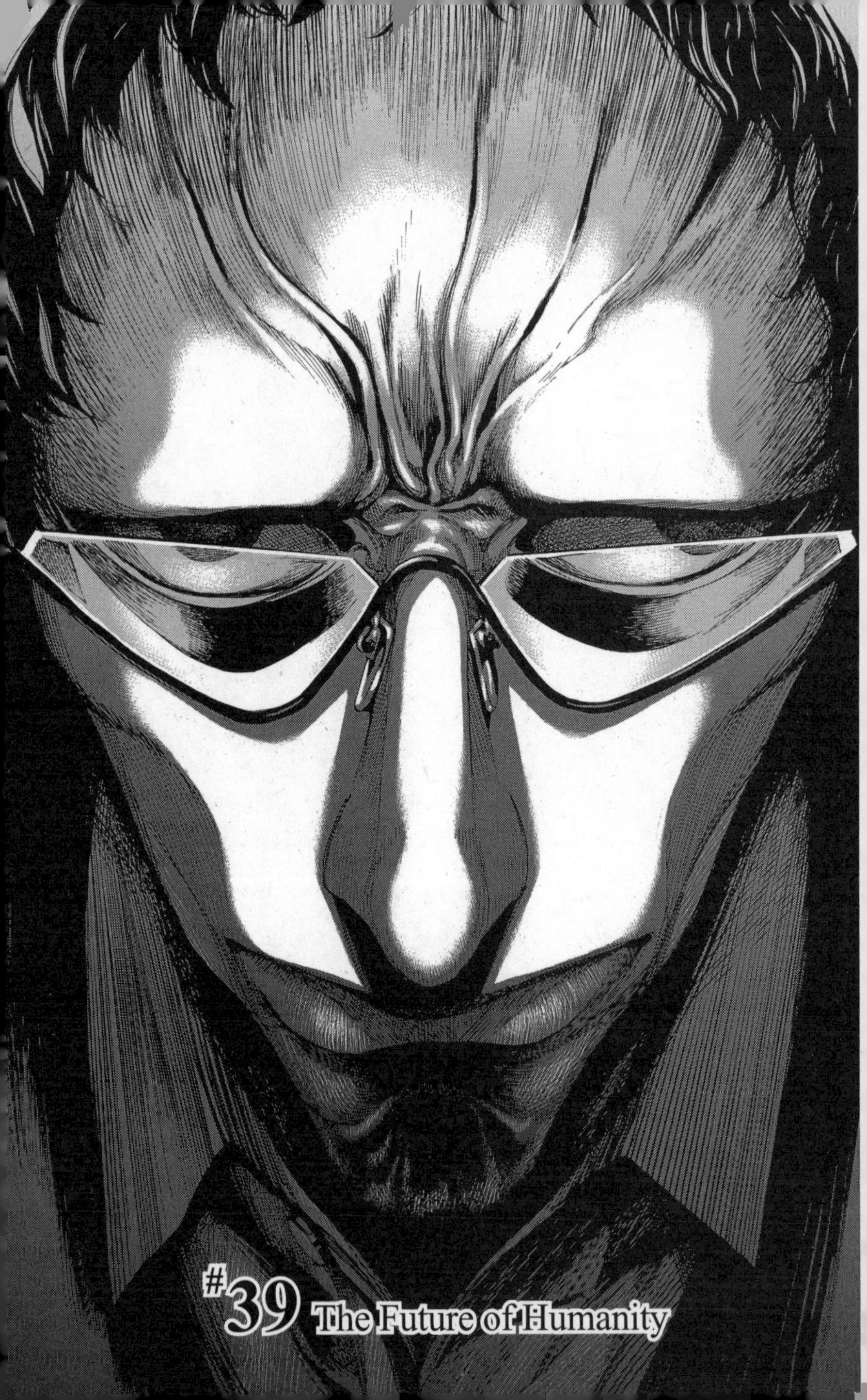
#39 The Future of Humanity

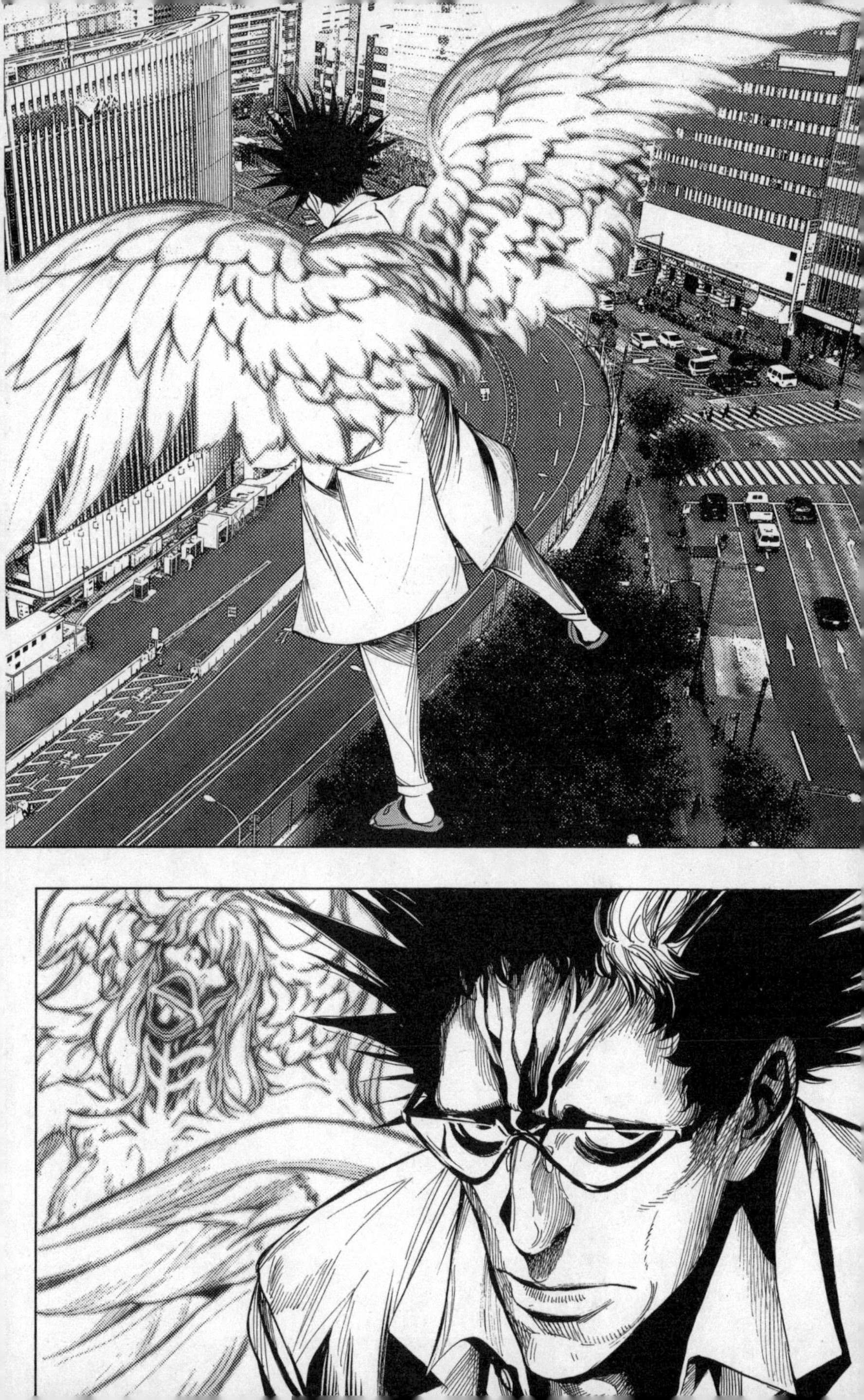

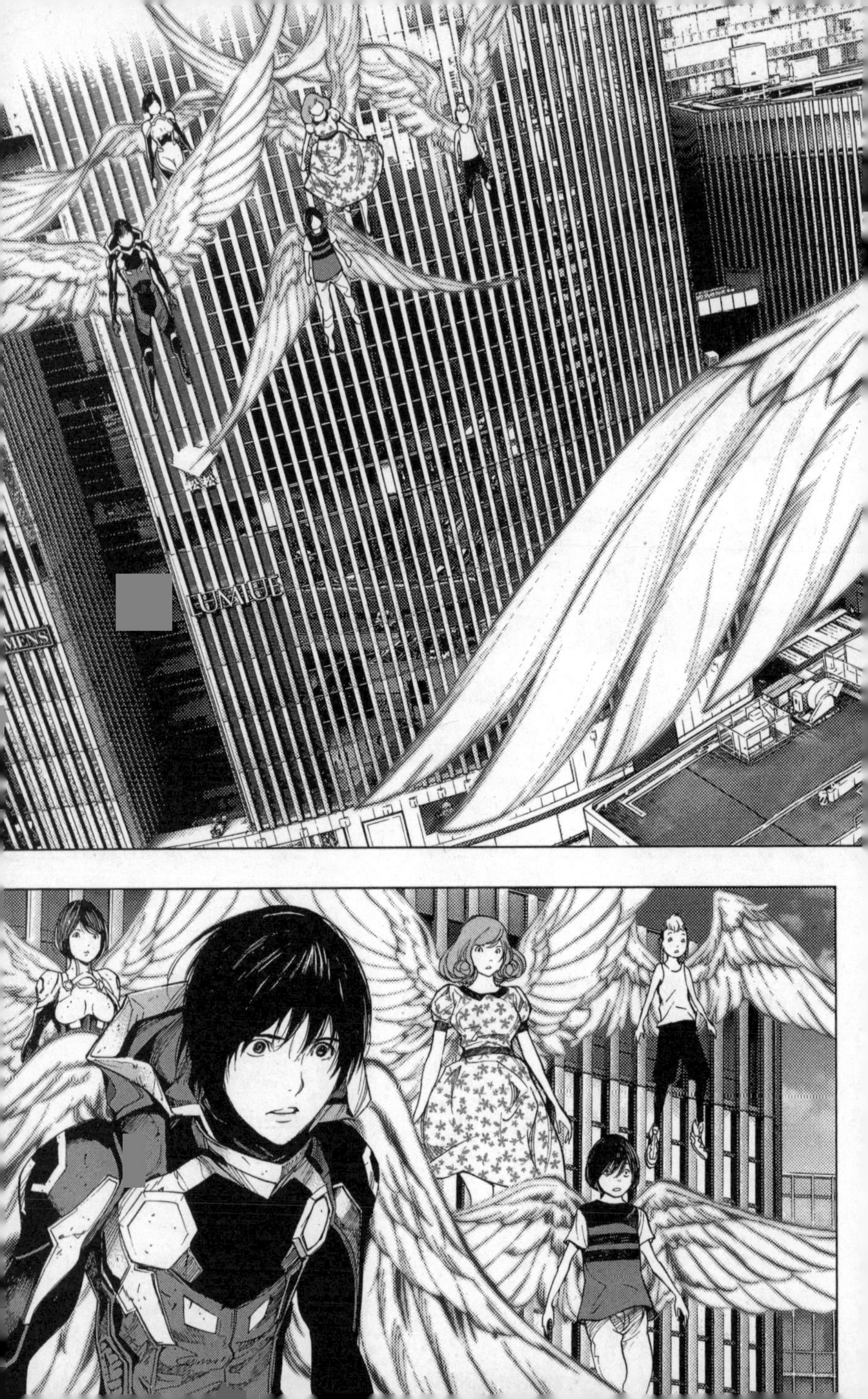
LUMIUE
MENS

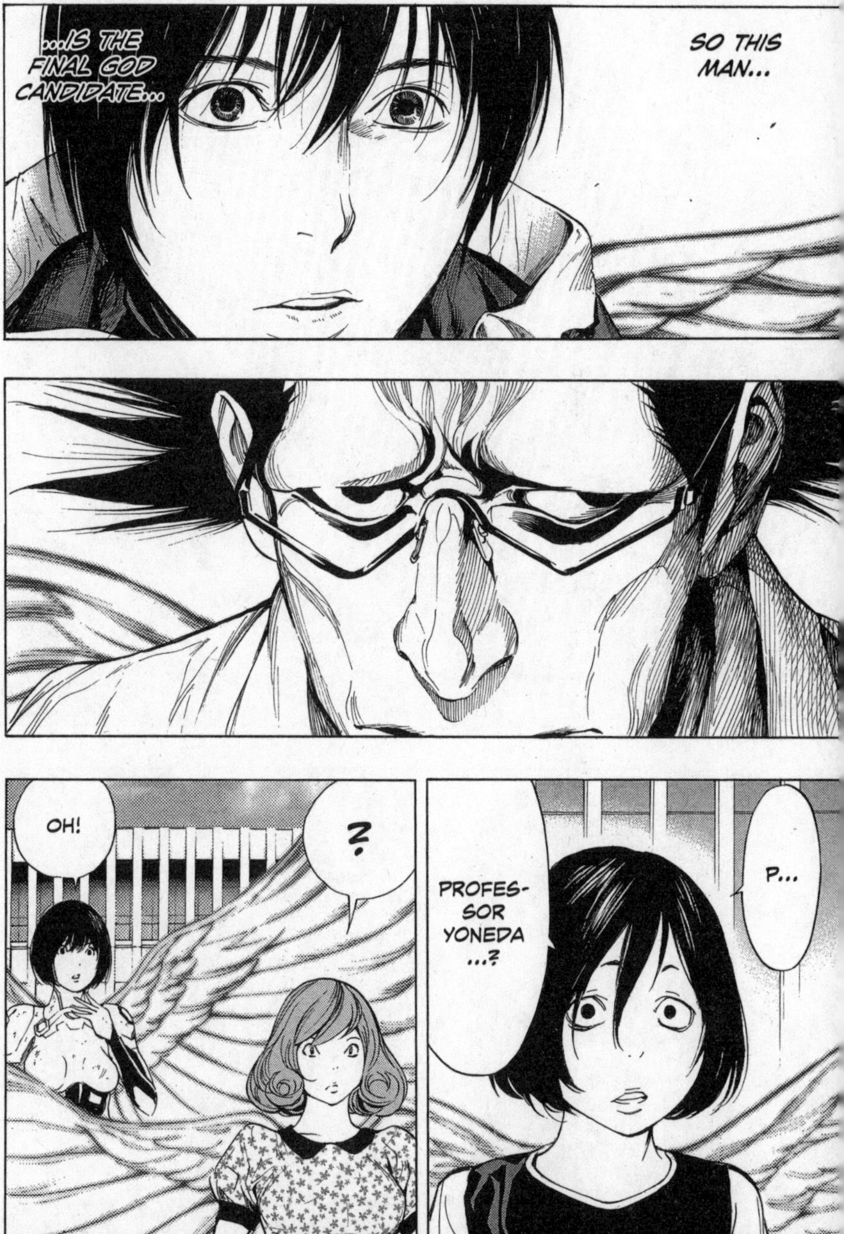
SO THIS MAN...
...IS THE FINAL GOD CANDIDATE...
P...
PROFES-SOR YONEDA ...?
?
OH!

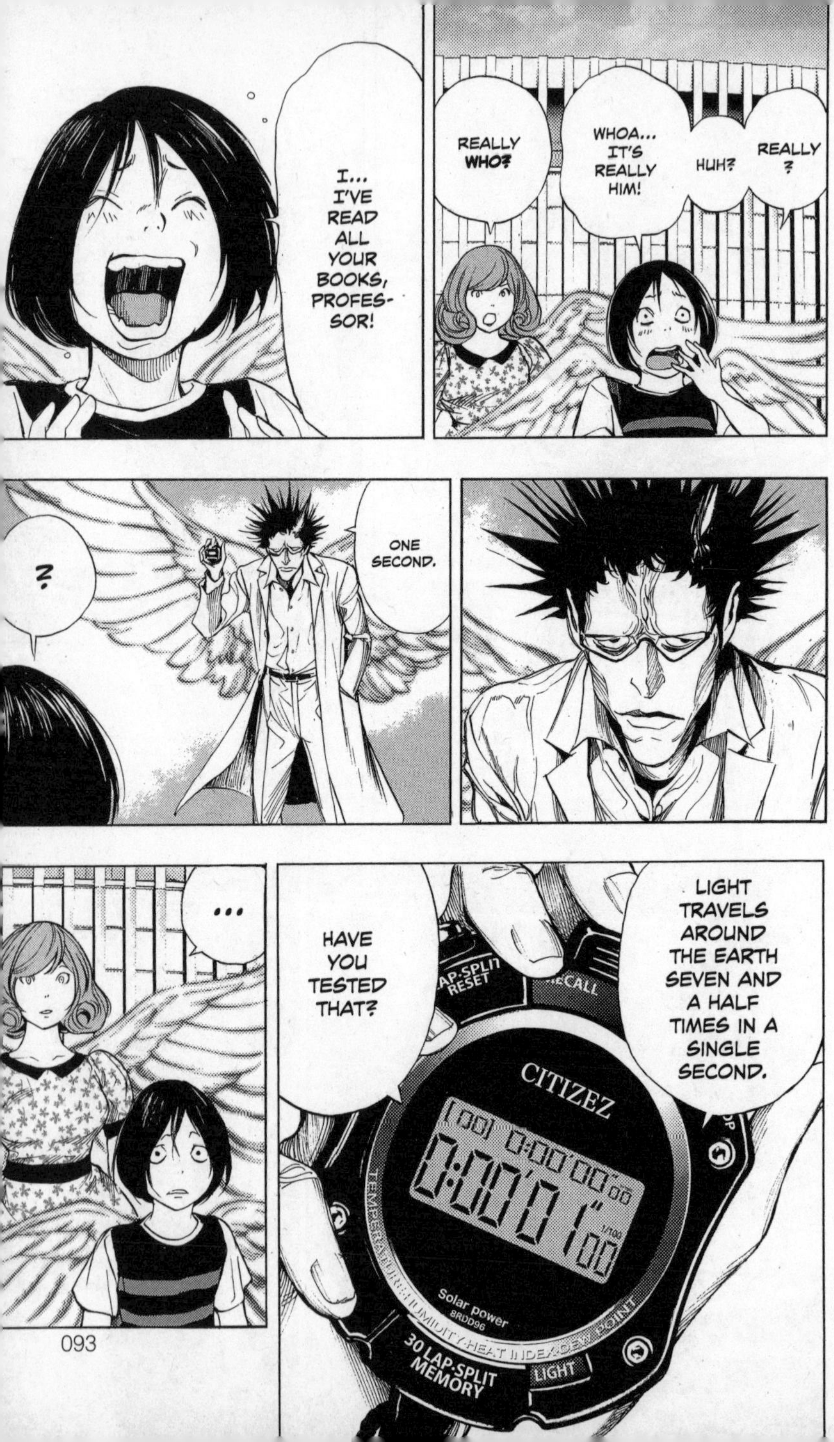
REALLY ?
HUH?
WHOA... IT'S REALLY HIM!
REALLY WHO?
I... I'VE READ ALL YOUR BOOKS, PROFES- SOR!
ONE SECOND.
?
LIGHT TRAVELS AROUND THE EARTH SEVEN AND A HALF TIMES IN A SINGLE SECOND.
HAVE YOU TESTED THAT?
LAP·SPLIT RESET
CITIZEZ
[00] 0:00'00"00
0:00'01"00
Solar power
8RDD96
30 LAP·SPLIT MEMORY
LIGHT
...

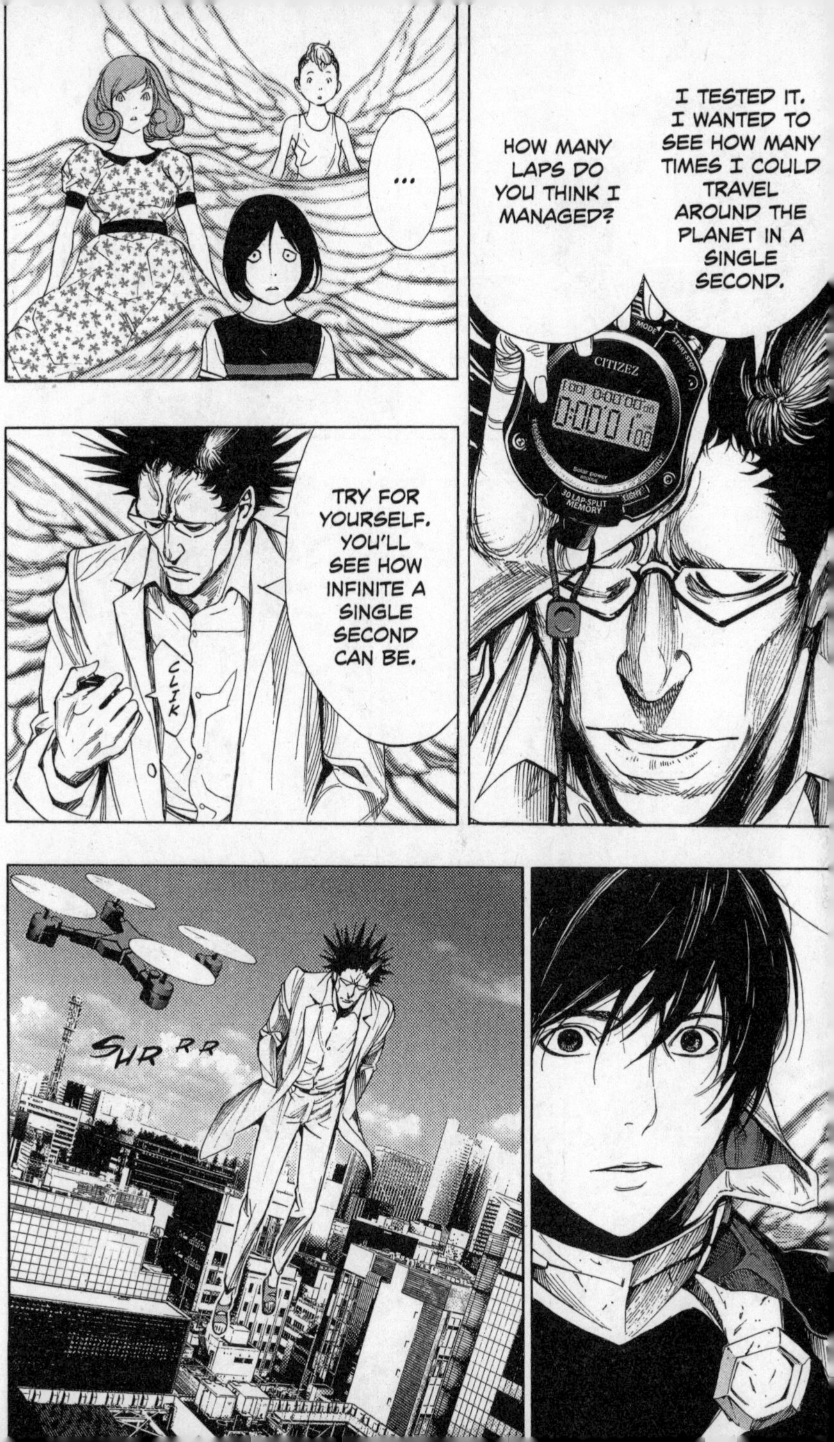
I TESTED IT. I WANTED TO SEE HOW MANY TIMES I COULD TRAVEL AROUND THE PLANET IN A SINGLE SECOND.
HOW MANY LAPS DO YOU THINK I MANAGED?
CITIZEZ
30 LAP-SPLIT MEMORY
...
TRY FOR YOURSELF. YOU'LL SEE HOW INFINITE A SINGLE SECOND CAN BE.
CLIK
SHRRR

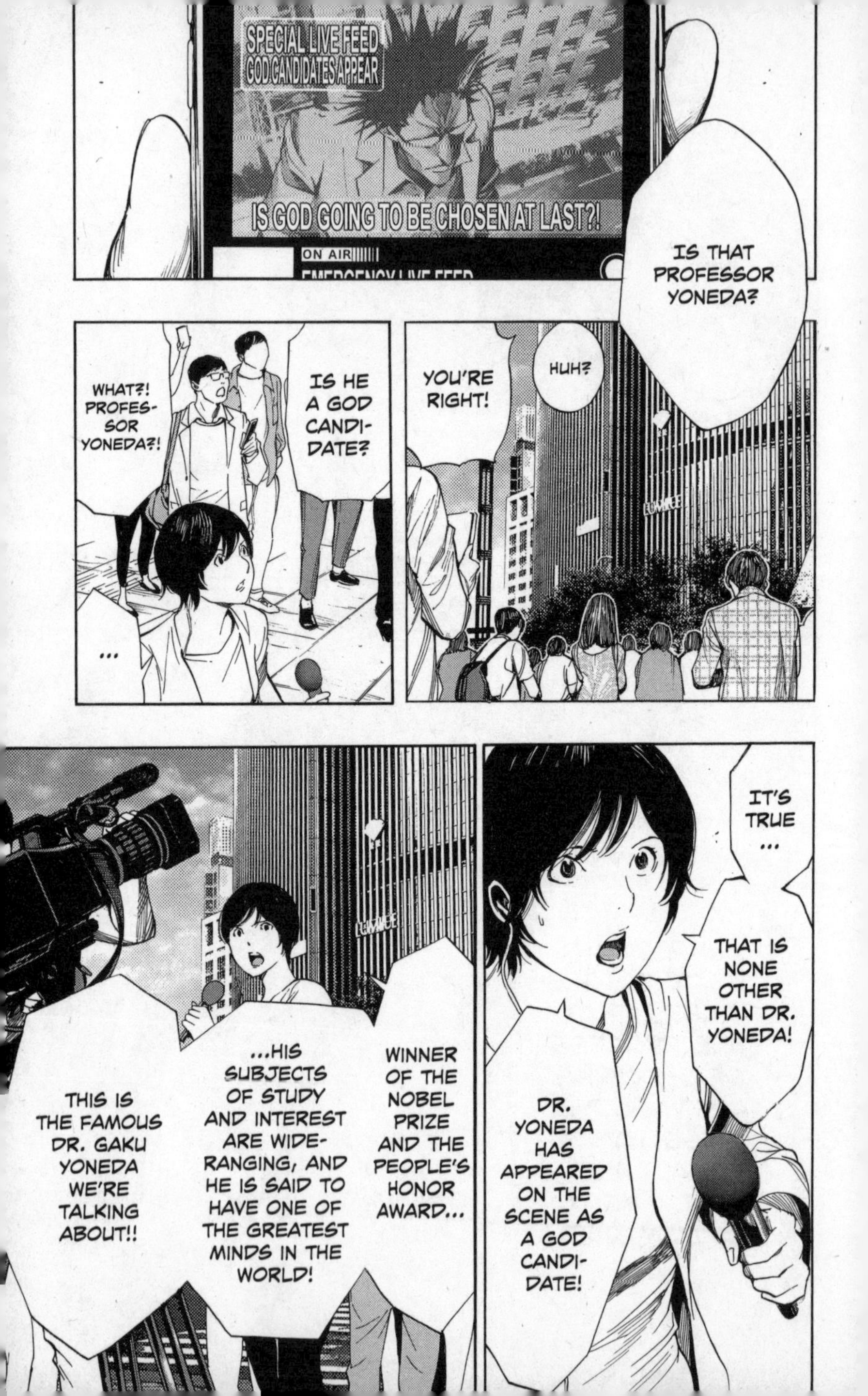
SPECIAL LIVE FEED
GOD CANDIDATES APPEAR
IS GOD GOING TO BE CHOSEN AT LAST?!
ON AIR
IS THAT PROFESSOR YONEDA?
HUH?
YOU'RE RIGHT!
IS HE A GOD CANDIDATE?
WHAT?! PROFESSOR YONEDA?!
...
IT'S TRUE...
THAT IS NONE OTHER THAN DR. YONEDA!
DR. YONEDA HAS APPEARED ON THE SCENE AS A GOD CANDIDATE!
WINNER OF THE NOBEL PRIZE AND THE PEOPLE'S HONOR AWARD...
...HIS SUBJECTS OF STUDY AND INTEREST ARE WIDE-RANGING, AND HE IS SAID TO HAVE ONE OF THE GREATEST MINDS IN THE WORLD!
THIS IS THE FAMOUS DR. GAKU YONEDA WE'RE TALKING ABOUT!!

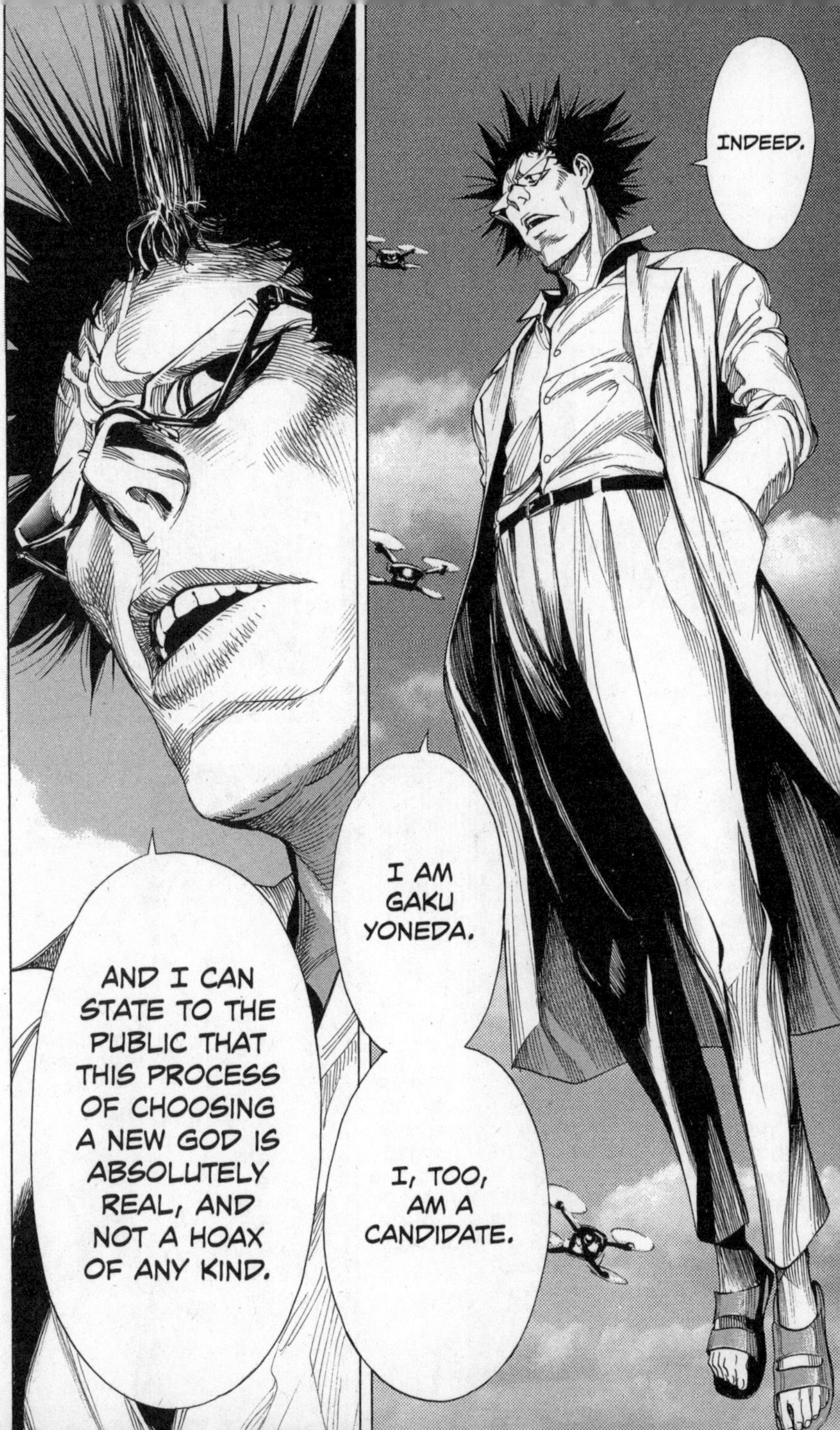
INDEED.
I AM GAKU YONEDA.
I, TOO, AM A CANDIDATE.
AND I CAN STATE TO THE PUBLIC THAT THIS PROCESS OF CHOOSING A NEW GOD IS ABSOLUTELY REAL, AND NOT A HOAX OF ANY KIND.

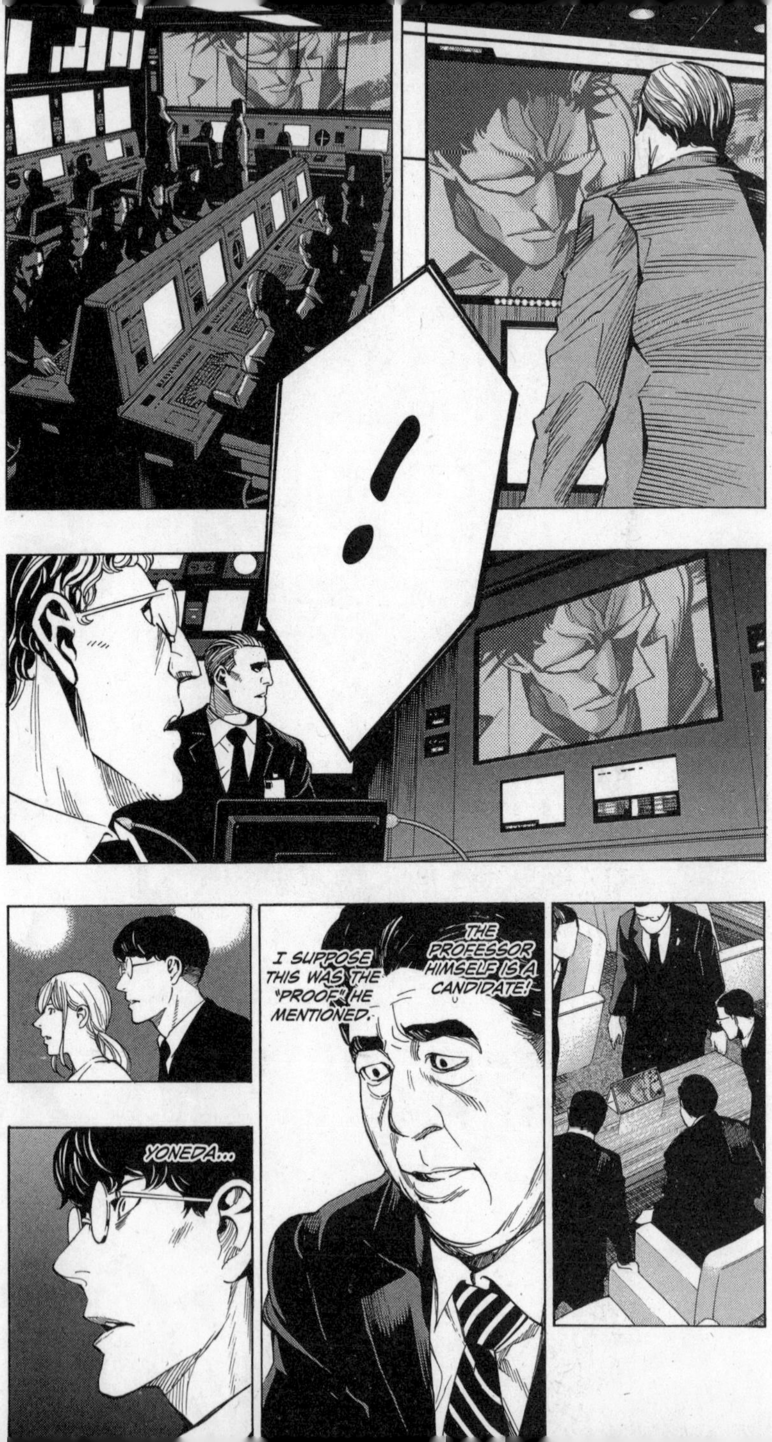
!
THE PROFESSOR HIMSELF IS A CANDIDATE!
I SUPPOSE THIS WAS THE "PROOF" HE MENTIONED.
YONEDA...

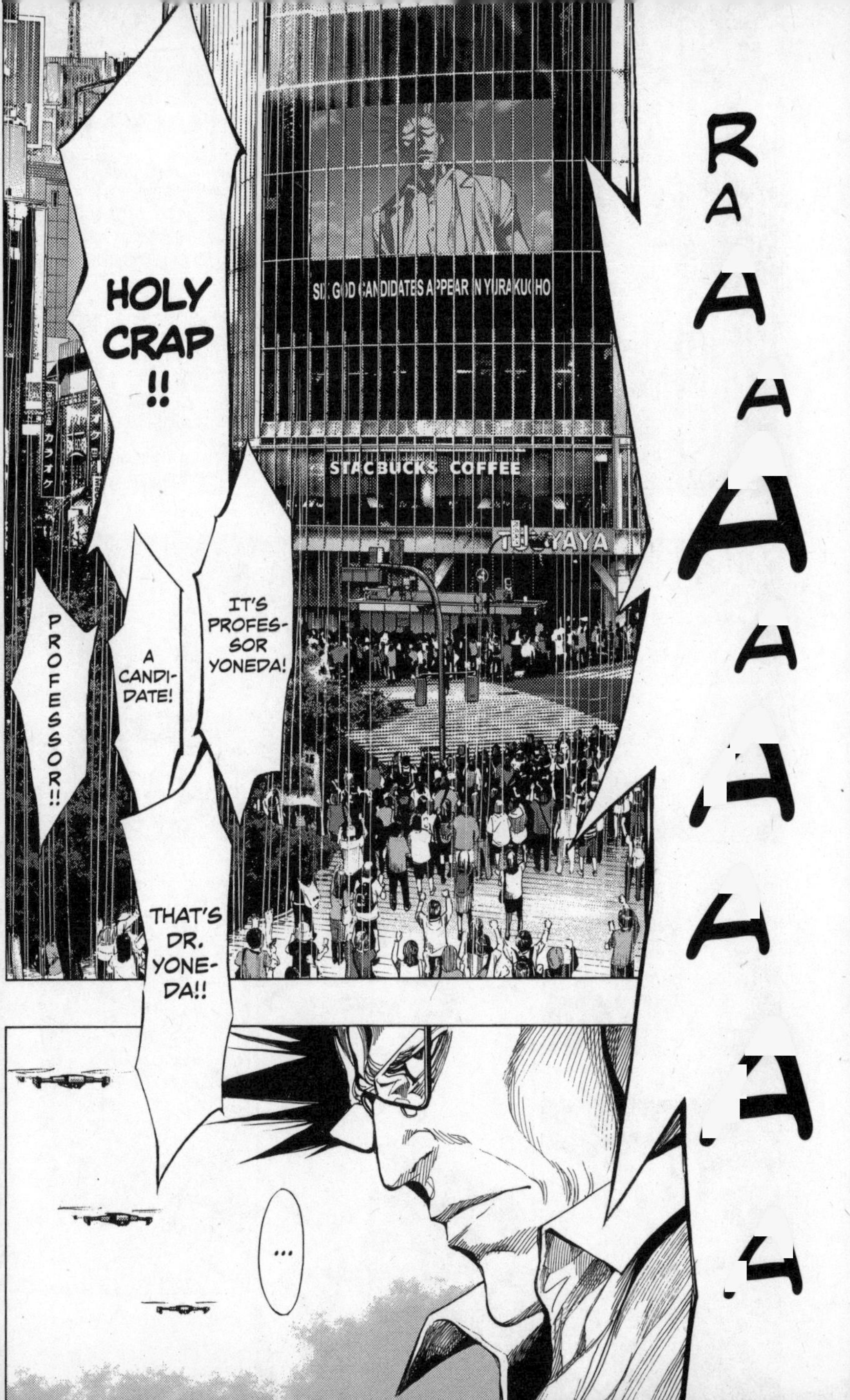
RAAAAAAAAA
SIX GOD CANDIDATES APPEAR IN YURAKUCHO
STACBUCKS COFFEE
IT'S PROFESSOR YONEDA!
A CANDIDATE!
HOLY CRAP!!
PROFESSOR!!
THAT'S DR. YONEDA!!
...

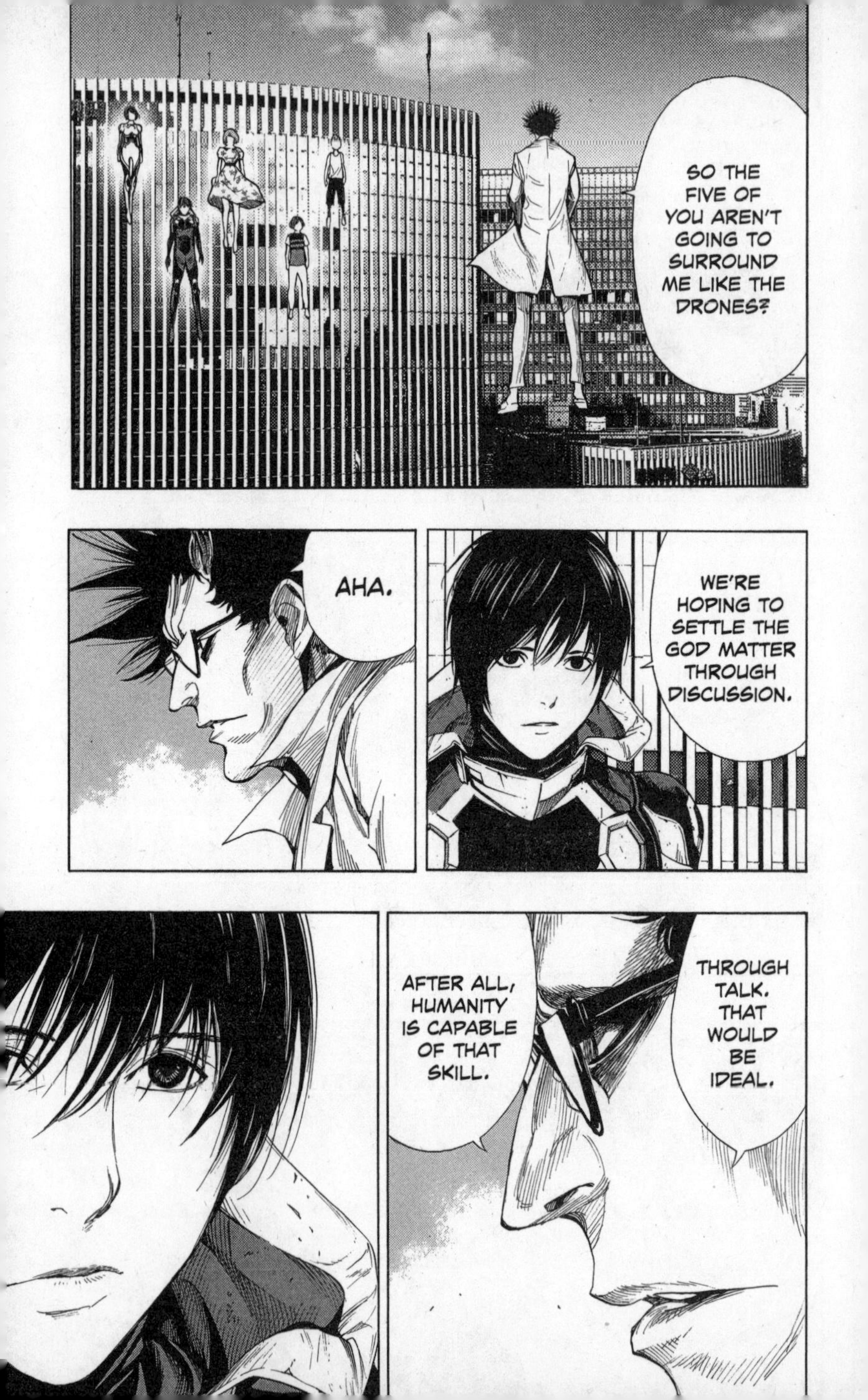
SO THE FIVE OF YOU AREN'T GOING TO SURROUND ME LIKE THE DRONES?
WE'RE HOPING TO SETTLE THE GOD MATTER THROUGH DISCUSSION.
AHA.
THROUGH TALK. THAT WOULD BE IDEAL.
AFTER ALL, HUMANITY IS CAPABLE OF THAT SKILL.

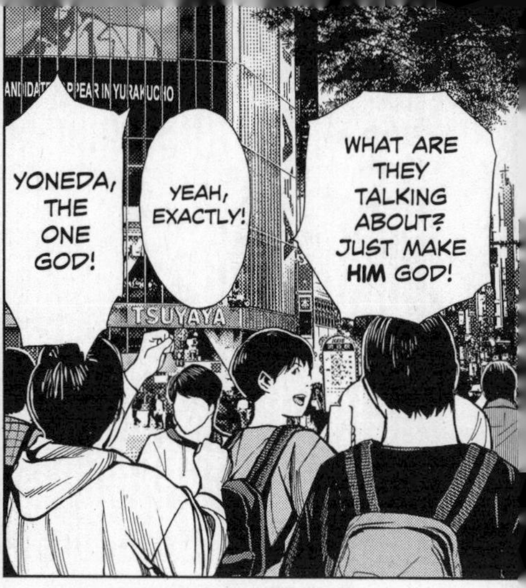
WHAT ARE THEY TALKING ABOUT? JUST MAKE HIM GOD!
YEAH, EXACTLY!
YONEDA, THE ONE GOD!
TSUYAYA

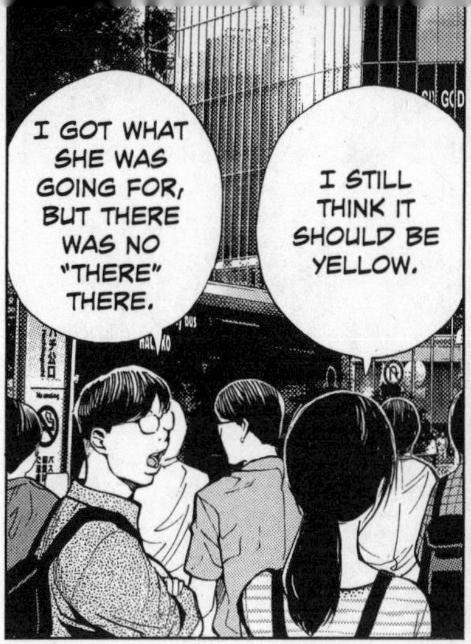
I STILL THINK IT SHOULD BE YELLOW.
I GOT WHAT SHE WAS GOING FOR, BUT THERE WAS NO "THERE" THERE.

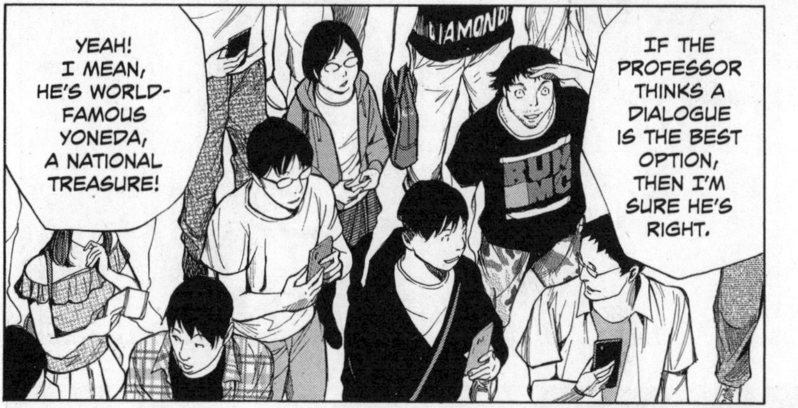
IF THE PROFESSOR THINKS A DIALOGUE IS THE BEST OPTION, THEN I'M SURE HE'S RIGHT.
YEAH! I MEAN, HE'S WORLD-FAMOUS YONEDA, A NATIONAL TREASURE!

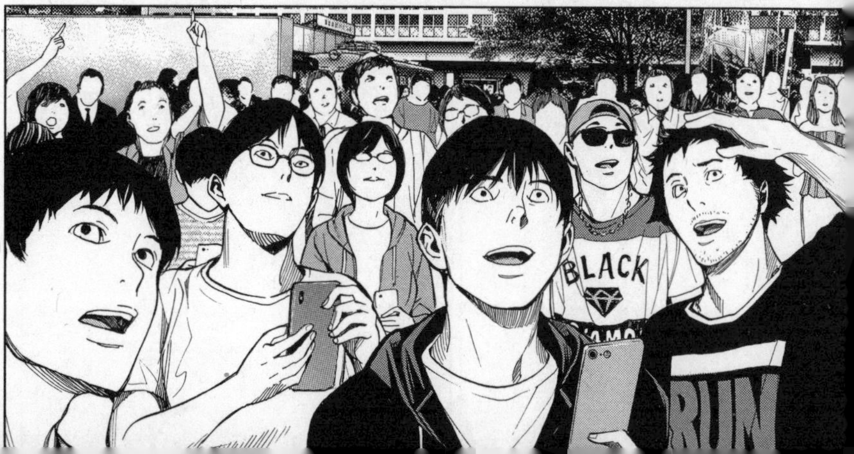
BLACK

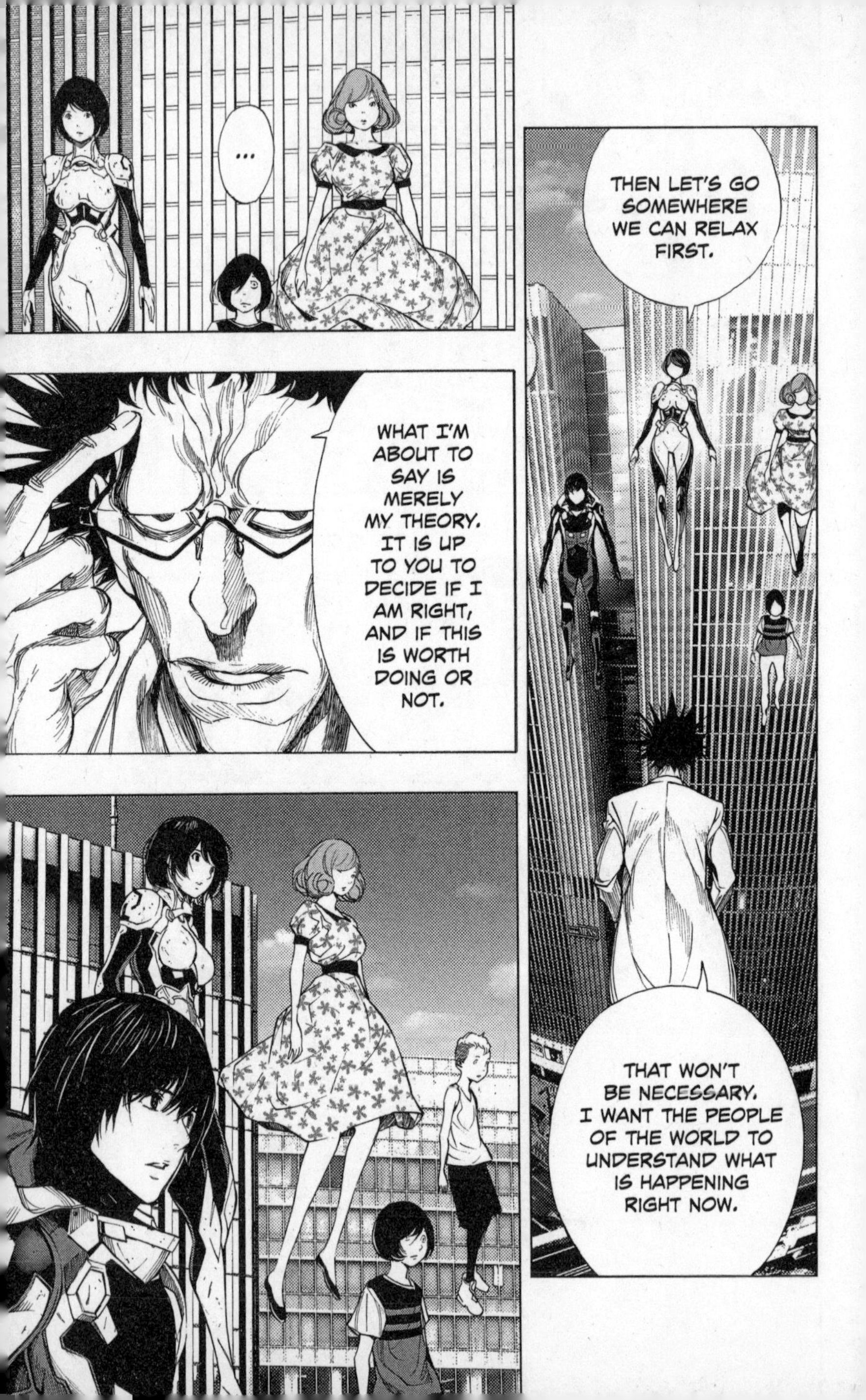
THEN LET'S GO SOMEWHERE WE CAN RELAX FIRST.
THAT WON'T BE NECESSARY. I WANT THE PEOPLE OF THE WORLD TO UNDERSTAND WHAT IS HAPPENING RIGHT NOW.
...
WHAT I'M ABOUT TO SAY IS MERELY MY THEORY. IT IS UP TO YOU TO DECIDE IF I AM RIGHT, AND IF THIS IS WORTH DOING OR NOT.

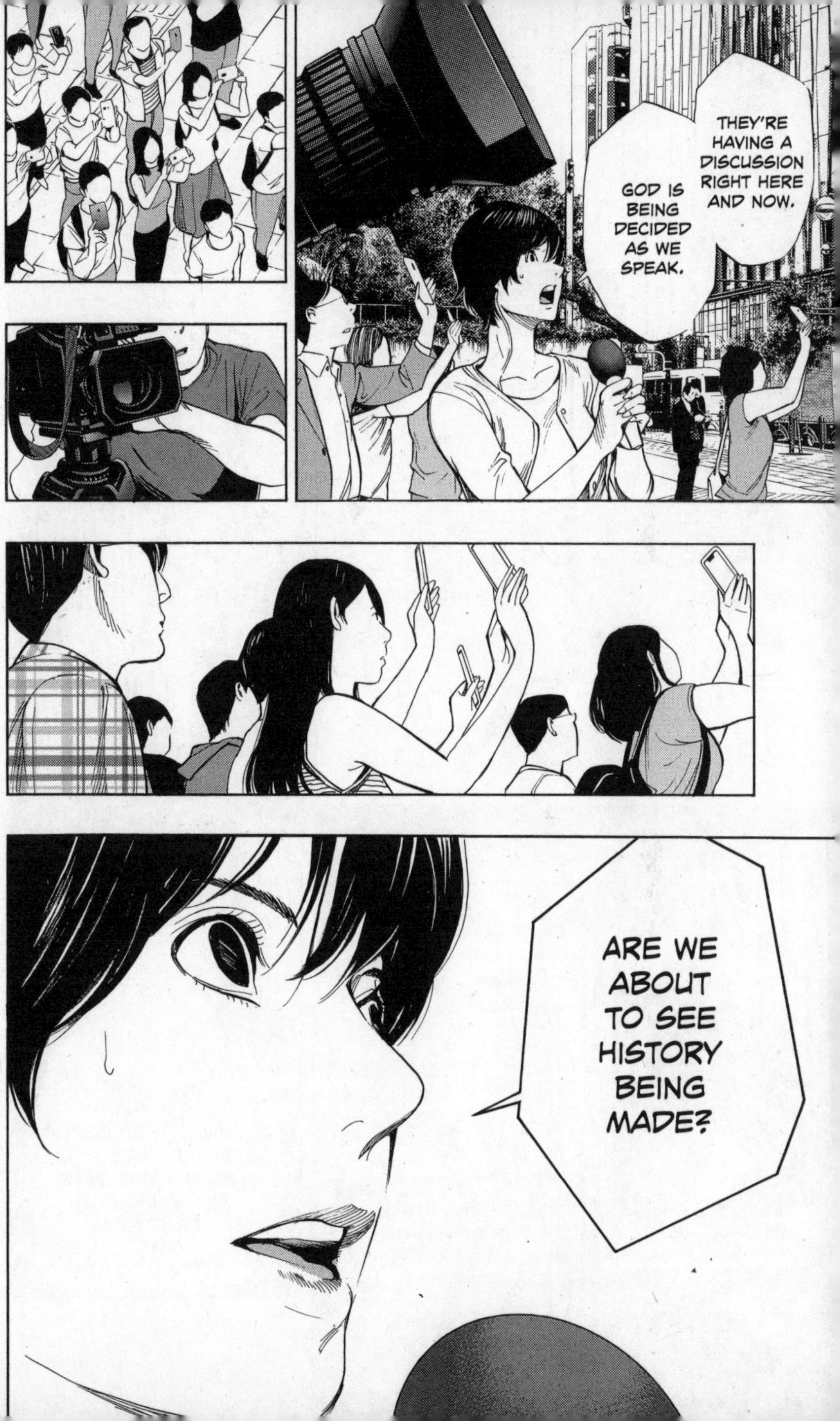
THEY'RE HAVING A DISCUSSION RIGHT HERE AND NOW.
GOD IS BEING DECIDED AS WE SPEAK.
ARE WE ABOUT TO SEE HISTORY BEING MADE?

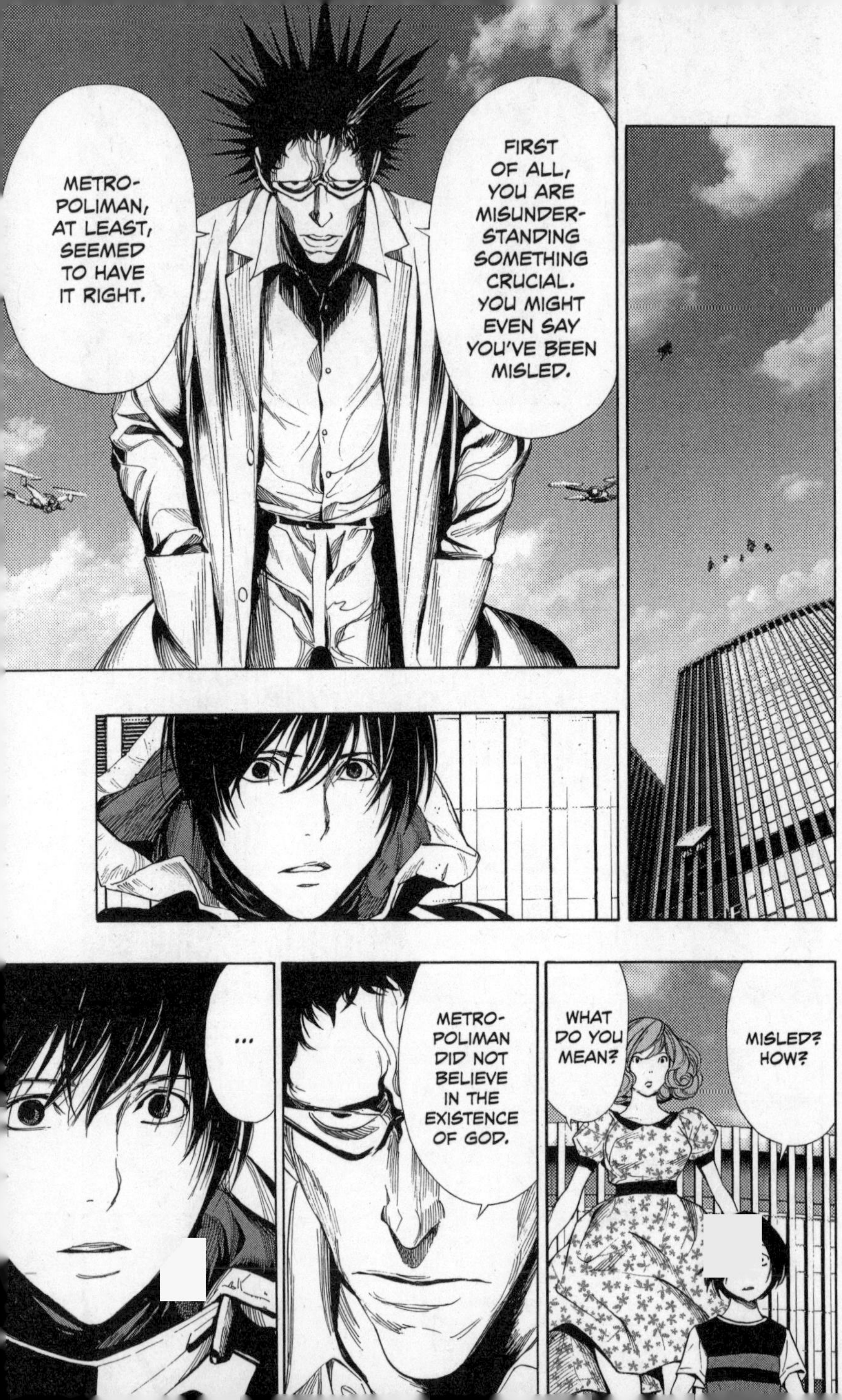
FIRST OF ALL, YOU ARE MISUNDER-STANDING SOMETHING CRUCIAL. YOU MIGHT EVEN SAY YOU'VE BEEN MISLED.
METRO-POLIMAN, AT LEAST, SEEMED TO HAVE IT RIGHT.
MISLED? HOW?
WHAT DO YOU MEAN?
METRO-POLIMAN DID NOT BELIEVE IN THE EXISTENCE OF GOD.
...

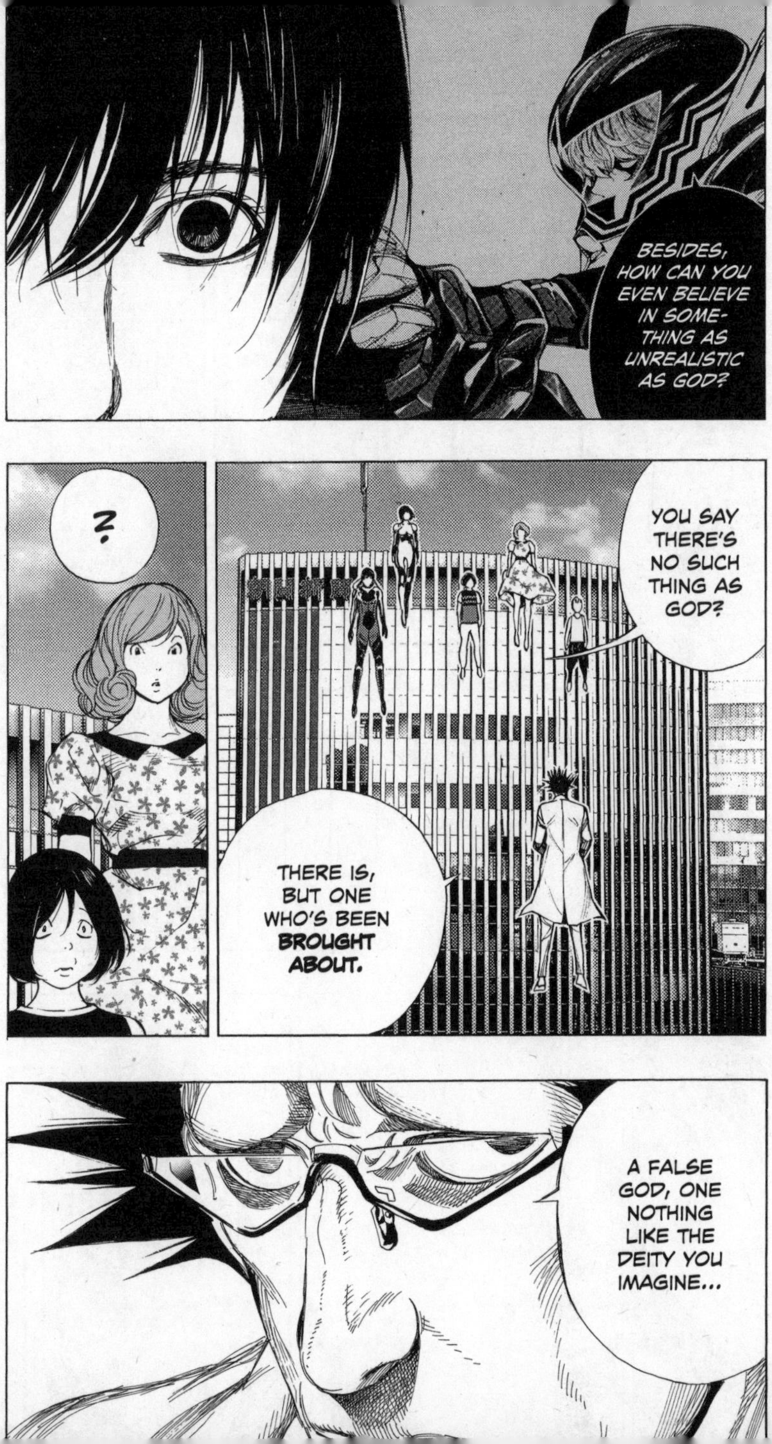
BESIDES, HOW CAN YOU EVEN BELIEVE IN SOME-THING AS UNREALISTIC AS GOD?
YOU SAY THERE'S NO SUCH THING AS GOD?
THERE IS, BUT ONE WHO'S BEEN **BROUGHT ABOUT.**
?
A FALSE GOD, ONE NOTHING LIKE THE DEITY YOU IMAGINE...

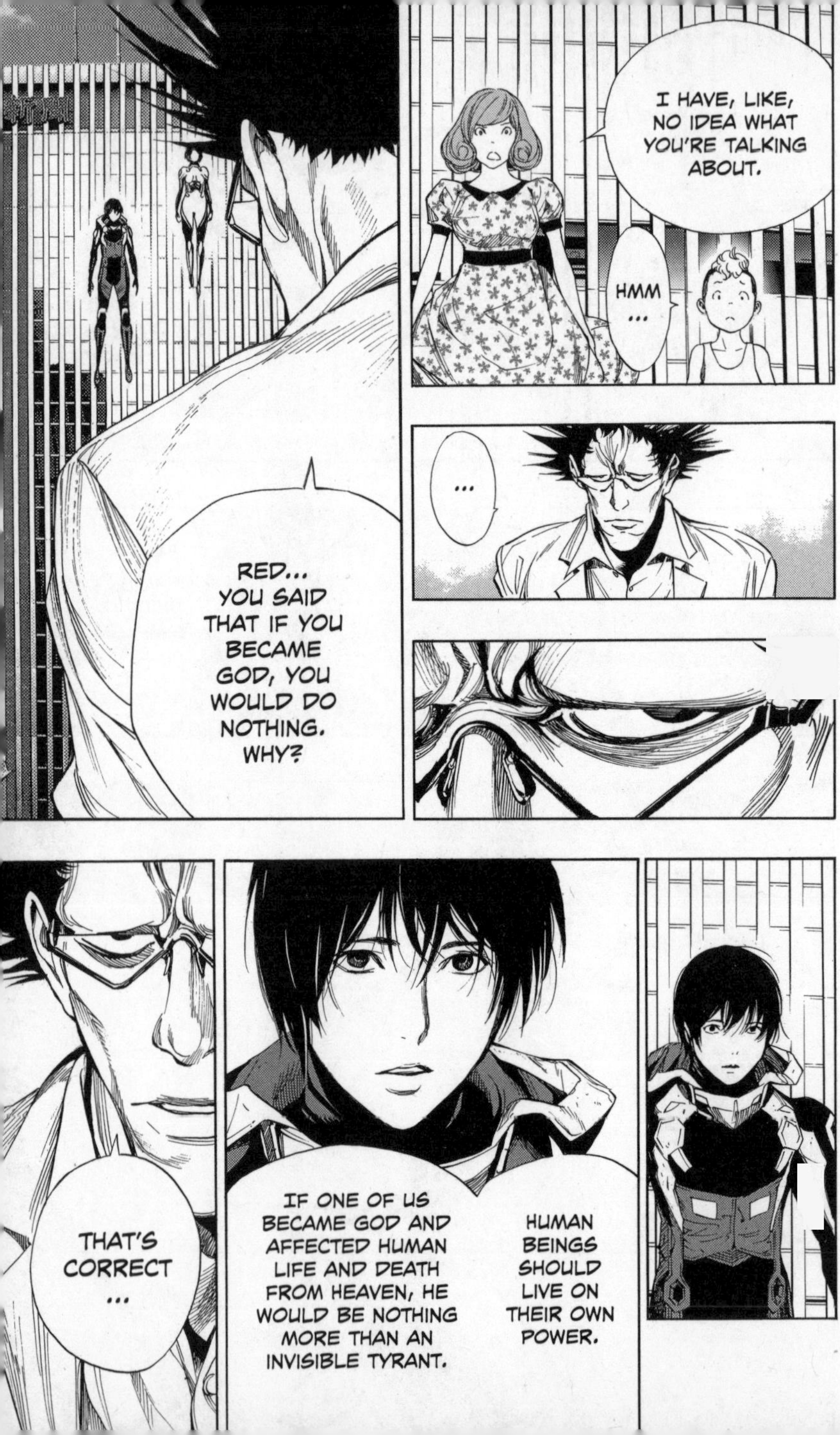
I HAVE, LIKE, NO IDEA WHAT YOU'RE TALKING ABOUT.
HMM ...
...
RED... YOU SAID THAT IF YOU BECAME GOD, YOU WOULD DO NOTHING. WHY?
IF ONE OF US BECAME GOD AND AFFECTED HUMAN LIFE AND DEATH FROM HEAVEN, HE WOULD BE NOTHING MORE THAN AN INVISIBLE TYRANT.
HUMAN BEINGS SHOULD LIVE ON THEIR OWN POWER.
THAT'S CORRECT ...

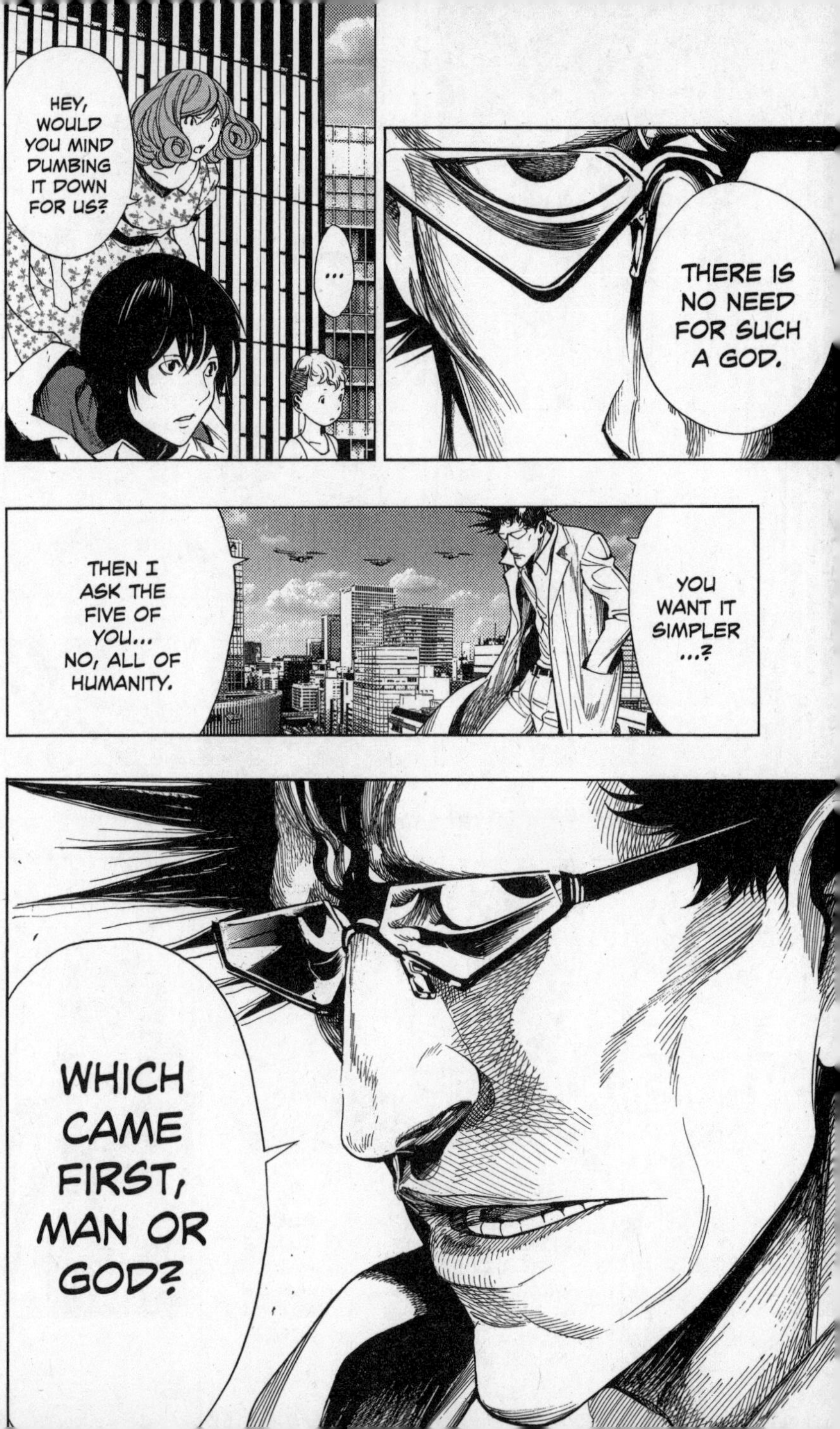
THERE IS NO NEED FOR SUCH A GOD.
HEY, WOULD YOU MIND DUMBING IT DOWN FOR US?
...
YOU WANT IT SIMPLER ...?
THEN I ASK THE FIVE OF YOU... NO, ALL OF HUMANITY.
WHICH CAME FIRST, MAN OR GOD?

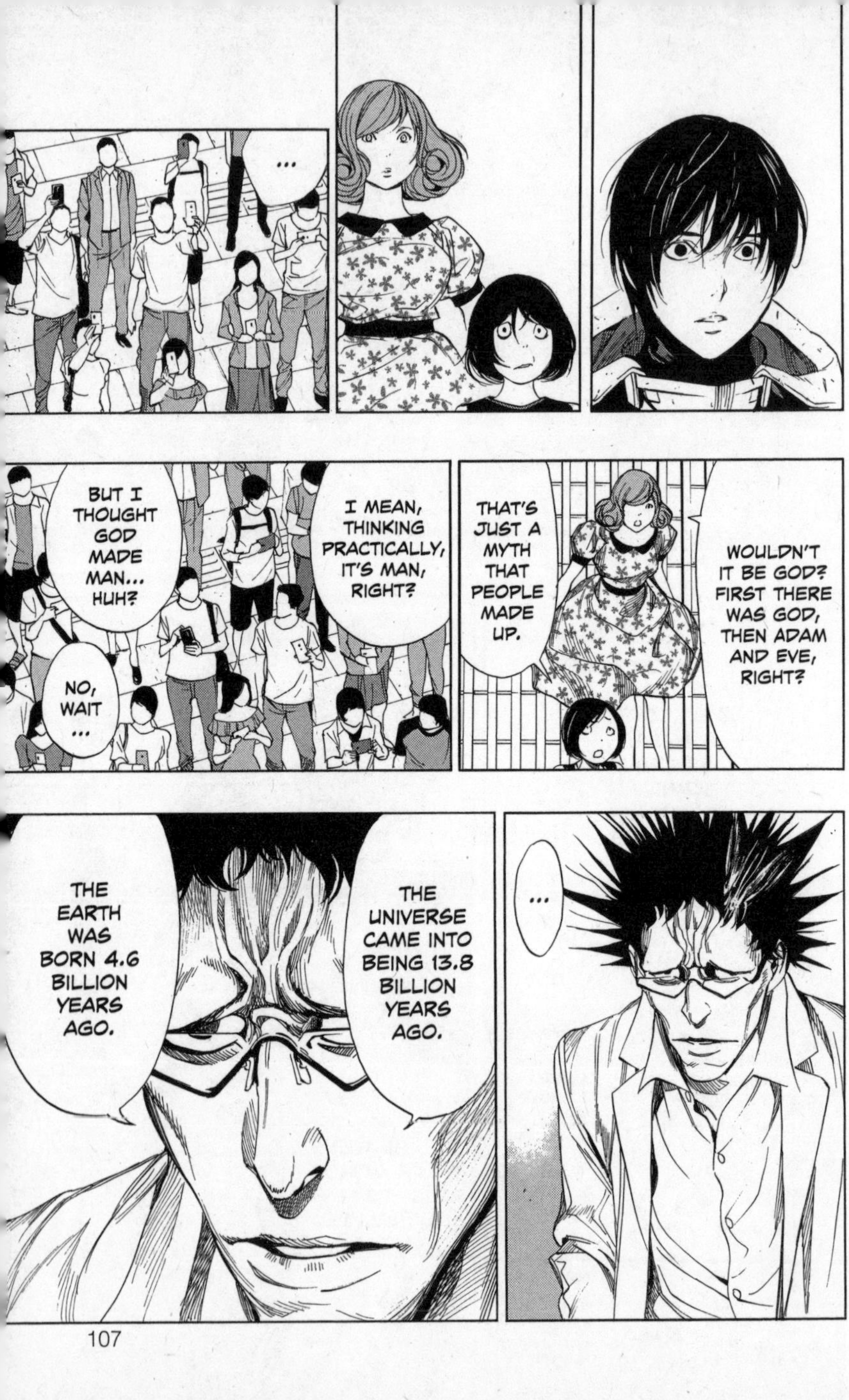
...
WOULDN'T IT BE GOD? FIRST THERE WAS GOD, THEN ADAM AND EVE, RIGHT?
THAT'S JUST A MYTH THAT PEOPLE MADE UP.
I MEAN, THINKING PRACTICALLY, IT'S MAN, RIGHT?
BUT I THOUGHT GOD MADE MAN... HUH?
NO, WAIT ...
...
THE UNIVERSE CAME INTO BEING 13.8 BILLION YEARS AGO.
THE EARTH WAS BORN 4.6 BILLION YEARS AGO.

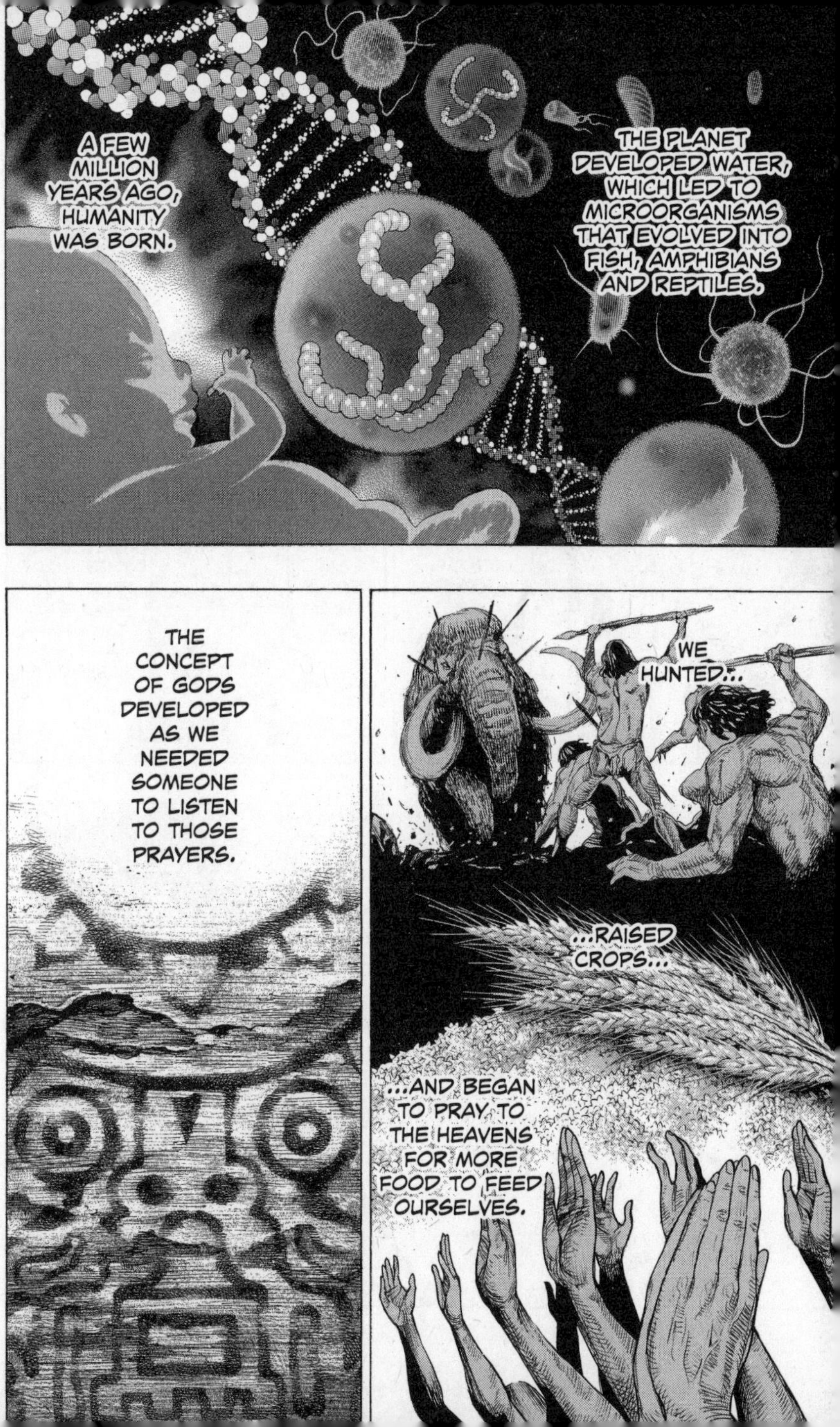
THE PLANET DEVELOPED WATER, WHICH LED TO MICROORGANISMS THAT EVOLVED INTO FISH, AMPHIBIANS AND REPTILES.
A FEW MILLION YEARS AGO, HUMANITY WAS BORN.
WE HUNTED...
...RAISED CROPS...
...AND BEGAN TO PRAY TO THE HEAVENS FOR MORE FOOD TO FEED OURSELVES.
THE CONCEPT OF GODS DEVELOPED AS WE NEEDED SOMEONE TO LISTEN TO THOSE PRAYERS.

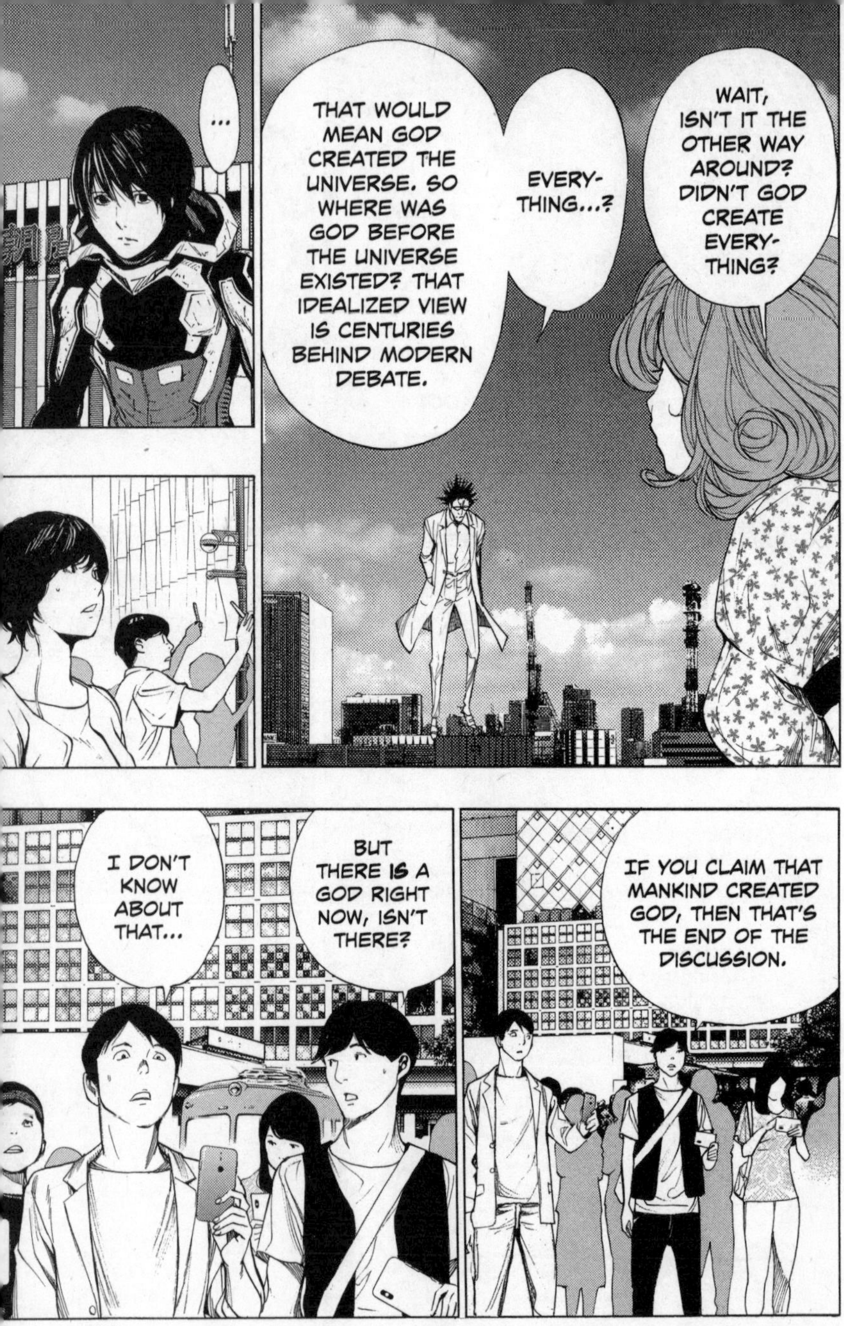
WAIT, ISN'T IT THE OTHER WAY AROUND? DIDN'T GOD CREATE EVERY-THING?
EVERY-THING...?
THAT WOULD MEAN GOD CREATED THE UNIVERSE. SO WHERE WAS GOD BEFORE THE UNIVERSE EXISTED? THAT IDEALIZED VIEW IS CENTURIES BEHIND MODERN DEBATE.
...
IF YOU CLAIM THAT MANKIND CREATED GOD, THEN THAT'S THE END OF THE DISCUSSION.
BUT THERE **IS** A GOD RIGHT NOW, ISN'T THERE?
I DON'T KNOW ABOUT THAT...

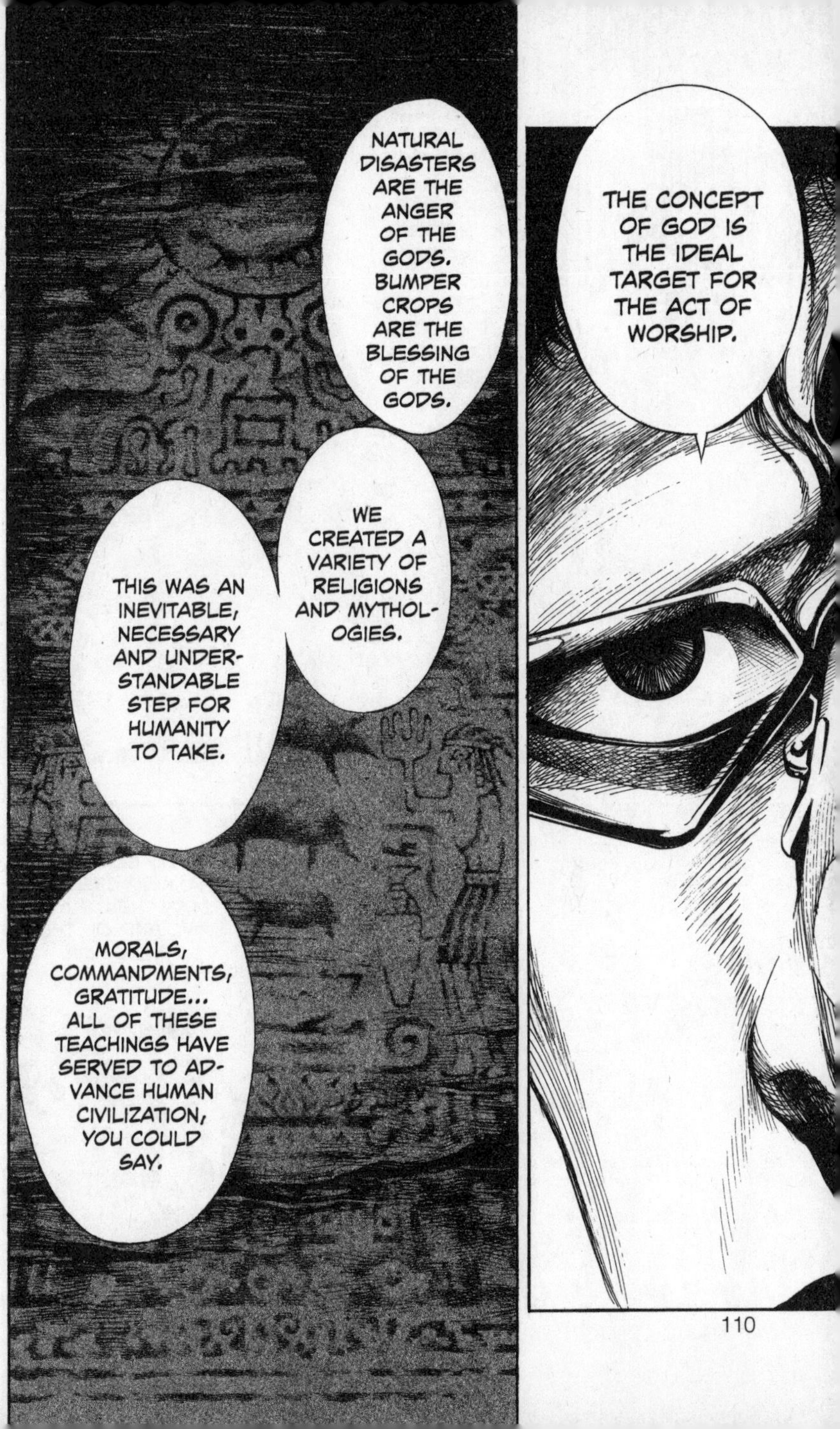
THE CONCEPT OF GOD IS THE IDEAL TARGET FOR THE ACT OF WORSHIP.
NATURAL DISASTERS ARE THE ANGER OF THE GODS. BUMPER CROPS ARE THE BLESSING OF THE GODS.
WE CREATED A VARIETY OF RELIGIONS AND MYTHOLOGIES.
THIS WAS AN INEVITABLE, NECESSARY AND UNDERSTANDABLE STEP FOR HUMANITY TO TAKE.
MORALS, COMMANDMENTS, GRATITUDE... ALL OF THESE TEACHINGS HAVE SERVED TO ADVANCE HUMAN CIVILIZATION, YOU COULD SAY.

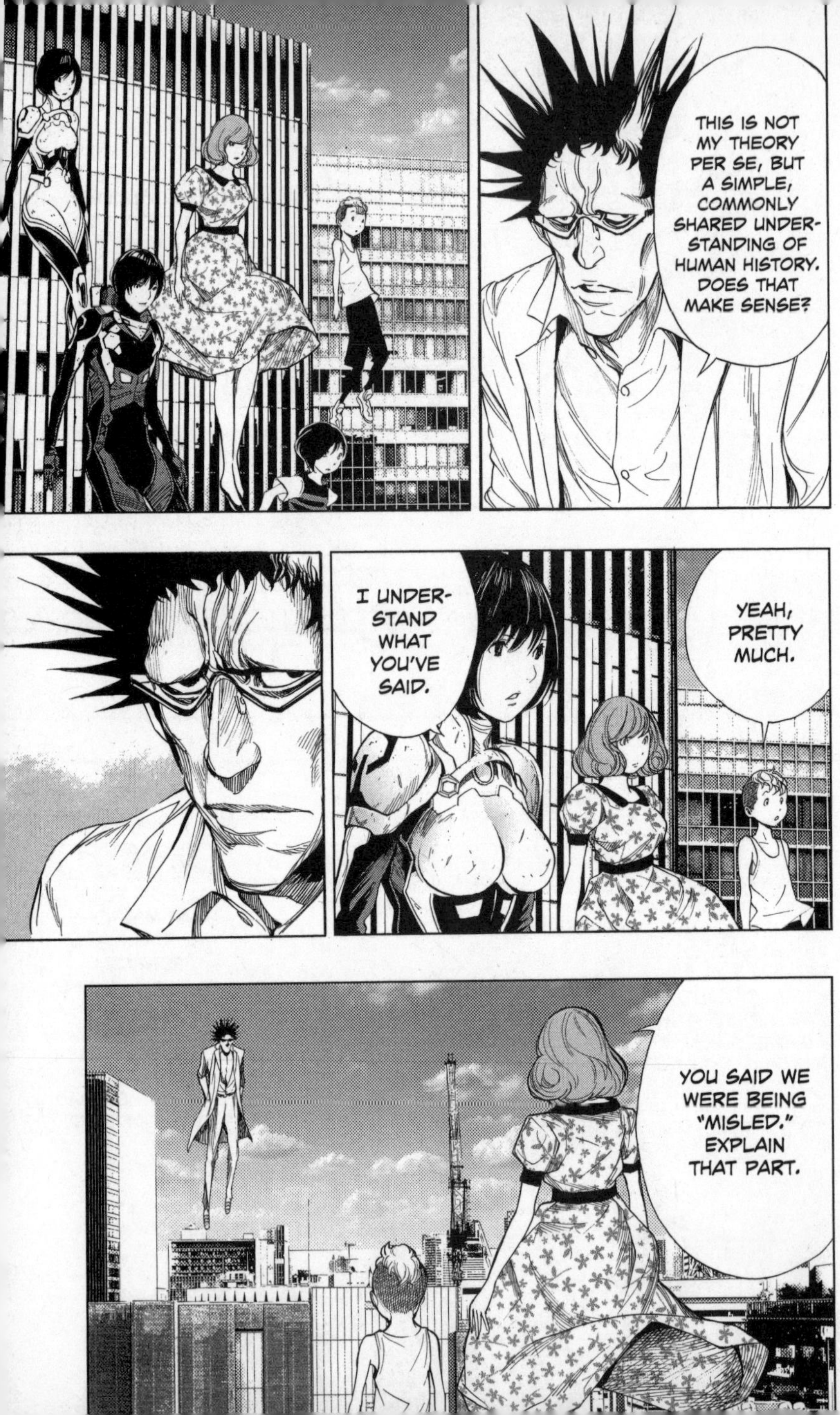
THIS IS NOT MY THEORY PER SE, BUT A SIMPLE, COMMONLY SHARED UNDER-STANDING OF HUMAN HISTORY. DOES THAT MAKE SENSE?
YEAH, PRETTY MUCH.
I UNDER-STAND WHAT YOU'VE SAID.
YOU SAID WE WERE BEING "MISLED." EXPLAIN THAT PART.

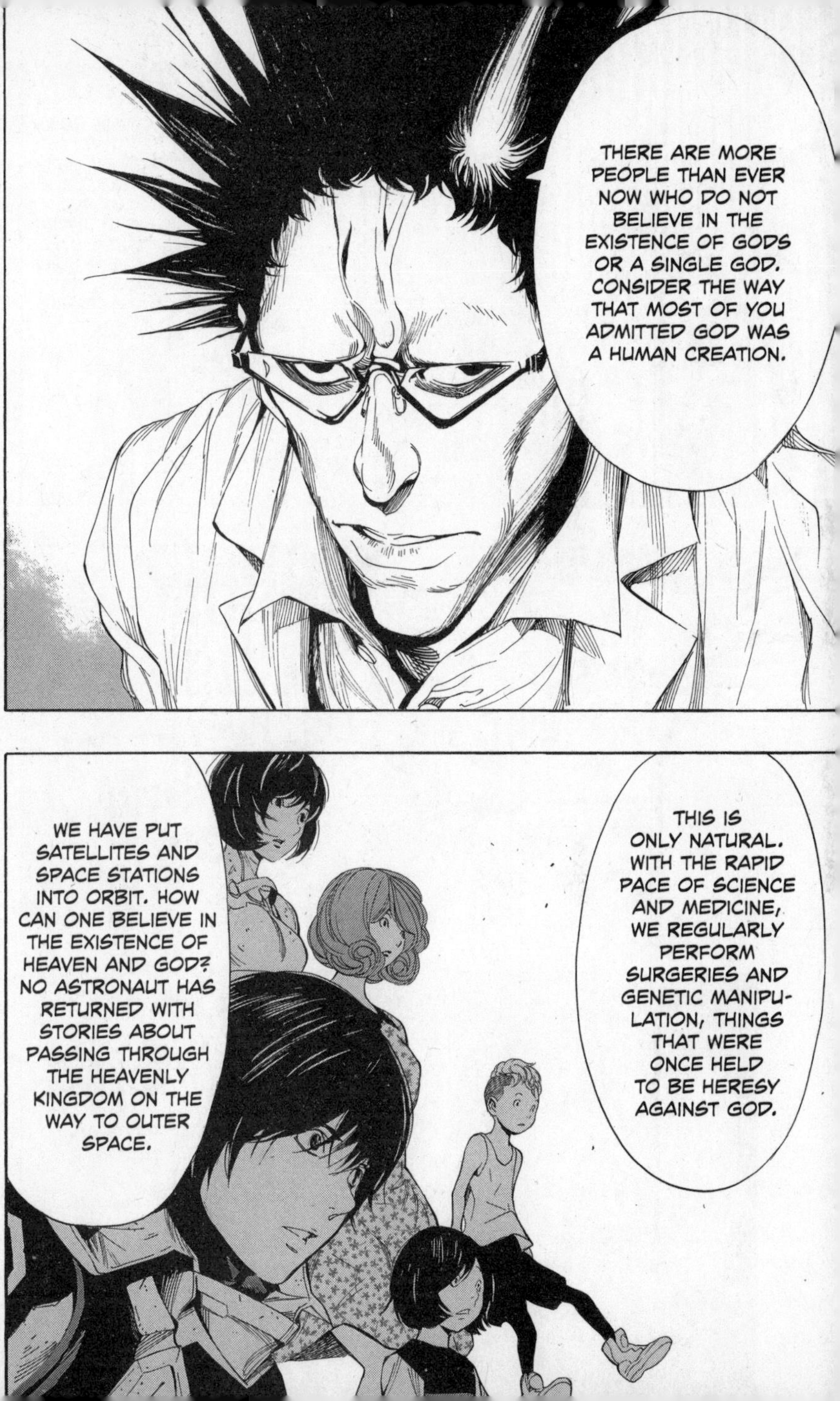
THERE ARE MORE PEOPLE THAN EVER NOW WHO DO NOT BELIEVE IN THE EXISTENCE OF GODS OR A SINGLE GOD. CONSIDER THE WAY THAT MOST OF YOU ADMITTED GOD WAS A HUMAN CREATION.
THIS IS ONLY NATURAL. WITH THE RAPID PACE OF SCIENCE AND MEDICINE, WE REGULARLY PERFORM SURGERIES AND GENETIC MANIPULATION, THINGS THAT WERE ONCE HELD TO BE HERESY AGAINST GOD.
WE HAVE PUT SATELLITES AND SPACE STATIONS INTO ORBIT. HOW CAN ONE BELIEVE IN THE EXISTENCE OF HEAVEN AND GOD? NO ASTRONAUT HAS RETURNED WITH STORIES ABOUT PASSING THROUGH THE HEAVENLY KINGDOM ON THE WAY TO OUTER SPACE.

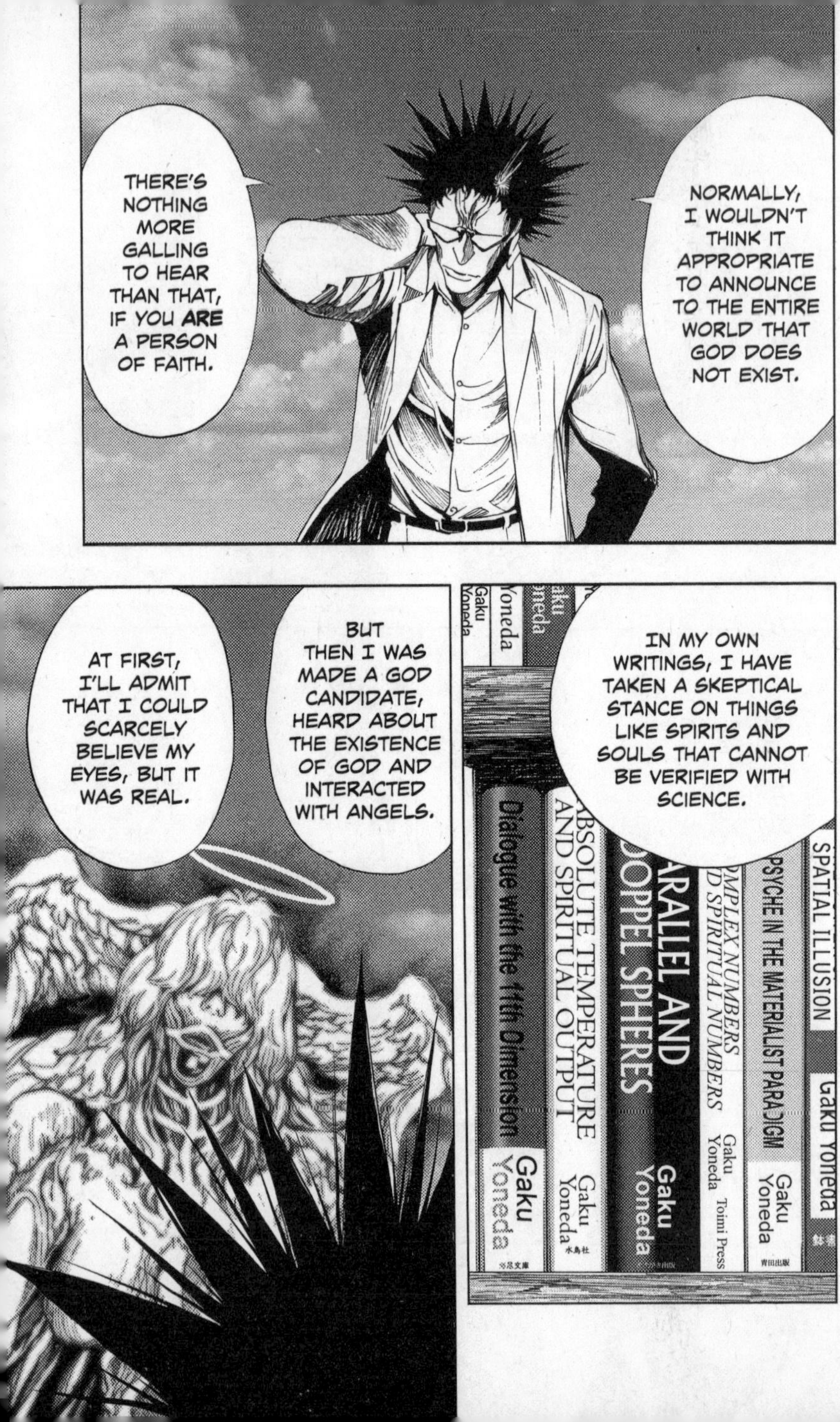
NORMALLY, I WOULDN'T THINK IT APPROPRIATE TO ANNOUNCE TO THE ENTIRE WORLD THAT GOD DOES NOT EXIST.
THERE'S NOTHING MORE GALLING TO HEAR THAN THAT, IF YOU **ARE** A PERSON OF FAITH.
IN MY OWN WRITINGS, I HAVE TAKEN A SKEPTICAL STANCE ON THINGS LIKE SPIRITS AND SOULS THAT CANNOT BE VERIFIED WITH SCIENCE.
SPATIAL ILLUSION
Gaku Yoneda
PSYCHE IN THE MATERIALIST PARADIGM
Gaku Yoneda
Gaku Yoneda
Toimi Press
Gaku Yoneda
ABSOLUTE TEMPERATURE AND SPIRITUAL OUTPUT
Gaku Yoneda
Dialogue with the 11th Dimension
Gaku Yoneda
BUT THEN I WAS MADE A GOD CANDIDATE, HEARD ABOUT THE EXISTENCE OF GOD AND INTERACTED WITH ANGELS.
AT FIRST, I'LL ADMIT THAT I COULD SCARCELY BELIEVE MY EYES, BUT IT WAS REAL.

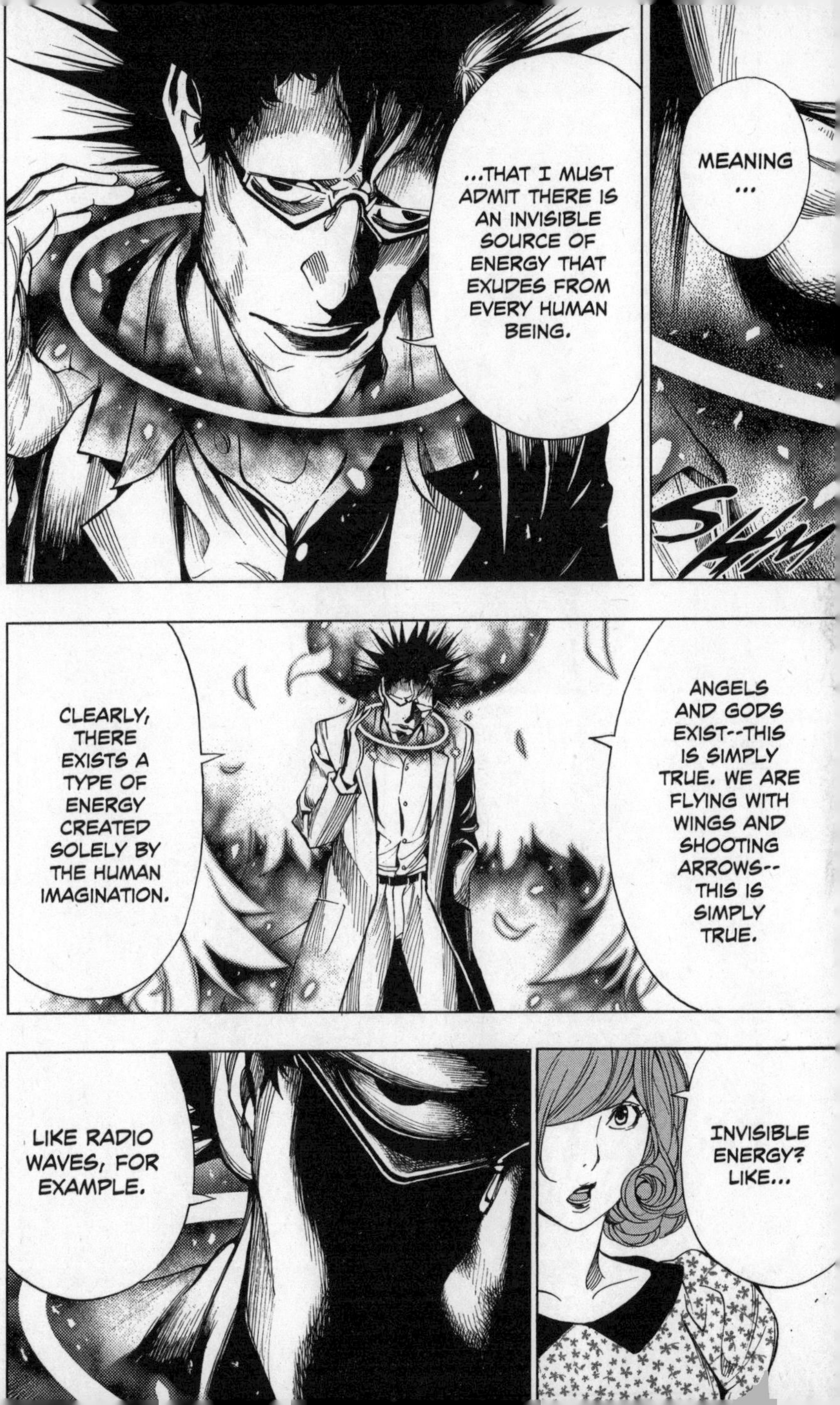
MEANING...
SHM
...THAT I MUST ADMIT THERE IS AN INVISIBLE SOURCE OF ENERGY THAT EXUDES FROM EVERY HUMAN BEING.
ANGELS AND GODS EXIST--THIS IS SIMPLY TRUE. WE ARE FLYING WITH WINGS AND SHOOTING ARROWS--THIS IS SIMPLY TRUE.
CLEARLY, THERE EXISTS A TYPE OF ENERGY CREATED SOLELY BY THE HUMAN IMAGINATION.
INVISIBLE ENERGY? LIKE...
LIKE RADIO WAVES, FOR EXAMPLE.

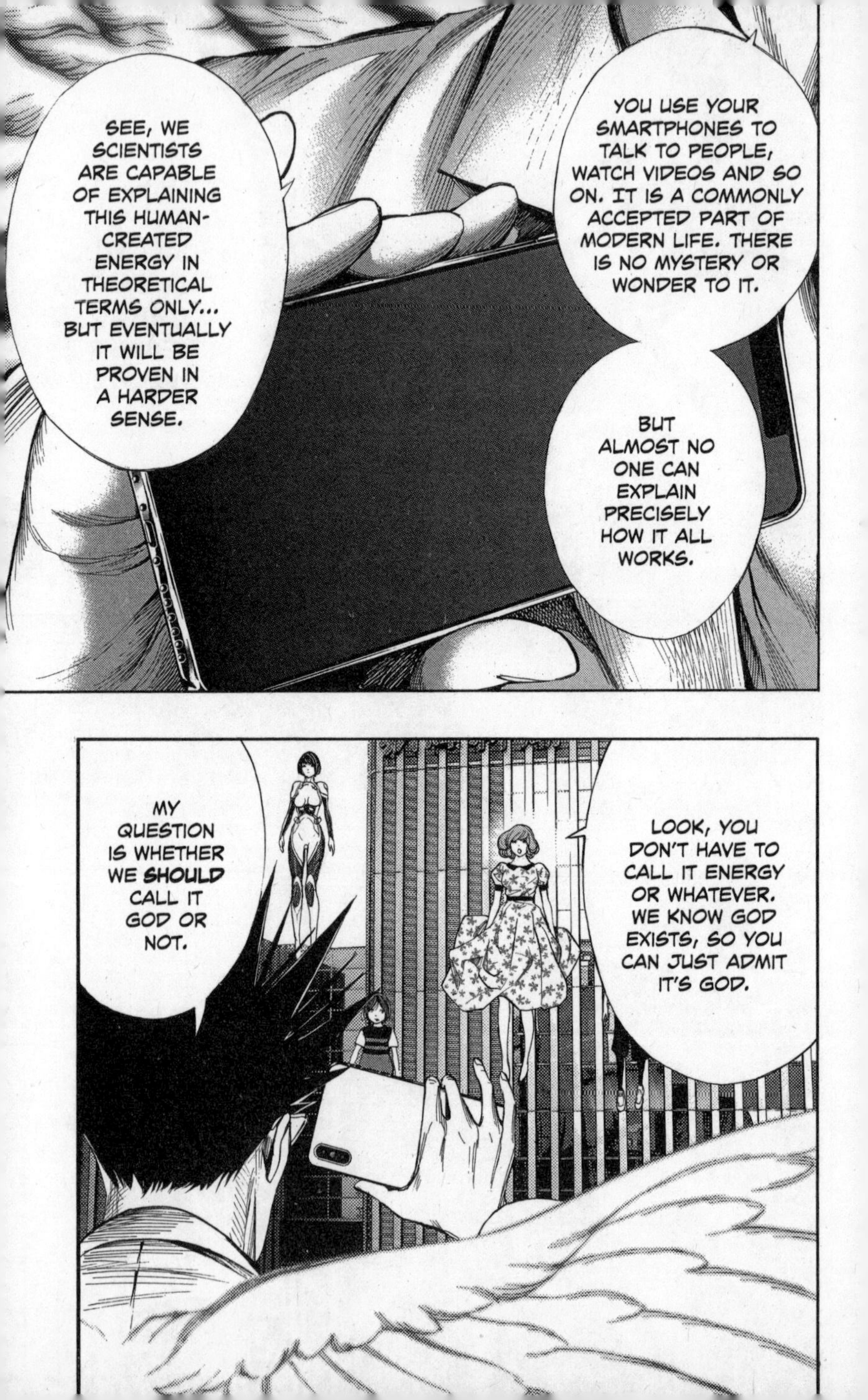
YOU USE YOUR SMARTPHONES TO TALK TO PEOPLE, WATCH VIDEOS AND SO ON. IT IS A COMMONLY ACCEPTED PART OF MODERN LIFE. THERE IS NO MYSTERY OR WONDER TO IT.
BUT ALMOST NO ONE CAN EXPLAIN PRECISELY HOW IT ALL WORKS.
SEE, WE SCIENTISTS ARE CAPABLE OF EXPLAINING THIS HUMAN-CREATED ENERGY IN THEORETICAL TERMS ONLY... BUT EVENTUALLY IT WILL BE PROVEN IN A HARDER SENSE.
LOOK, YOU DON'T HAVE TO CALL IT ENERGY OR WHATEVER. WE KNOW GOD EXISTS, SO YOU CAN JUST ADMIT IT'S GOD.
MY QUESTION IS WHETHER WE **SHOULD** CALL IT GOD OR NOT.

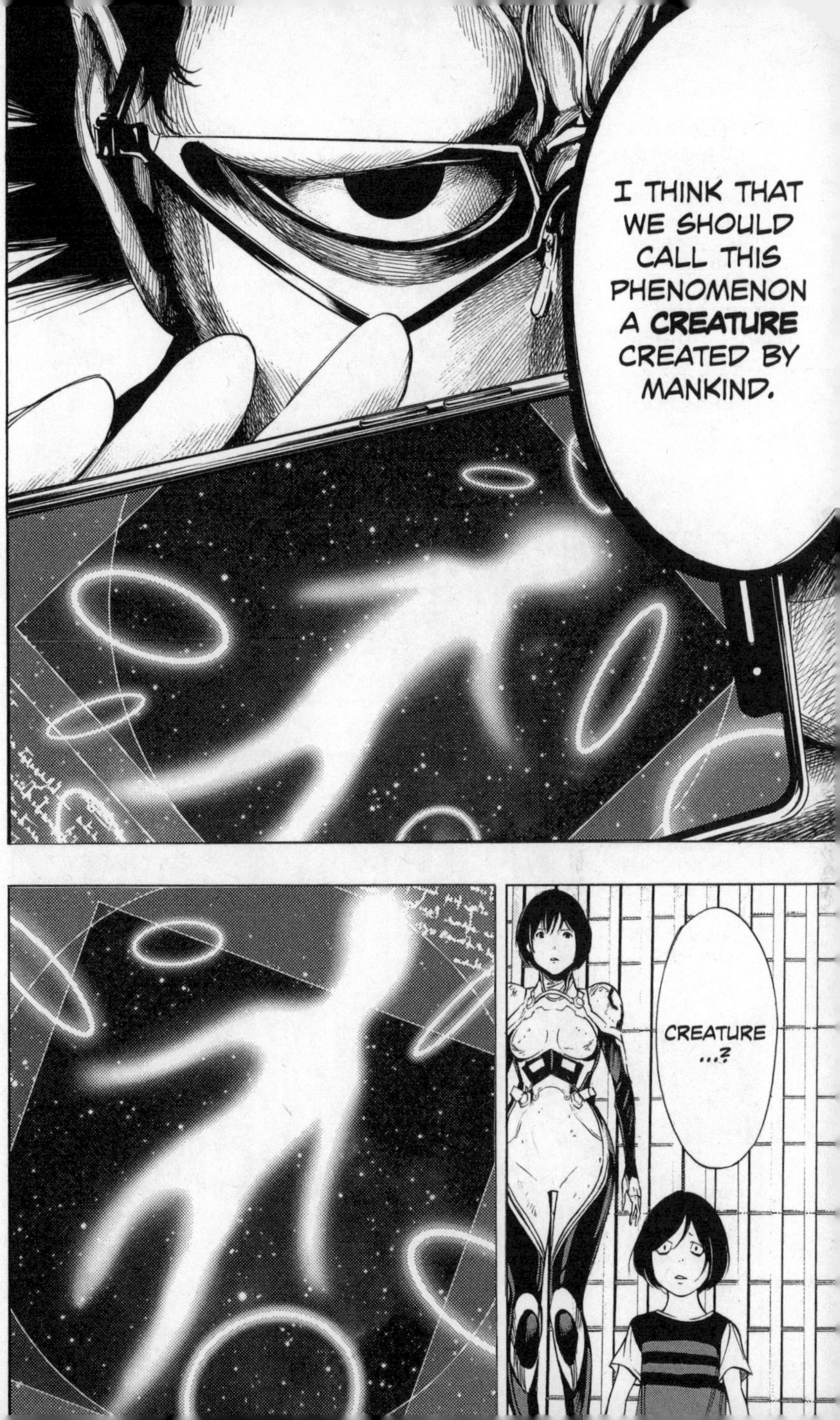
I THINK THAT WE SHOULD CALL THIS PHENOMENON A **CREATURE** CREATED BY MANKIND.
CREATURE ...?

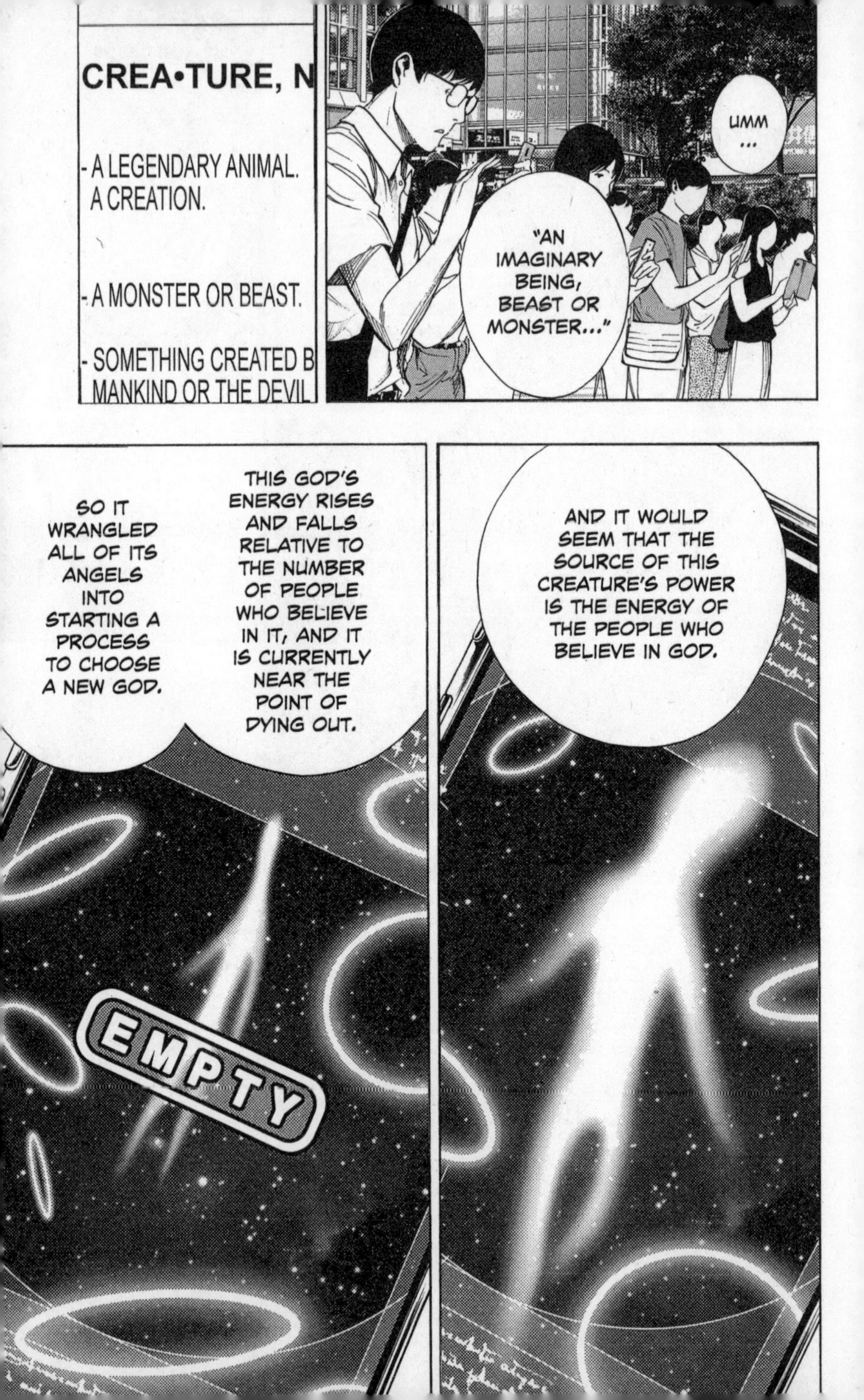
UMM ...
"AN IMAGINARY BEING, BEAST OR MONSTER..."
CREA•TURE, N
- A LEGENDARY ANIMAL. A CREATION.
- A MONSTER OR BEAST.
- SOMETHING CREATED B
MANKIND OR THE DEVIL
AND IT WOULD SEEM THAT THE SOURCE OF THIS CREATURE'S POWER IS THE ENERGY OF THE PEOPLE WHO BELIEVE IN GOD.
THIS GOD'S ENERGY RISES AND FALLS RELATIVE TO THE NUMBER OF PEOPLE WHO BELIEVE IN IT, AND IT IS CURRENTLY NEAR THE POINT OF DYING OUT.
SO IT WRANGLED ALL OF ITS ANGELS INTO STARTING A PROCESS TO CHOOSE A NEW GOD.
EMPTY

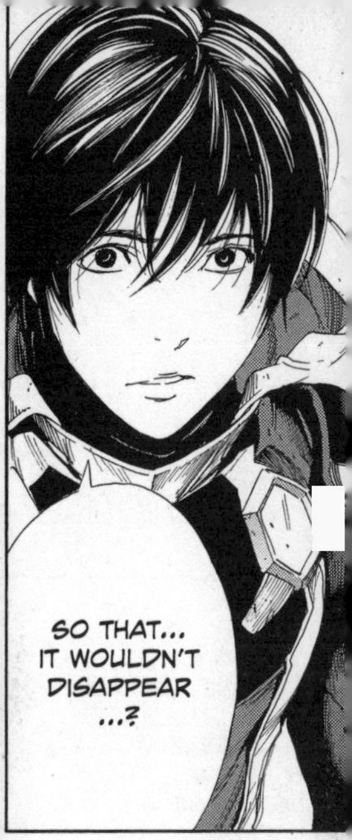
SO THAT... IT WOULDN'T DISAPPEAR ...?
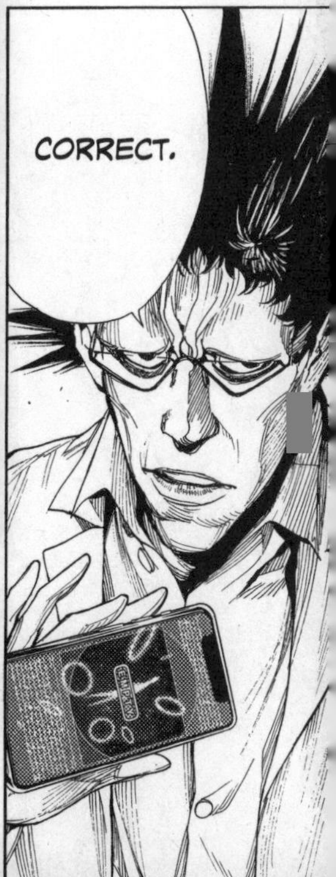
CORRECT.
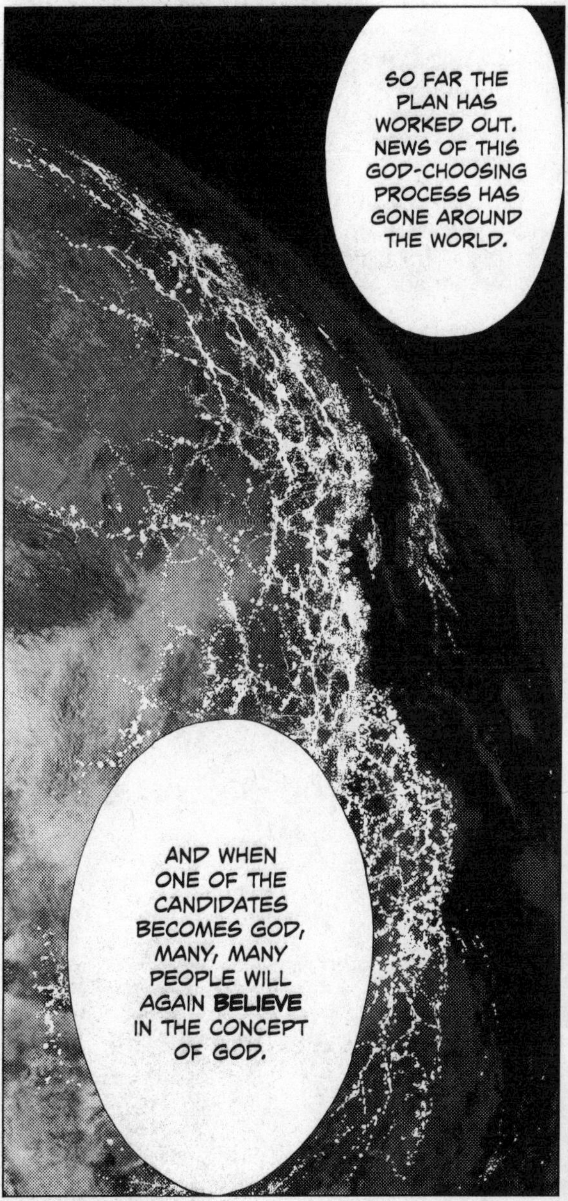
SO FAR THE PLAN HAS WORKED OUT. NEWS OF THIS GOD-CHOOSING PROCESS HAS GONE AROUND THE WORLD.
AND WHEN ONE OF THE CANDIDATES BECOMES GOD, MANY, MANY PEOPLE WILL AGAIN **BELIEVE** IN THE CONCEPT OF GOD.

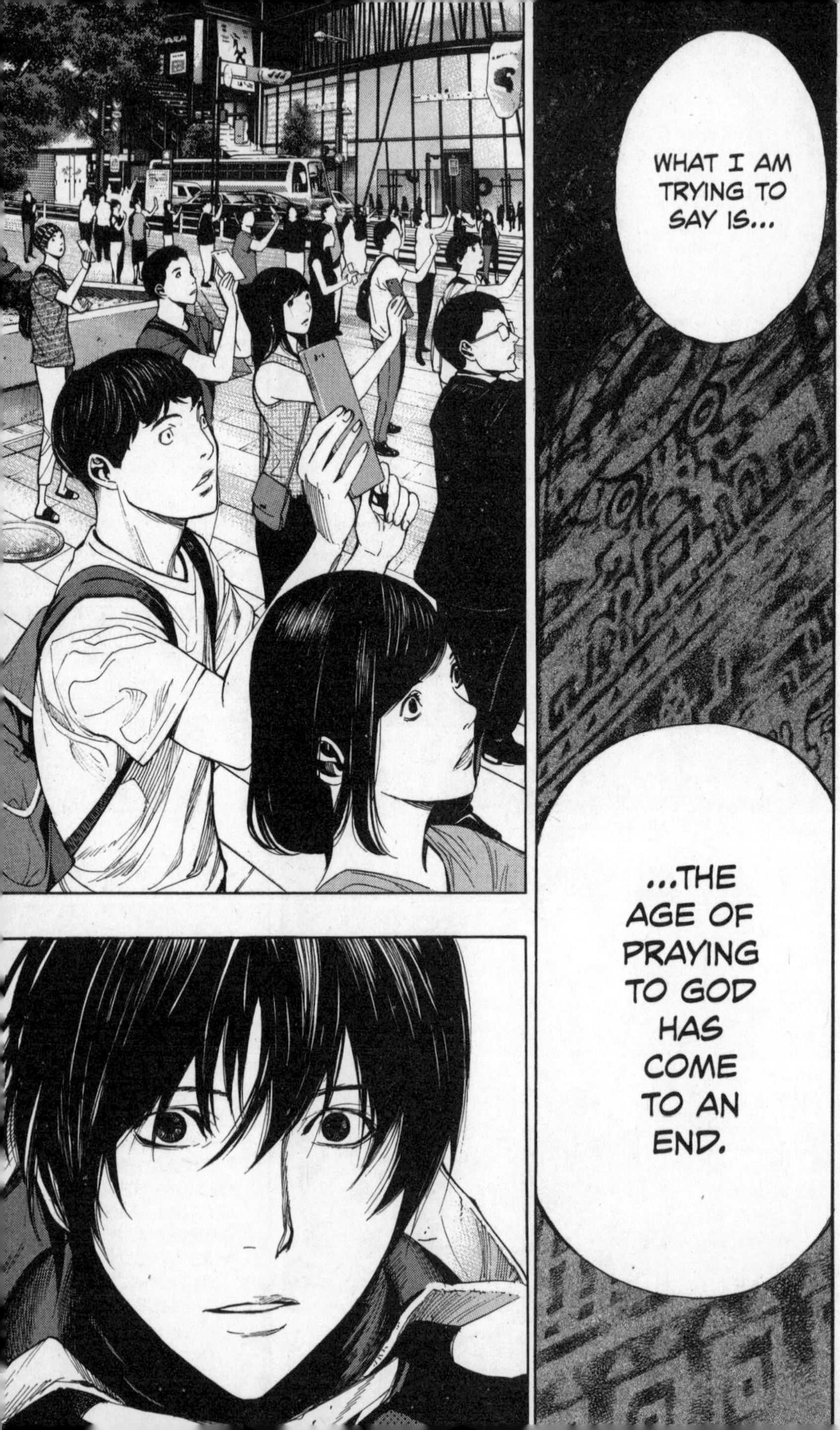
WHAT I AM TRYING TO SAY IS...
...THE AGE OF PRAYING TO GOD HAS COME TO AN END.

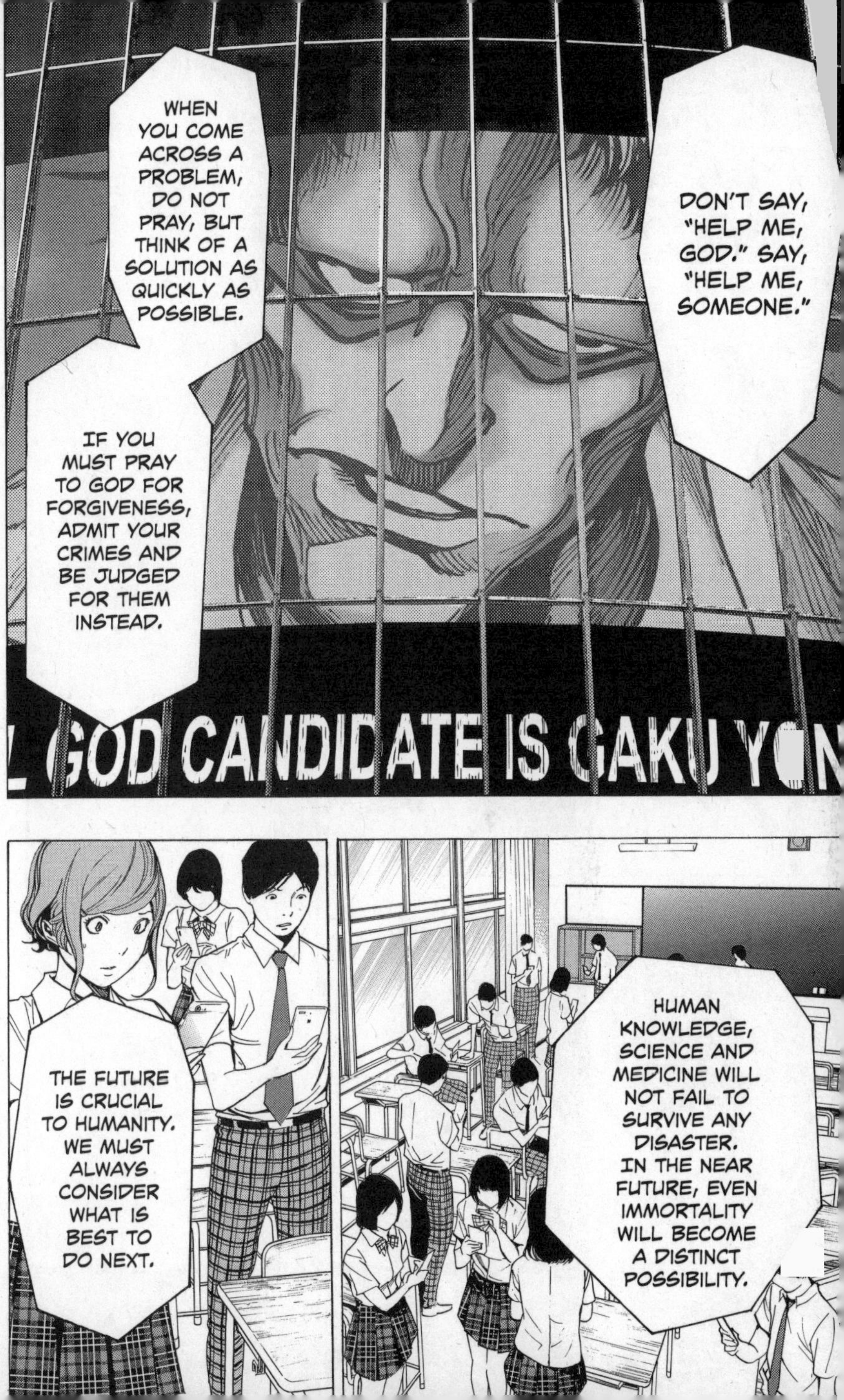
DON'T SAY, "HELP ME, GOD." SAY, "HELP ME, SOMEONE."
WHEN YOU COME ACROSS A PROBLEM, DO NOT PRAY, BUT THINK OF A SOLUTION AS QUICKLY AS POSSIBLE.
IF YOU MUST PRAY TO GOD FOR FORGIVENESS, ADMIT YOUR CRIMES AND BE JUDGED FOR THEM INSTEAD.
GOD CANDIDATE IS GAKU
HUMAN KNOWLEDGE, SCIENCE AND MEDICINE WILL NOT FAIL TO SURVIVE ANY DISASTER. IN THE NEAR FUTURE, EVEN IMMORTALITY WILL BECOME A DISTINCT POSSIBILITY.
THE FUTURE IS CRUCIAL TO HUMANITY. WE MUST ALWAYS CONSIDER WHAT IS BEST TO DO NEXT.

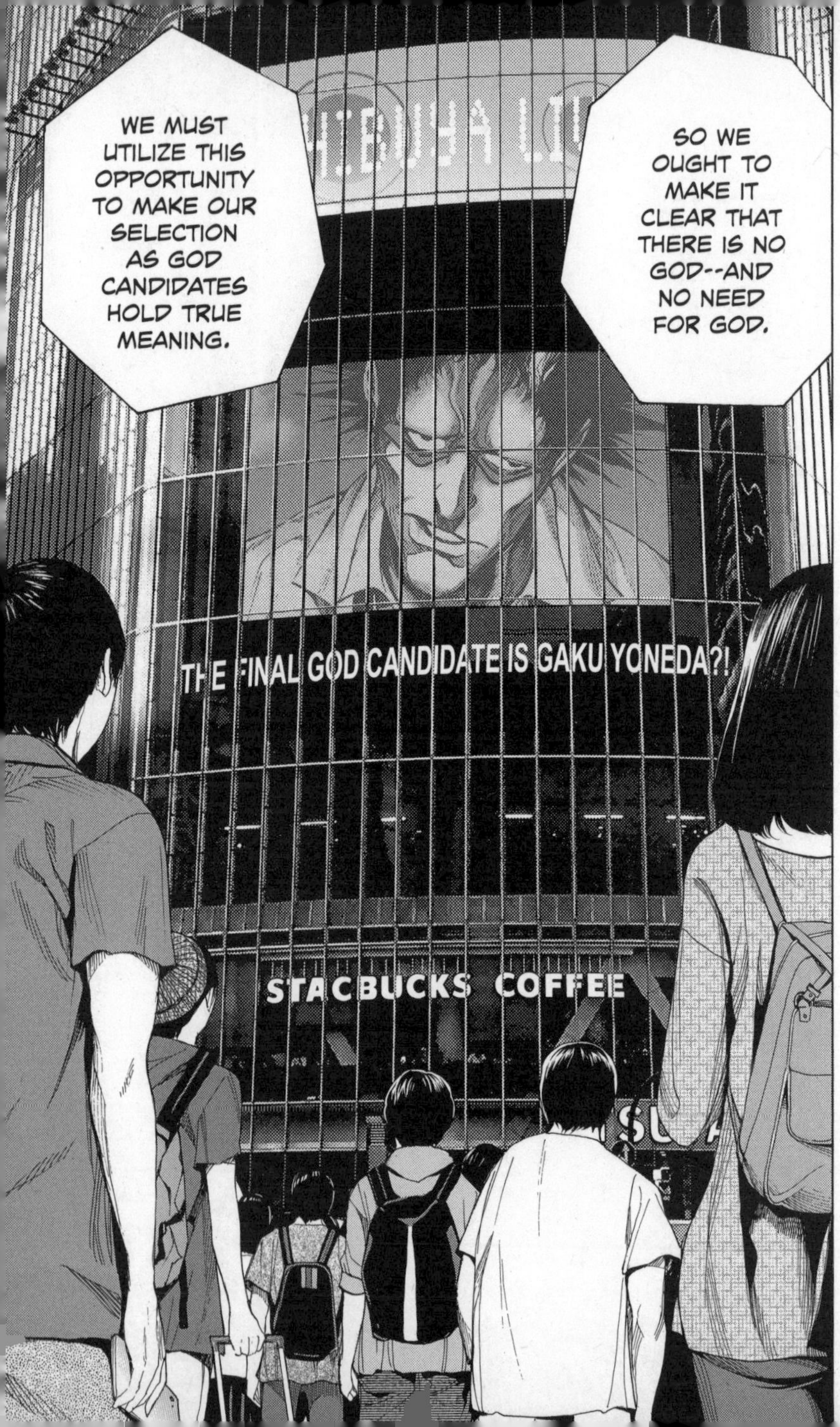
WE MUST UTILIZE THIS OPPORTUNITY TO MAKE OUR SELECTION AS GOD CANDIDATES HOLD TRUE MEANING.
SO WE OUGHT TO MAKE IT CLEAR THAT THERE IS NO GOD--AND NO NEED FOR GOD.
THE FINAL GOD CANDIDATE IS GAKU YONEDA?!
STACBUCKS COFFEE

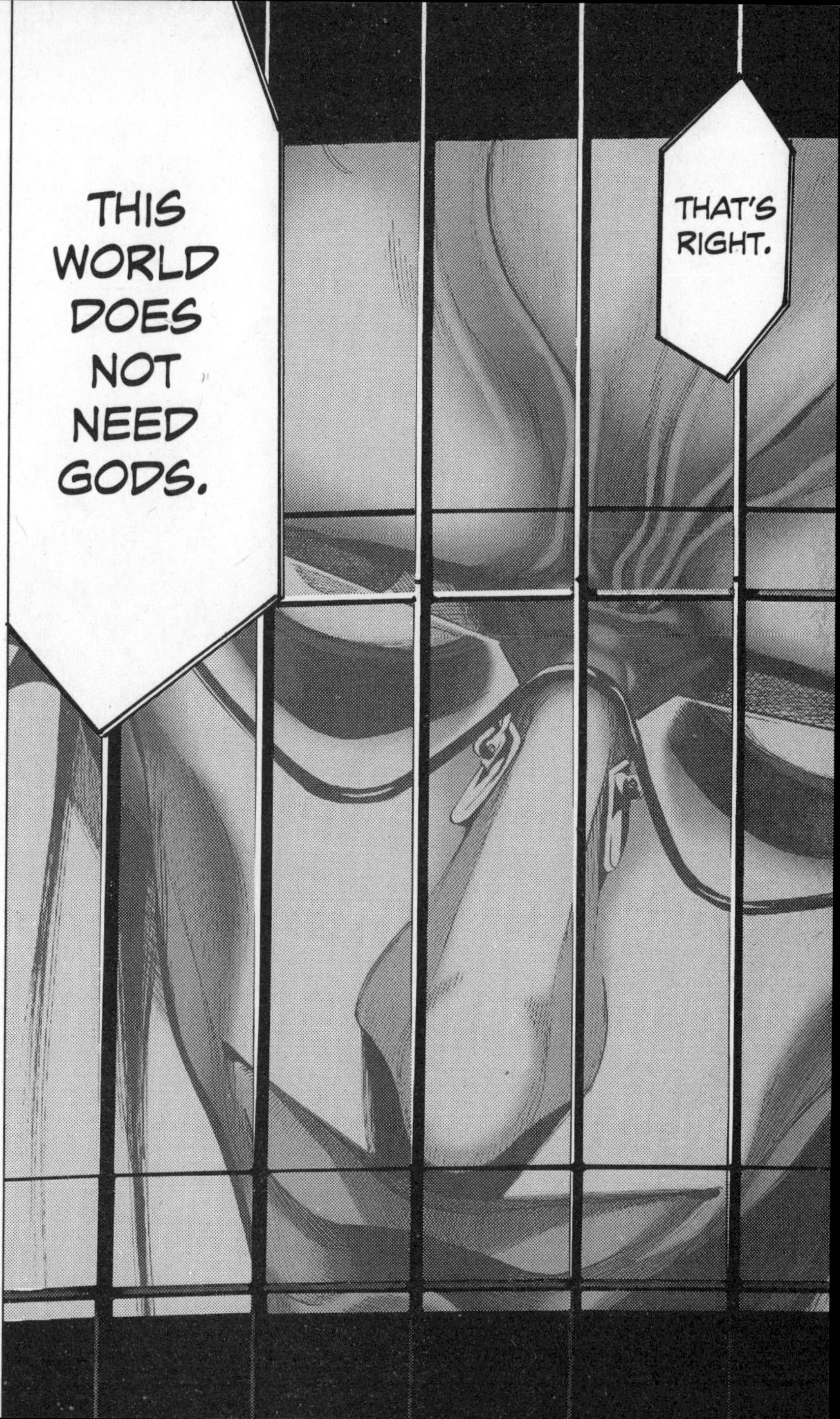
THAT'S RIGHT.
THIS WORLD DOES NOT NEED GODS.

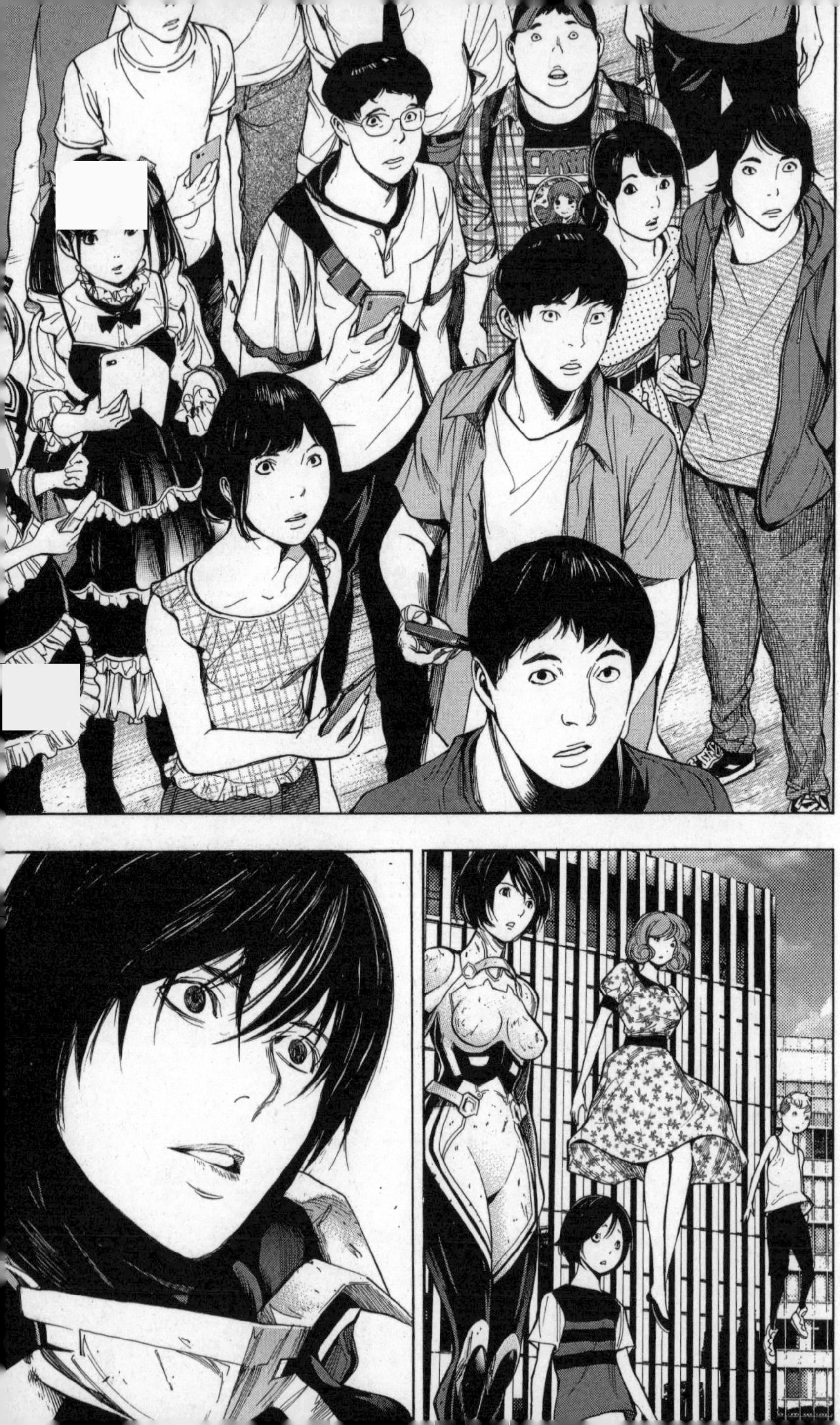

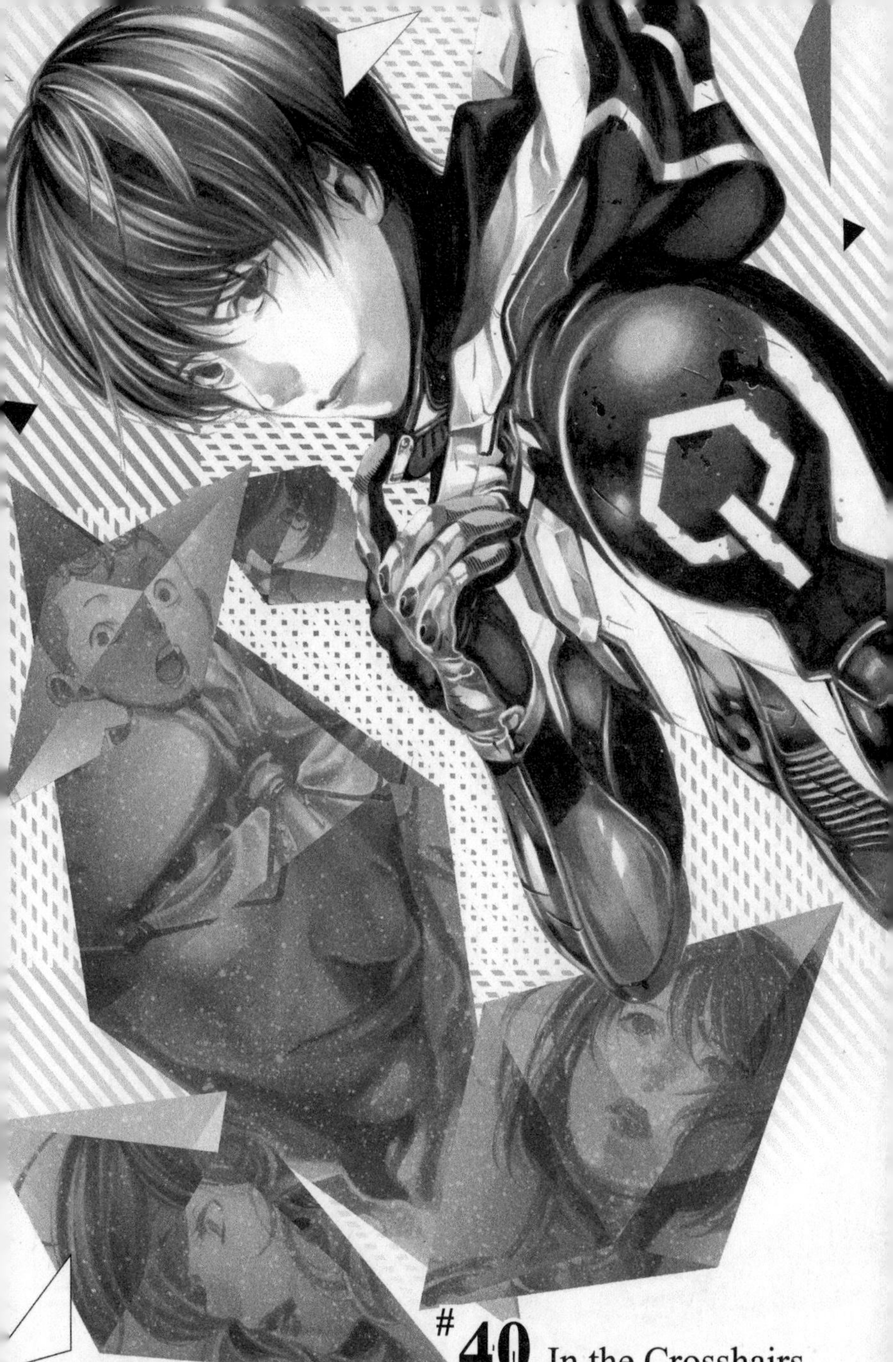

#40 In the Crosshairs

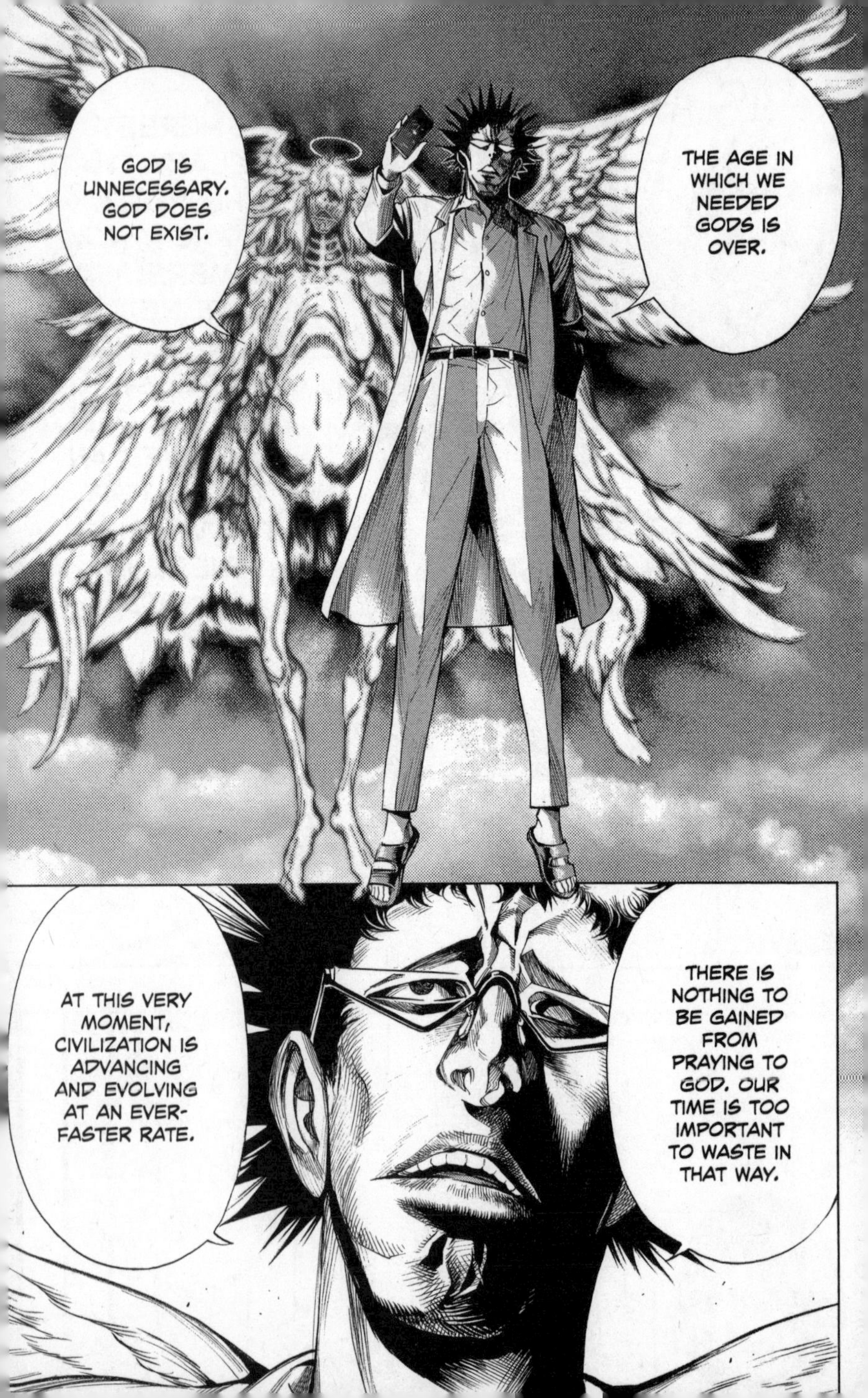
THE AGE IN WHICH WE NEEDED GODS IS OVER.
GOD IS UNNECESSARY. GOD DOES NOT EXIST.
THERE IS NOTHING TO BE GAINED FROM PRAYING TO GOD. OUR TIME IS TOO IMPORTANT TO WASTE IN THAT WAY.
AT THIS VERY MOMENT, CIVILIZATION IS ADVANCING AND EVOLVING AT AN EVER-FASTER RATE.

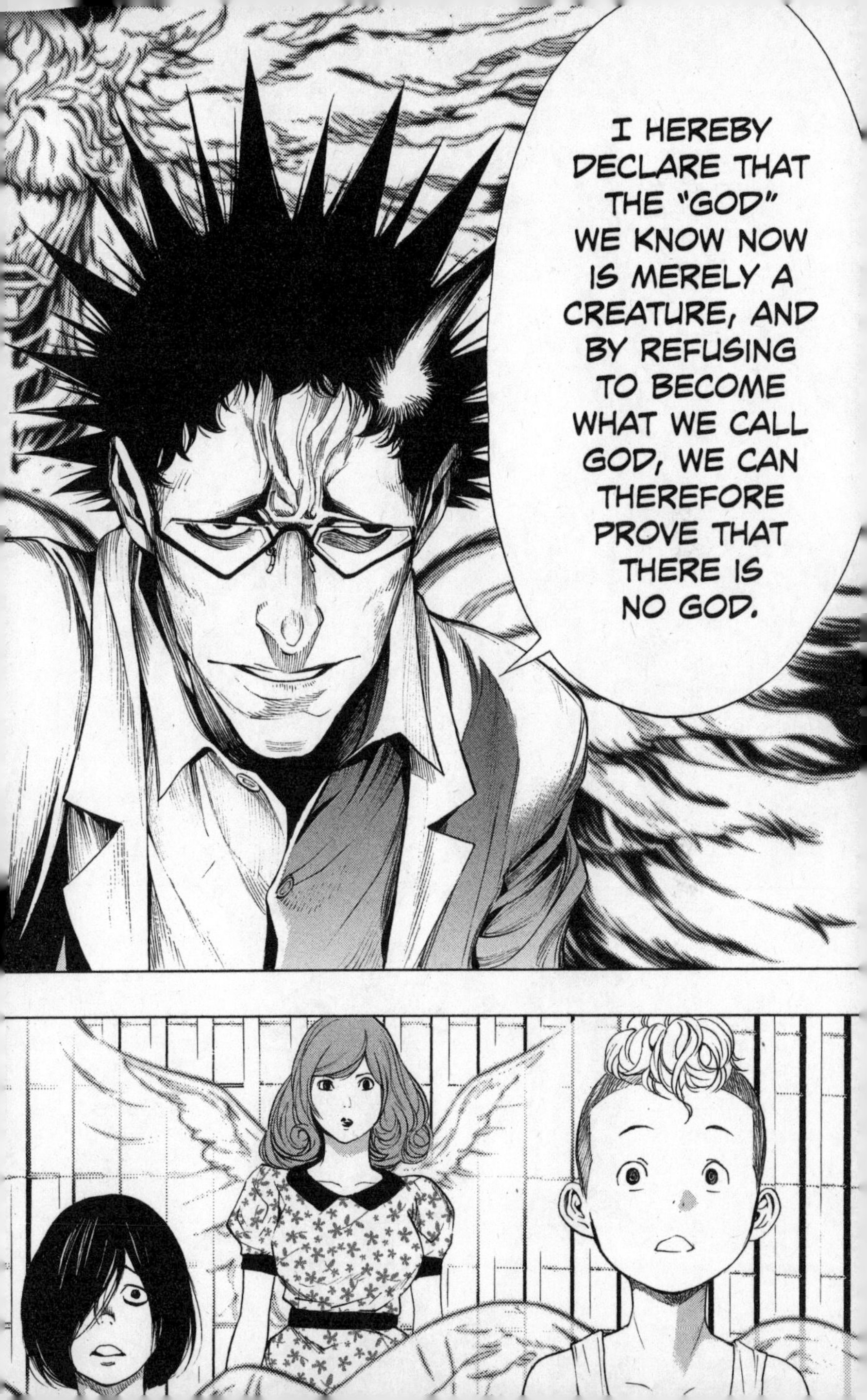
I HEREBY DECLARE THAT THE "GOD" WE KNOW NOW IS MERELY A CREATURE, AND BY REFUSING TO BECOME WHAT WE CALL GOD, WE CAN THEREFORE PROVE THAT THERE IS NO GOD.

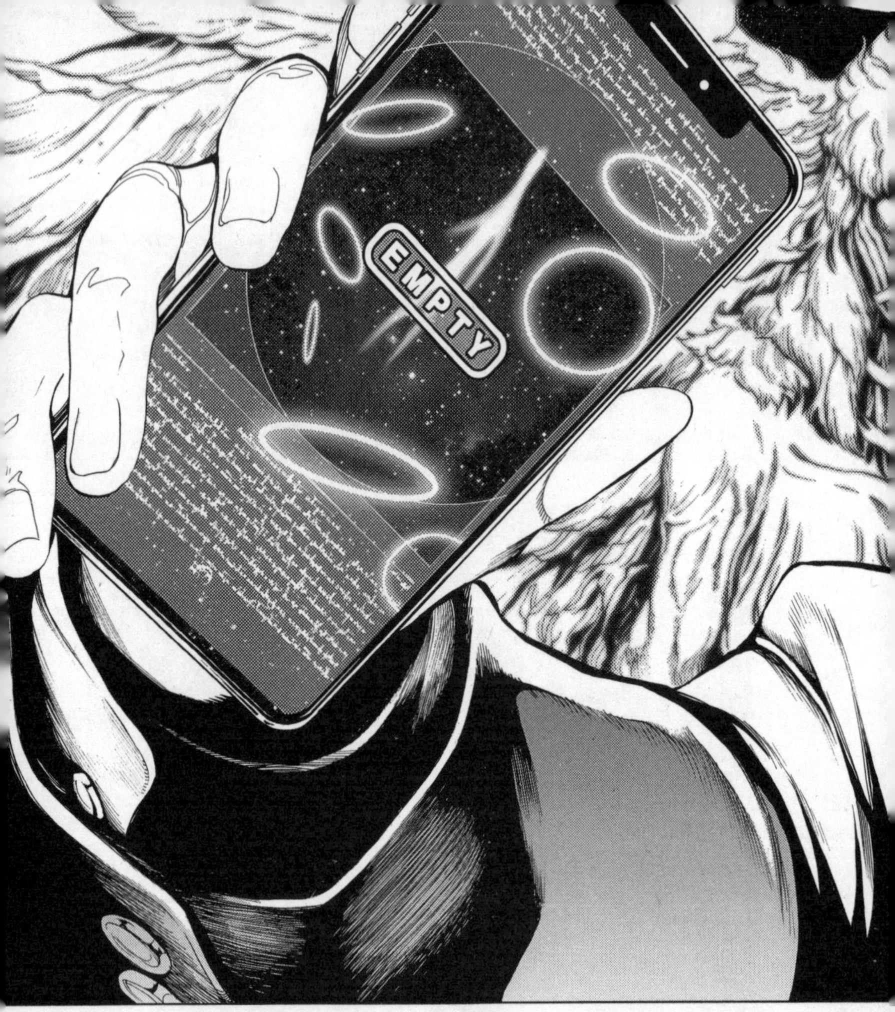
EMPTY
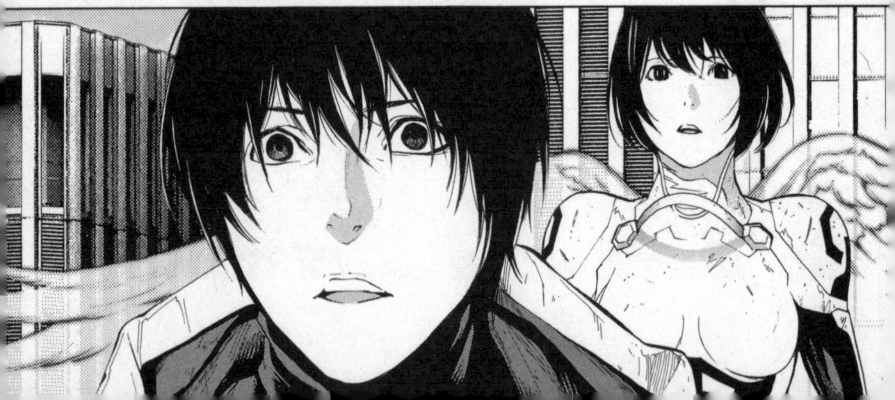

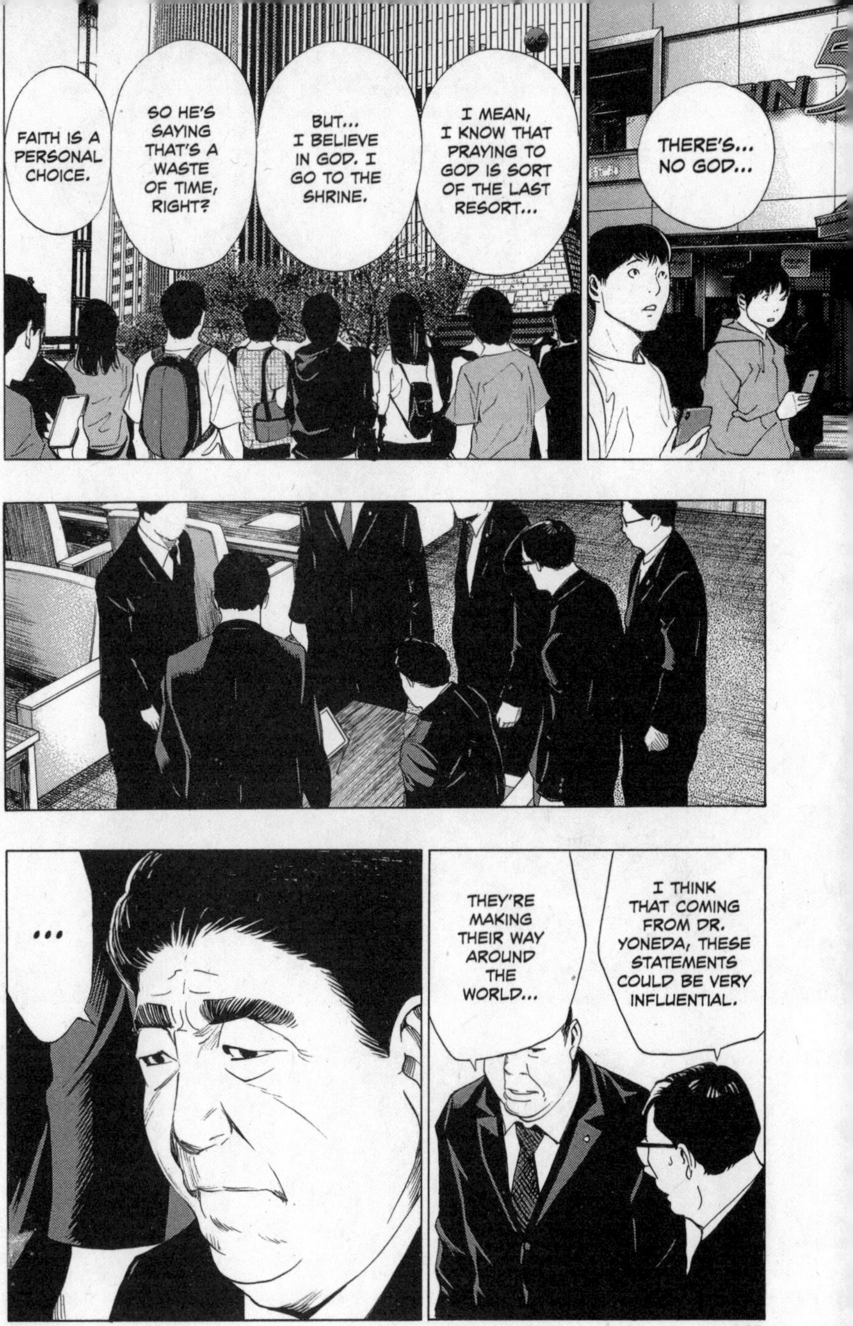
THERE'S... NO GOD...
I MEAN, I KNOW THAT PRAYING TO GOD IS SORT OF THE LAST RESORT...
BUT... I BELIEVE IN GOD. I GO TO THE SHRINE.
SO HE'S SAYING THAT'S A WASTE OF TIME, RIGHT?
FAITH IS A PERSONAL CHOICE.
I THINK THAT COMING FROM DR. YONEDA, THESE STATEMENTS COULD BE VERY INFLUENTIAL.
THEY'RE MAKING THEIR WAY AROUND THE WORLD...
...

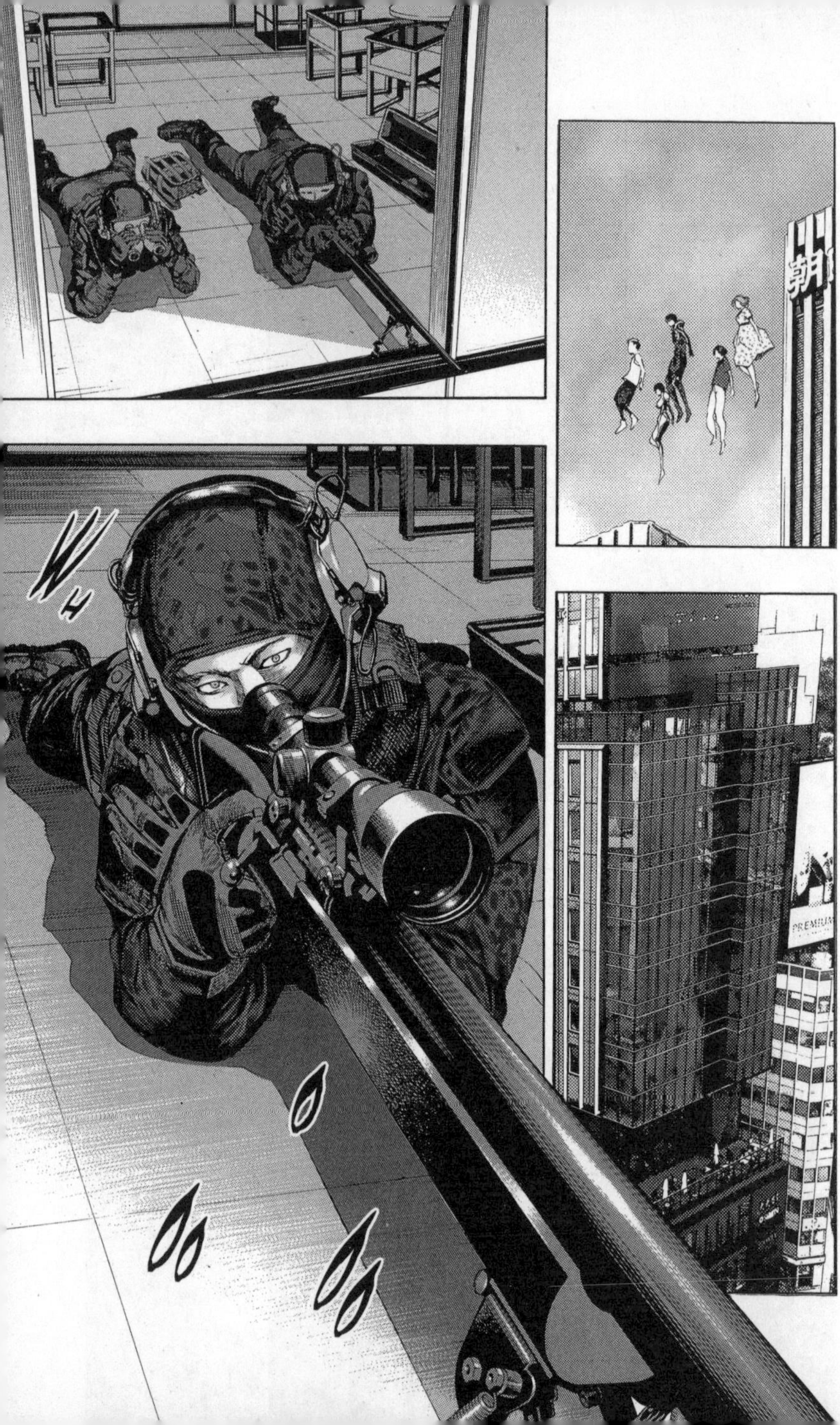
PREMIUM

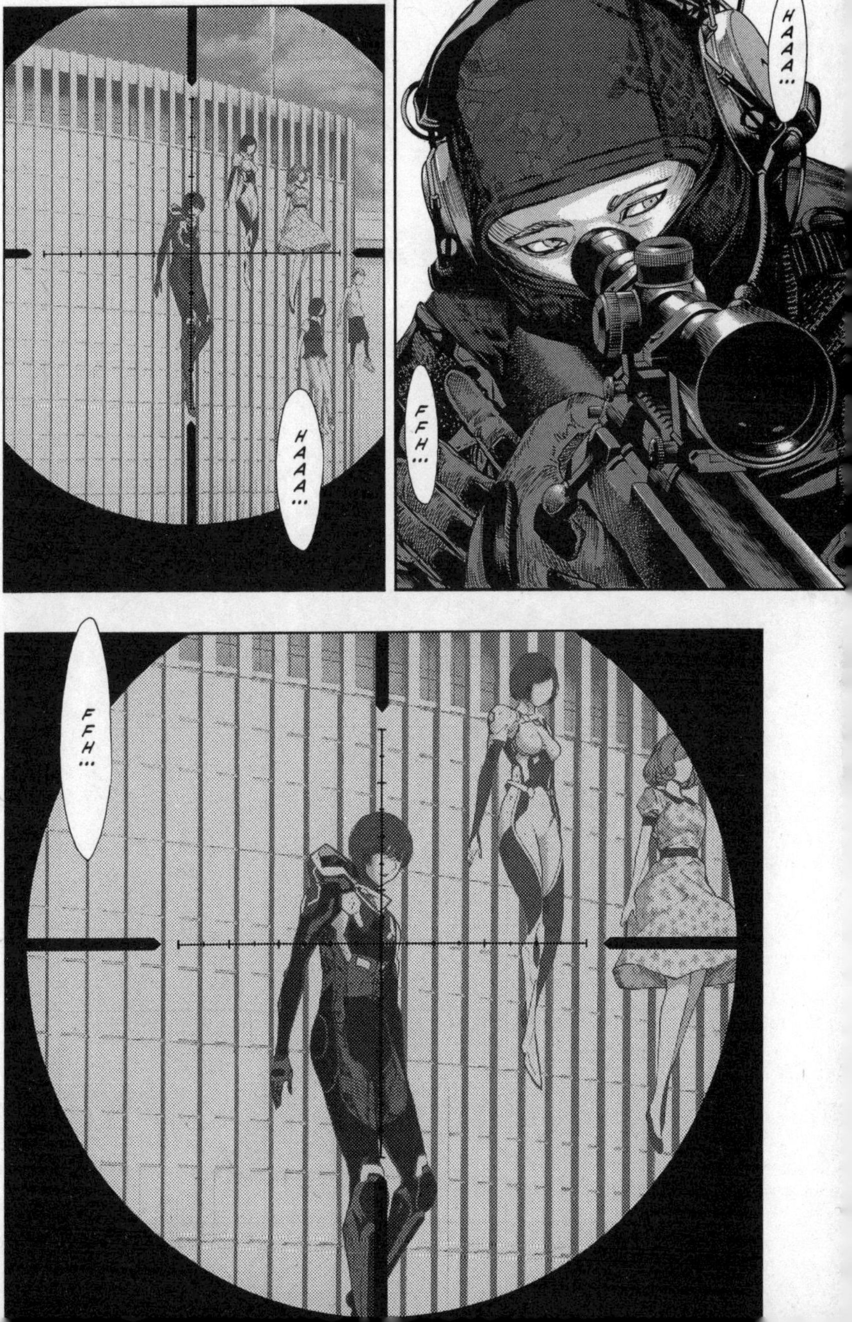
HAAA...
FFH...
HAAA...
FFH...

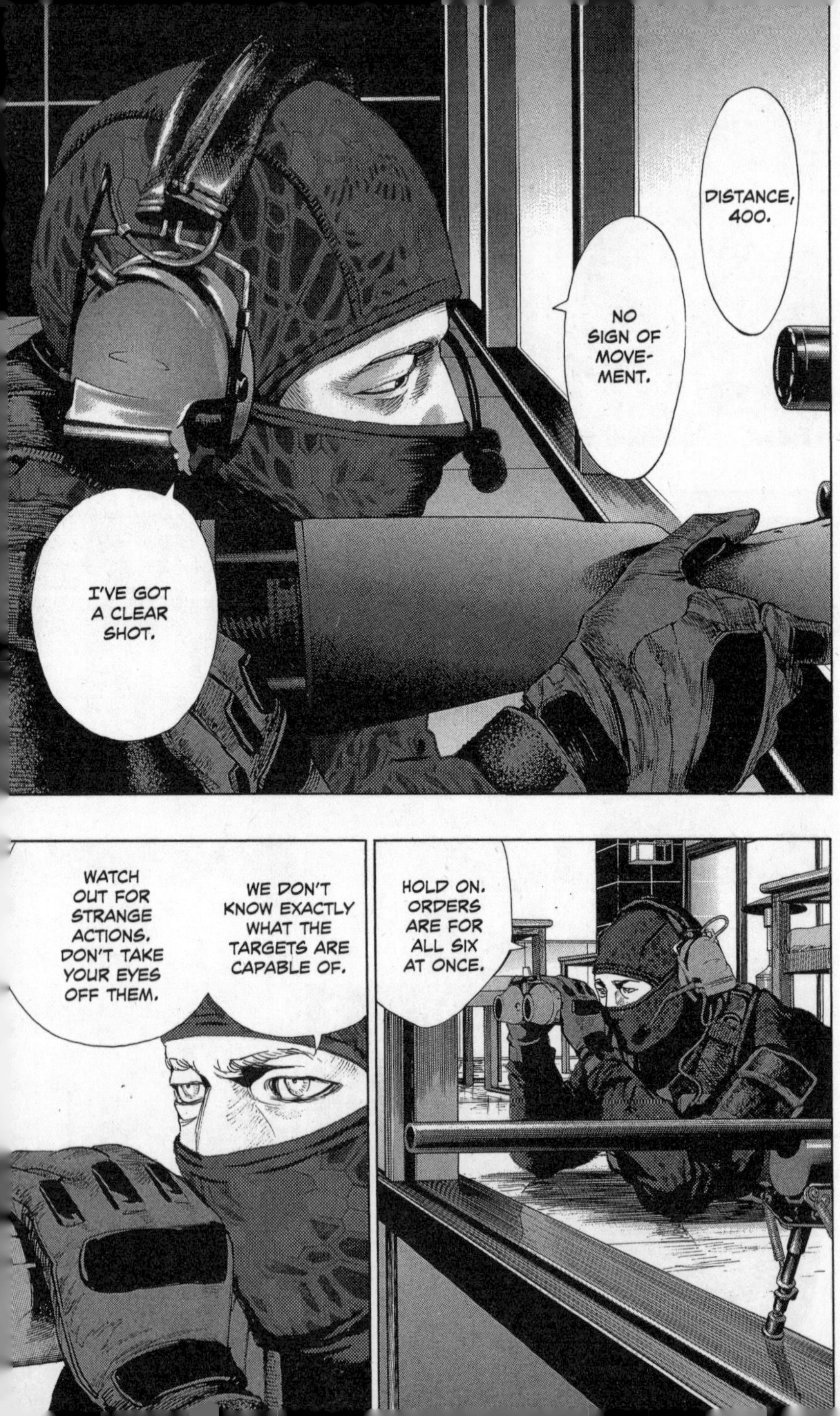
DISTANCE, 400.
NO SIGN OF MOVE-MENT.
I'VE GOT A CLEAR SHOT.
HOLD ON. ORDERS ARE FOR ALL SIX AT ONCE.
WE DON'T KNOW EXACTLY WHAT THE TARGETS ARE CAPABLE OF.
WATCH OUT FOR STRANGE ACTIONS. DON'T TAKE YOUR EYES OFF THEM.

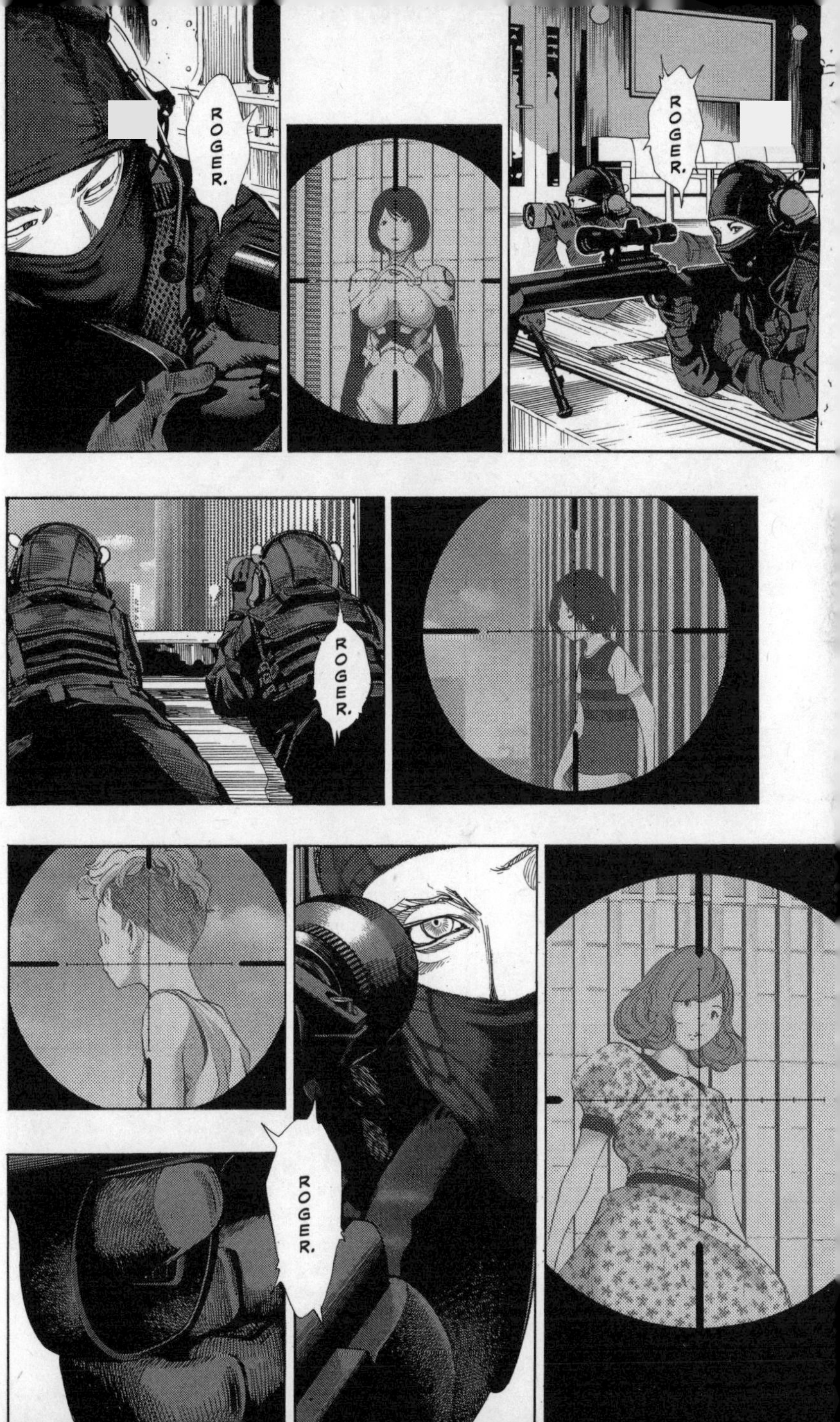
ROGER.
ROGER.
ROGER.
ROGER.

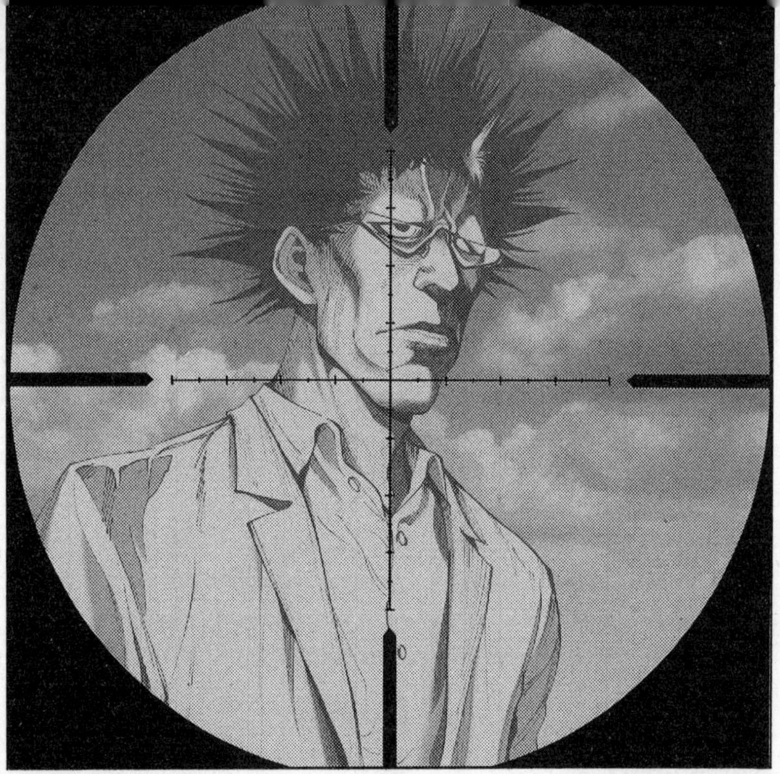
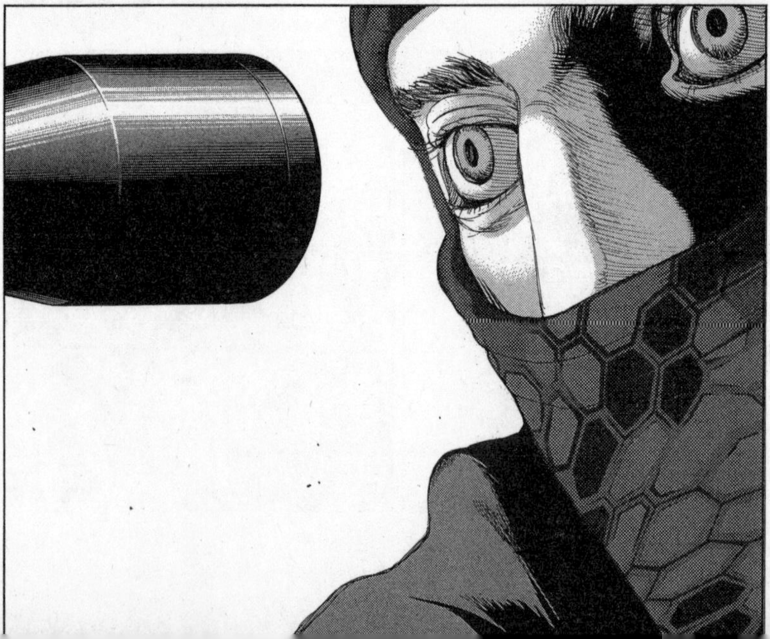

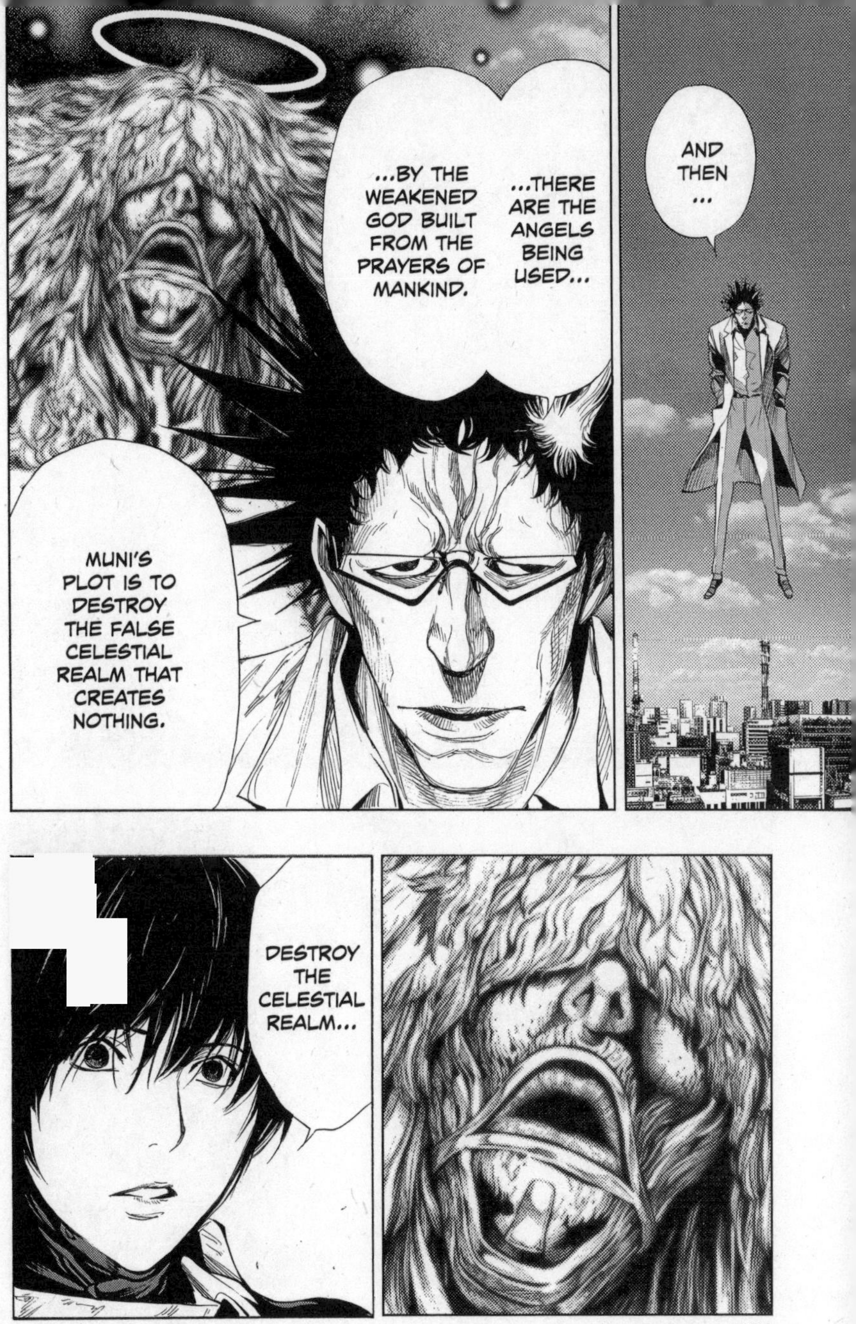
AND THEN ...
...THERE ARE THE ANGELS BEING USED...
...BY THE WEAKENED GOD BUILT FROM THE PRAYERS OF MANKIND.
MUNI'S PLOT IS TO DESTROY THE FALSE CELESTIAL REALM THAT CREATES NOTHING.
DESTROY THE CELESTIAL REALM...

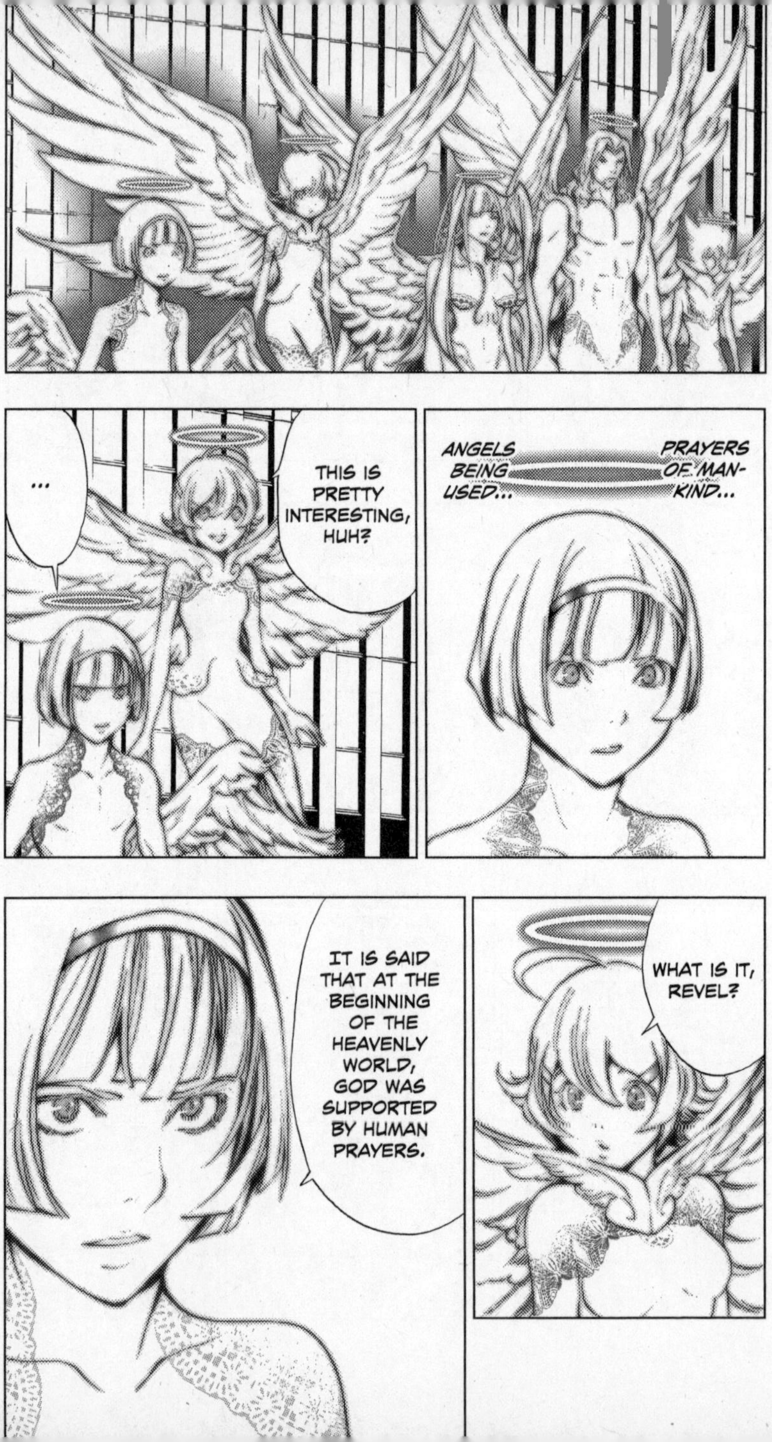
PRAYERS OF MAN-KIND...
ANGELS BEING USED...
THIS IS PRETTY INTERESTING, HUH?
...
WHAT IS IT, REVEL?
IT IS SAID THAT AT THE BEGINNING OF THE HEAVENLY WORLD, GOD WAS SUPPORTED BY HUMAN PRAYERS.

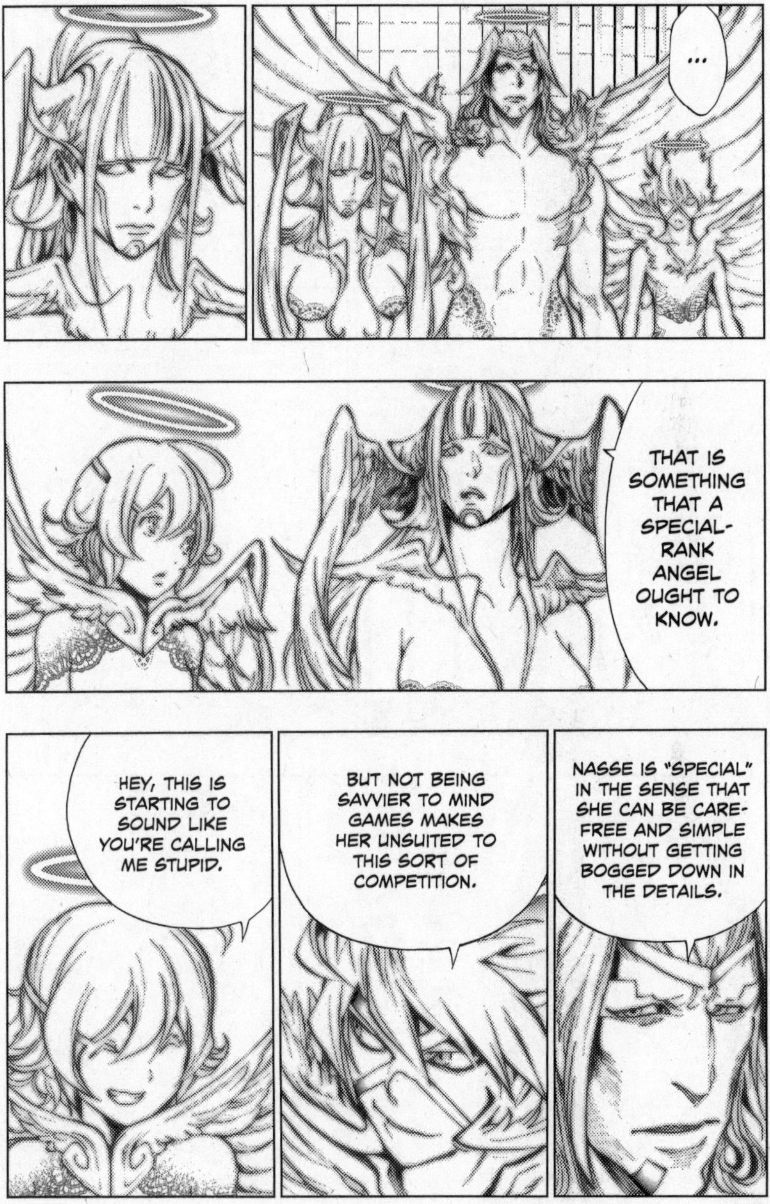
...
THAT IS SOMETHING THAT A SPECIAL-RANK ANGEL OUGHT TO KNOW.
NASSE IS "SPECIAL" IN THE SENSE THAT SHE CAN BE CARE-FREE AND SIMPLE WITHOUT GETTING BOGGED DOWN IN THE DETAILS.
BUT NOT BEING SAVVIER TO MIND GAMES MAKES HER UNSUITED TO THIS SORT OF COMPETITION.
HEY, THIS IS STARTING TO SOUND LIKE YOU'RE CALLING ME STUPID.

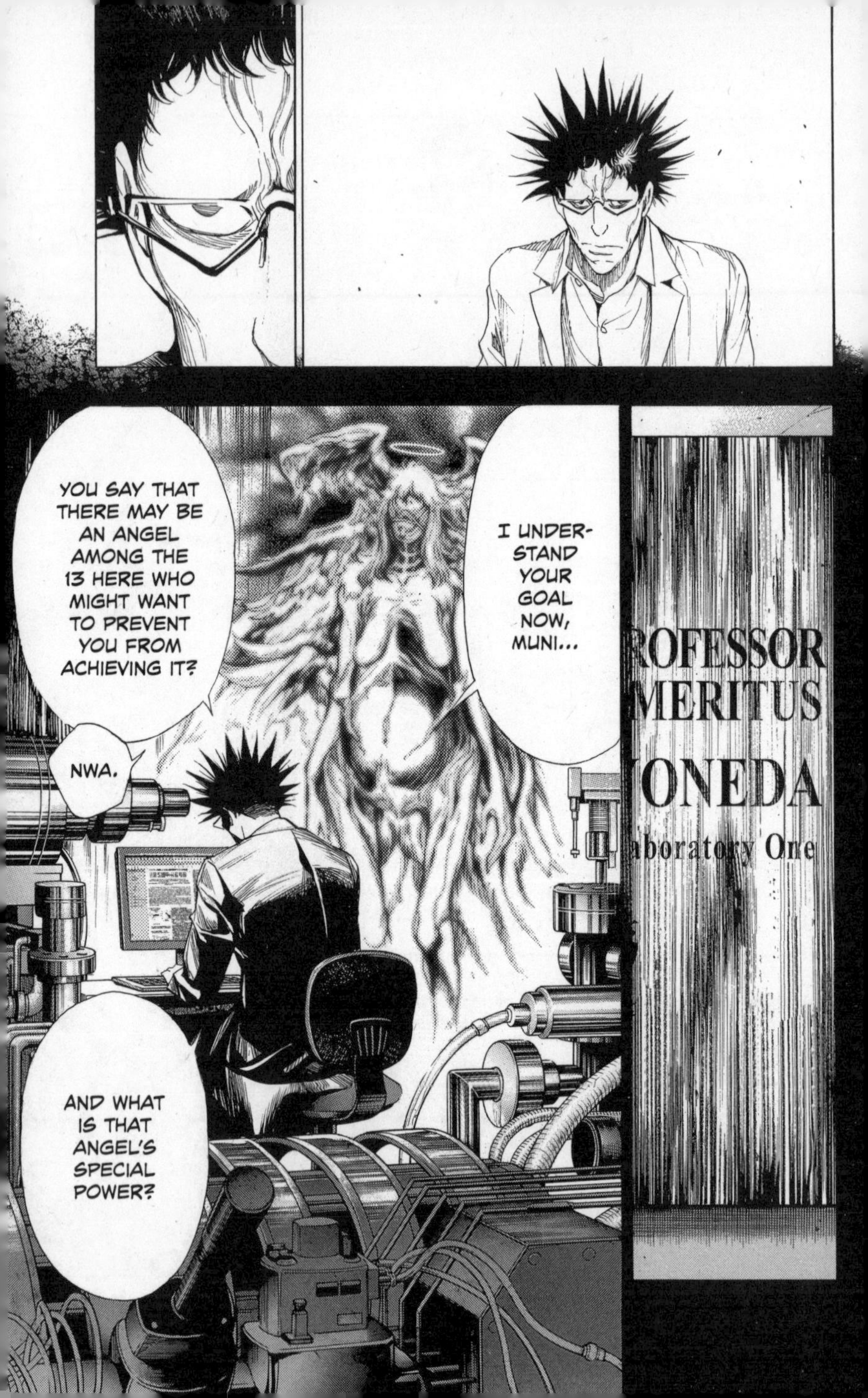
ROFESSOR
MERITUS
ONEDA
aboratory One
I UNDER-STAND YOUR GOAL NOW, MUNI...
YOU SAY THAT THERE MAY BE AN ANGEL AMONG THE 13 HERE WHO MIGHT WANT TO PREVENT YOU FROM ACHIEVING IT?
NWA.
AND WHAT IS THAT ANGEL'S SPECIAL POWER?

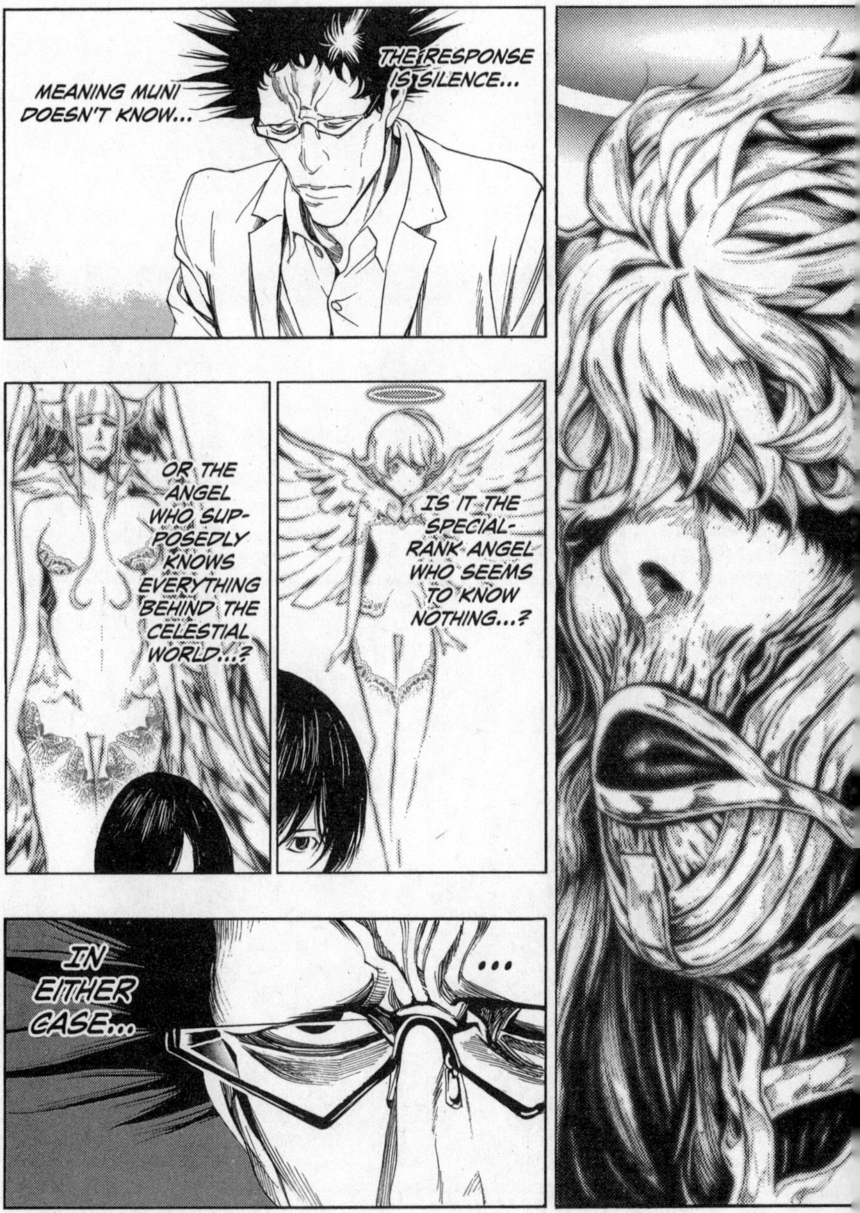
THE RESPONSE IS SILENCE...
MEANING MUNI DOESN'T KNOW...
IS IT THE SPECIAL-RANK ANGEL WHO SEEMS TO KNOW NOTHING...?
OR THE ANGEL WHO SUPPOSEDLY KNOWS EVERYTHING BEHIND THE CELESTIAL WORLD...?
...
IN EITHER CASE...

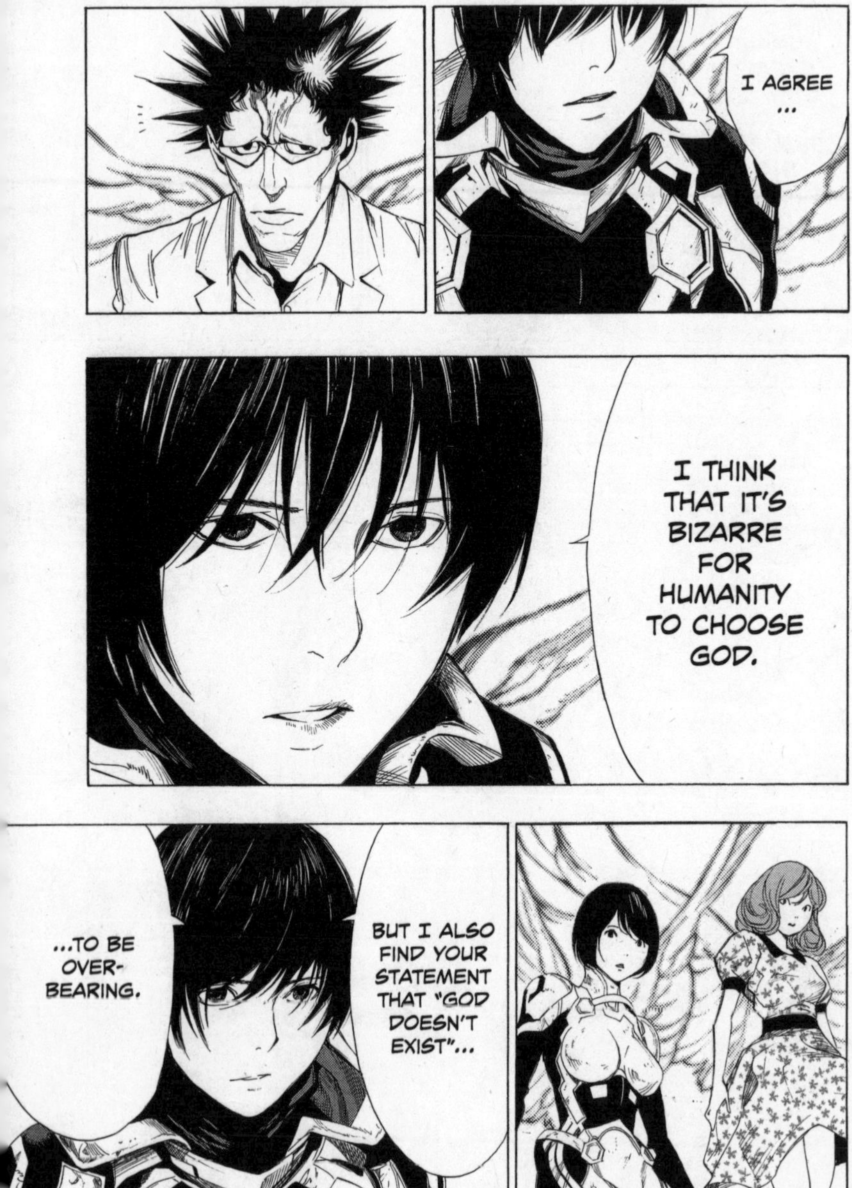
I AGREE ...
I THINK THAT IT'S BIZARRE FOR HUMANITY TO CHOOSE GOD.
BUT I ALSO FIND YOUR STATEMENT THAT "GOD DOESN'T EXIST"...
...TO BE OVER-BEARING.

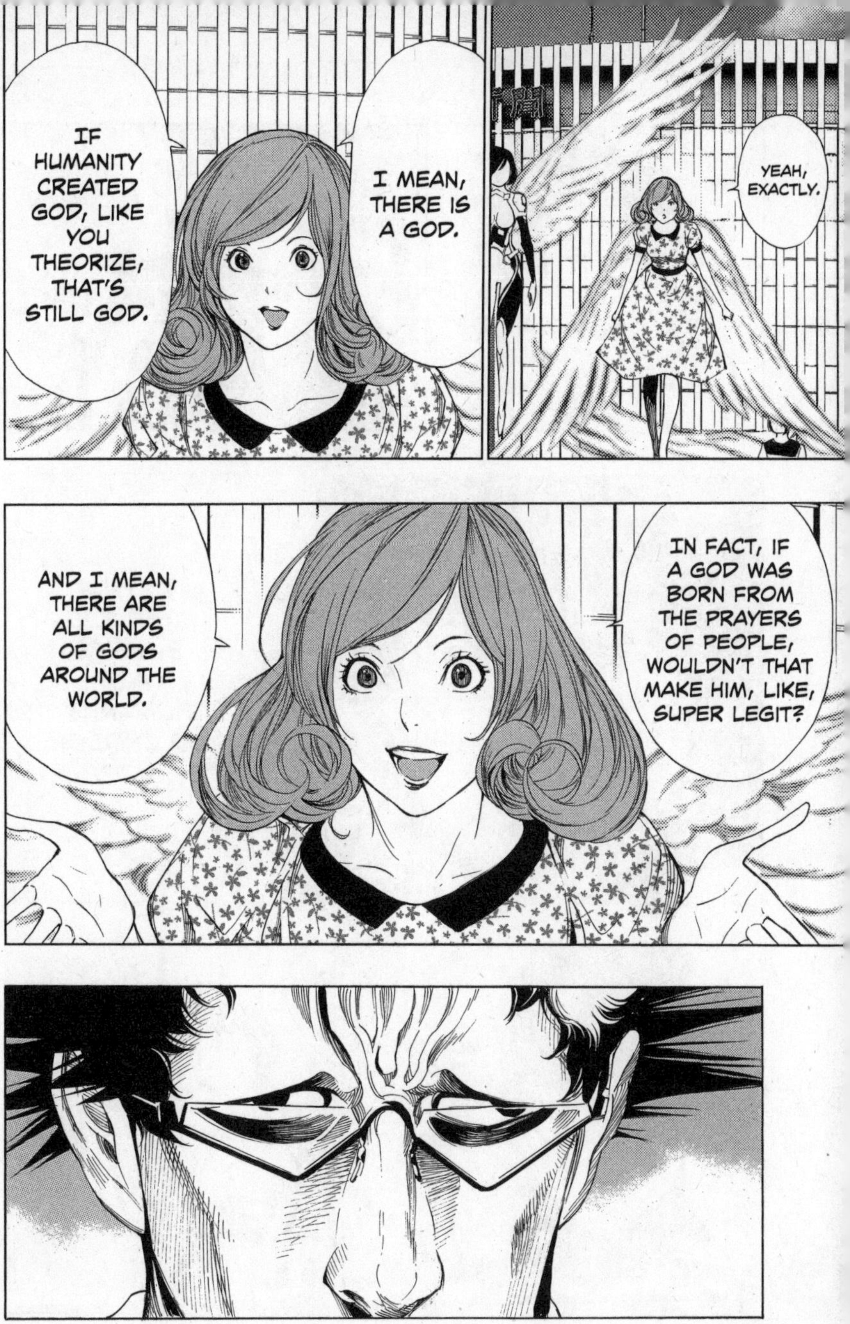
YEAH, EXACTLY.
I MEAN, THERE IS A GOD.
IF HUMANITY CREATED GOD, LIKE YOU THEORIZE, THAT'S STILL GOD.
IN FACT, IF A GOD WAS BORN FROM THE PRAYERS OF PEOPLE, WOULDN'T THAT MAKE HIM, LIKE, SUPER LEGIT?
AND I MEAN, THERE ARE ALL KINDS OF GODS AROUND THE WORLD.

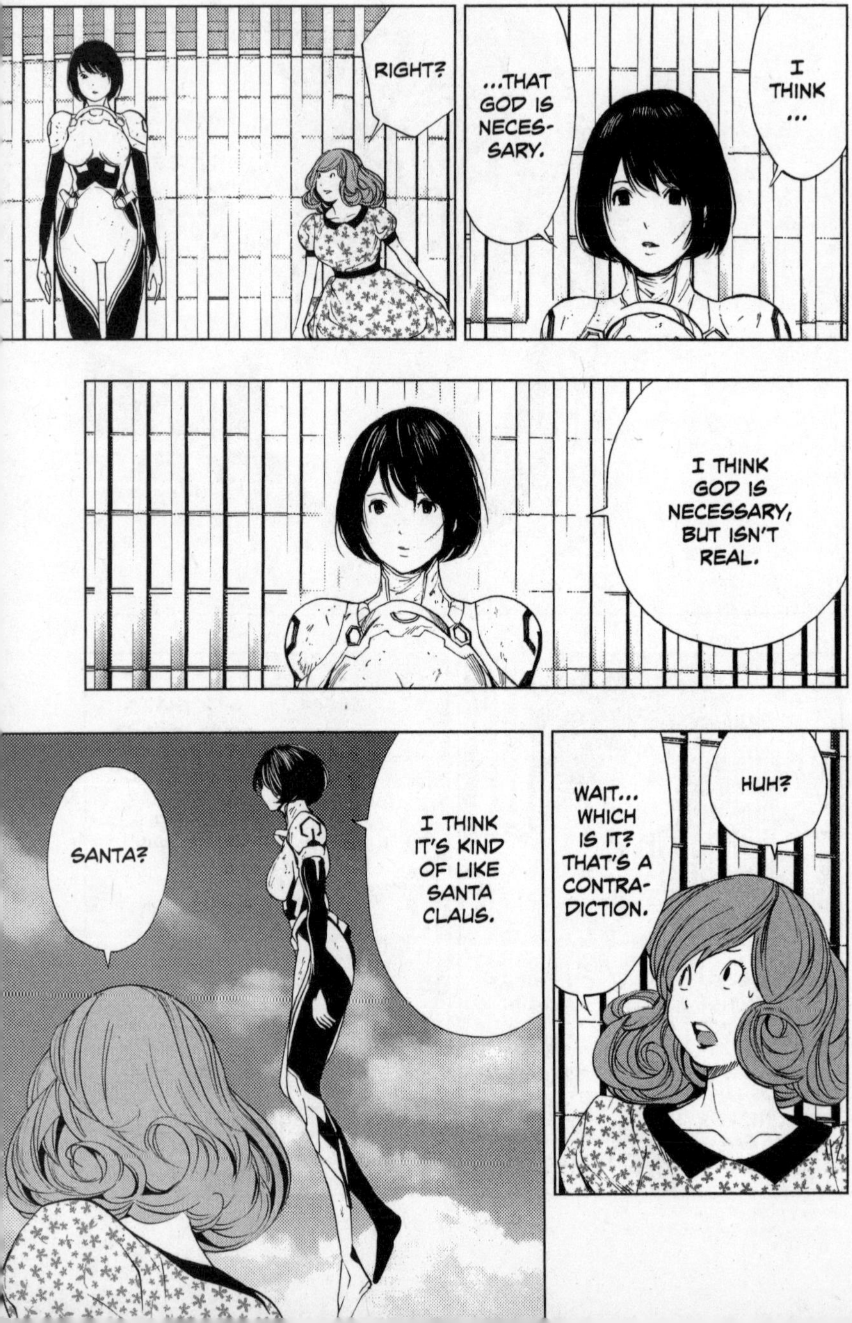
I THINK...
...THAT GOD IS NECESSARY.
RIGHT?
I THINK GOD IS NECESSARY, BUT ISN'T REAL.
HUH?
WAIT... WHICH IS IT? THAT'S A CONTRADICTION.
I THINK IT'S KIND OF LIKE SANTA CLAUS.
SANTA?

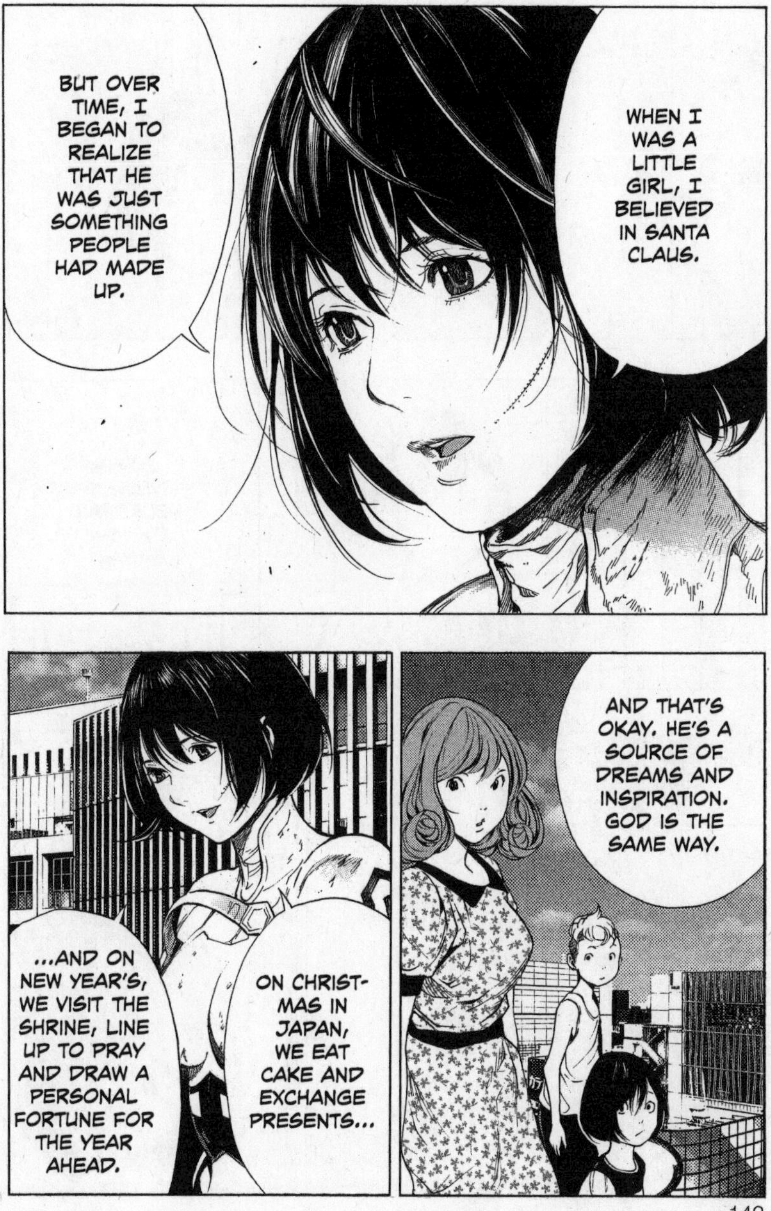
WHEN I WAS A LITTLE GIRL, I BELIEVED IN SANTA CLAUS.
BUT OVER TIME, I BEGAN TO REALIZE THAT HE WAS JUST SOMETHING PEOPLE HAD MADE UP.
AND THAT'S OKAY. HE'S A SOURCE OF DREAMS AND INSPIRATION. GOD IS THE SAME WAY.
ON CHRIST-MAS IN JAPAN, WE EAT CAKE AND EXCHANGE PRESENTS...
...AND ON NEW YEAR'S, WE VISIT THE SHRINE, LINE UP TO PRAY AND DRAW A PERSONAL FORTUNE FOR THE YEAR AHEAD.

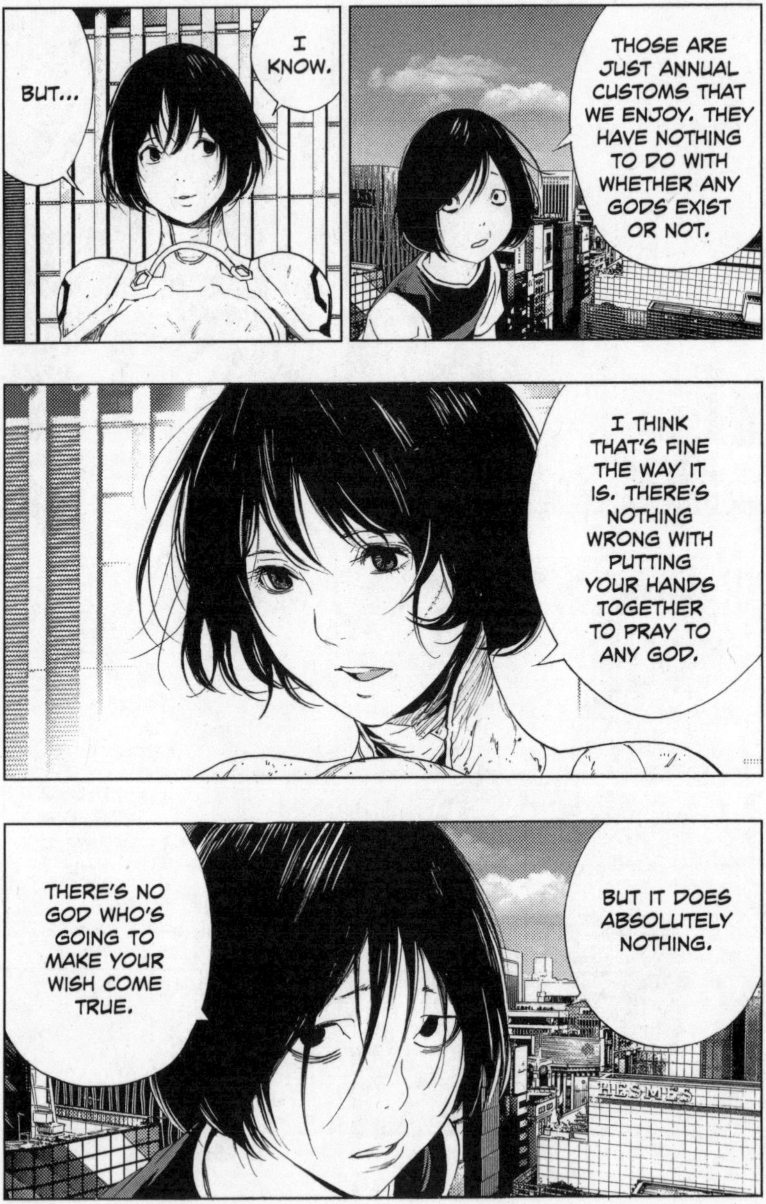
THOSE ARE JUST ANNUAL CUSTOMS THAT WE ENJOY. THEY HAVE NOTHING TO DO WITH WHETHER ANY GODS EXIST OR NOT.
I KNOW.
BUT...
I THINK THAT'S FINE THE WAY IT IS. THERE'S NOTHING WRONG WITH PUTTING YOUR HANDS TOGETHER TO PRAY TO ANY GOD.
BUT IT DOES ABSOLUTELY NOTHING.
THERE'S NO GOD WHO'S GOING TO MAKE YOUR WISH COME TRUE.

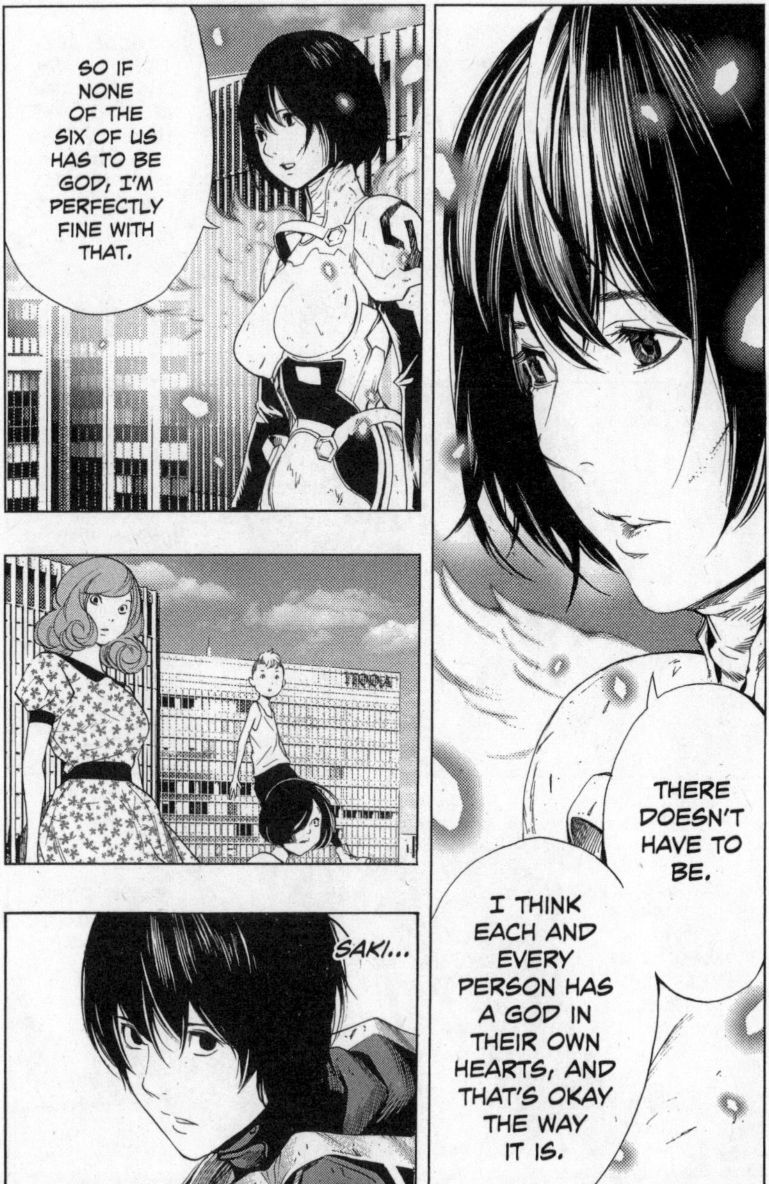
THERE DOESN'T HAVE TO BE.
I THINK EACH AND EVERY PERSON HAS A GOD IN THEIR OWN HEARTS, AND THAT'S OKAY THE WAY IT IS.
SO IF NONE OF THE SIX OF US HAS TO BE GOD, I'M PERFECTLY FINE WITH THAT.
SAKI...

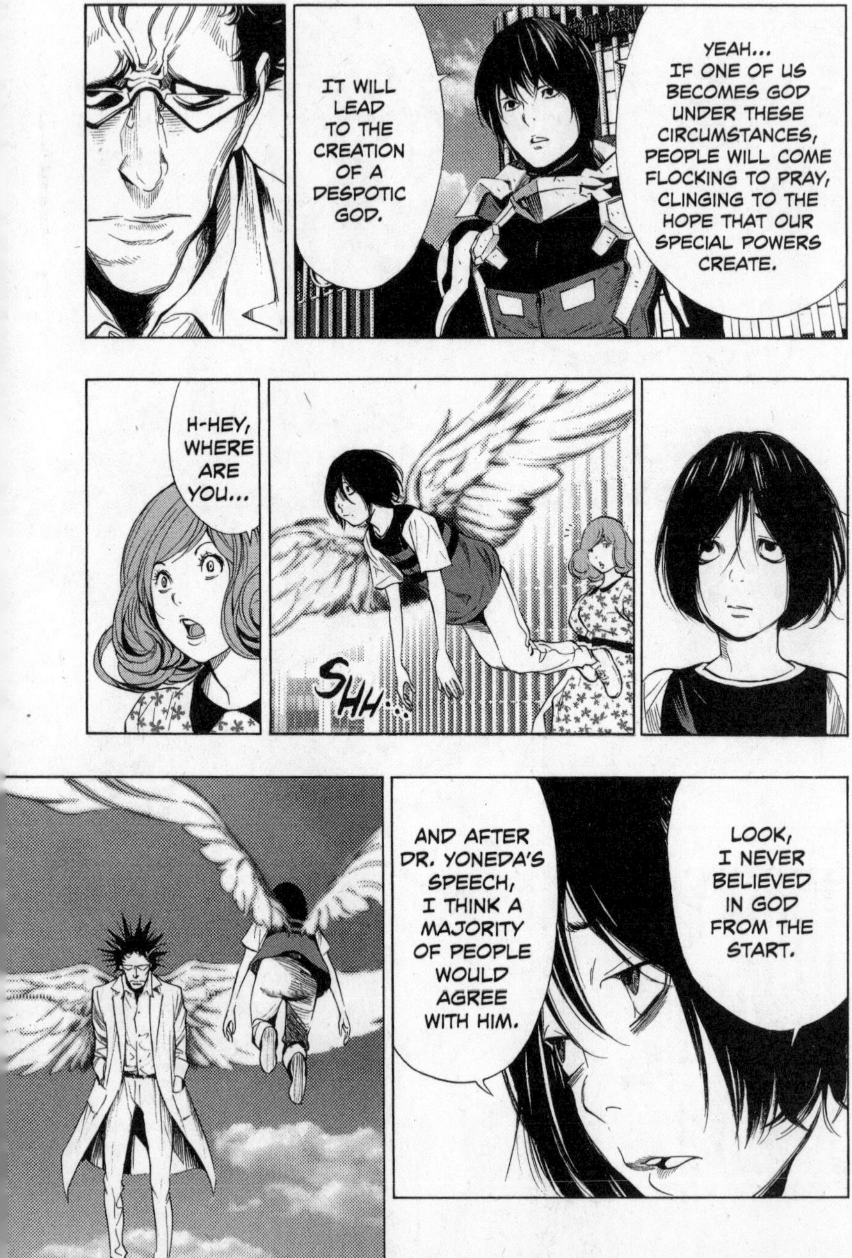
YEAH... IF ONE OF US BECOMES GOD UNDER THESE CIRCUMSTANCES, PEOPLE WILL COME FLOCKING TO PRAY, CLINGING TO THE HOPE THAT OUR SPECIAL POWERS CREATE.
IT WILL LEAD TO THE CREATION OF A DESPOTIC GOD.
SHH...
H-HEY, WHERE ARE YOU...
LOOK, I NEVER BELIEVED IN GOD FROM THE START.
AND AFTER DR. YONEDA'S SPEECH, I THINK A MAJORITY OF PEOPLE WOULD AGREE WITH HIM.

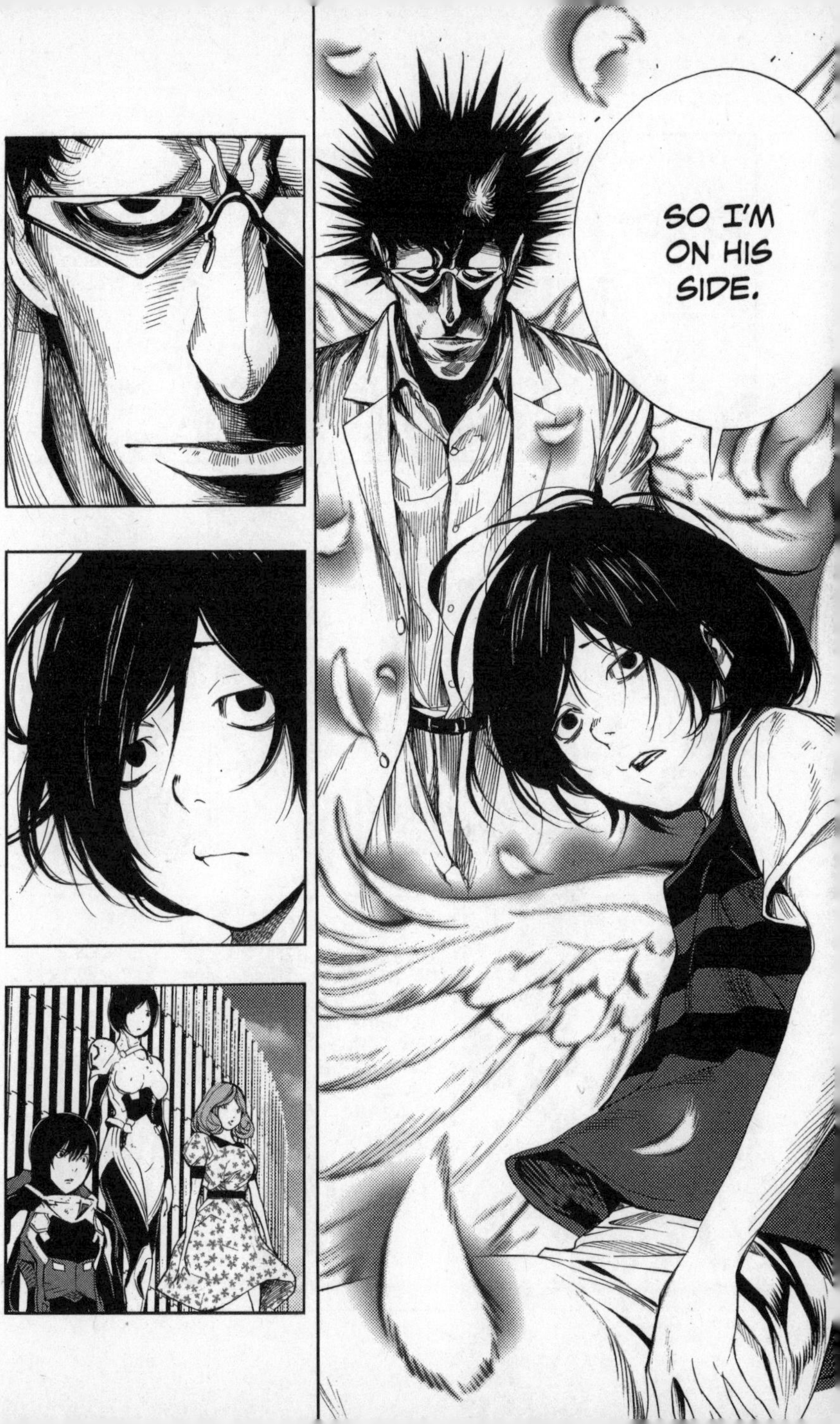
SO I'M ON HIS SIDE.

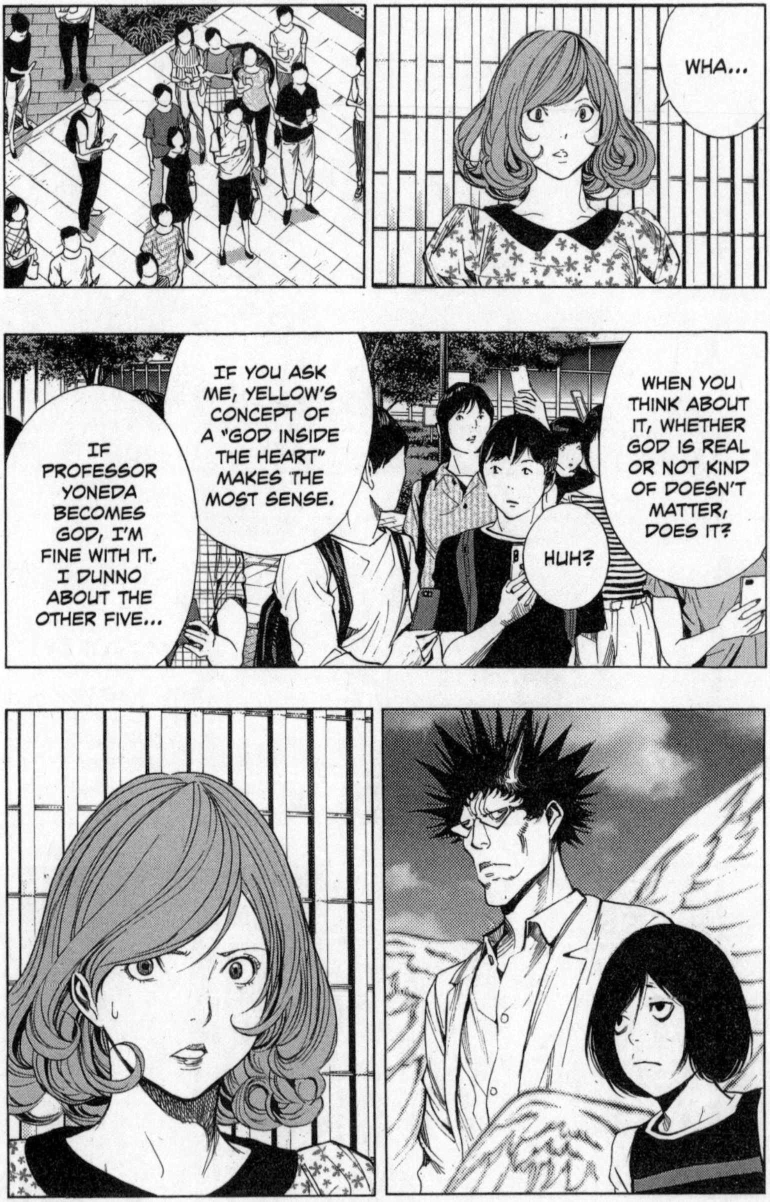
WHA...
WHEN YOU THINK ABOUT IT, WHETHER GOD IS REAL OR NOT KIND OF DOESN'T MATTER, DOES IT?
IF YOU ASK ME, YELLOW'S CONCEPT OF A "GOD INSIDE THE HEART" MAKES THE MOST SENSE.
HUH?
IF PROFESSOR YONEDA BECOMES GOD, I'M FINE WITH IT. I DUNNO ABOUT THE OTHER FIVE...

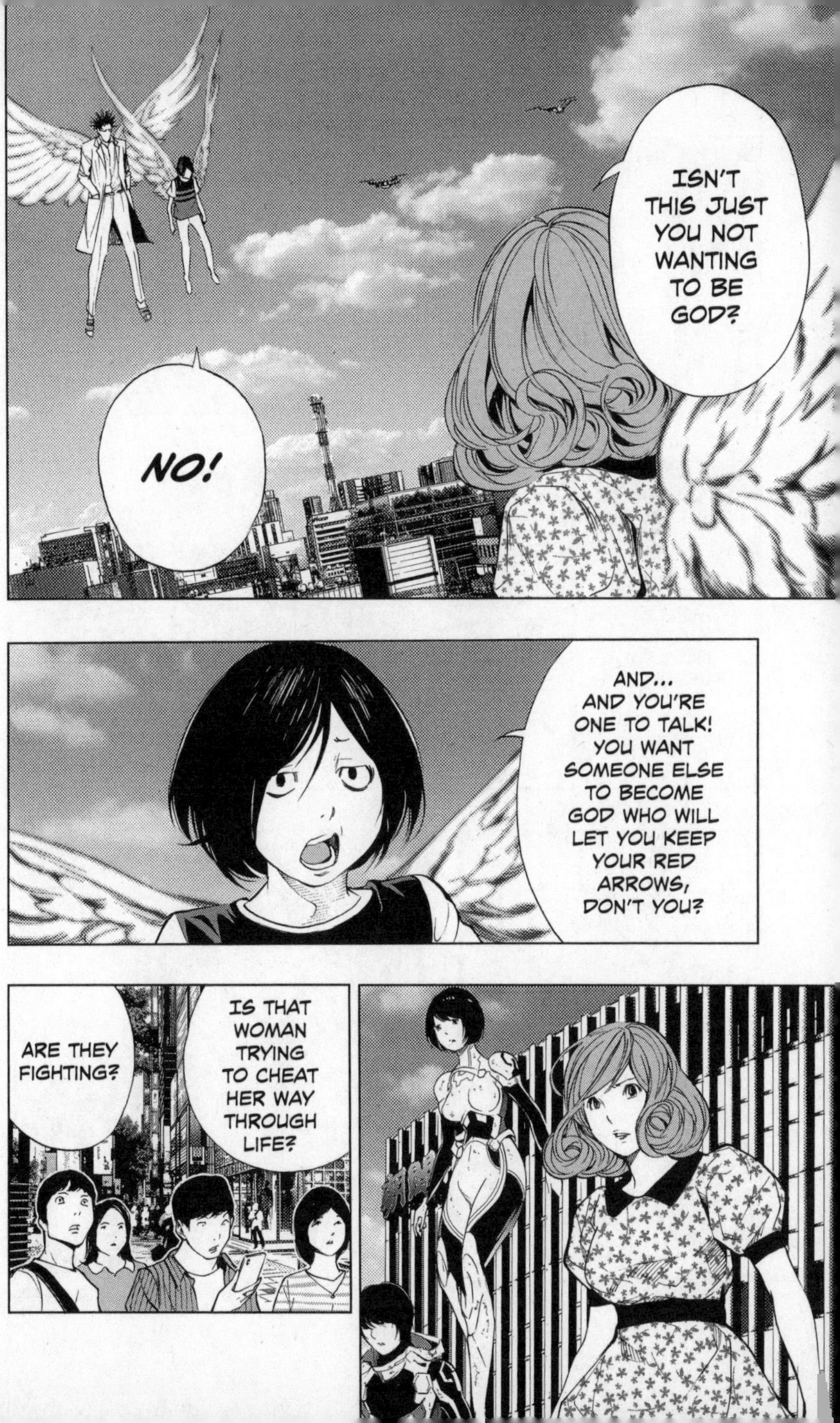
ISN'T THIS JUST YOU NOT WANTING TO BE GOD?
NO!
AND... AND YOU'RE ONE TO TALK! YOU WANT SOMEONE ELSE TO BECOME GOD WHO WILL LET YOU KEEP YOUR RED ARROWS, DON'T YOU?
IS THAT WOMAN TRYING TO CHEAT HER WAY THROUGH LIFE?
ARE THEY FIGHTING?

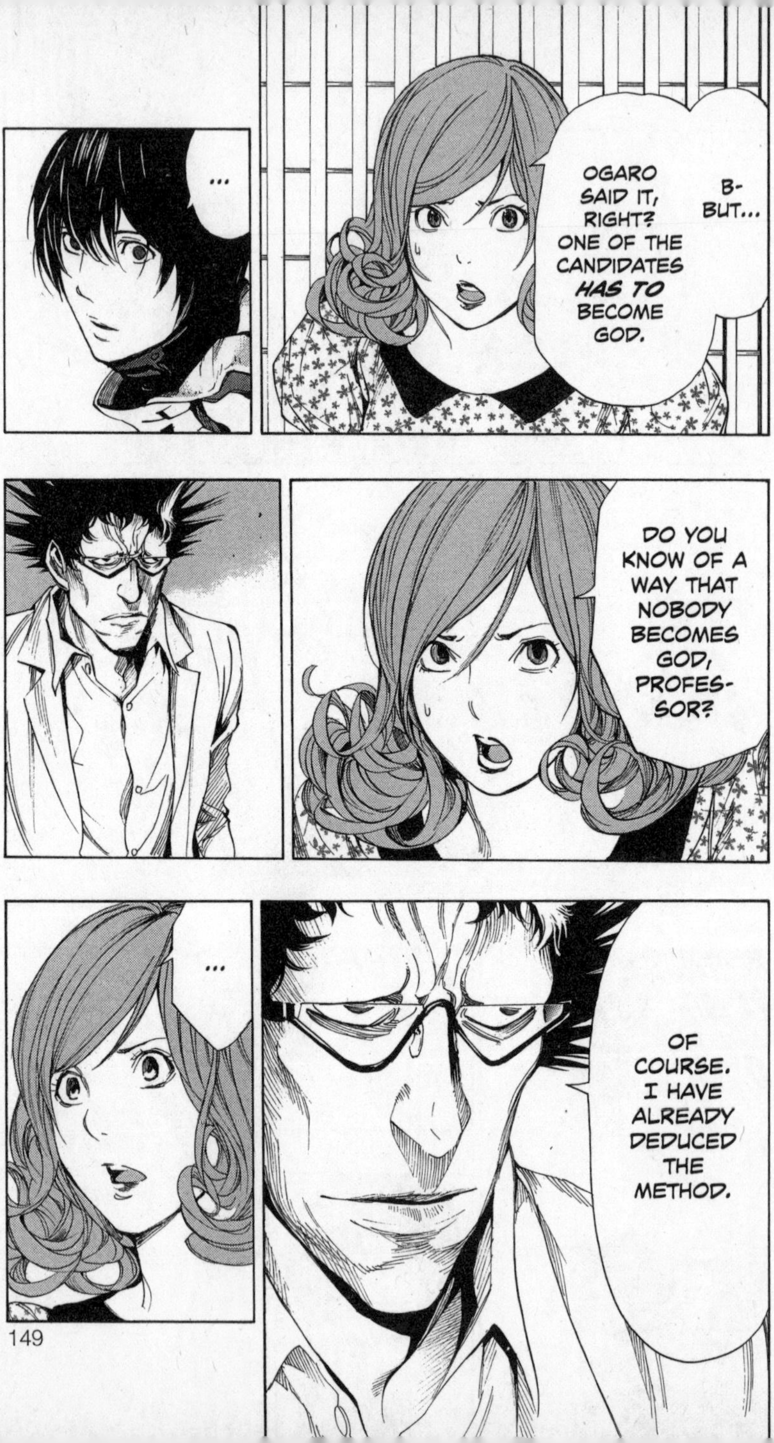
B-BUT...
OGARO SAID IT, RIGHT? ONE OF THE CANDIDATES **HAS TO** BECOME GOD.
...
DO YOU KNOW OF A WAY THAT NOBODY BECOMES GOD, PROFESSOR?
OF COURSE. I HAVE ALREADY DEDUCED THE METHOD.
...

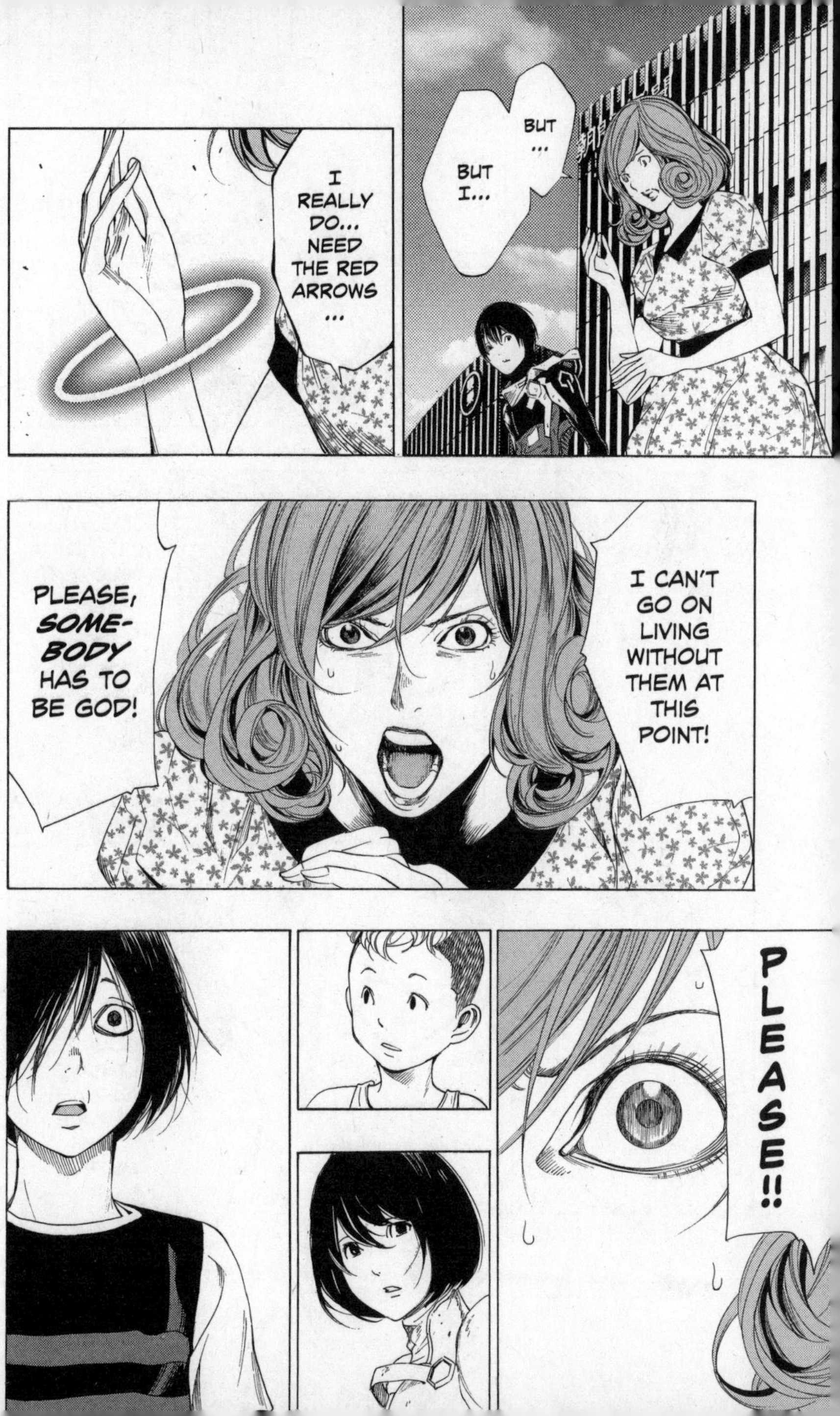
BUT ...
BUT I...
I REALLY DO... NEED THE RED ARROWS ...
I CAN'T GO ON LIVING WITHOUT THEM AT THIS POINT!
PLEASE, *SOMEBODY* HAS TO BE GOD!
PLEASE!!

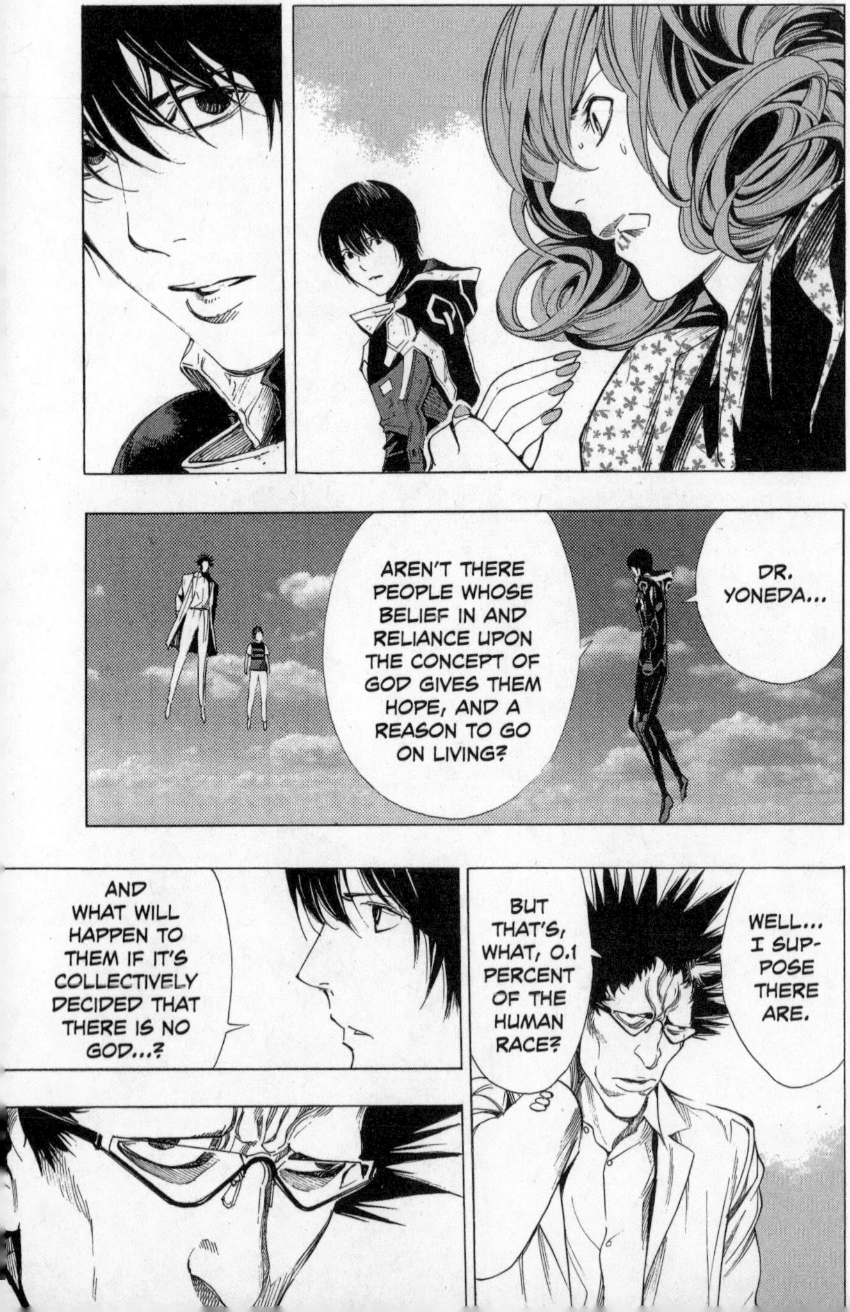
DR. YONEDA...
AREN'T THERE PEOPLE WHOSE BELIEF IN AND RELIANCE UPON THE CONCEPT OF GOD GIVES THEM HOPE, AND A REASON TO GO ON LIVING?
WELL... I SUP-POSE THERE ARE.
BUT THAT'S, WHAT, 0.1 PERCENT OF THE HUMAN RACE?
AND WHAT WILL HAPPEN TO THEM IF IT'S COLLECTIVELY DECIDED THAT THERE IS NO GOD...?

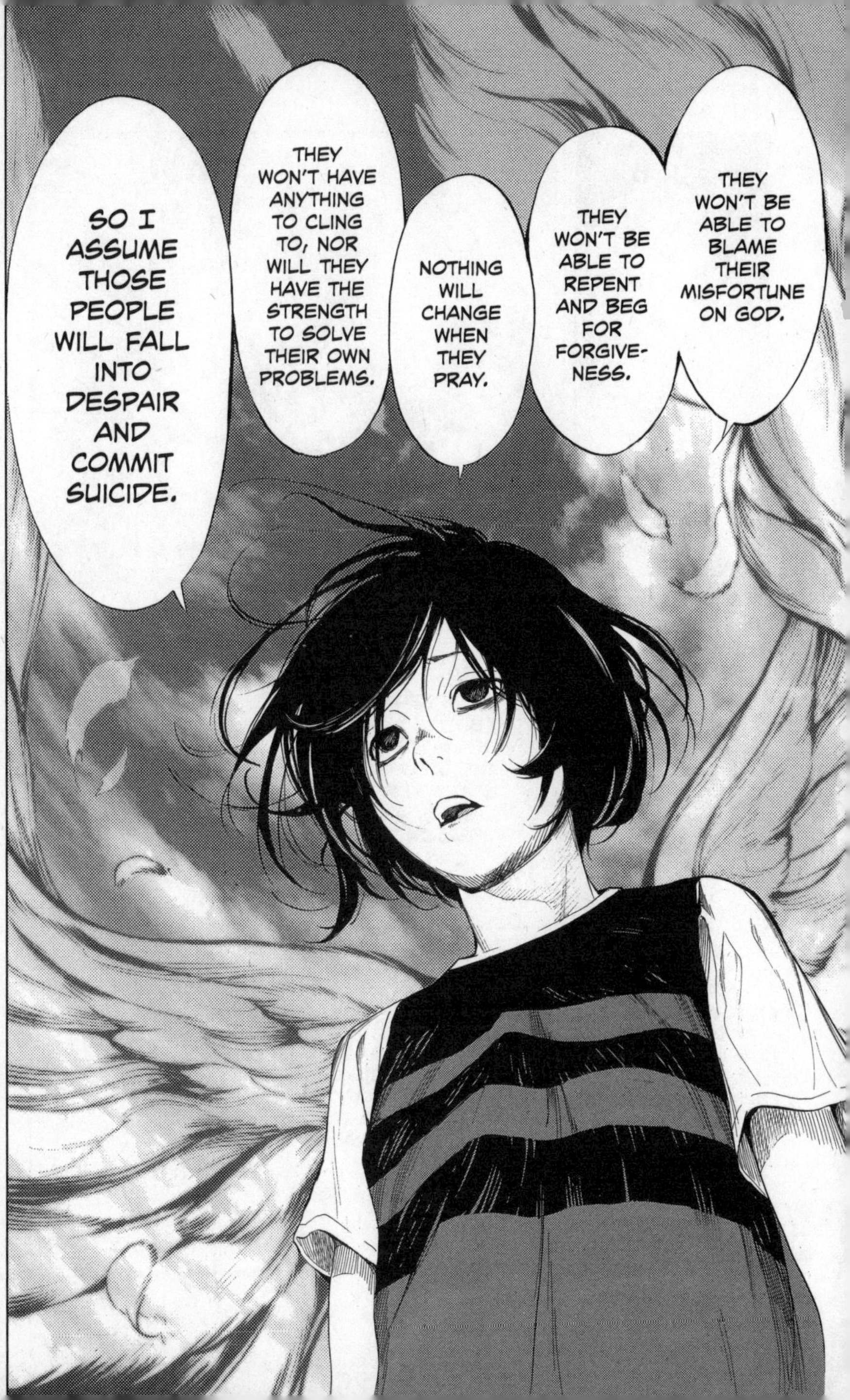
THEY WON'T BE ABLE TO BLAME THEIR MISFORTUNE ON GOD.
THEY WON'T BE ABLE TO REPENT AND BEG FOR FORGIVE-NESS.
NOTHING WILL CHANGE WHEN THEY PRAY.
THEY WON'T HAVE ANYTHING TO CLING TO, NOR WILL THEY HAVE THE STRENGTH TO SOLVE THEIR OWN PROBLEMS.
SO I ASSUME THOSE PEOPLE WILL FALL INTO DESPAIR AND COMMIT SUICIDE.

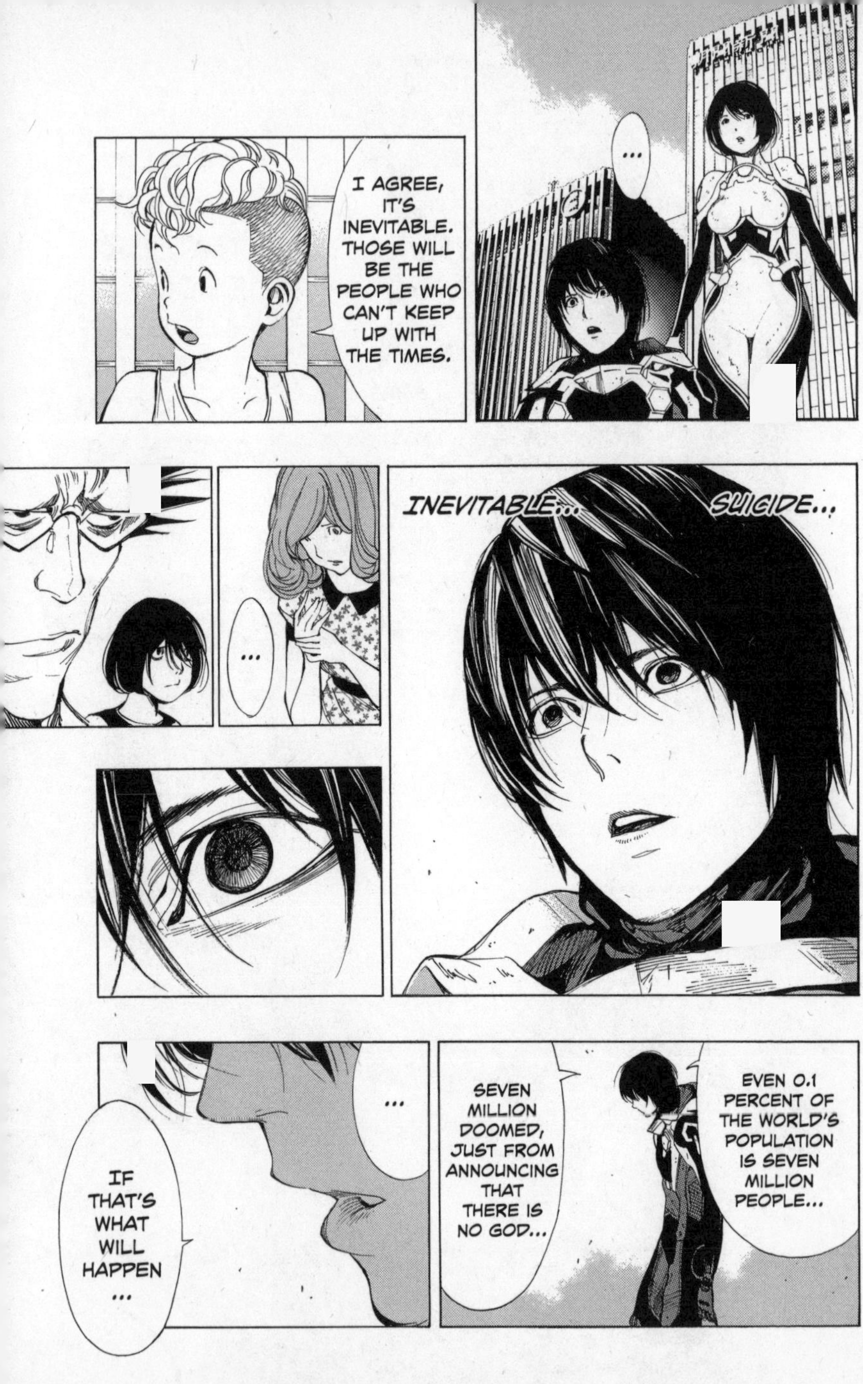
...
I AGREE, IT'S INEVITABLE. THOSE WILL BE THE PEOPLE WHO CAN'T KEEP UP WITH THE TIMES.
SUICIDE...
INEVITABLE...
...
EVEN 0.1 PERCENT OF THE WORLD'S POPULATION IS SEVEN MILLION PEOPLE...
SEVEN MILLION DOOMED, JUST FROM ANNOUNCING THAT THERE IS NO GOD...
...
IF THAT'S WHAT WILL HAPPEN ...

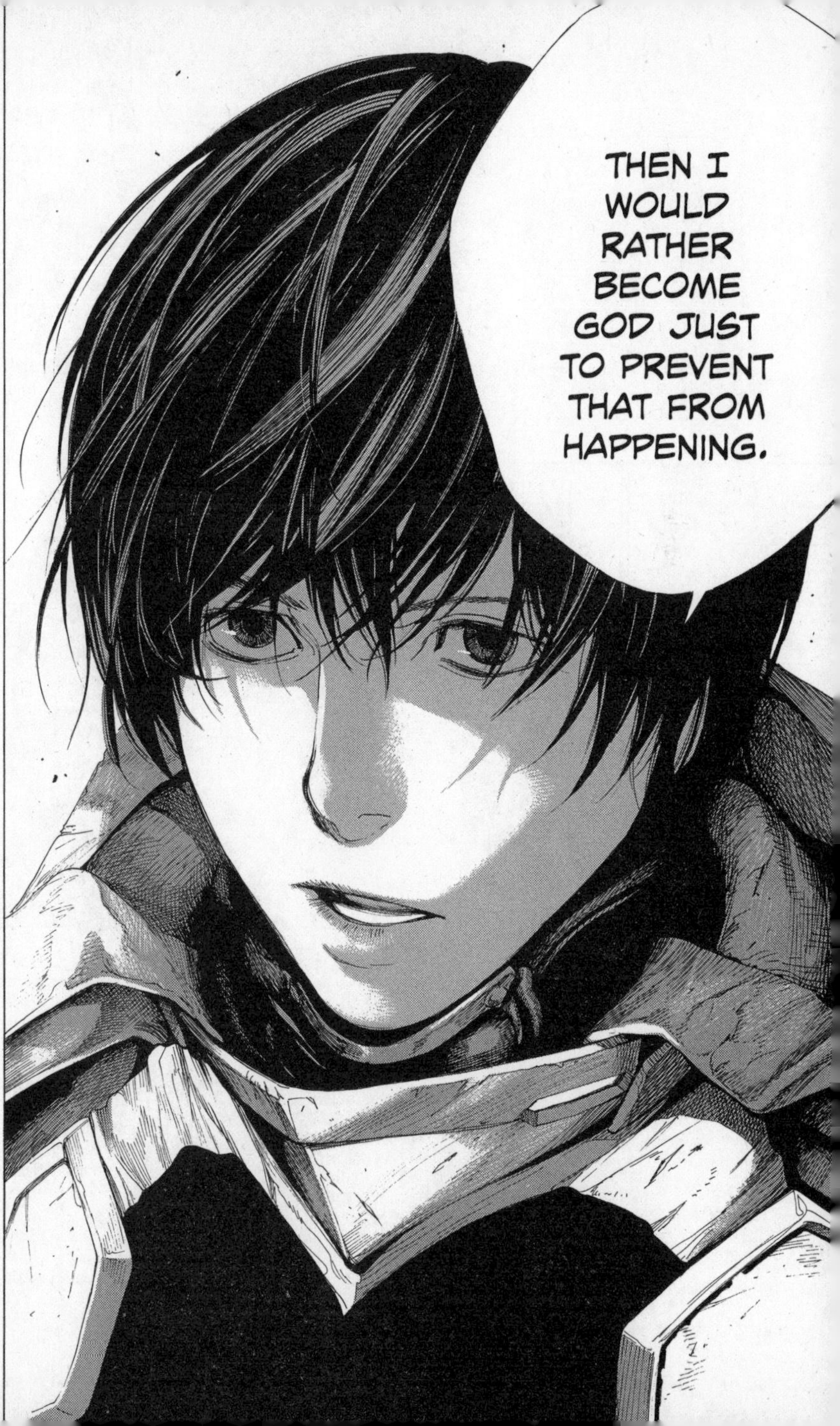
THEN I WOULD RATHER BECOME GOD JUST TO PREVENT THAT FROM HAPPENING.

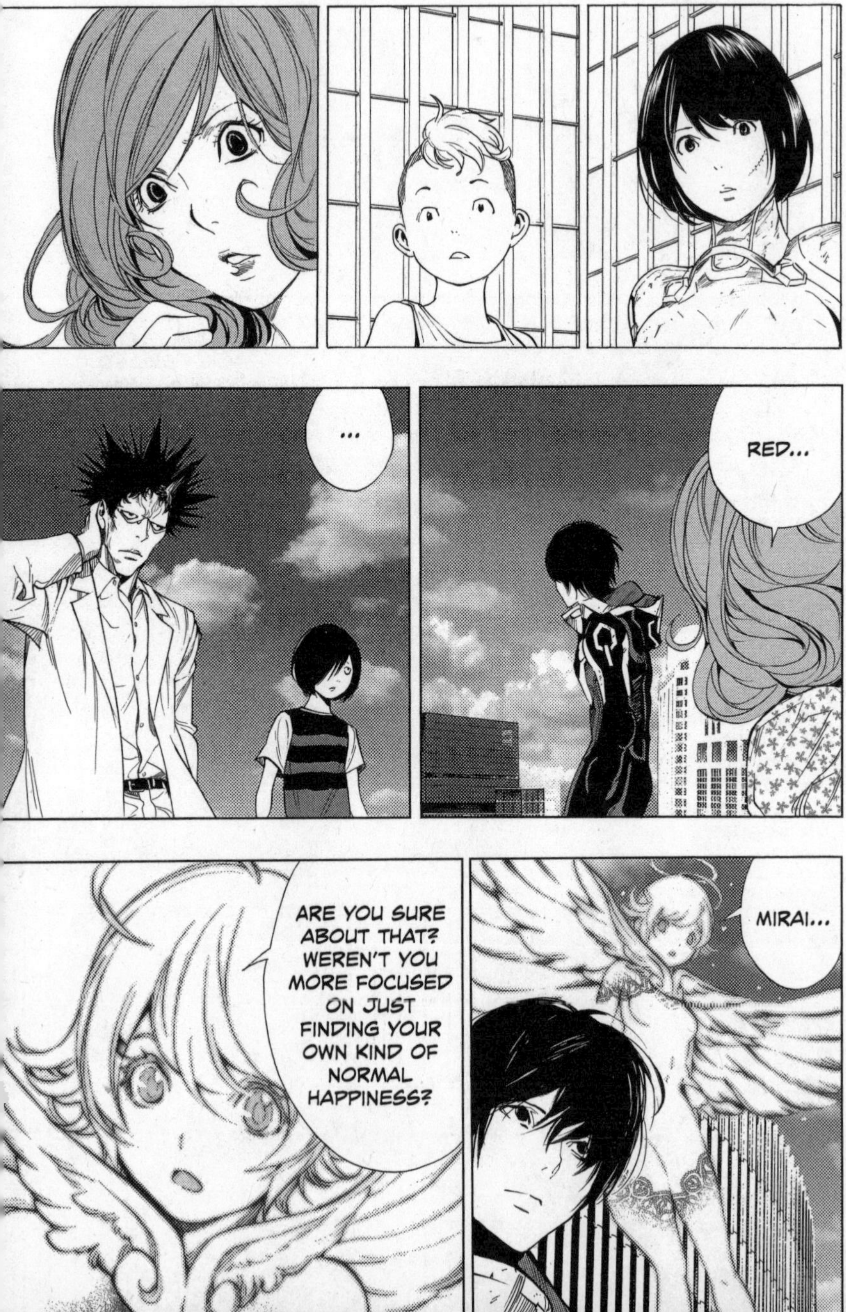
RED...
...
MIRAI...
ARE YOU SURE ABOUT THAT? WEREN'T YOU MORE FOCUSED ON JUST FINDING YOUR OWN KIND OF NORMAL HAPPINESS?

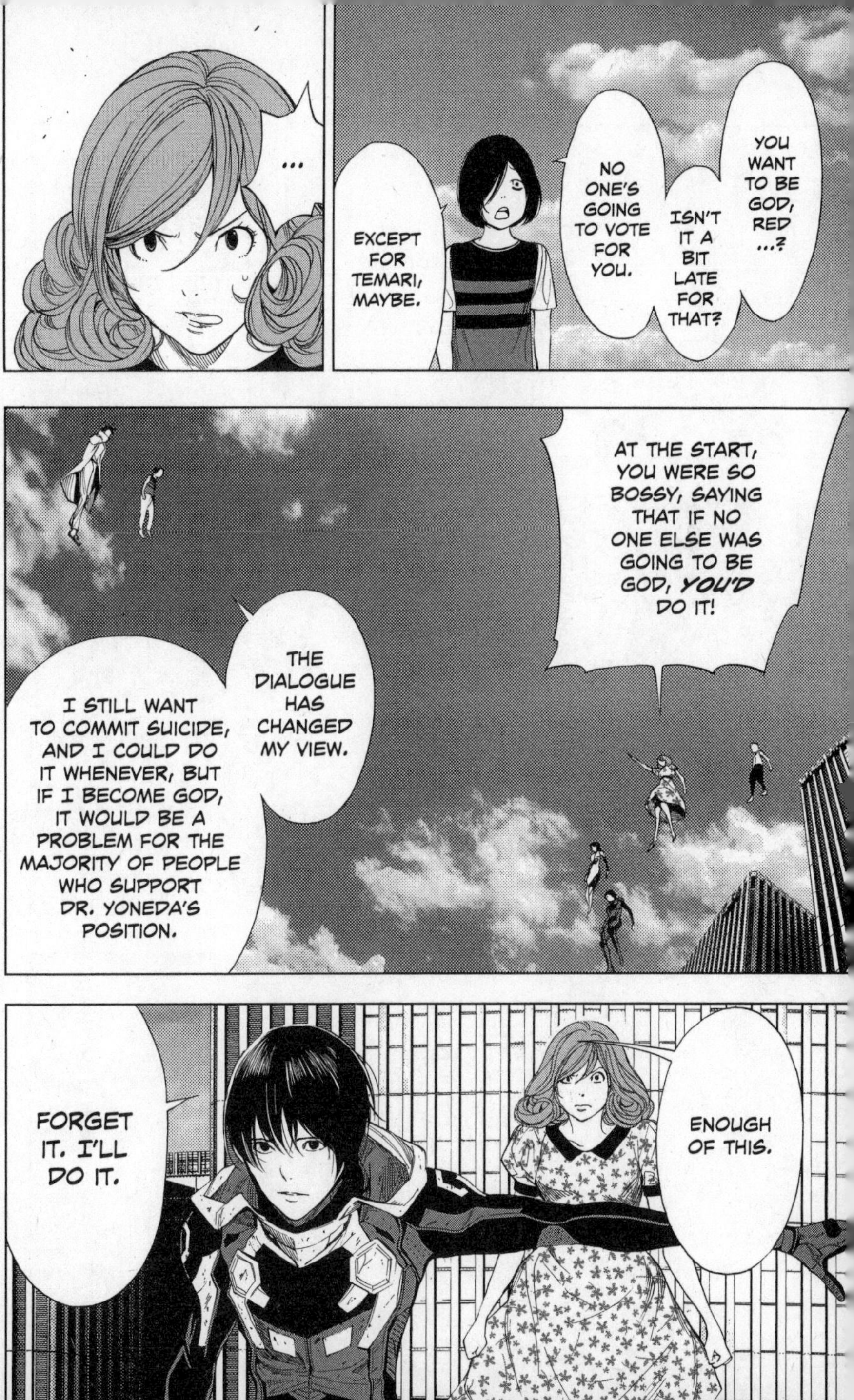

YOU WANT TO BE GOD, RED ...?
ISN'T IT A BIT LATE FOR THAT?
NO ONE'S GOING TO VOTE FOR YOU.
EXCEPT FOR TEMARI, MAYBE.
...
AT THE START, YOU WERE SO BOSSY, SAYING THAT IF NO ONE ELSE WAS GOING TO BE GOD, *YOU'D* DO IT!
THE DIALOGUE HAS CHANGED MY VIEW.
I STILL WANT TO COMMIT SUICIDE, AND I COULD DO IT WHENEVER, BUT IF I BECOME GOD, IT WOULD BE A PROBLEM FOR THE MAJORITY OF PEOPLE WHO SUPPORT DR. YONEDA'S POSITION.
ENOUGH OF THIS.
FORGET IT. I'LL DO IT.

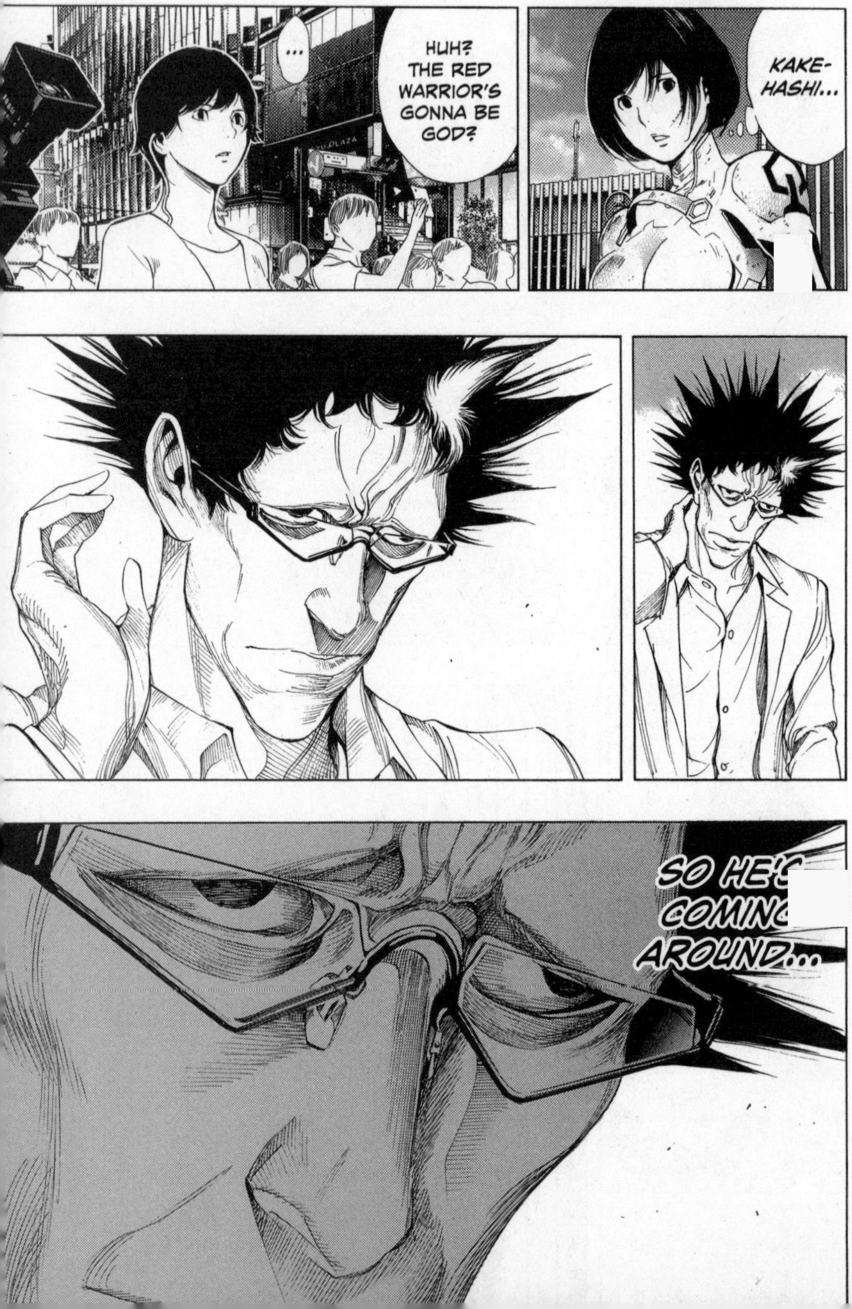
KAKE-HASHI...
HUH? THE RED WARRIOR'S GONNA BE GOD?
...
SO HE'S COMIN AROUND...

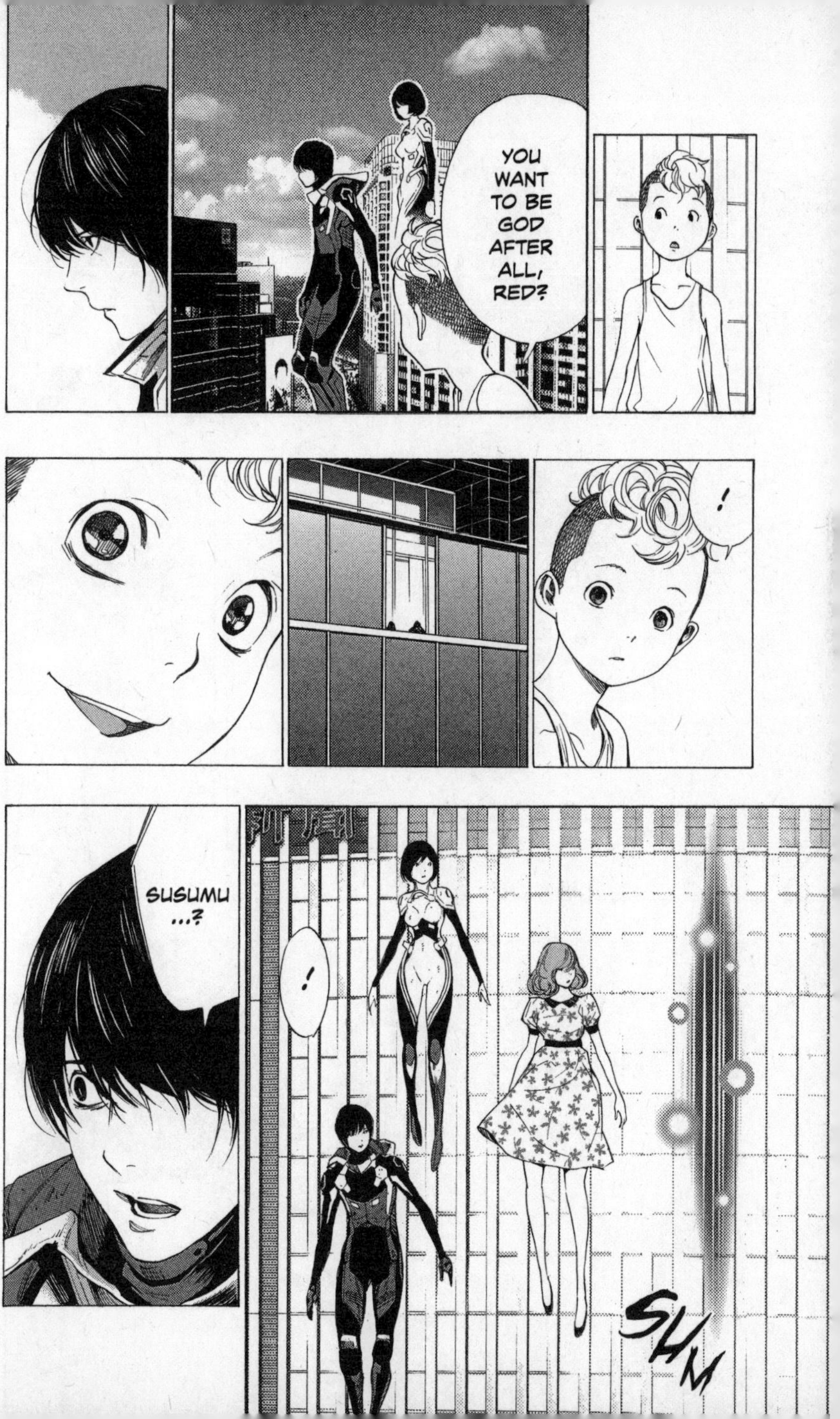
YOU WANT TO BE GOD AFTER ALL, RED?
!
!
SUSUMU ...?
SHM

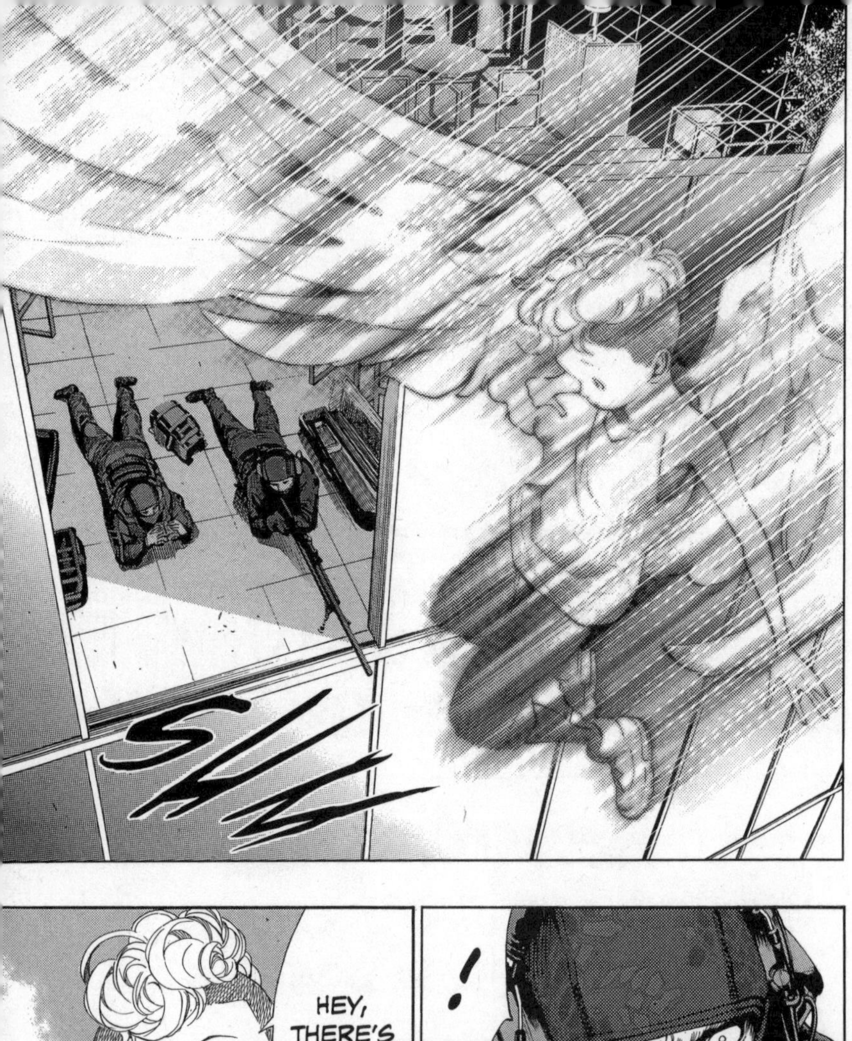

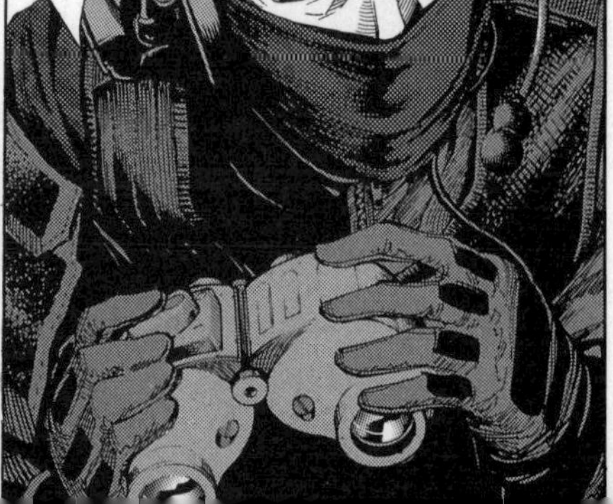
!

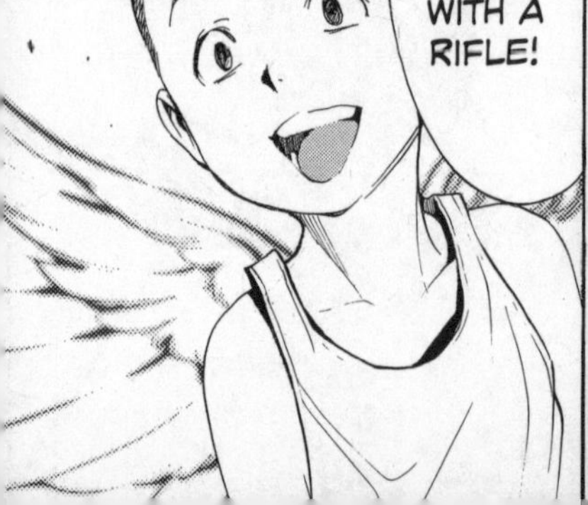
HEY, THERE'S A GUY WITH A RIFLE!

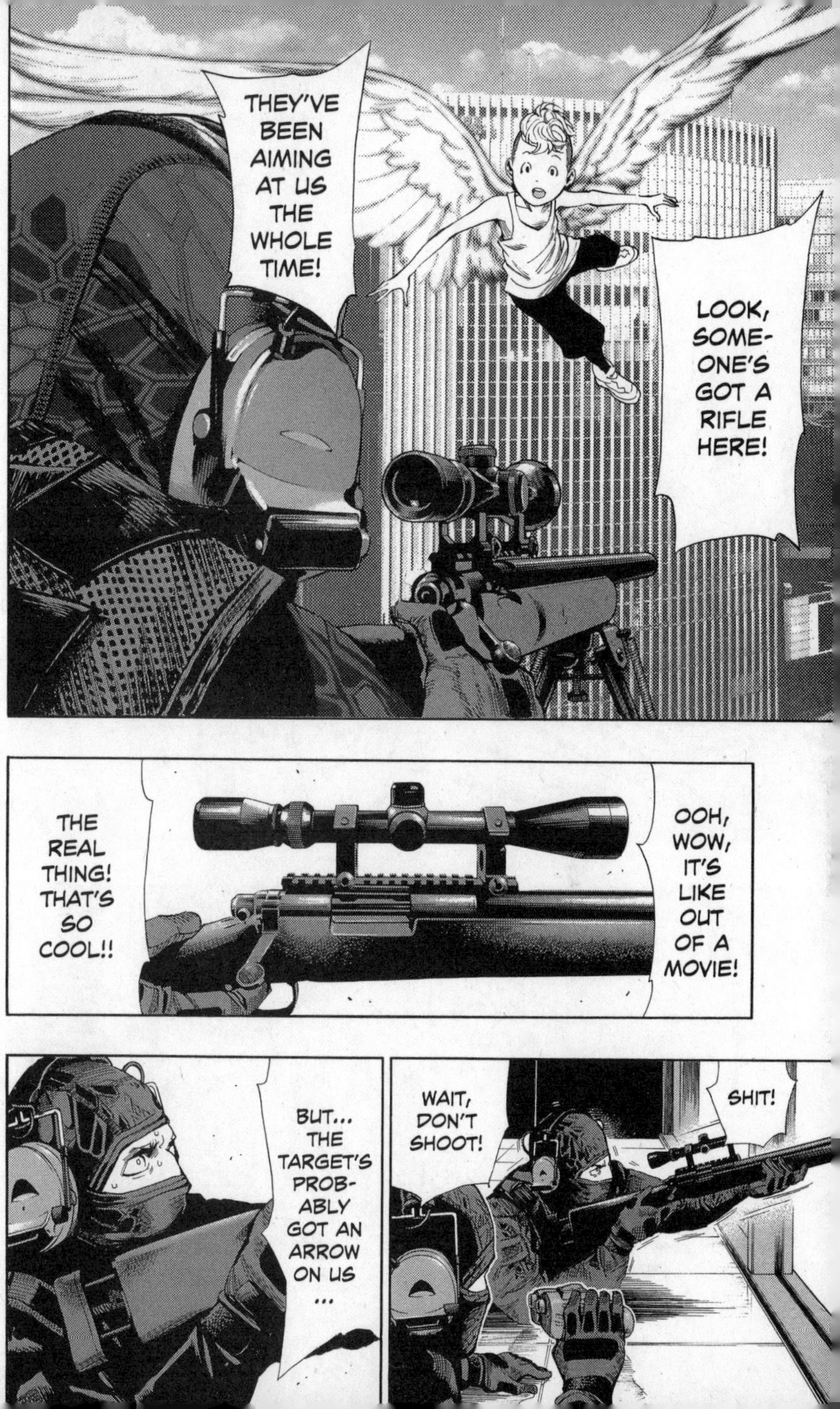
LOOK, SOME-ONE'S GOT A RIFLE HERE!
THEY'VE BEEN AIMING AT US THE WHOLE TIME!
OOH, WOW, IT'S LIKE OUT OF A MOVIE!
THE REAL THING! THAT'S SO COOL!!
SHIT!
WAIT, DON'T SHOOT!
BUT... THE TARGET'S PROB-ABLY GOT AN ARROW ON US ...

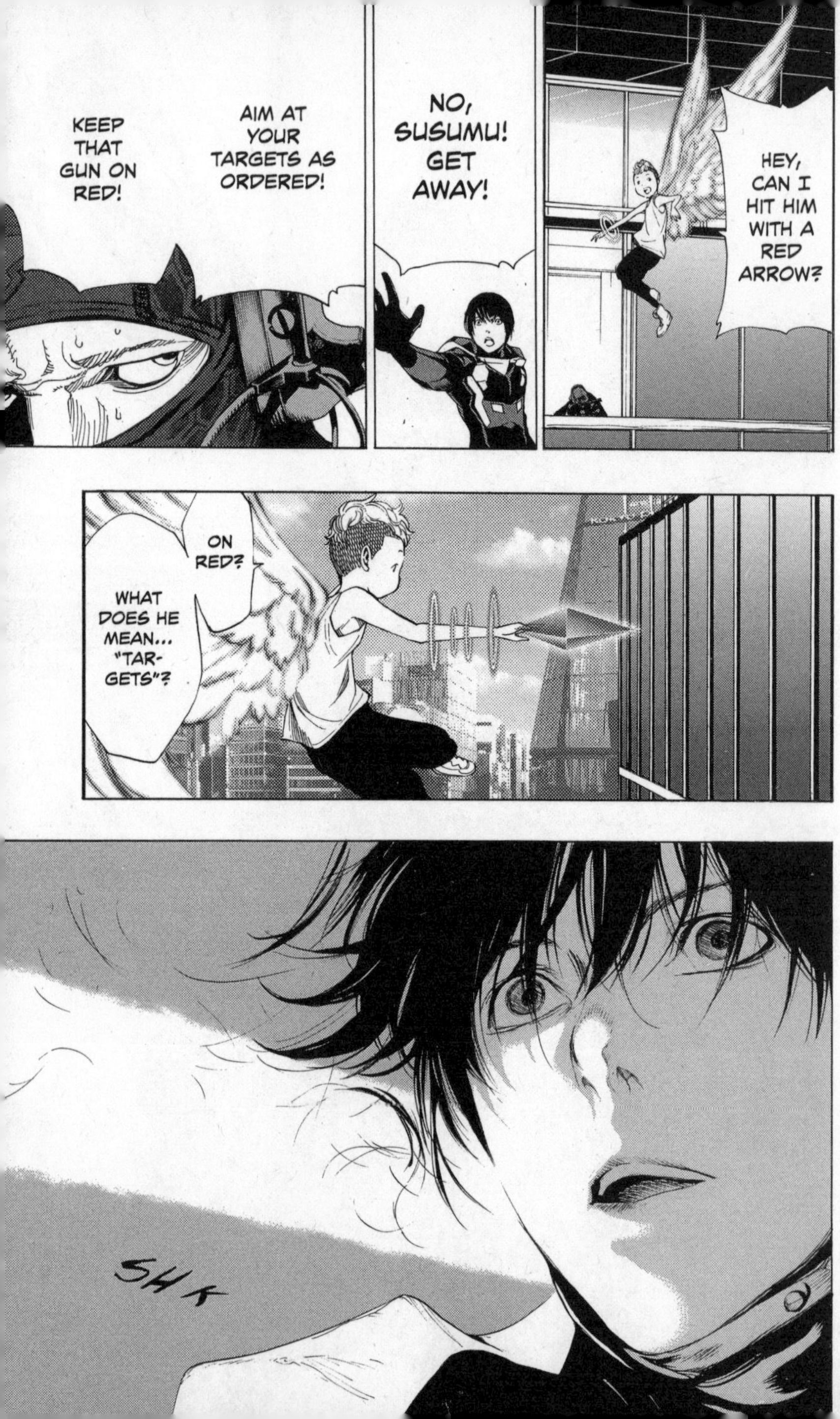
HEY, CAN I HIT HIM WITH A RED ARROW?
NO, SUSUMU! GET AWAY!
AIM AT YOUR TARGETS AS ORDERED!
KEEP THAT GUN ON RED!
ON RED?
WHAT DOES HE MEAN... "TAR-GETS"?
SHK

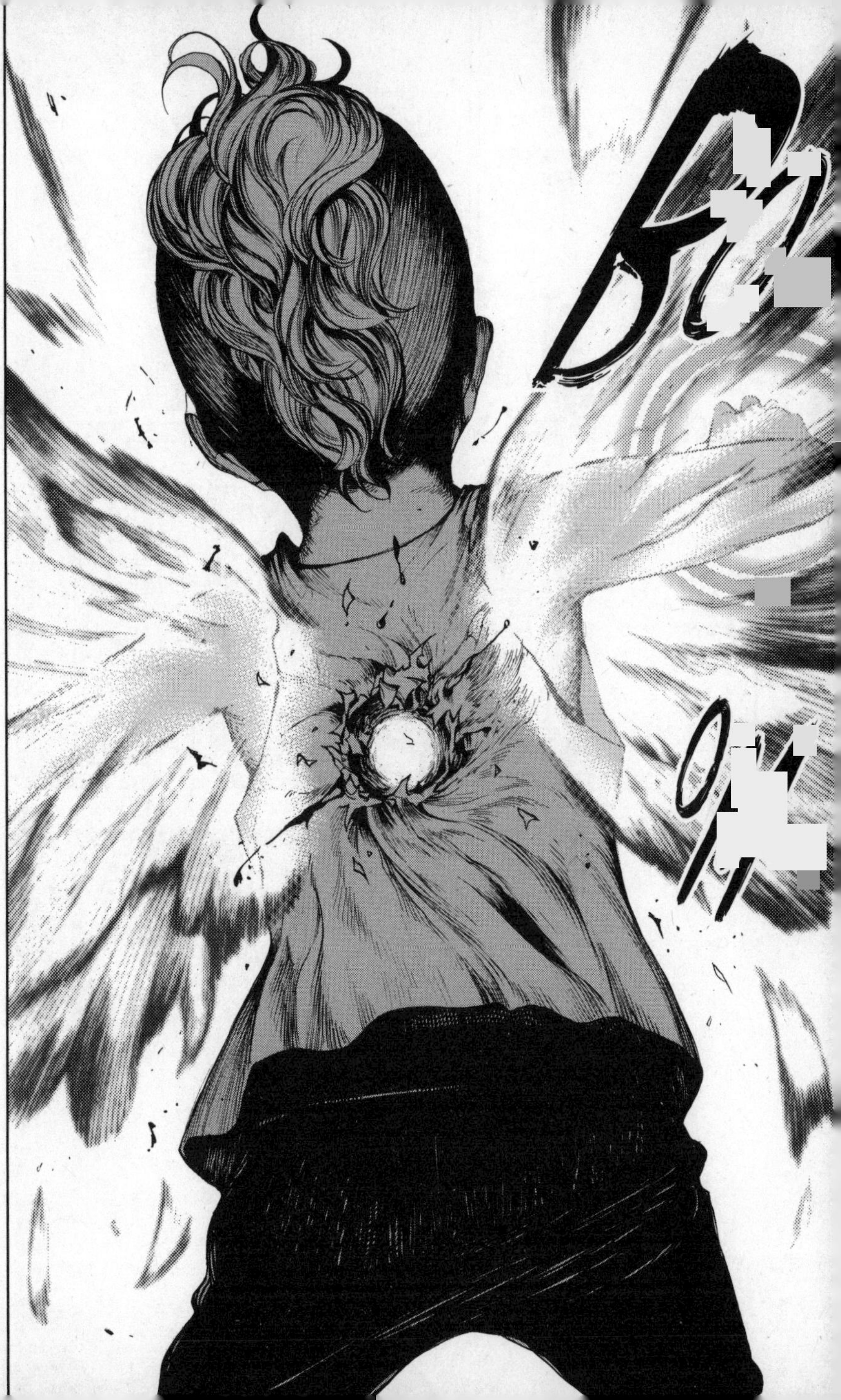

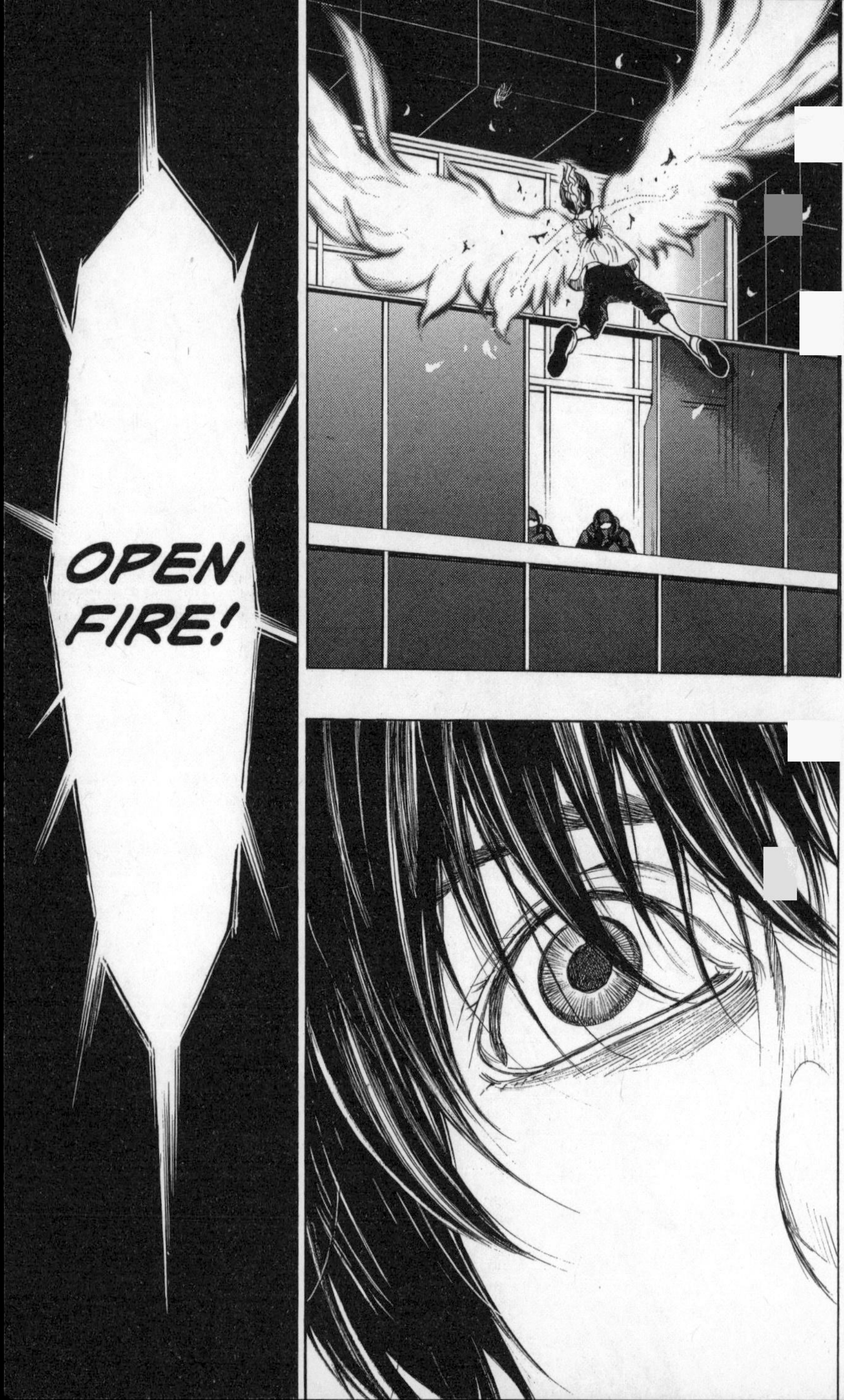
OPEN FIRE!

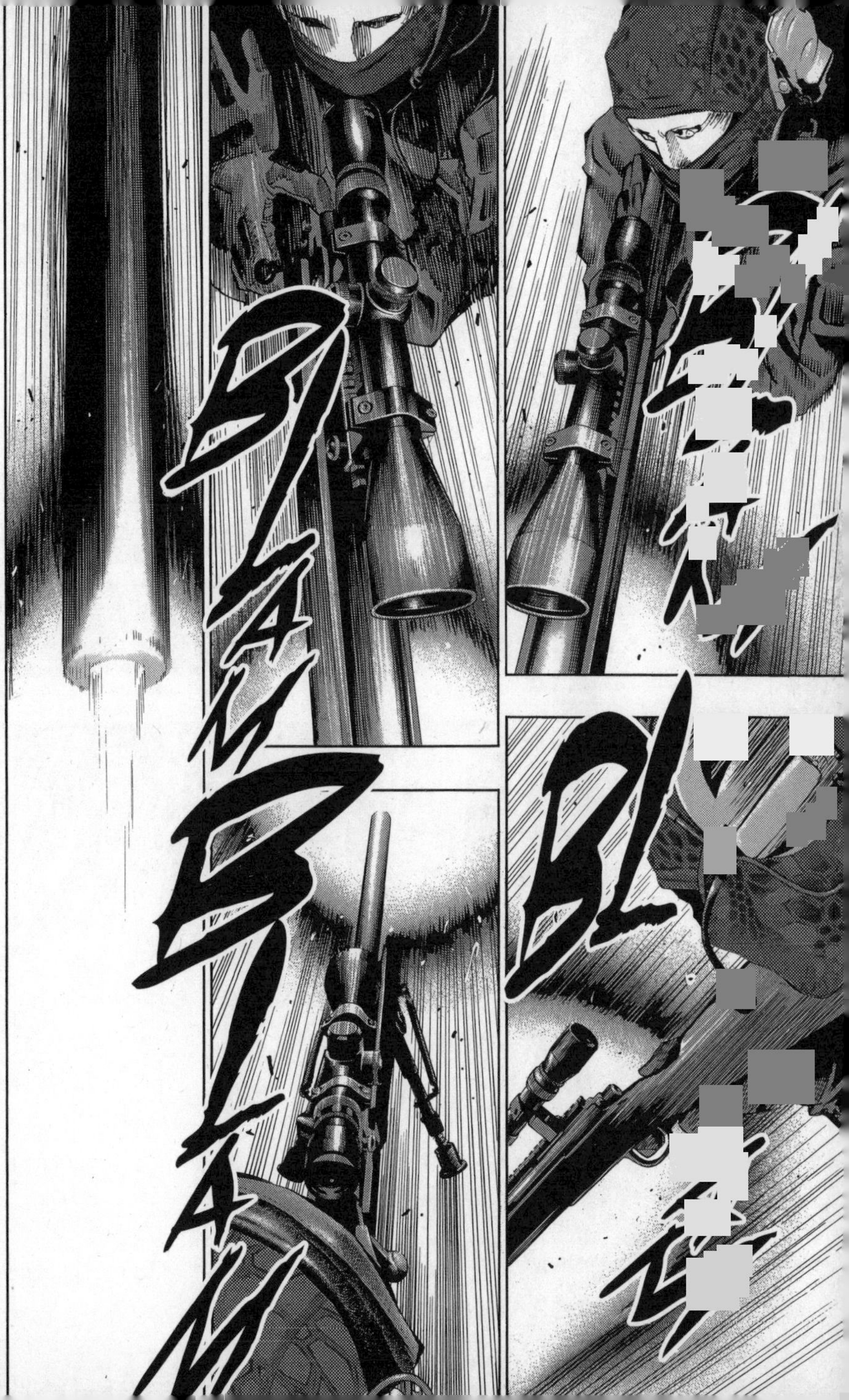
BLAM BLAM

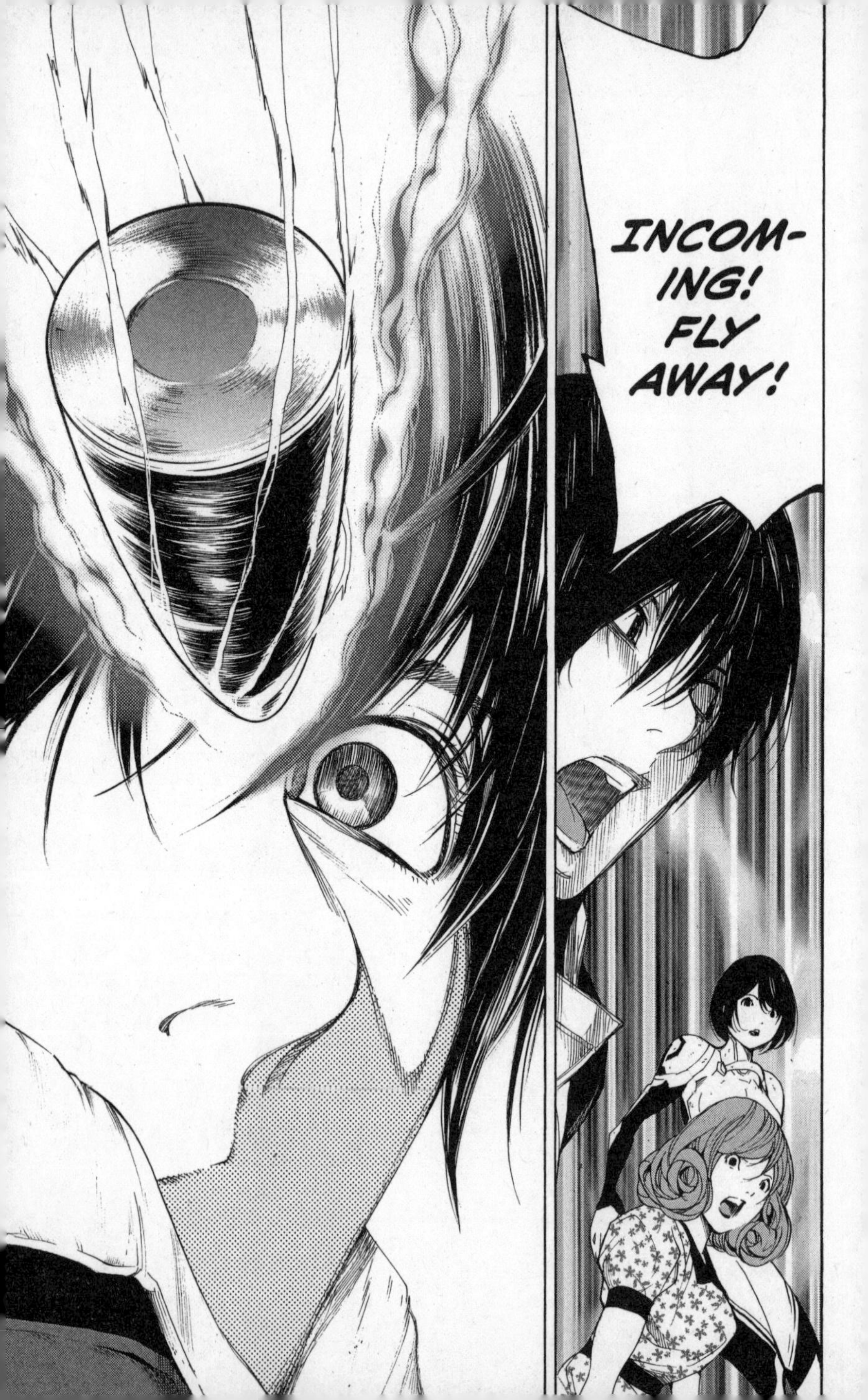
INCOM-
ING!
FLY
AWAY!

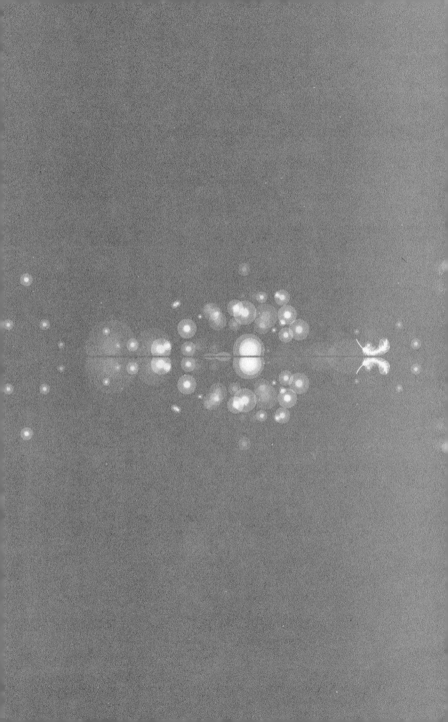

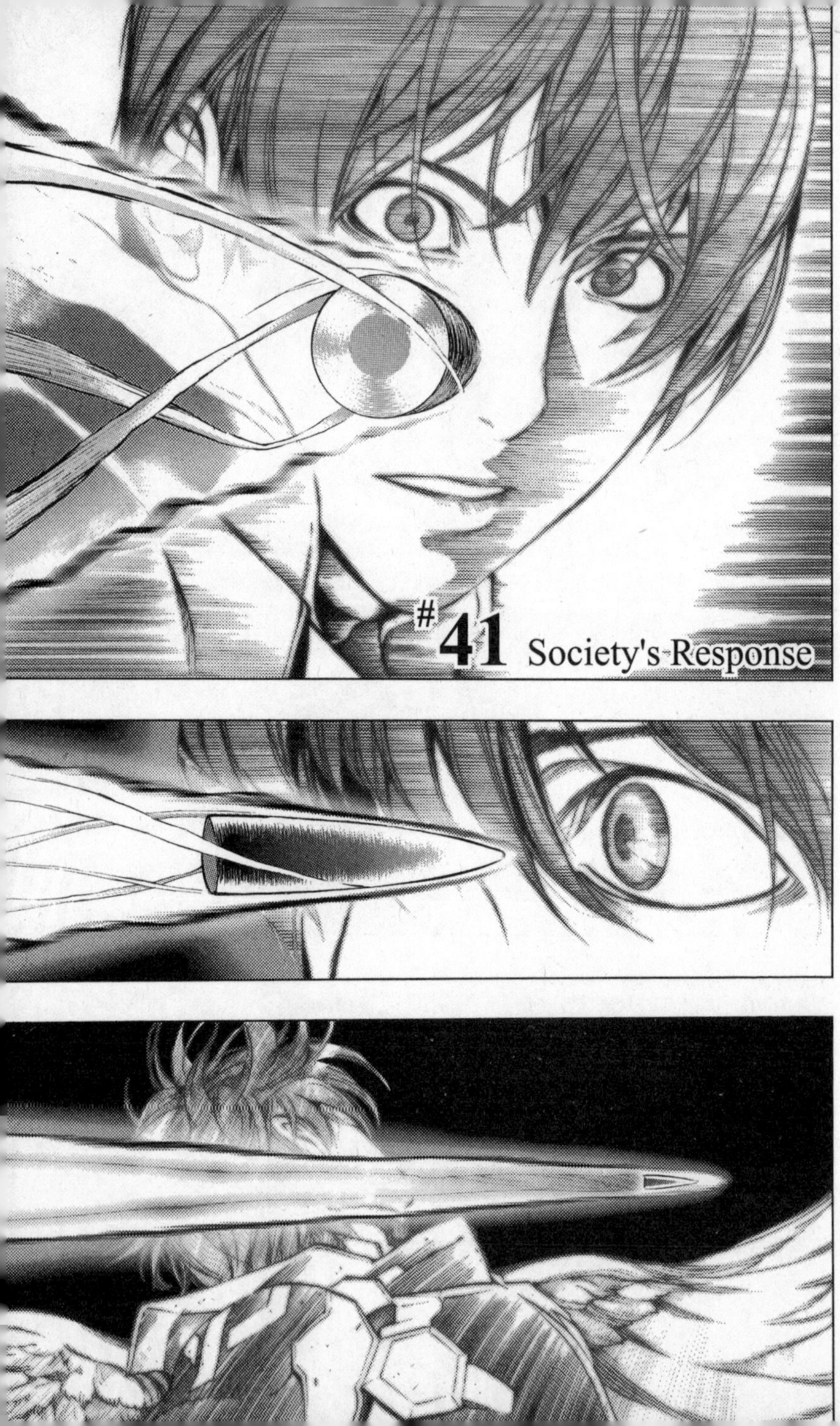
#41 Society's Response

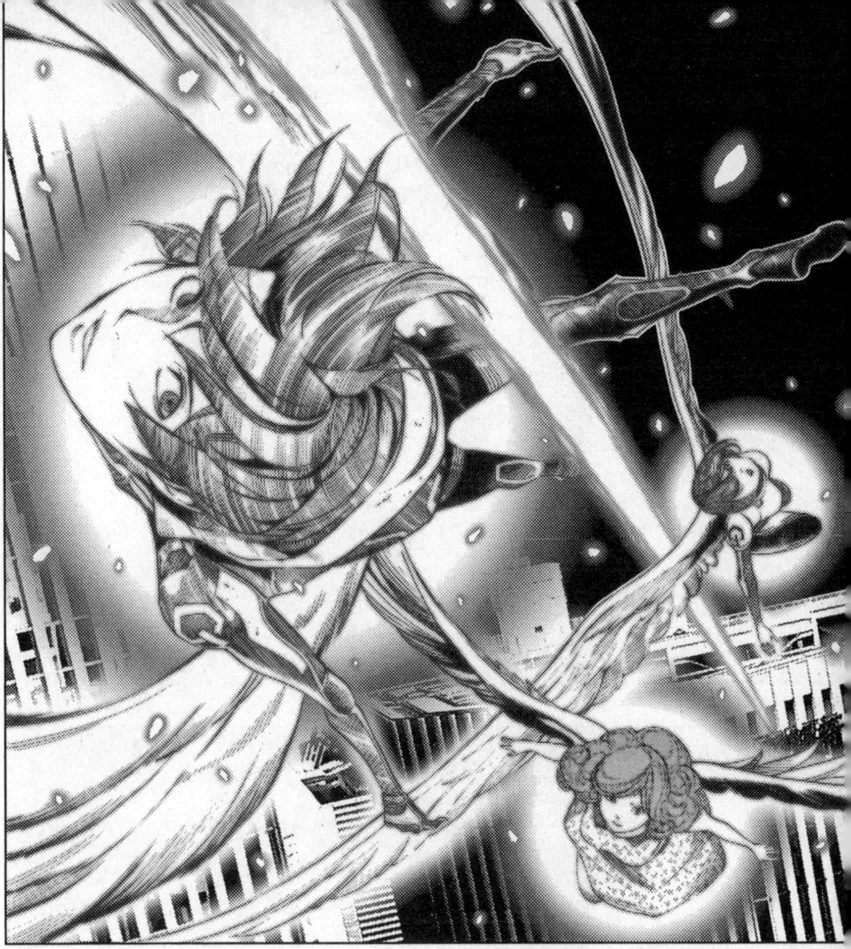

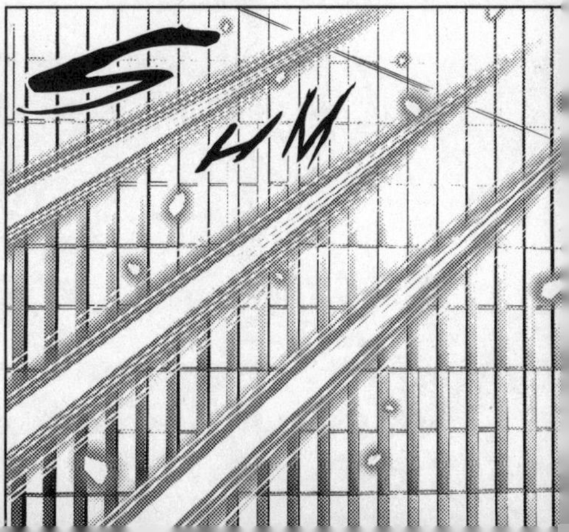
SHM

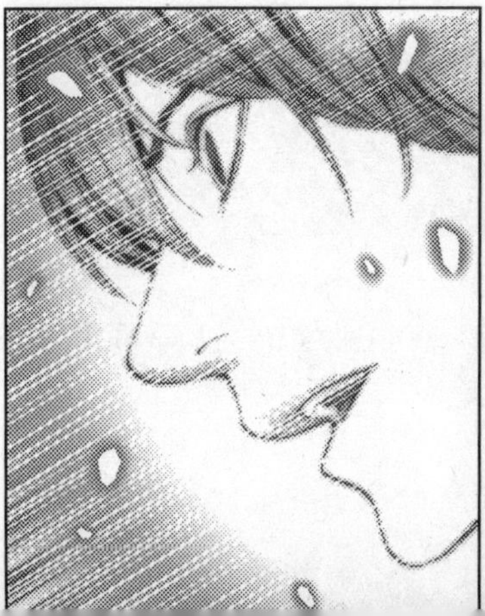

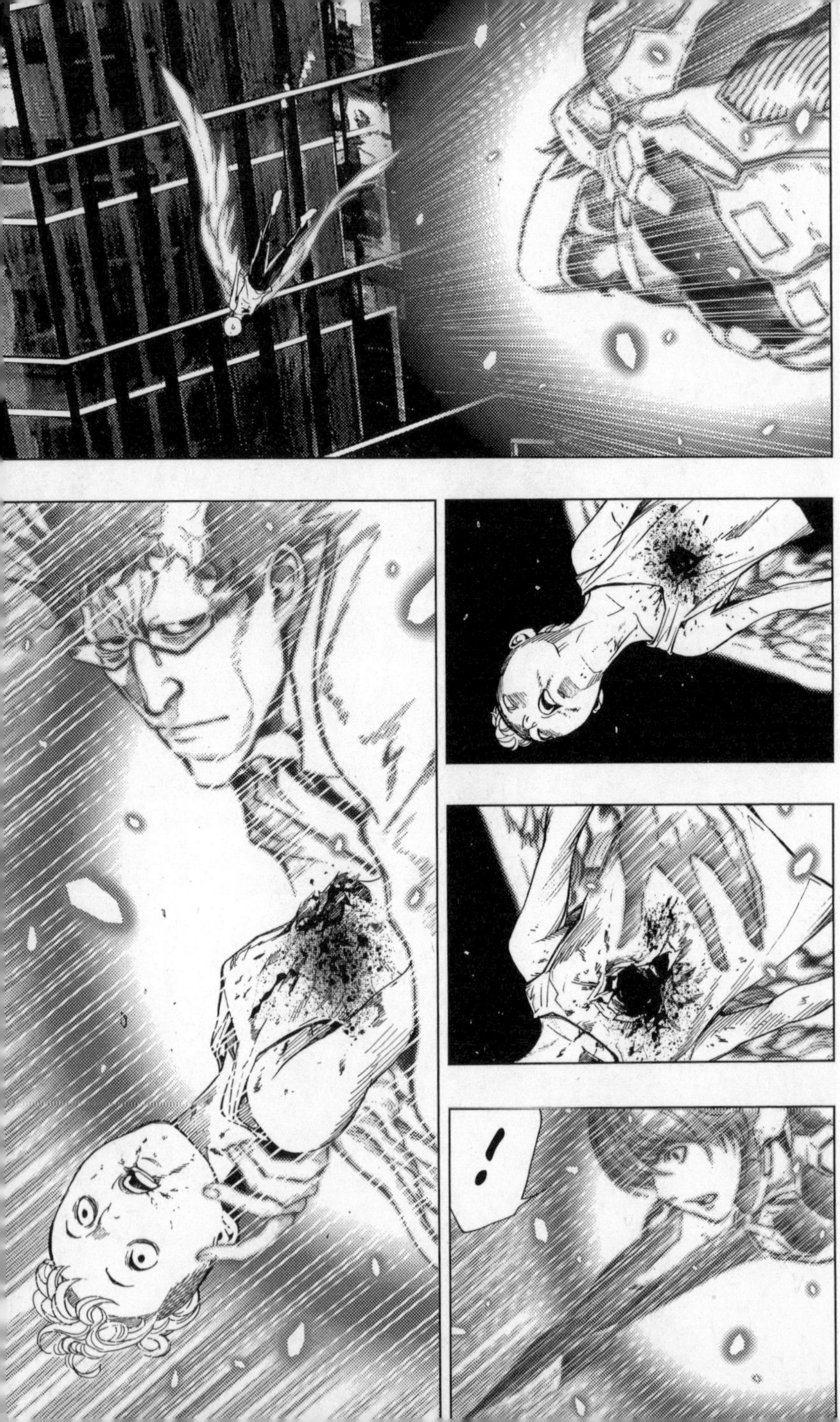
!

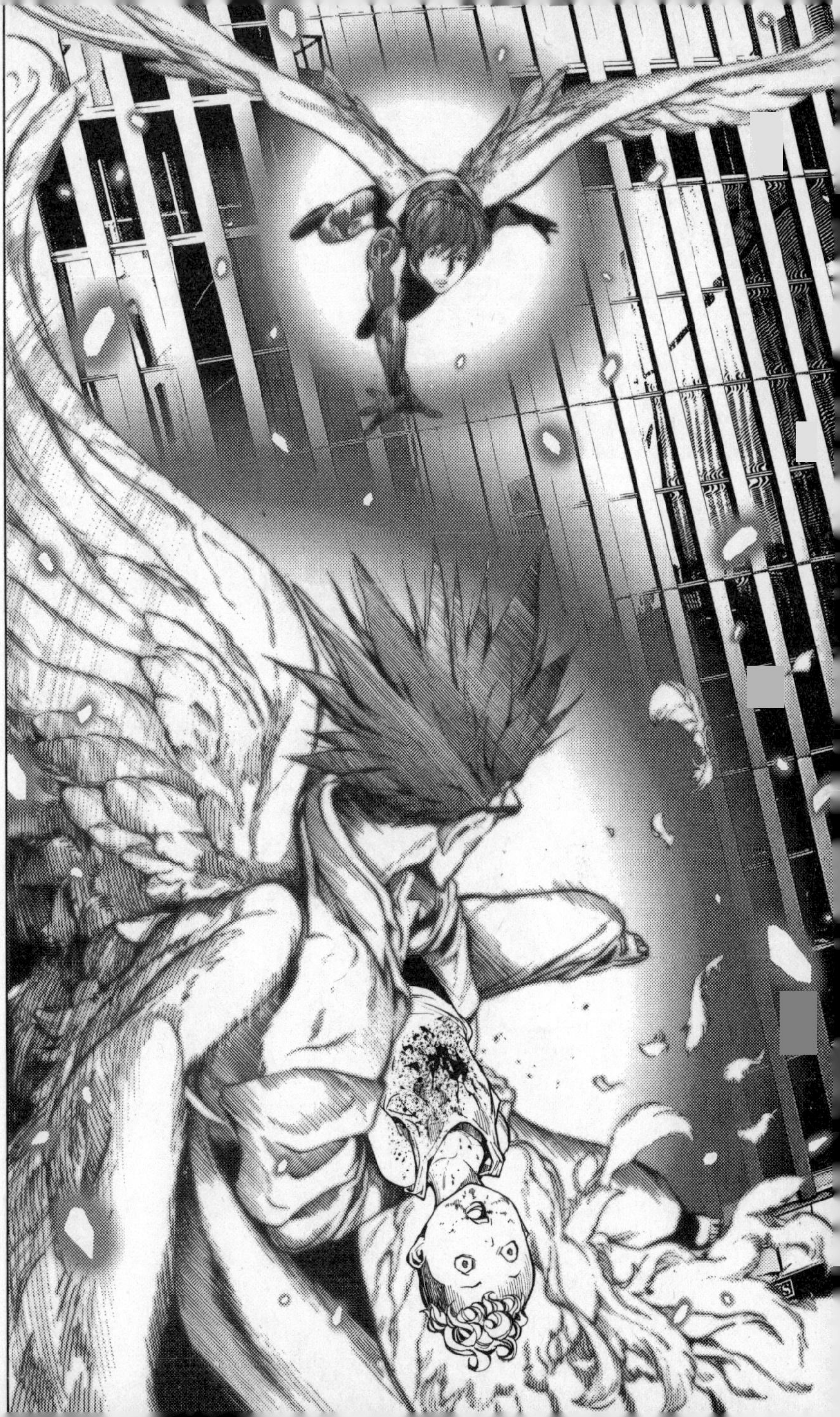

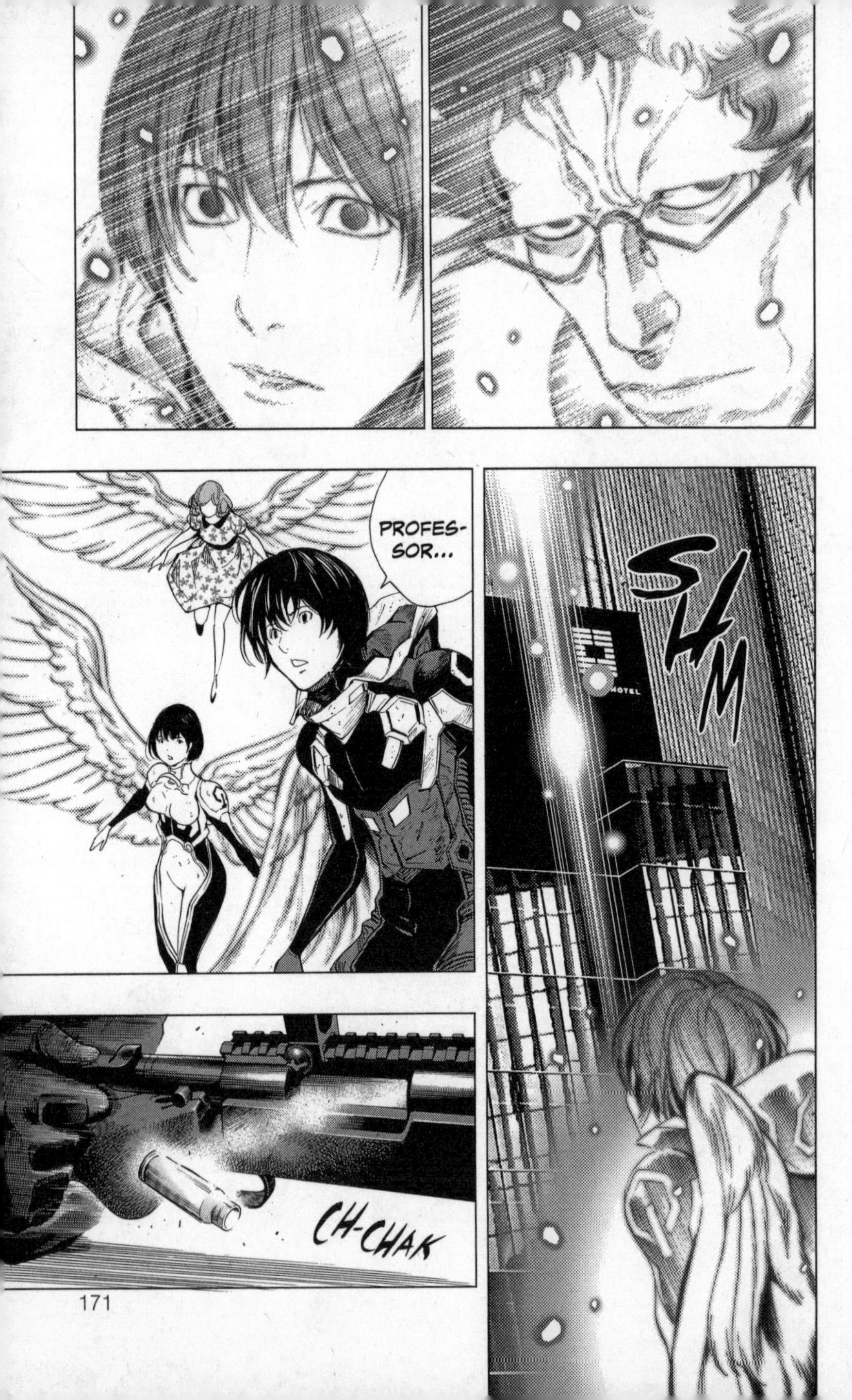
SHM
PROFES-
SOR...
CH-CHAK

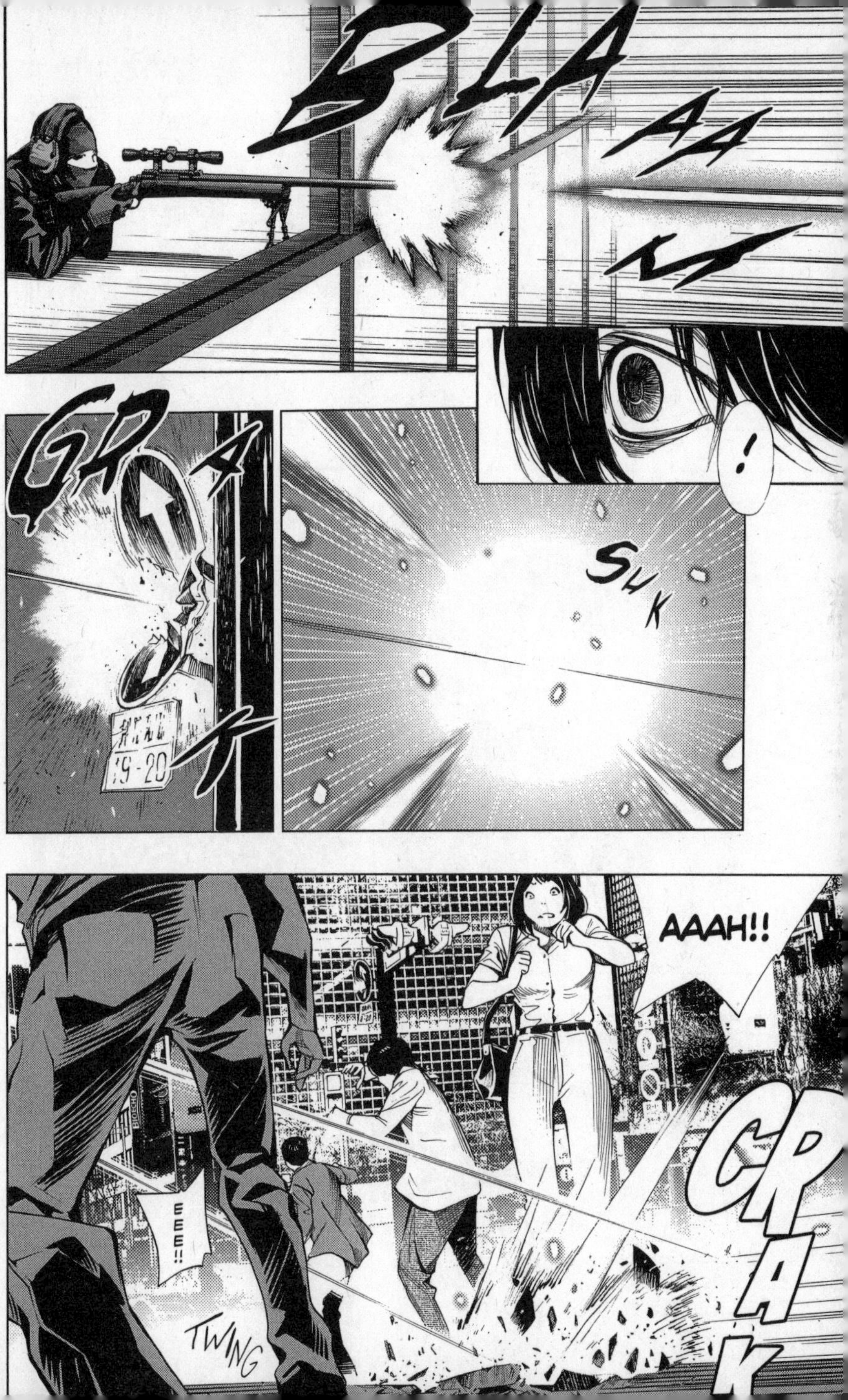
BLAAAANT
!
SHK
GRAK
AAAH!!
CRAK
EEE!!
TWING

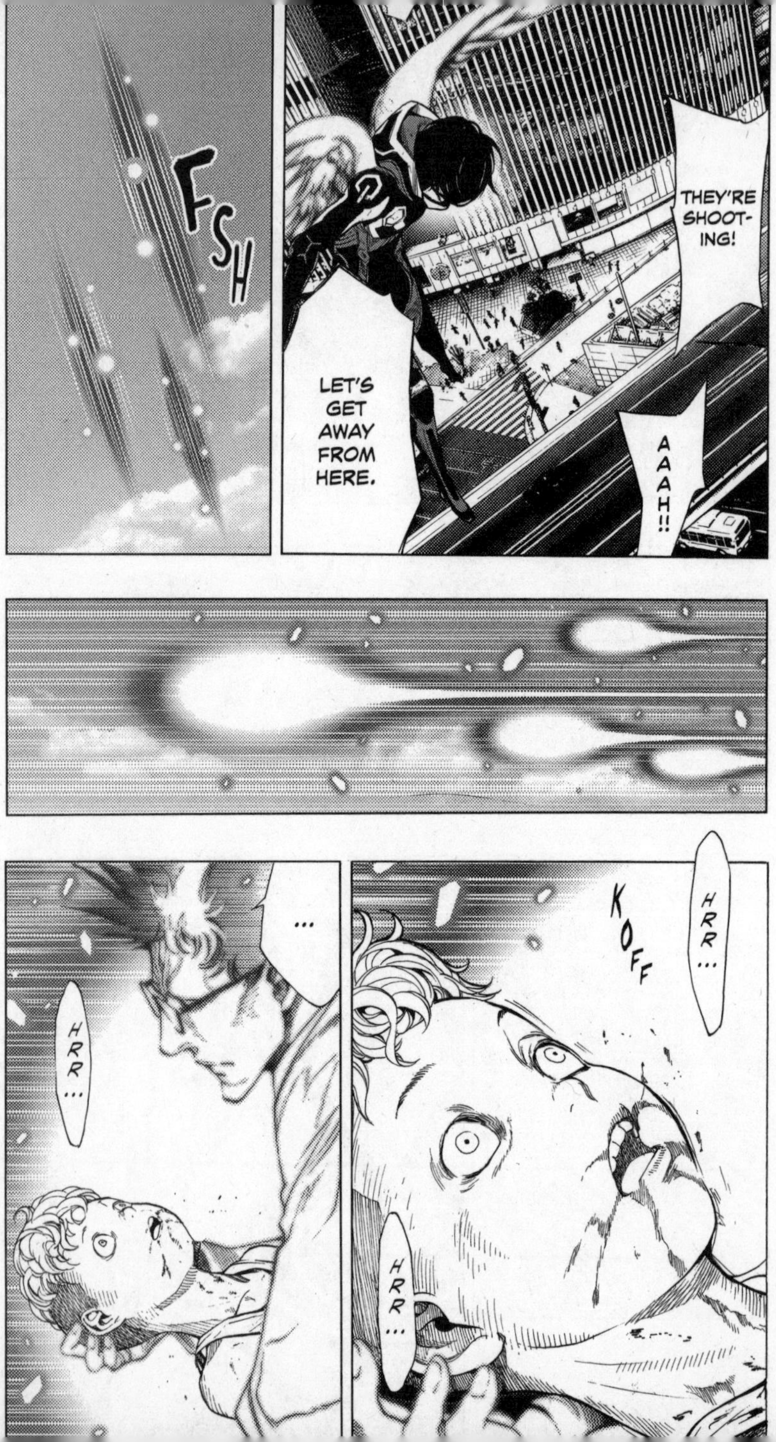
THEY'RE SHOOT-ING!
AAAAH!!
LET'S GET AWAY FROM HERE.
FSH
HRR...
KOFF
HRR...
...
HRR...

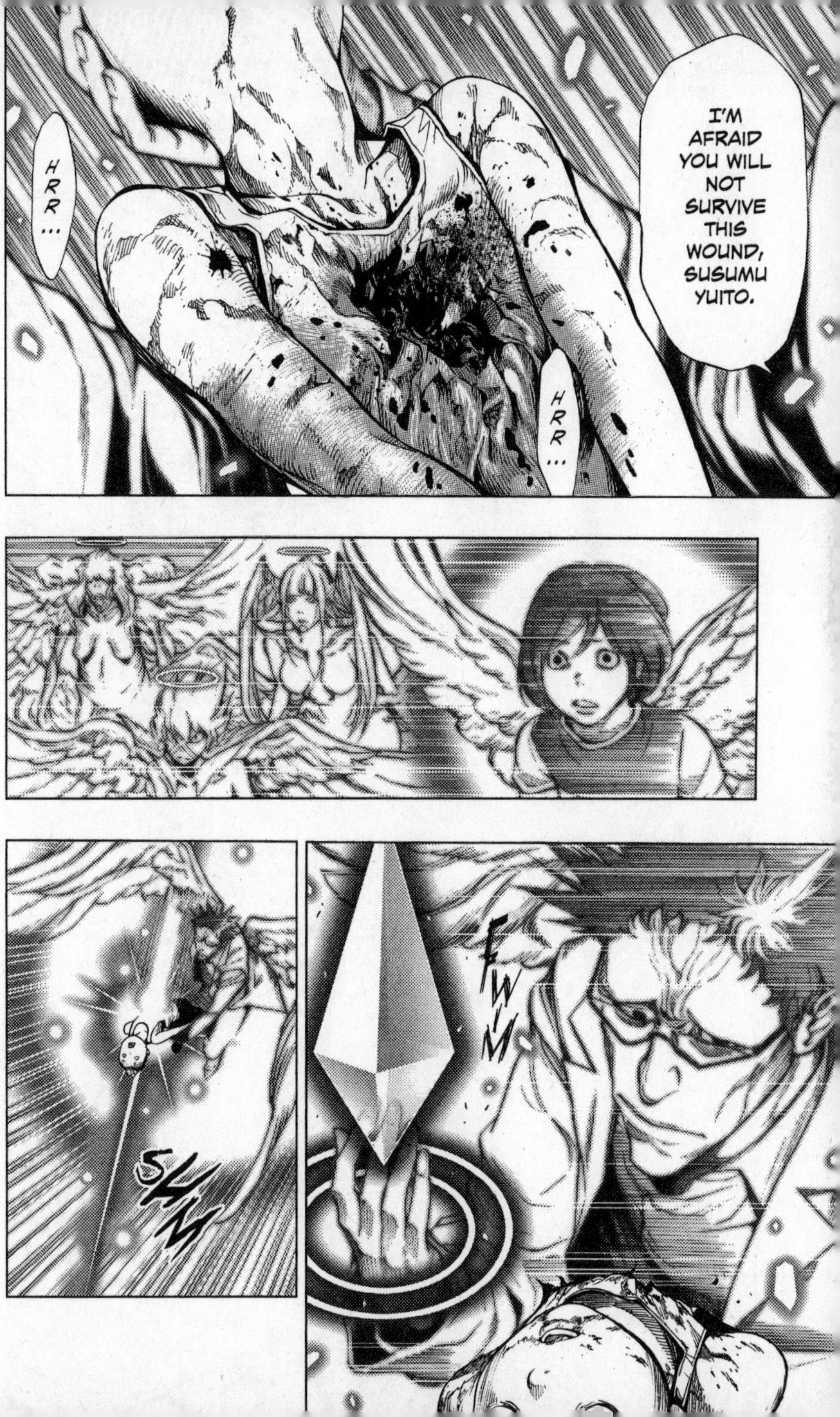
I'M AFRAID YOU WILL NOT SURVIVE THIS WOUND, SUSUMU YUITO.
HRR...
HRR...
FWIM
SHM

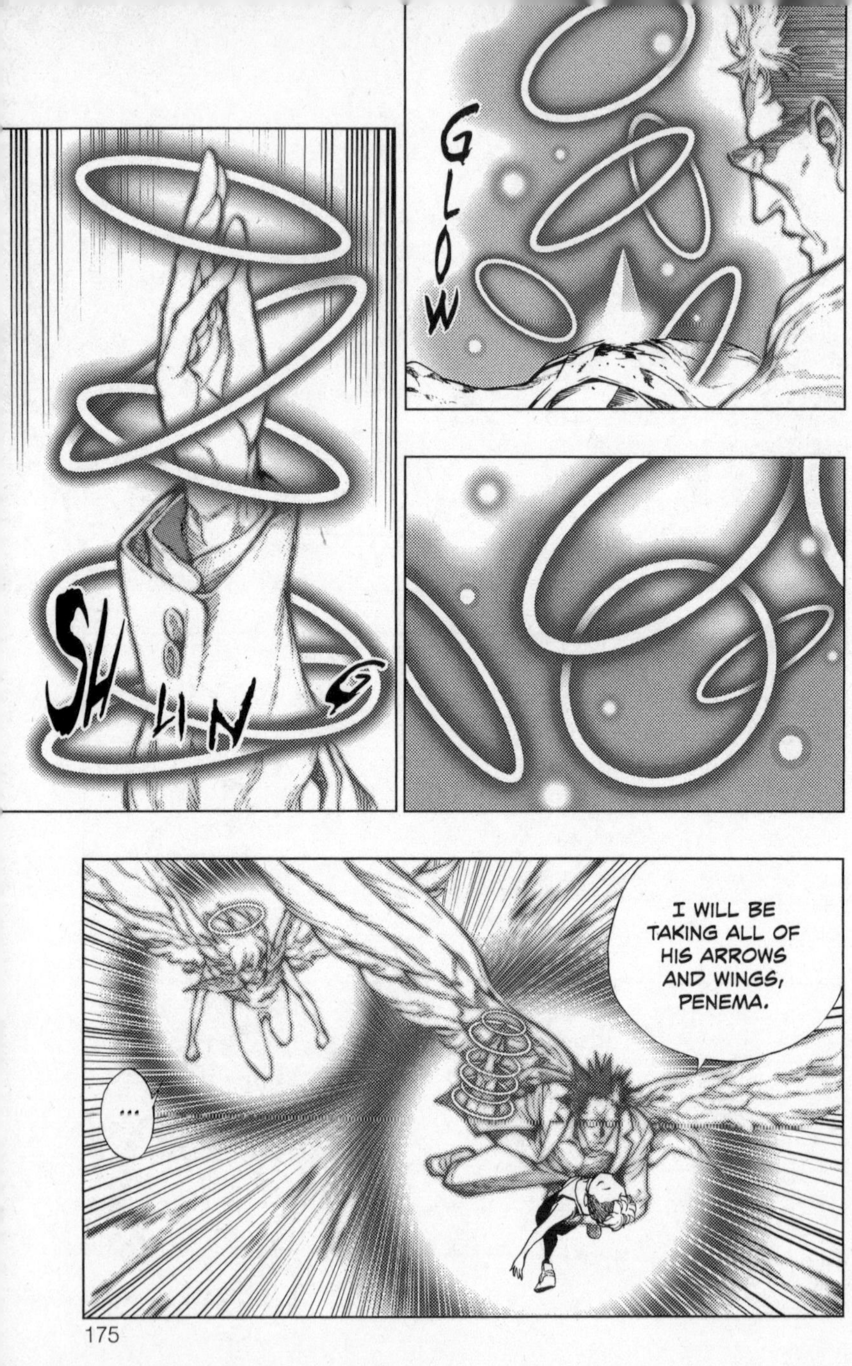
GLOW
SHLING
I WILL BE TAKING ALL OF HIS ARROWS AND WINGS, PENEMA.
...

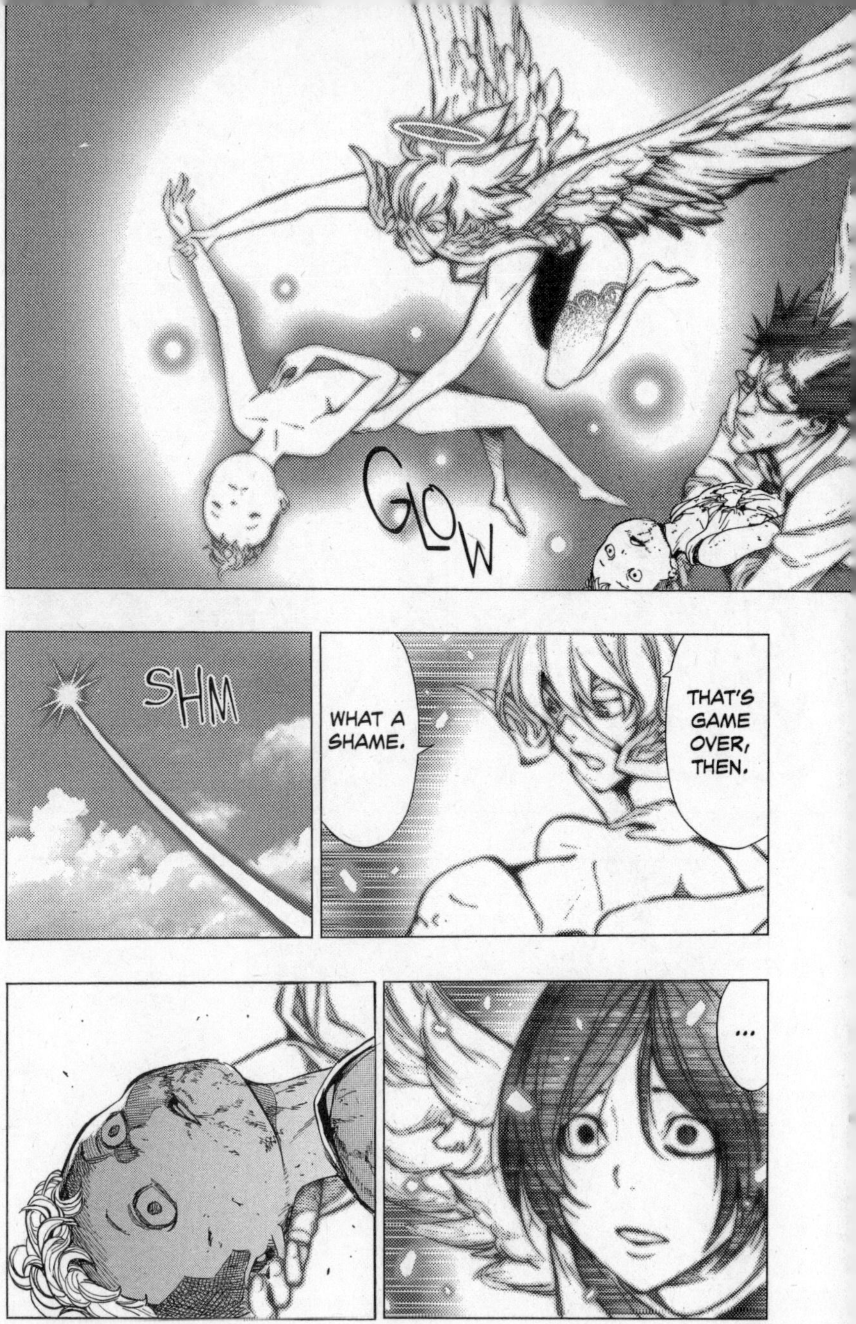
GLOW
THAT'S GAME OVER, THEN.
WHAT A SHAME.
SHM
...

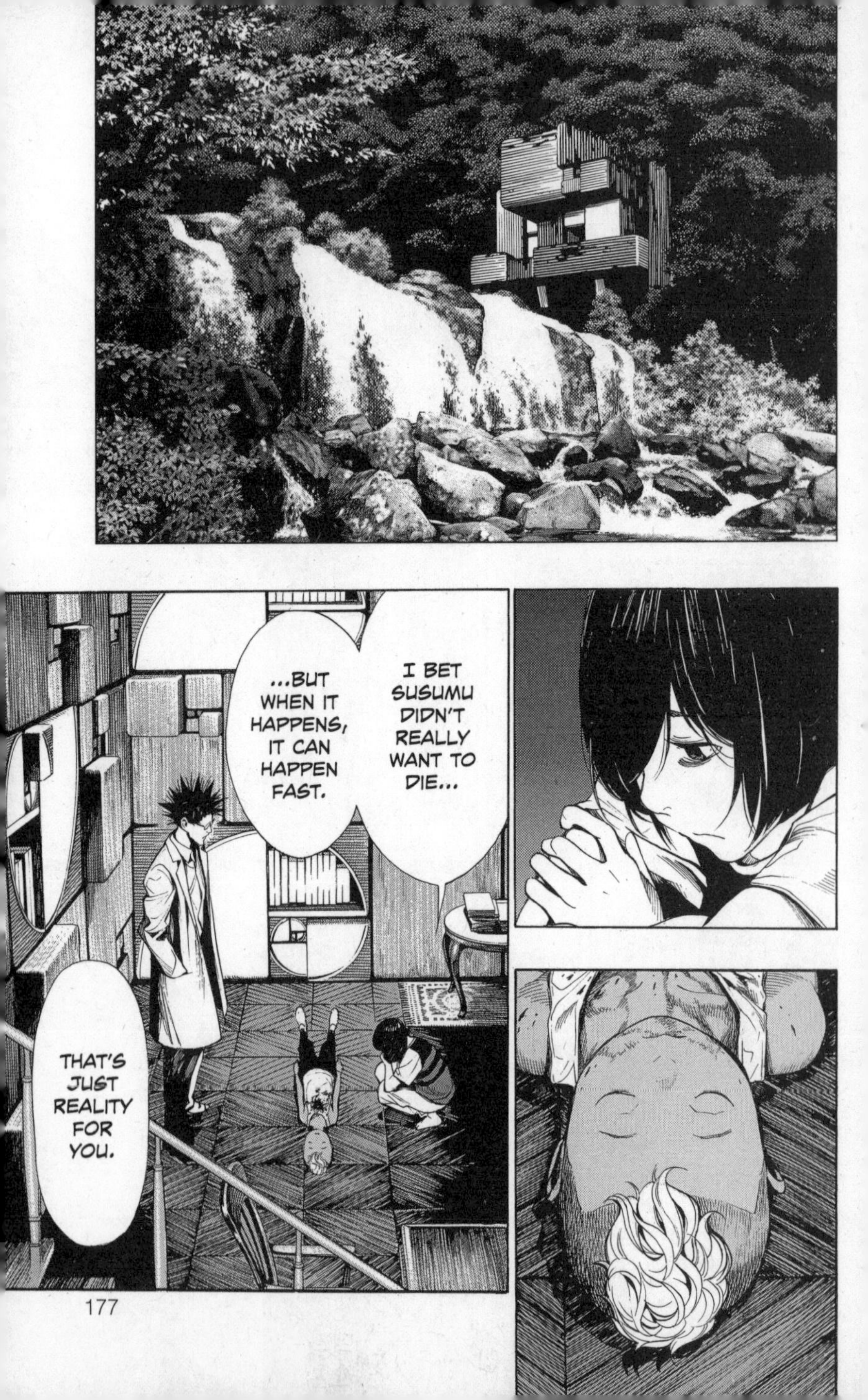
I BET SUSUMU DIDN'T REALLY WANT TO DIE...
...BUT WHEN IT HAPPENS, IT CAN HAPPEN FAST.
THAT'S JUST REALITY FOR YOU.

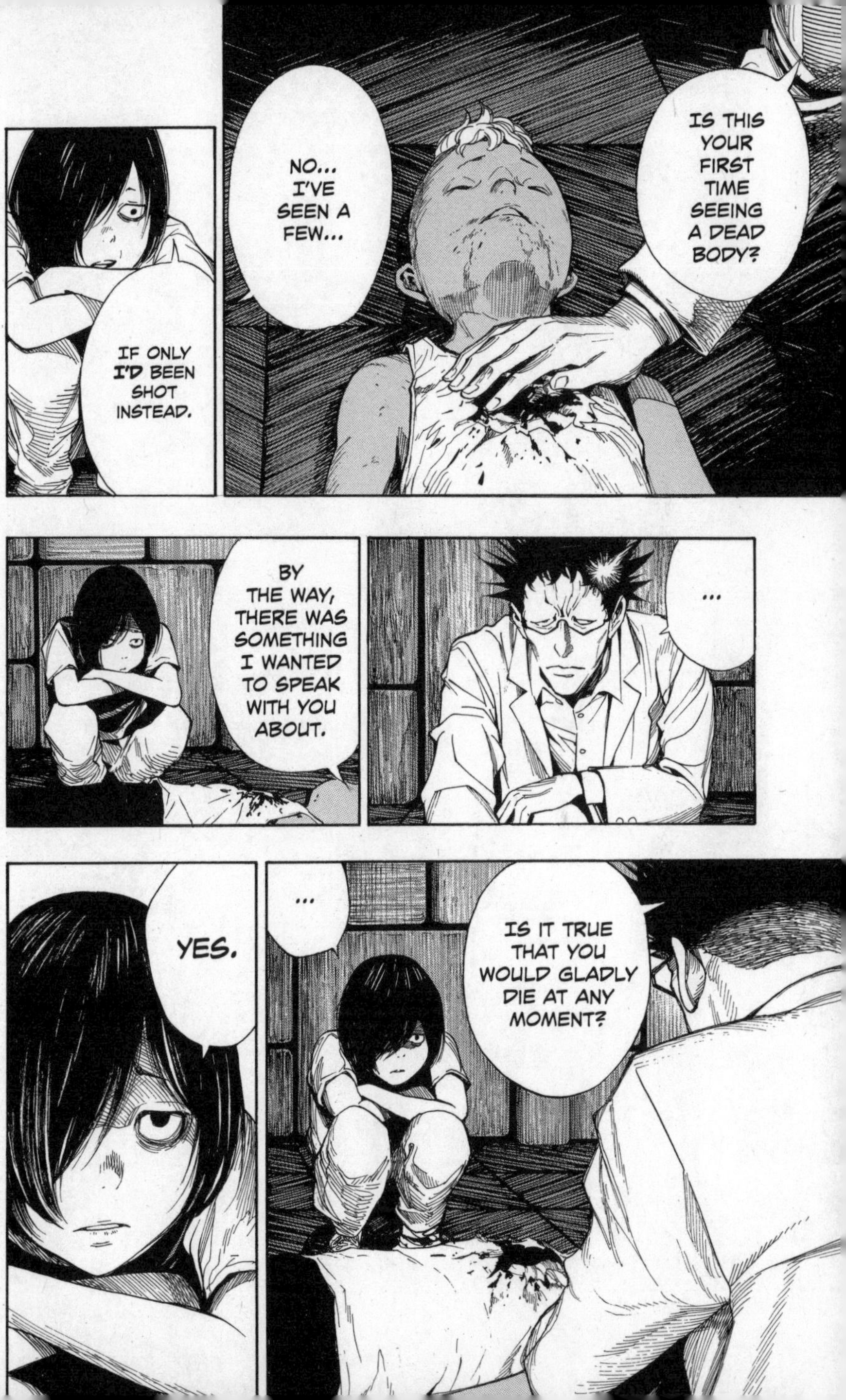
IS THIS YOUR FIRST TIME SEEING A DEAD BODY?
NO... I'VE SEEN A FEW...
IF ONLY I'D BEEN SHOT INSTEAD.
...
BY THE WAY, THERE WAS SOMETHING I WANTED TO SPEAK WITH YOU ABOUT.
IS IT TRUE THAT YOU WOULD GLADLY DIE AT ANY MOMENT?
...
YES.

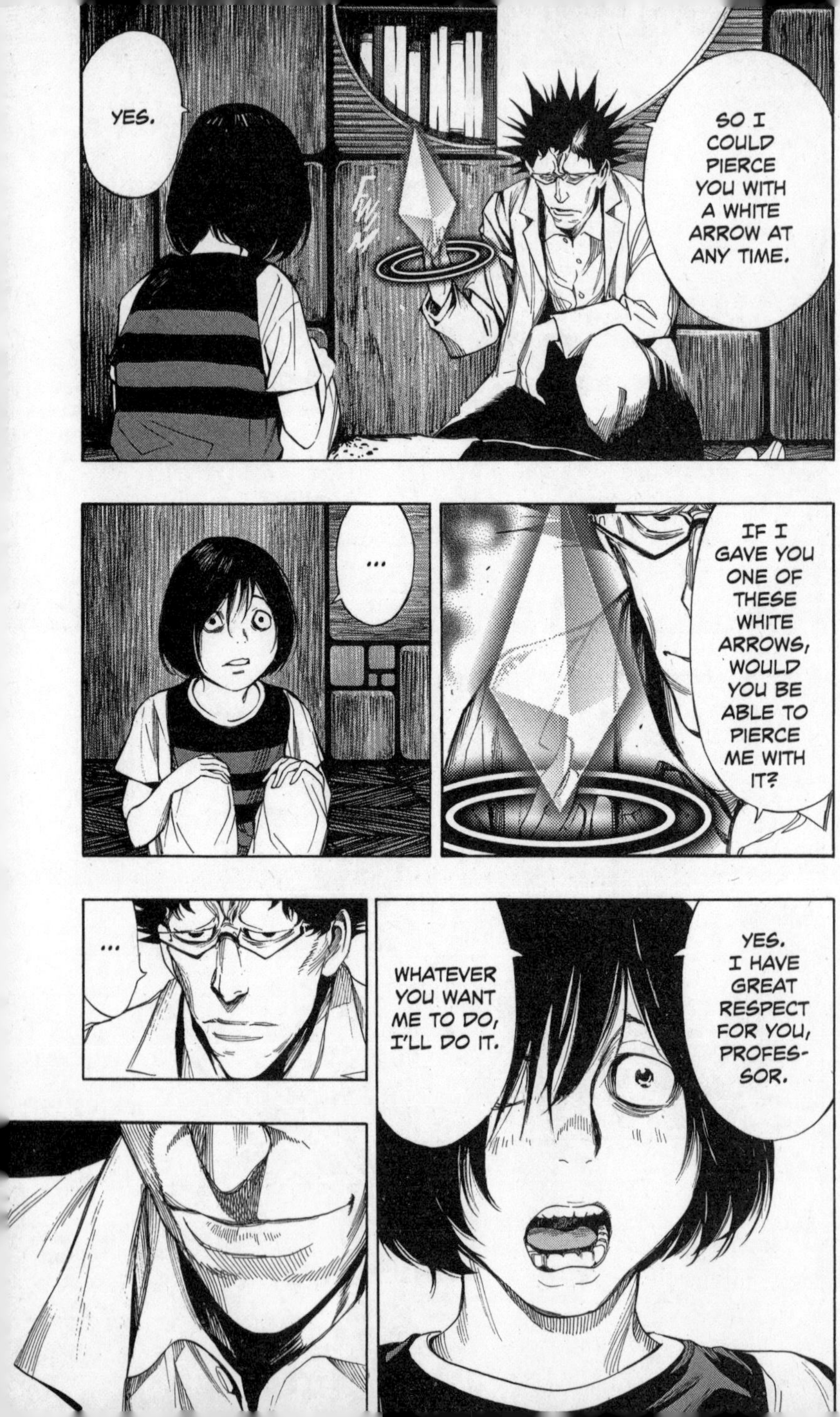
SO I COULD PIERCE YOU WITH A WHITE ARROW AT ANY TIME.
YES.
IF I GAVE YOU ONE OF THESE WHITE ARROWS, WOULD YOU BE ABLE TO PIERCE ME WITH IT?
...
YES. I HAVE GREAT RESPECT FOR YOU, PROFES-SOR.
WHATEVER YOU WANT ME TO DO, I'LL DO IT.
...

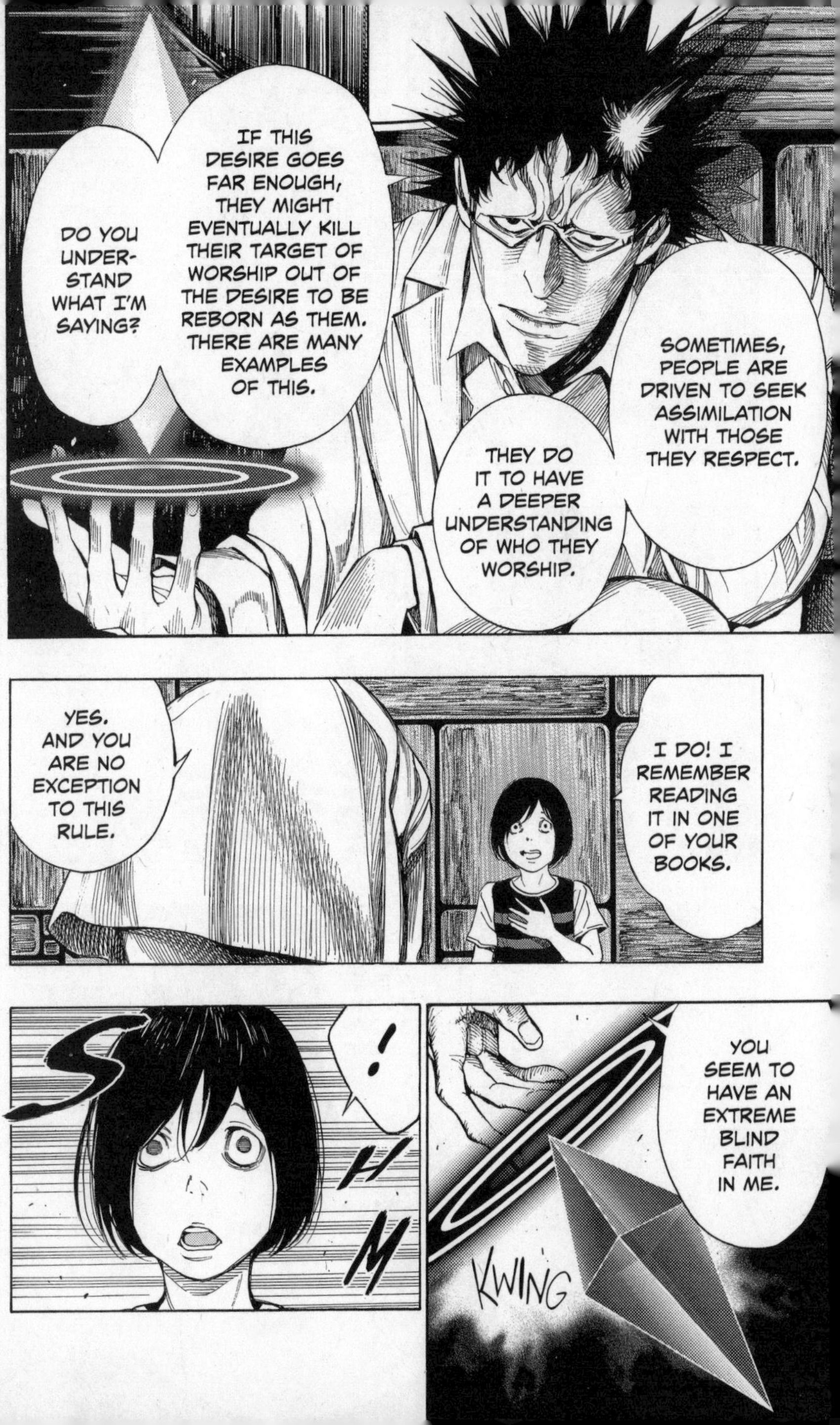
SOMETIMES, PEOPLE ARE DRIVEN TO SEEK ASSIMILATION WITH THOSE THEY RESPECT.
THEY DO IT TO HAVE A DEEPER UNDERSTANDING OF WHO THEY WORSHIP.
IF THIS DESIRE GOES FAR ENOUGH, THEY MIGHT EVENTUALLY KILL THEIR TARGET OF WORSHIP OUT OF THE DESIRE TO BE REBORN AS THEM. THERE ARE MANY EXAMPLES OF THIS.
DO YOU UNDER-STAND WHAT I'M SAYING?
I DO! I REMEMBER READING IT IN ONE OF YOUR BOOKS.
YES. AND YOU ARE NO EXCEPTION TO THIS RULE.
YOU SEEM TO HAVE AN EXTREME BLIND FAITH IN ME.
KWING
!
SHM

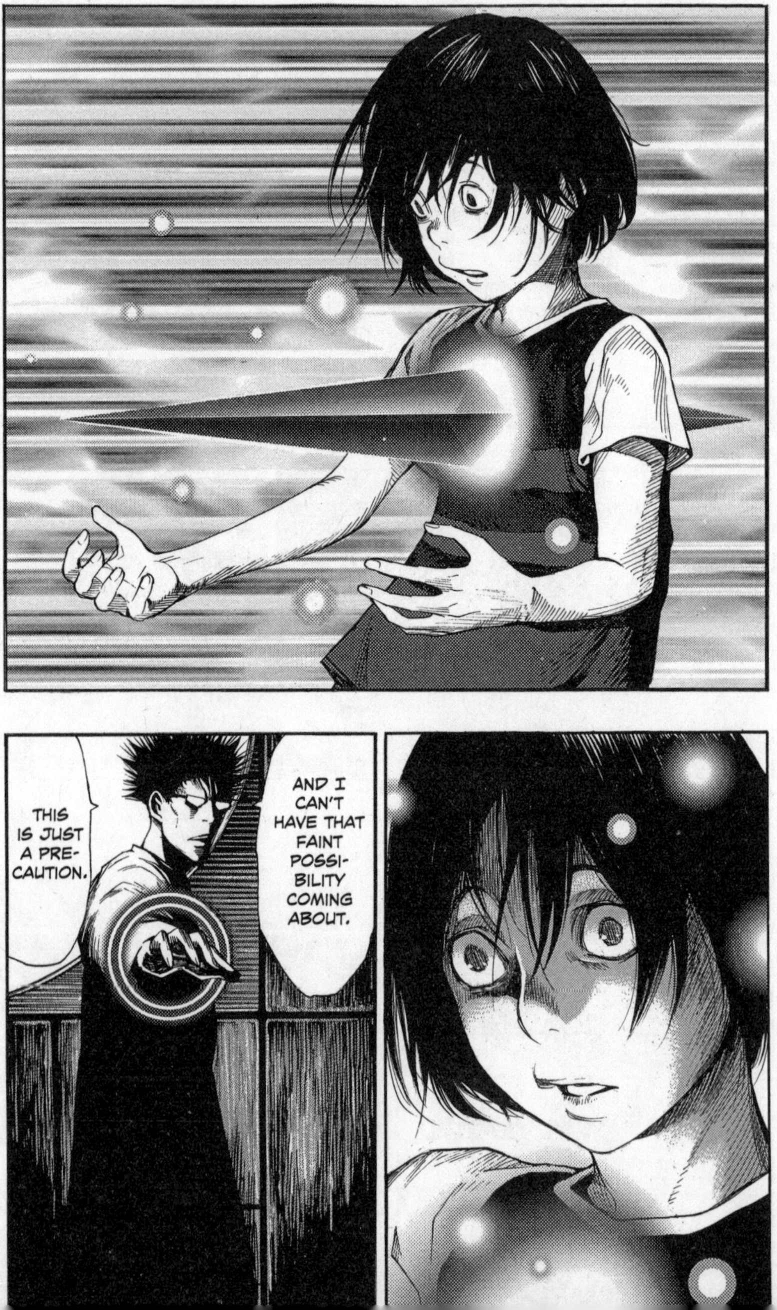
THIS IS JUST A PRE-CAUTION.
AND I CAN'T HAVE THAT FAINT POSSI-BILITY COMING ABOUT.

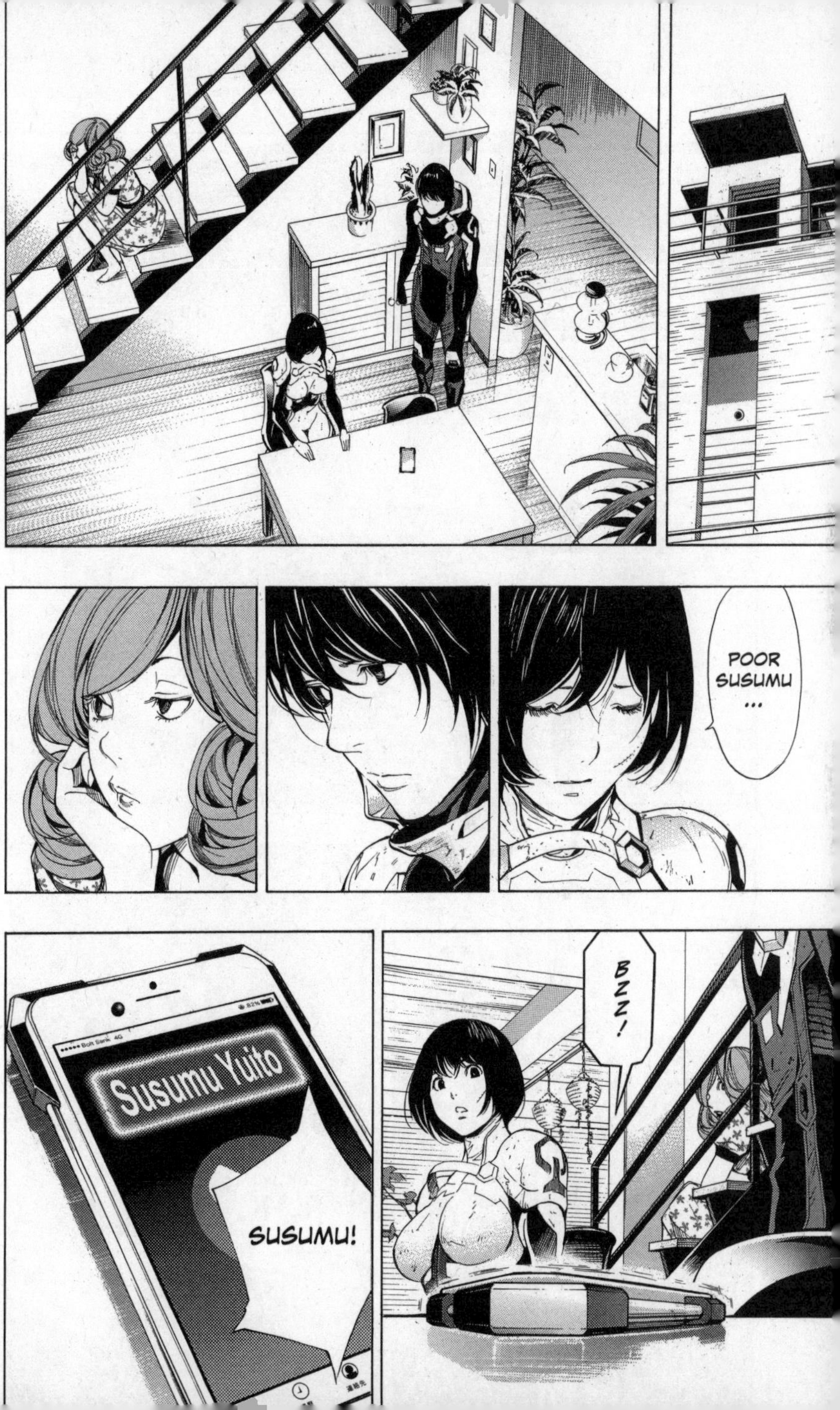
POOR SUSUMU ...
BZZ!
Susumu Yuito
SUSUMU!

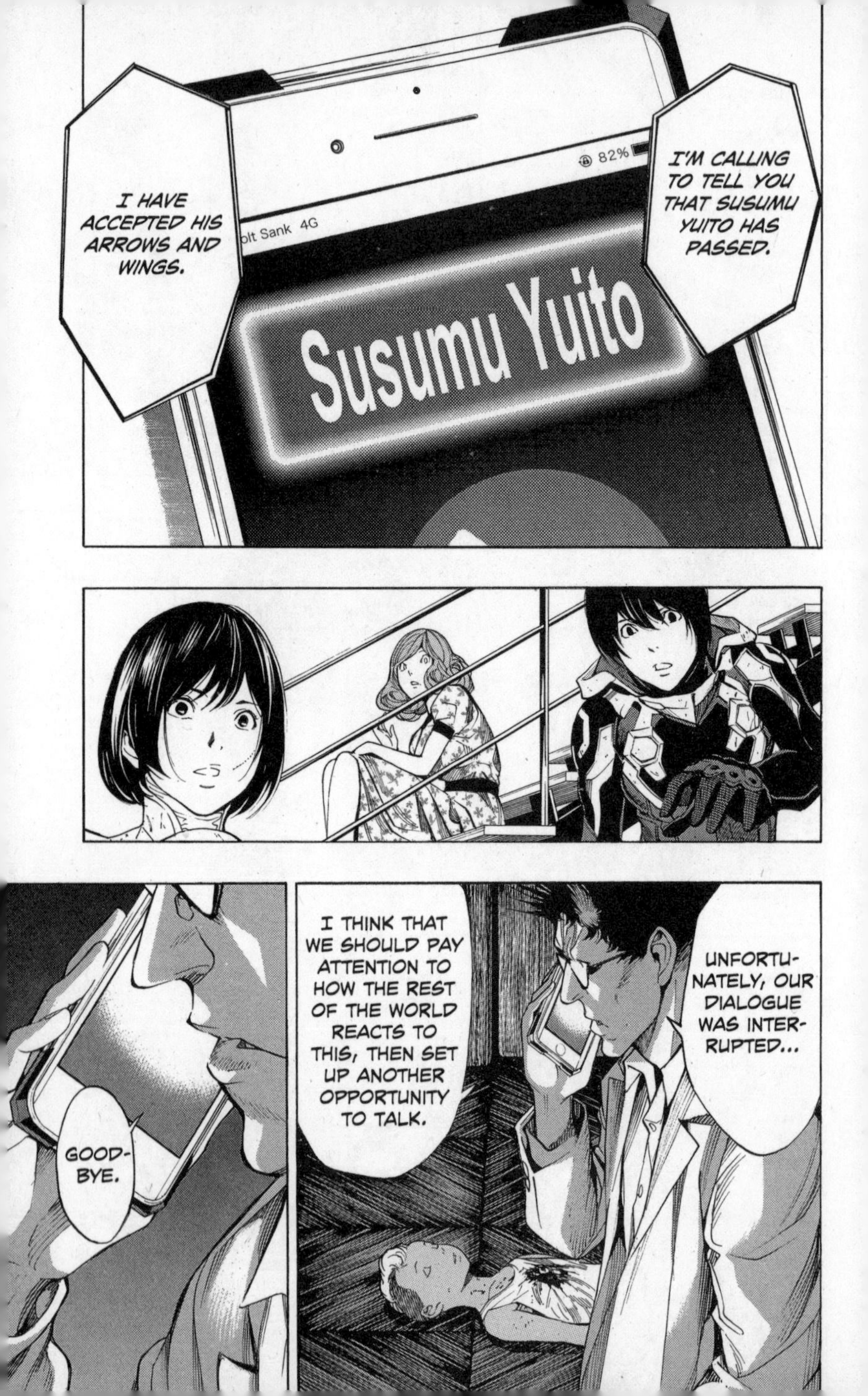
I'M CALLING TO TELL YOU THAT SUSUMU YUITO HAS PASSED.
82%
olt Sank 4G
Susumu Yuito
I HAVE ACCEPTED HIS ARROWS AND WINGS.
UNFORTU-NATELY, OUR DIALOGUE WAS INTER-RUPTED...
I THINK THAT WE SHOULD PAY ATTENTION TO HOW THE REST OF THE WORLD REACTS TO THIS, THEN SET UP ANOTHER OPPORTUNITY TO TALK.
GOOD-BYE.

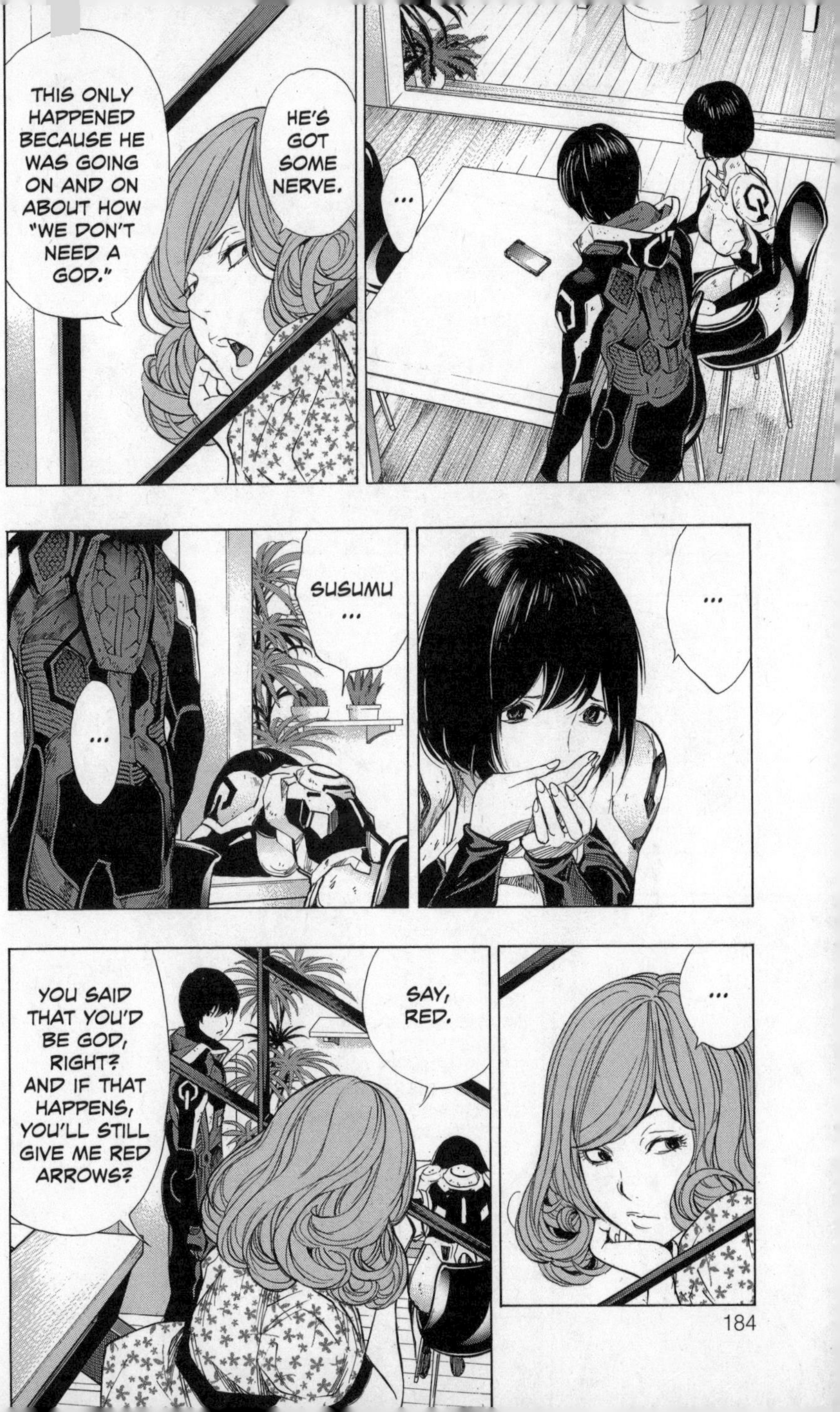
...
HE'S GOT SOME NERVE.
THIS ONLY HAPPENED BECAUSE HE WAS GOING ON AND ON ABOUT HOW "WE DON'T NEED A GOD."
...
SUSUMU ...
...
...
SAY, RED.
YOU SAID THAT YOU'D BE GOD, RIGHT? AND IF THAT HAPPENS, YOU'LL STILL GIVE ME RED ARROWS?

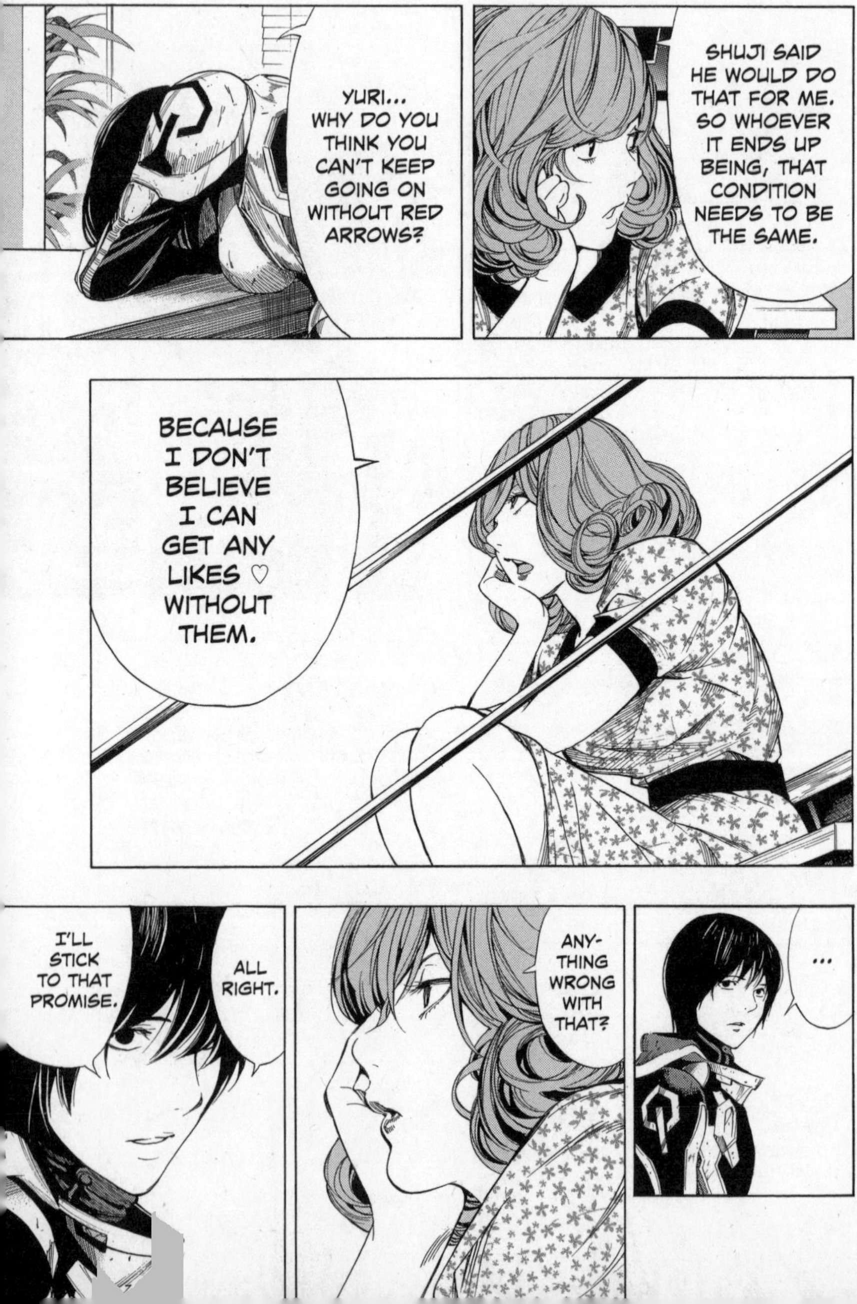
SHUJI SAID HE WOULD DO THAT FOR ME. SO WHOEVER IT ENDS UP BEING, THAT CONDITION NEEDS TO BE THE SAME.
YURI... WHY DO YOU THINK YOU CAN'T KEEP GOING ON WITHOUT RED ARROWS?
BECAUSE I DON'T BELIEVE I CAN GET ANY LIKES ♡ WITHOUT THEM.
...
ANY-THING WRONG WITH THAT?
ALL RIGHT.
I'LL STICK TO THAT PROMISE.

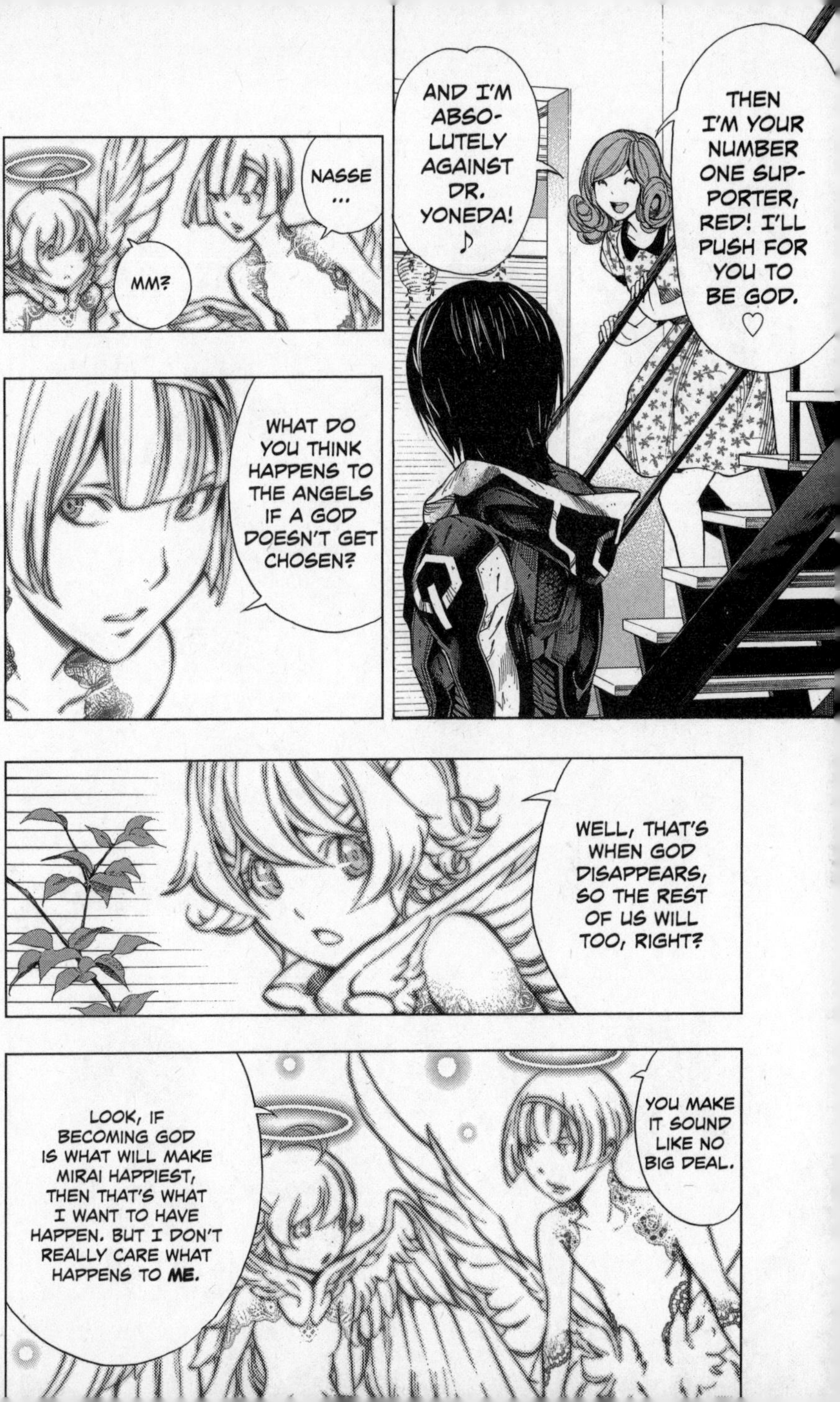
THEN I'M YOUR NUMBER ONE SUPPORTER, RED! I'LL PUSH FOR YOU TO BE GOD. ♡
AND I'M ABSOLUTELY AGAINST DR. YONEDA! ♪
NASSE ...
MM?
WHAT DO YOU THINK HAPPENS TO THE ANGELS IF A GOD DOESN'T GET CHOSEN?
WELL, THAT'S WHEN GOD DISAPPEARS, SO THE REST OF US WILL TOO, RIGHT?
YOU MAKE IT SOUND LIKE NO BIG DEAL.
LOOK, IF BECOMING GOD IS WHAT WILL MAKE MIRAI HAPPIEST, THEN THAT'S WHAT I WANT TO HAVE HAPPEN. BUT I DON'T REALLY CARE WHAT HAPPENS TO ME.

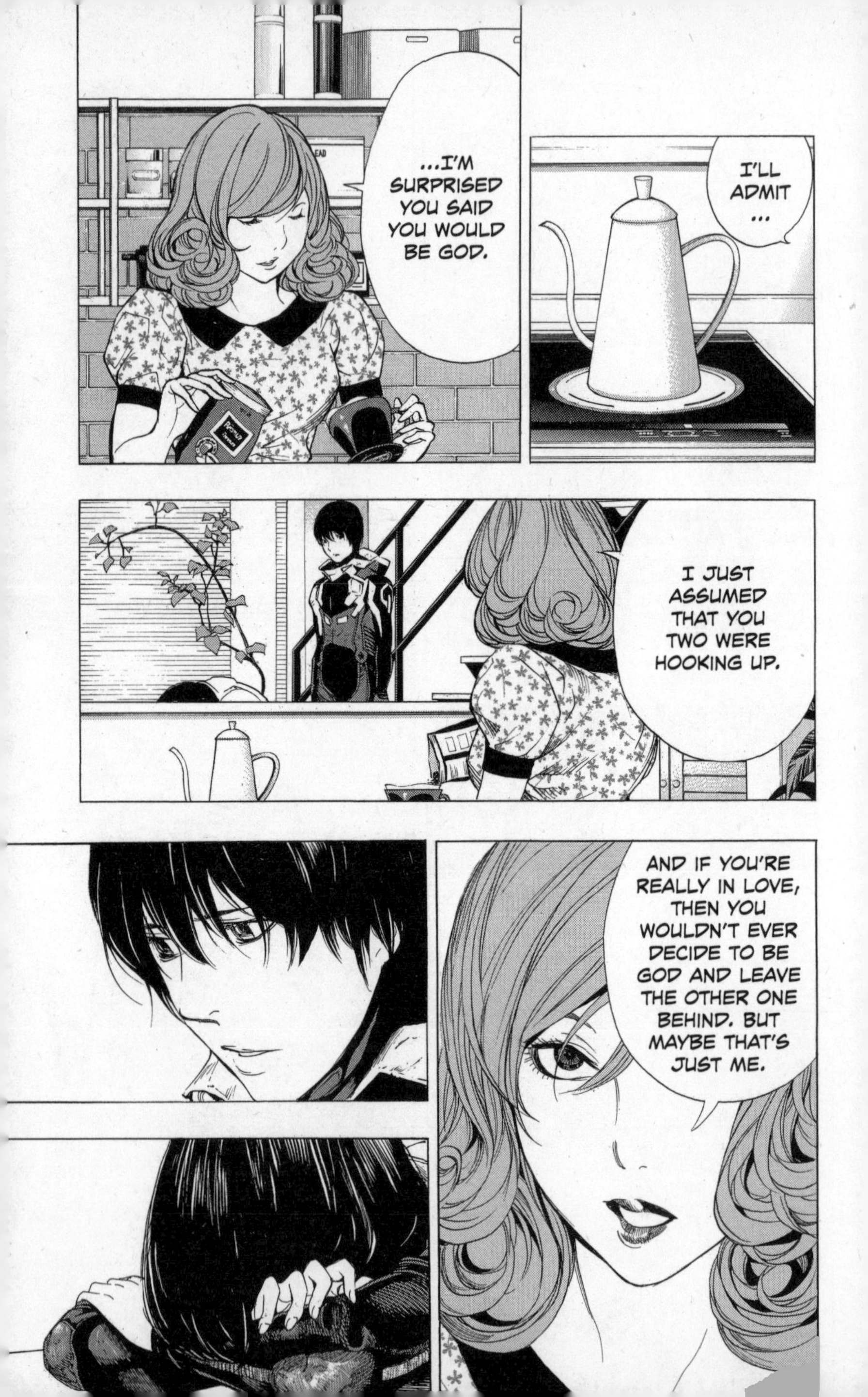
I'LL ADMIT ...
...I'M SURPRISED YOU SAID YOU WOULD BE GOD.
I JUST ASSUMED THAT YOU TWO WERE HOOKING UP.
AND IF YOU'RE REALLY IN LOVE, THEN YOU WOULDN'T EVER DECIDE TO BE GOD AND LEAVE THE OTHER ONE BEHIND. BUT MAYBE THAT'S JUST ME.

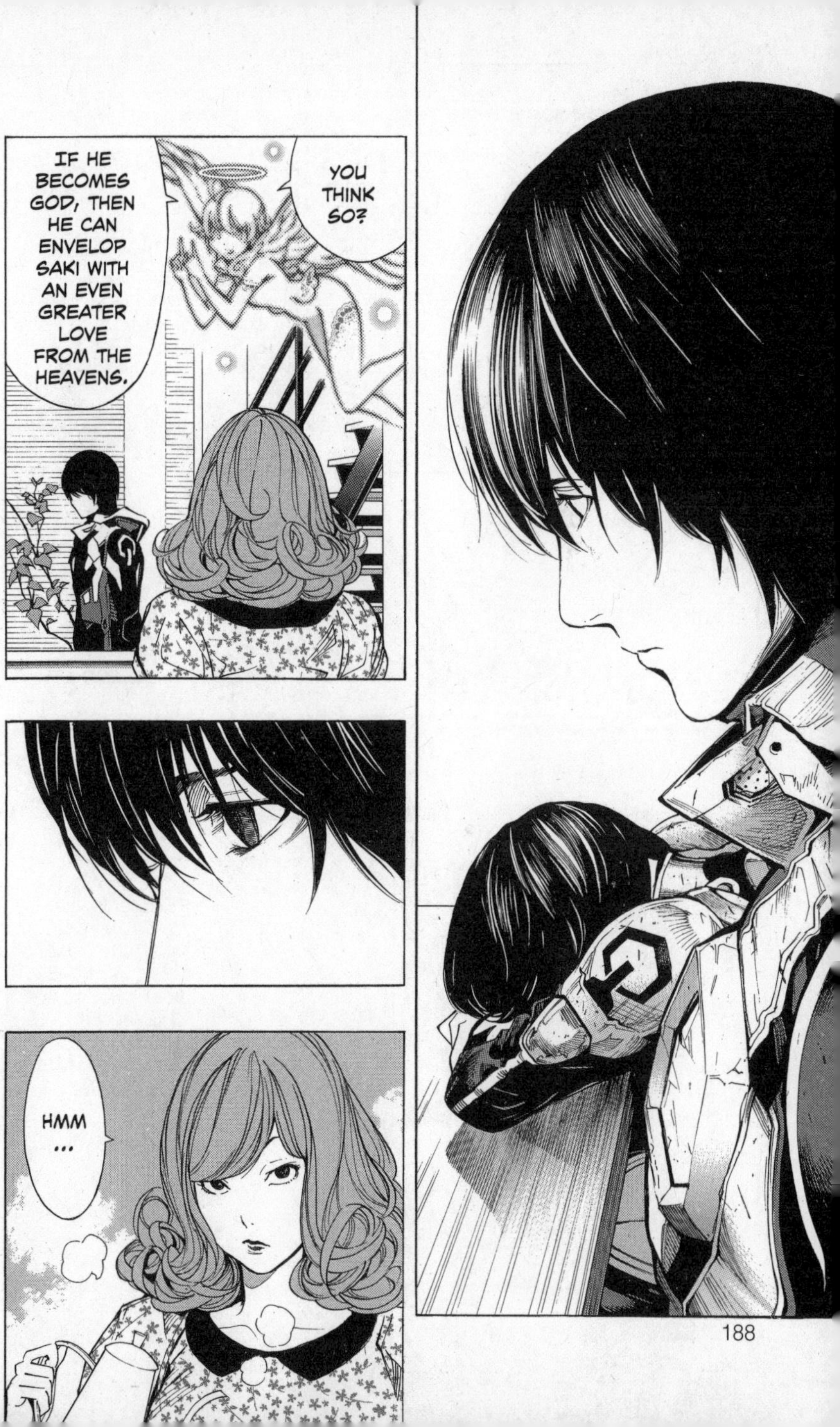
IF HE BECOMES GOD, THEN HE CAN ENVELOP SAKI WITH AN EVEN GREATER LOVE FROM THE HEAVENS.
YOU THINK SO?
HMM ...

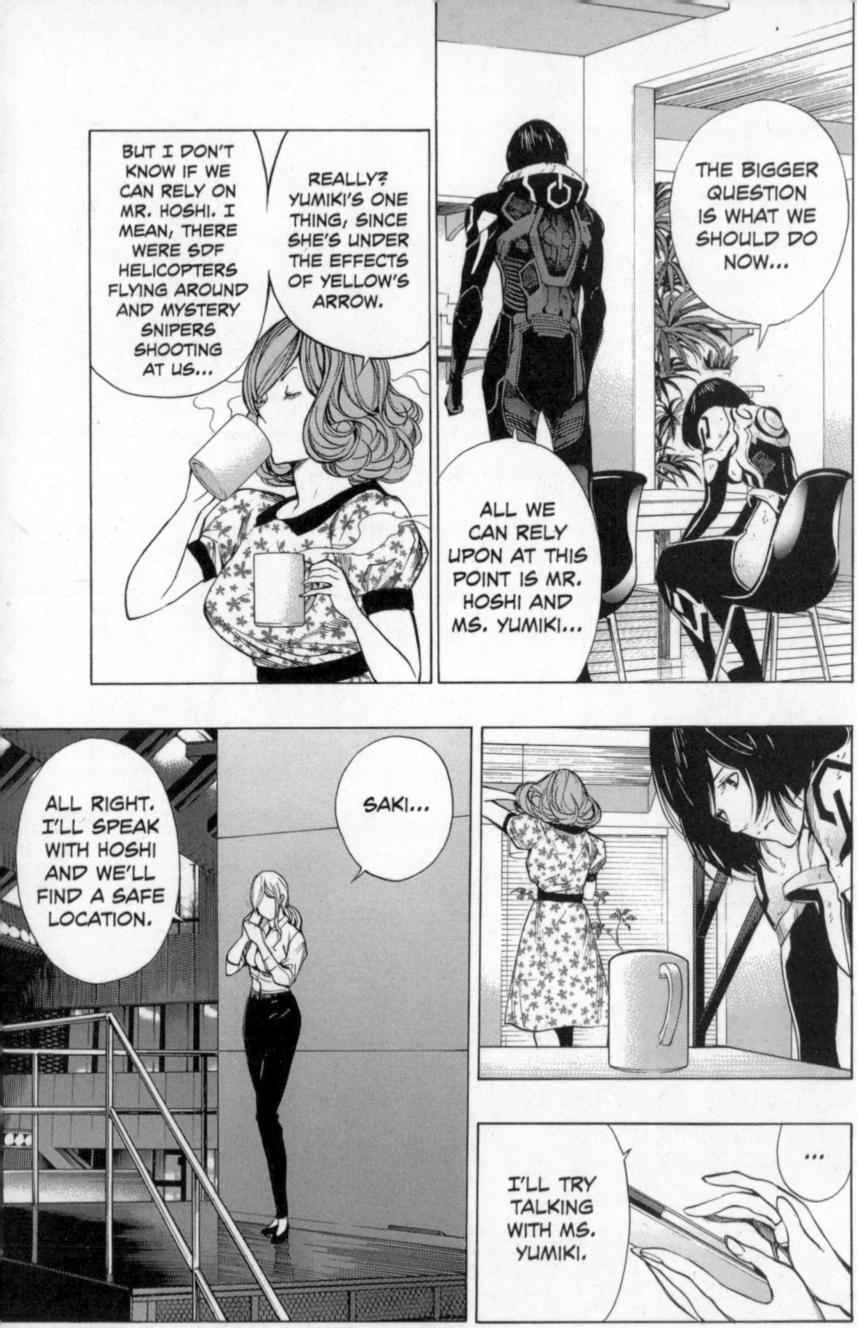
THE BIGGER QUESTION IS WHAT WE SHOULD DO NOW...
ALL WE CAN RELY UPON AT THIS POINT IS MR. HOSHI AND MS. YUMIKI...
REALLY? YUMIKI'S ONE THING, SINCE SHE'S UNDER THE EFFECTS OF YELLOW'S ARROW.
BUT I DON'T KNOW IF WE CAN RELY ON MR. HOSHI. I MEAN, THERE WERE SDF HELICOPTERS FLYING AROUND AND MYSTERY SNIPERS SHOOTING AT US...
...
I'LL TRY TALKING WITH MS. YUMIKI.
SAKI...
ALL RIGHT. I'LL SPEAK WITH HOSHI AND WE'LL FIND A SAFE LOCATION.

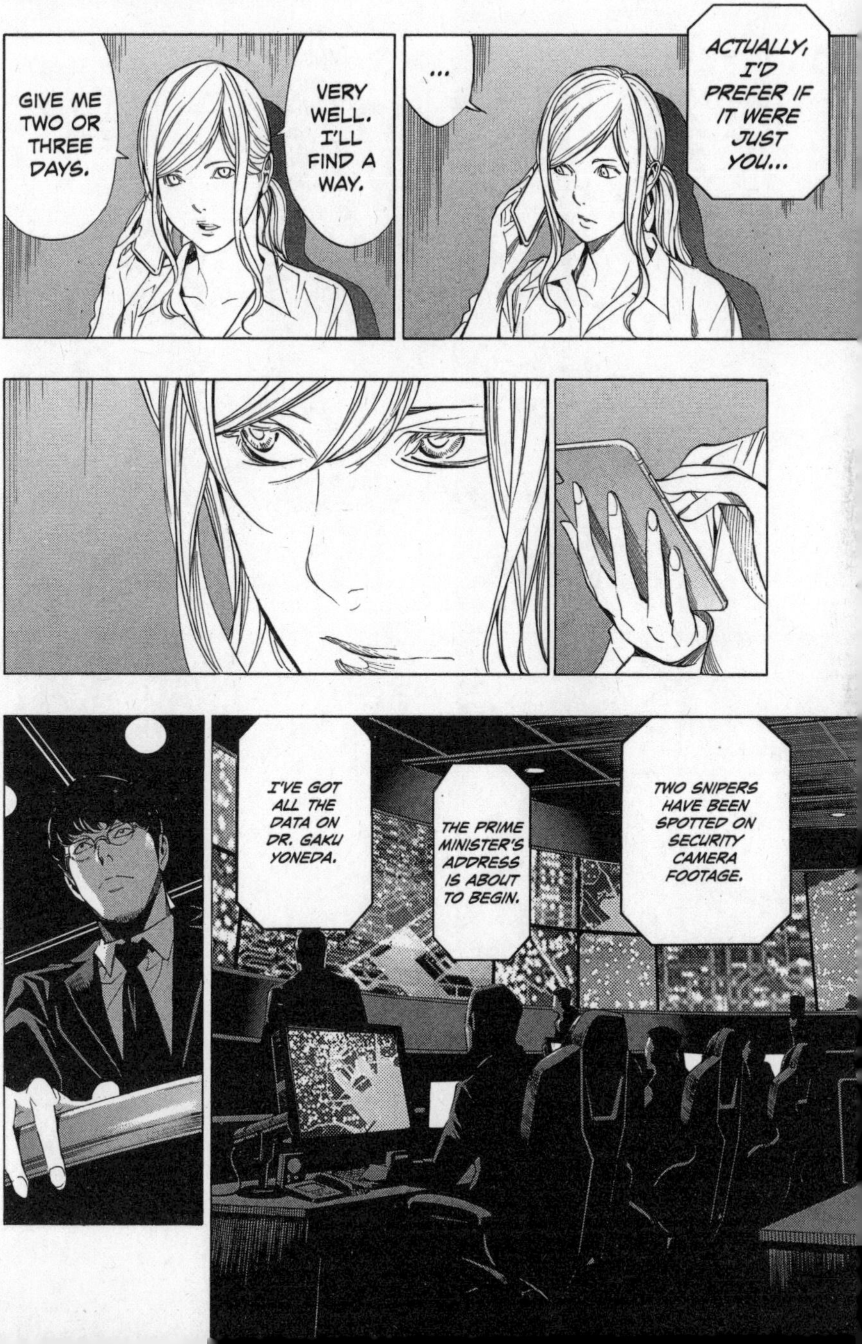
ACTUALLY, I'D PREFER IF IT WERE JUST YOU...
...
VERY WELL. I'LL FIND A WAY.
GIVE ME TWO OR THREE DAYS.
TWO SNIPERS HAVE BEEN SPOTTED ON SECURITY CAMERA FOOTAGE.
THE PRIME MINISTER'S ADDRESS IS ABOUT TO BEGIN.
I'VE GOT ALL THE DATA ON DR. GAKU YONEDA.

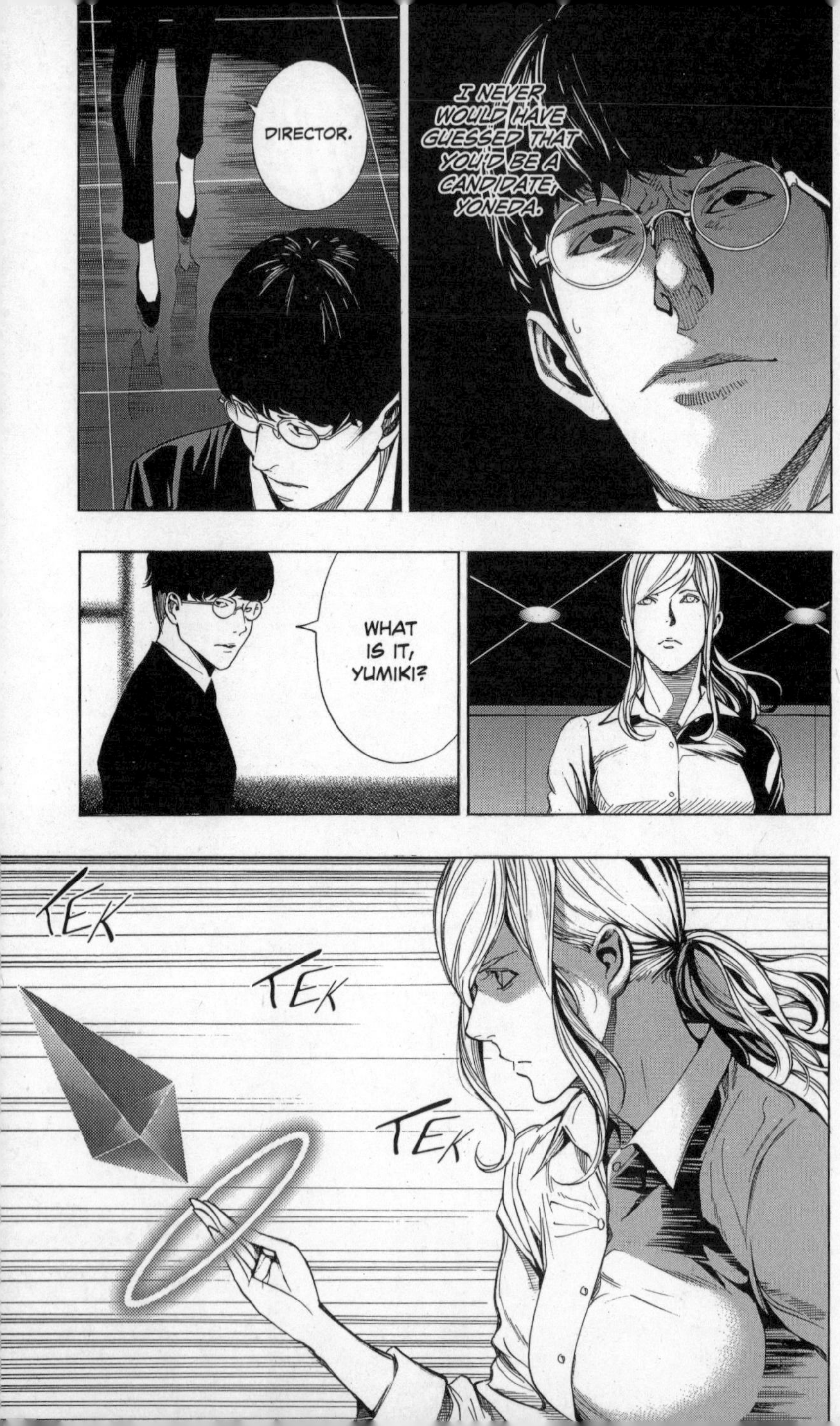
I NEVER WOULD HAVE GUESSED THAT YOU'D BE A CANDIDATE, YONEDA.
DIRECTOR.
WHAT IS IT, YUMIKI?
TEK
TEK
TEK

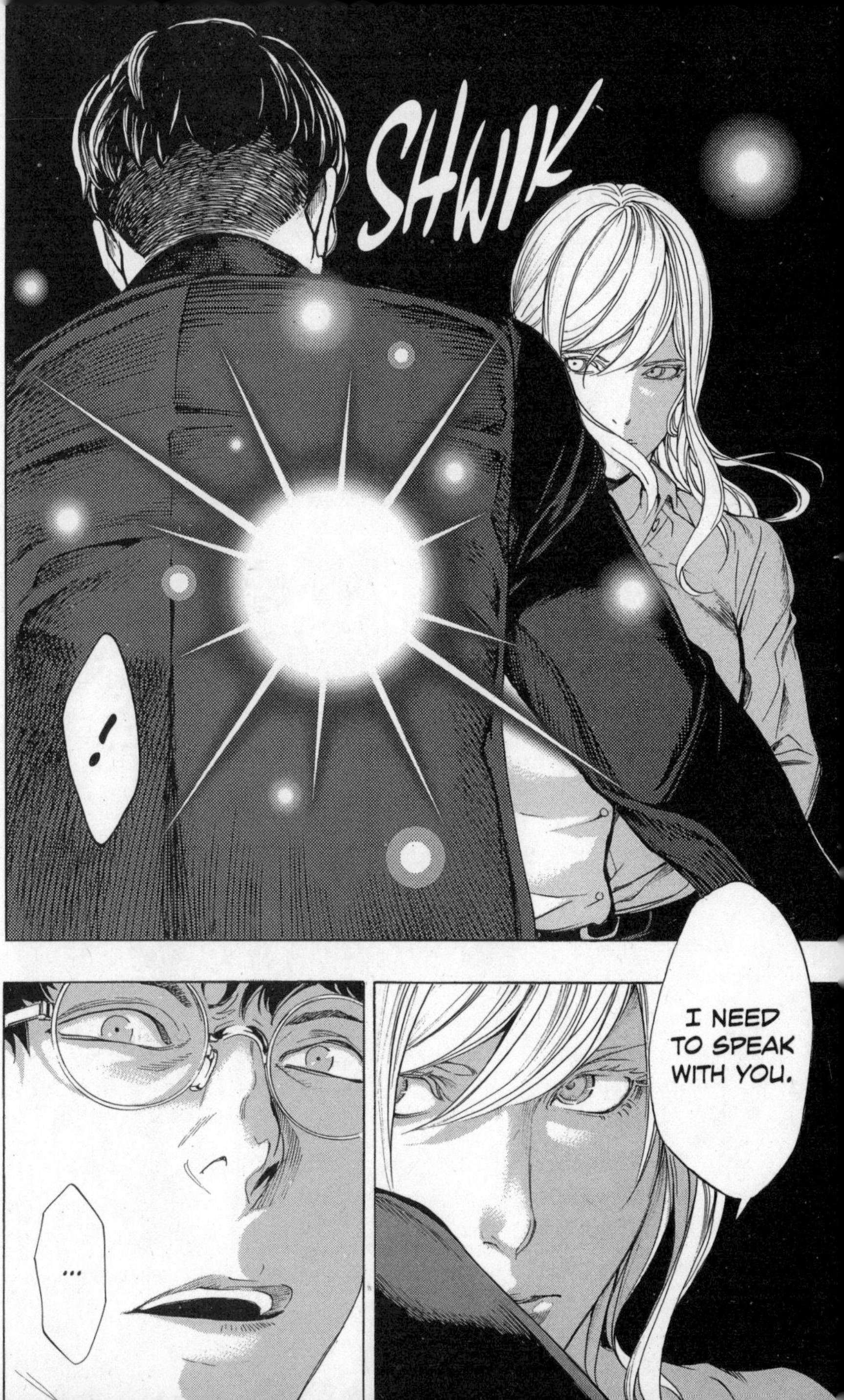
SHWIK
!
I NEED TO SPEAK WITH YOU.
...

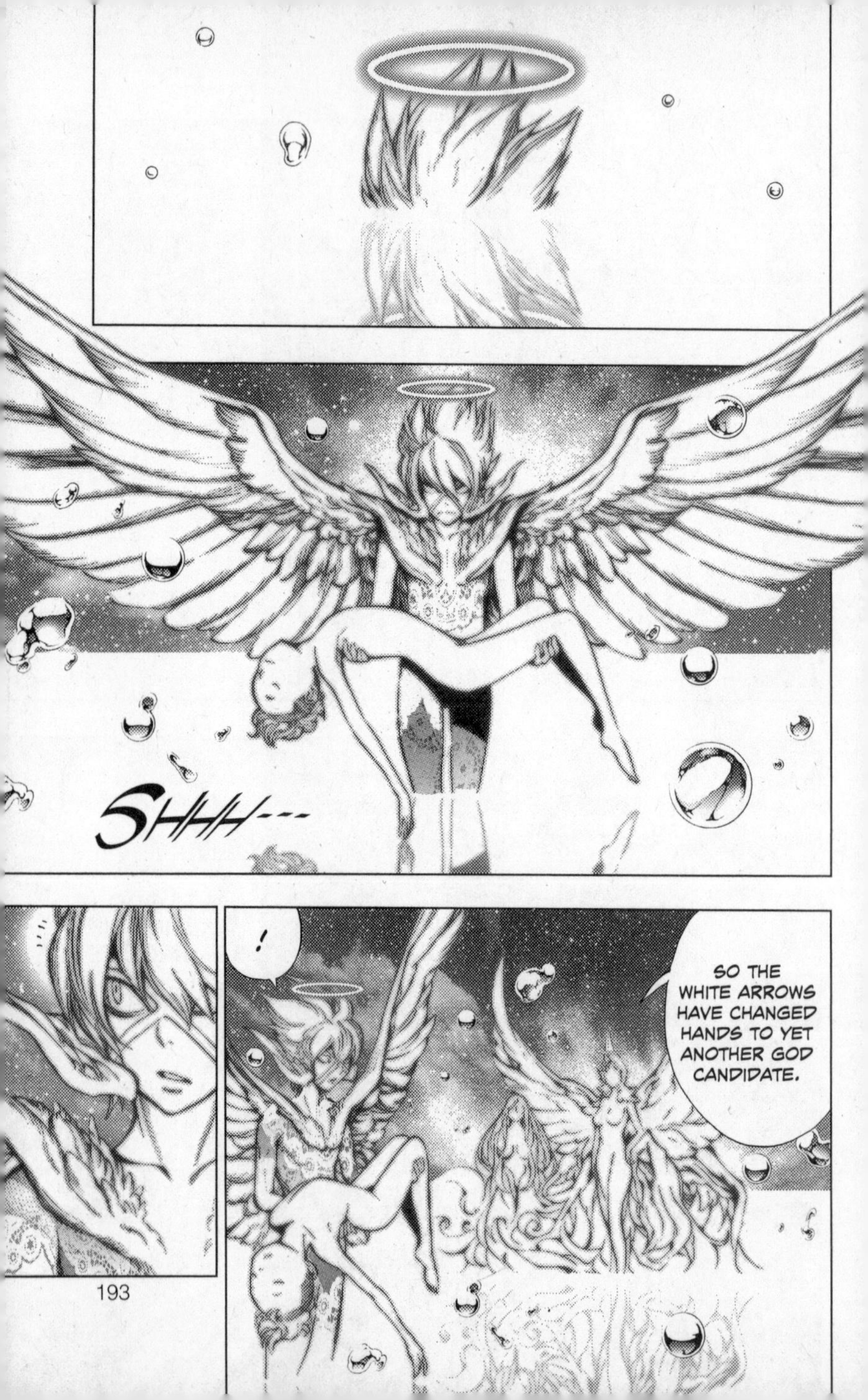
SHHH---
SO THE WHITE ARROWS HAVE CHANGED HANDS TO YET ANOTHER GOD CANDIDATE.
!
!!!

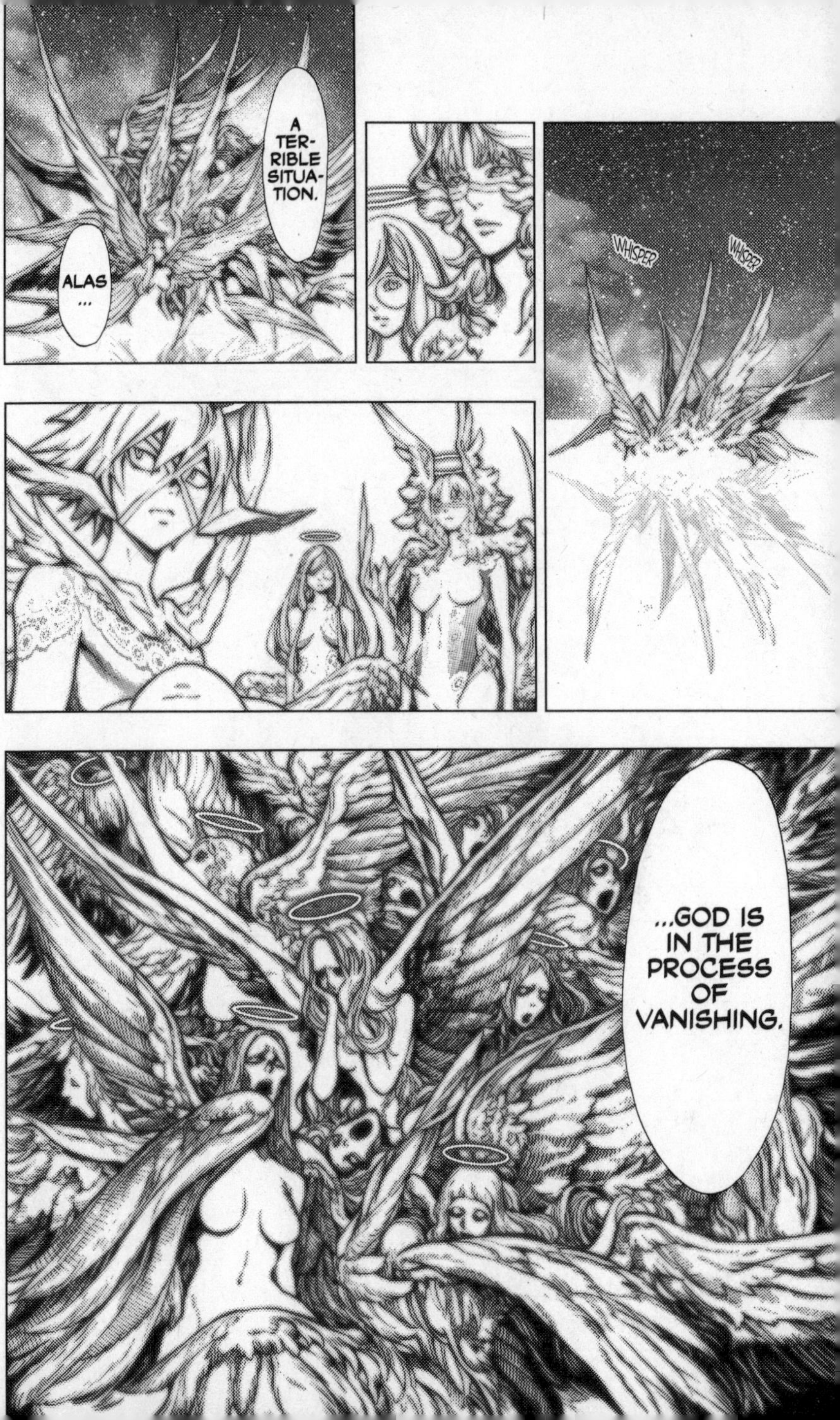
WHISPER
WHISPER
A TERRIBLE SITUATION.
ALAS...
...GOD IS IN THE PROCESS OF VANISHING.

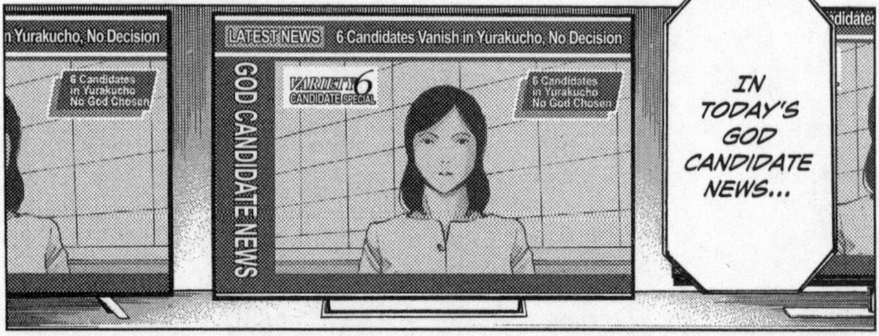
IN TODAY'S GOD CANDIDATE NEWS...
LATEST NEWS 6 Candidates Vanish in Yurakucho, No Decision
6 Candidates in Yurakucho No God Chosen
VARIETY 6 CANDIDATE SPECIAL
GOD CANDIDATE NEWS
6 Candidates in Yurakucho No God Chosen
n Yurakucho, No Decision

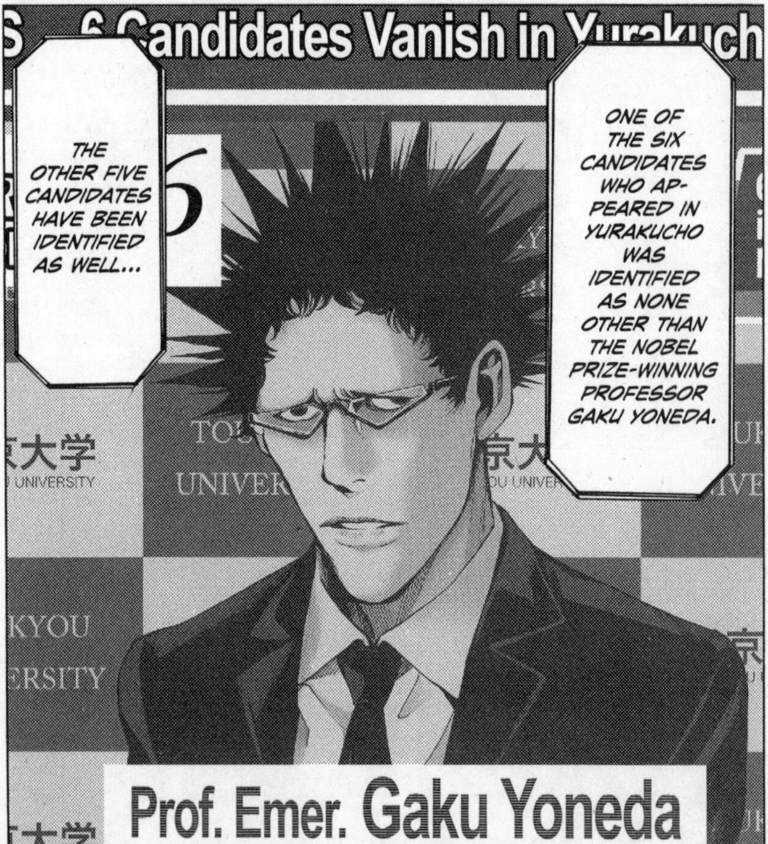
Candidates Vanish in
ONE OF THE SIX CANDIDATES WHO APPEARED IN YURAKUCHO WAS IDENTIFIED AS NONE OTHER THAN THE NOBEL PRIZE-WINNING PROFESSOR GAKU YONEDA.
THE OTHER FIVE CANDIDATES HAVE BEEN IDENTIFIED AS WELL...
Prof. Emer. Gaku Yoneda

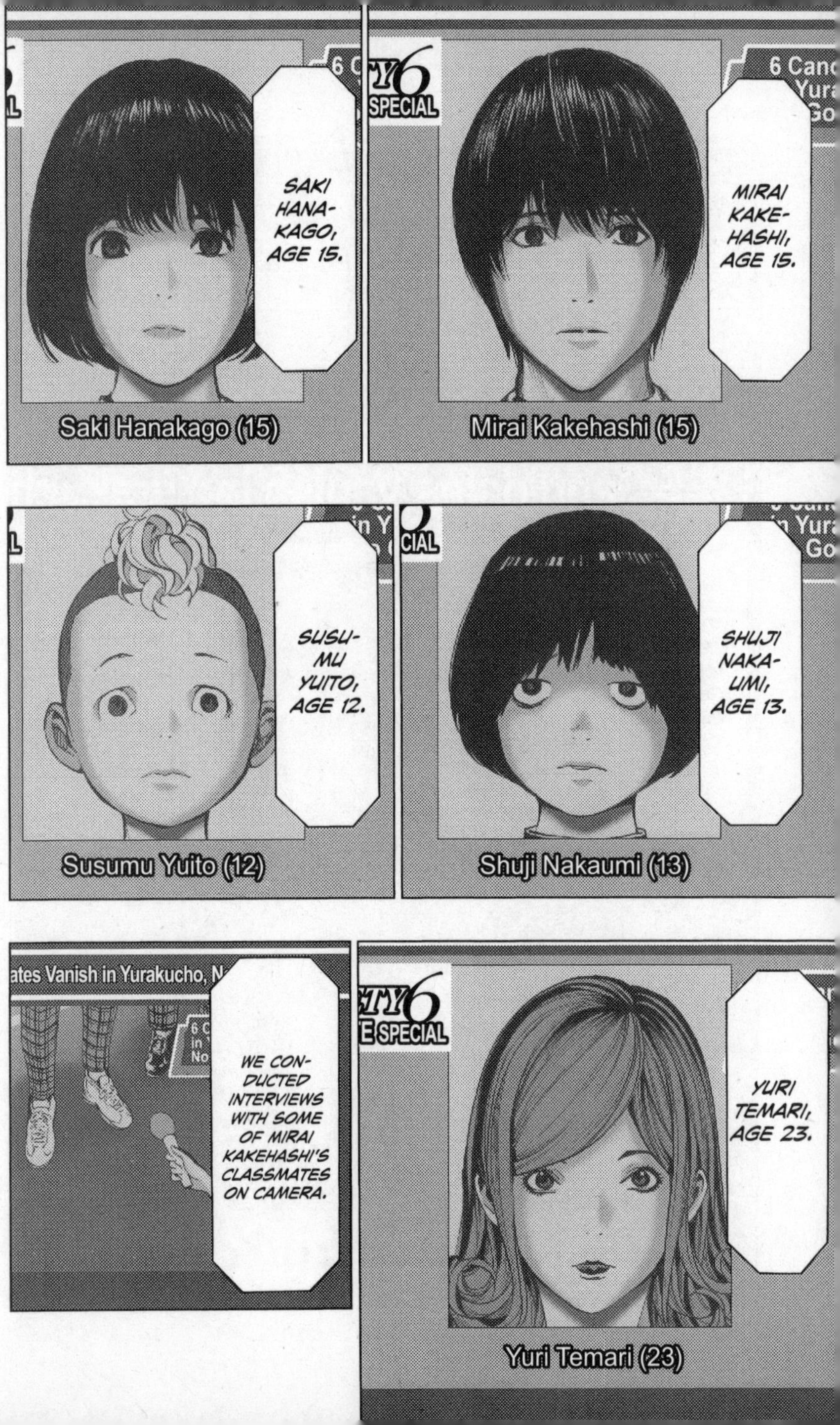
MIRAI KAKE-HASHI, AGE 15.
Mirai Kakehashi (15)
SAKI HANA-KAGO, AGE 15.
Saki Hanakago (15)
SHUJI NAKA-UMI, AGE 13.
Shuji Nakaumi (13)
SUSU-MU YUITO, AGE 12.
Susumu Yuito (12)
YURI TEMARI, AGE 23.
Yuri Temari (23)
WE CON-DUCTED INTERVIEWS WITH SOME OF MIRAI KAKEHASHI'S CLASSMATES ON CAMERA.

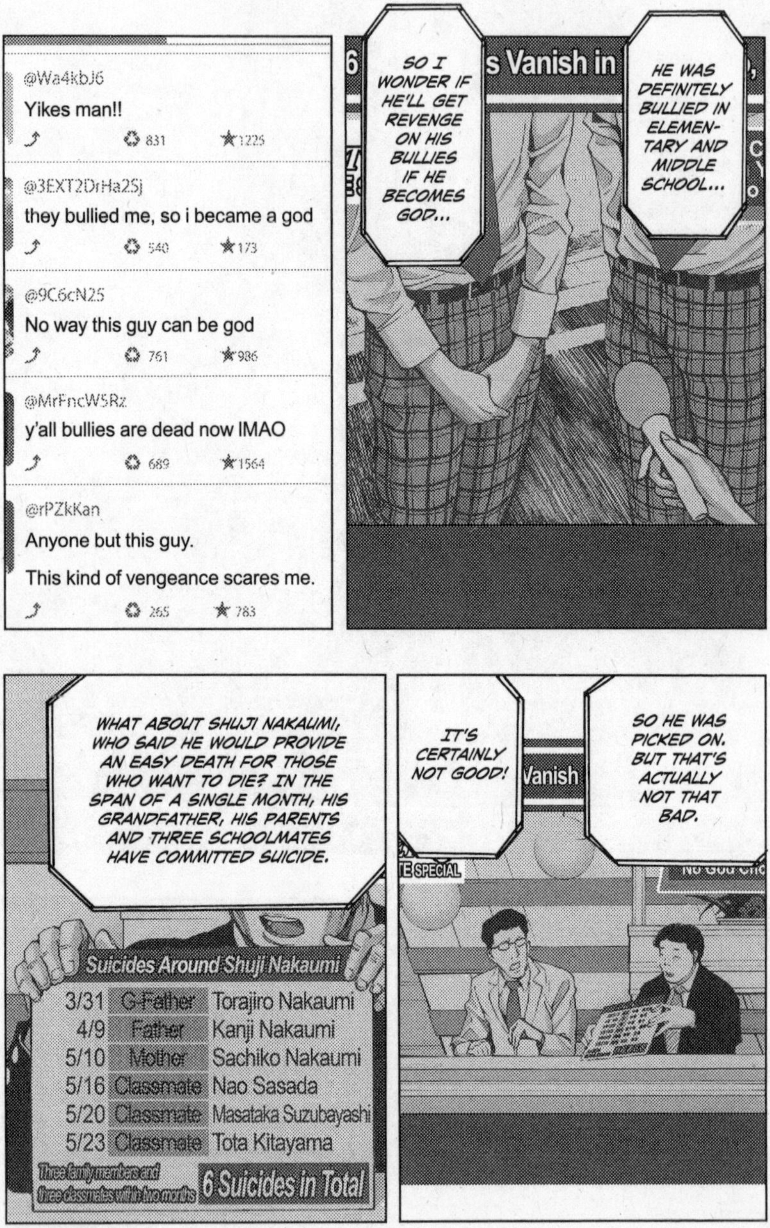
s Vanish in
HE WAS DEFINITELY BULLIED IN ELEMENTARY AND MIDDLE SCHOOL...
SO I WONDER IF HE'LL GET REVENGE ON HIS BULLIES IF HE BECOMES GOD...
@Wa4kbJ6
Yikes man!!
831 1225
@3EXT2DrHa2Sj
they bullied me, so i became a god
540 173
@9C6cN25
No way this guy can be god
761 986
@MrFncW5Rz
y'all bullies are dead now lMAO
689 1564
@rPZkKan
Anyone but this guy.
This kind of vengeance scares me.
265 783
SO HE WAS PICKED ON. BUT THAT'S ACTUALLY NOT THAT BAD.
IT'S CERTAINLY NOT GOOD!
Vanish
WHAT ABOUT SHUJI NAKAUMI, WHO SAID HE WOULD PROVIDE AN EASY DEATH FOR THOSE WHO WANT TO DIE? IN THE SPAN OF A SINGLE MONTH, HIS GRANDFATHER, HIS PARENTS AND THREE SCHOOLMATES HAVE COMMITTED SUICIDE.
Suicides Around Shuji Nakaumi
3/31 G-Father Torajiro Nakaumi
4/9 Father Kanji Nakaumi
5/10 Mother Sachiko Nakaumi
5/16 Classmate Nao Sasada
5/20 Classmate Masataka Suzubayashi
5/23 Classmate Tota Kitayama
Three family members and three classmates within two months
6 Suicides in Total

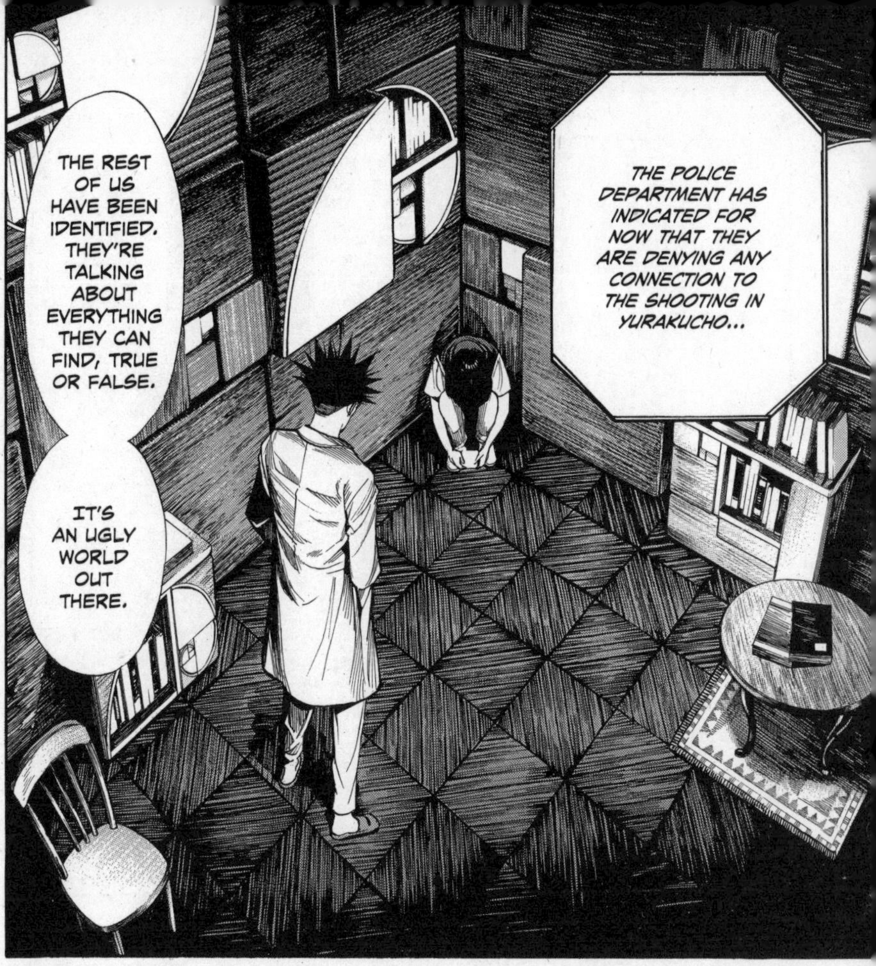
THE POLICE DEPARTMENT HAS INDICATED FOR NOW THAT THEY ARE DENYING ANY CONNECTION TO THE SHOOTING IN YURAKUCHO...
THE REST OF US HAVE BEEN IDENTIFIED. THEY'RE TALKING ABOUT EVERYTHING THEY CAN FIND, TRUE OR FALSE.
IT'S AN UGLY WORLD OUT THERE.

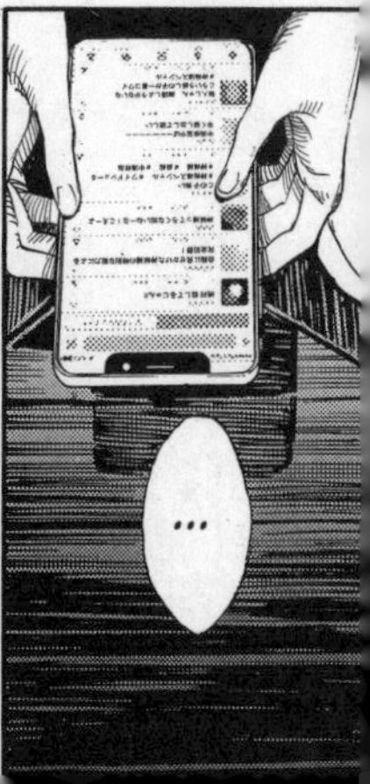
...

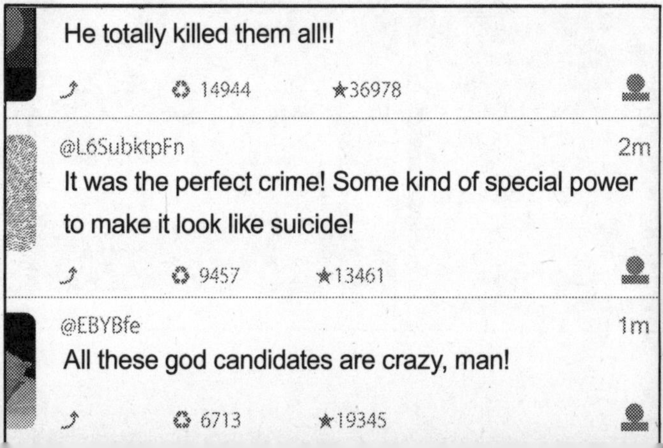
He totally killed them all!!
14944
36978
@L6SubktpFn
2m
It was the perfect crime! Some kind of special power to make it look like suicide!
9457
13461
@EBYBfe
1m
All these god candidates are crazy, man!
6713
19345

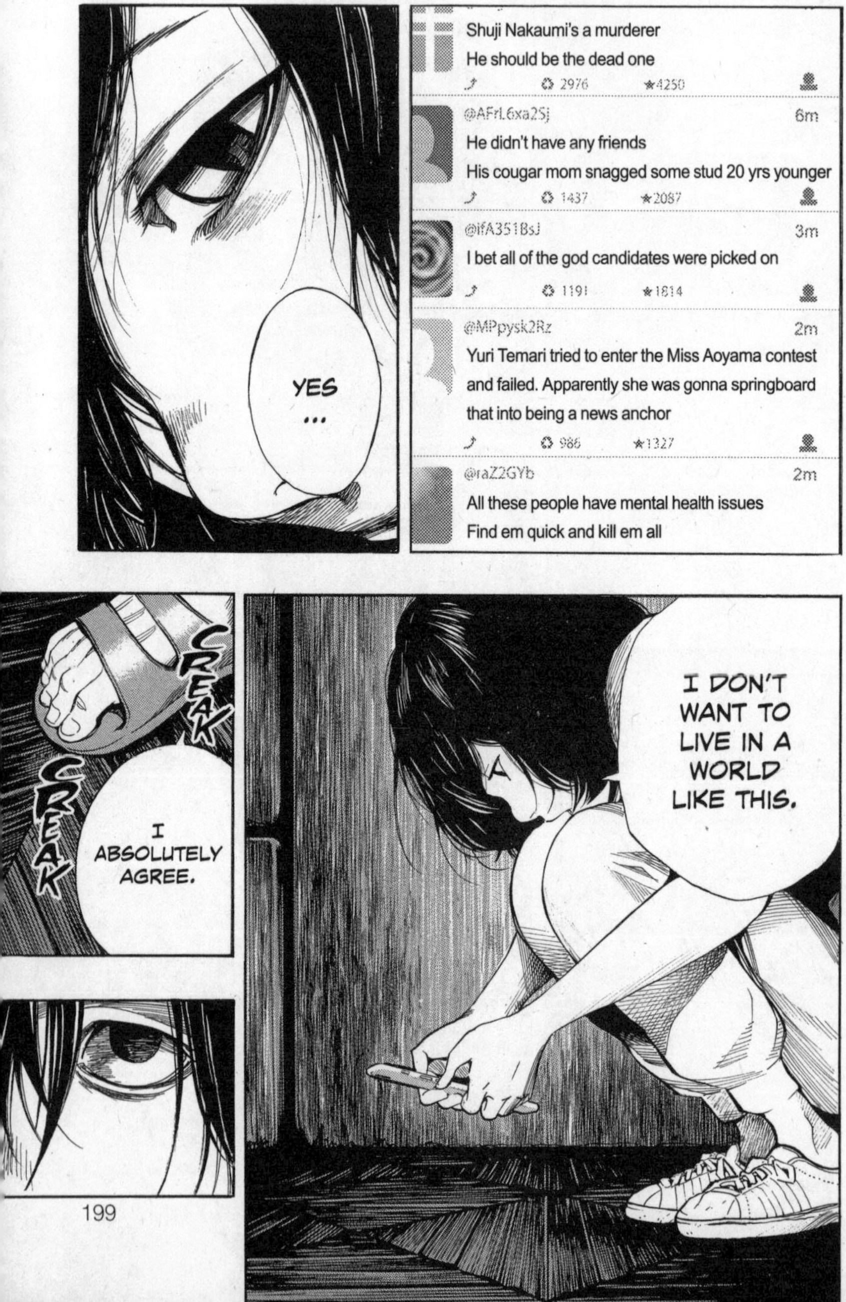
Shuji Nakaumi's a murderer
He should be the dead one
2976 ★4250
@AFrL6xa2Sj 6m
He didn't have any friends
His cougar mom snagged some stud 20 yrs younger
1437 ★2087
@ifA351BsJ 3m
I bet all of the god candidates were picked on
1191 ★1814
@MPpysk2Rz 2m
Yuri Temari tried to enter the Miss Aoyama contest and failed. Apparently she was gonna springboard that into being a news anchor
986 ★1327
@raZ2GYb 2m
All these people have mental health issues
Find em quick and kill em all
YES ...
I DON'T WANT TO LIVE IN A WORLD LIKE THIS.
CREAK
CREAK
I ABSOLUTELY AGREE.

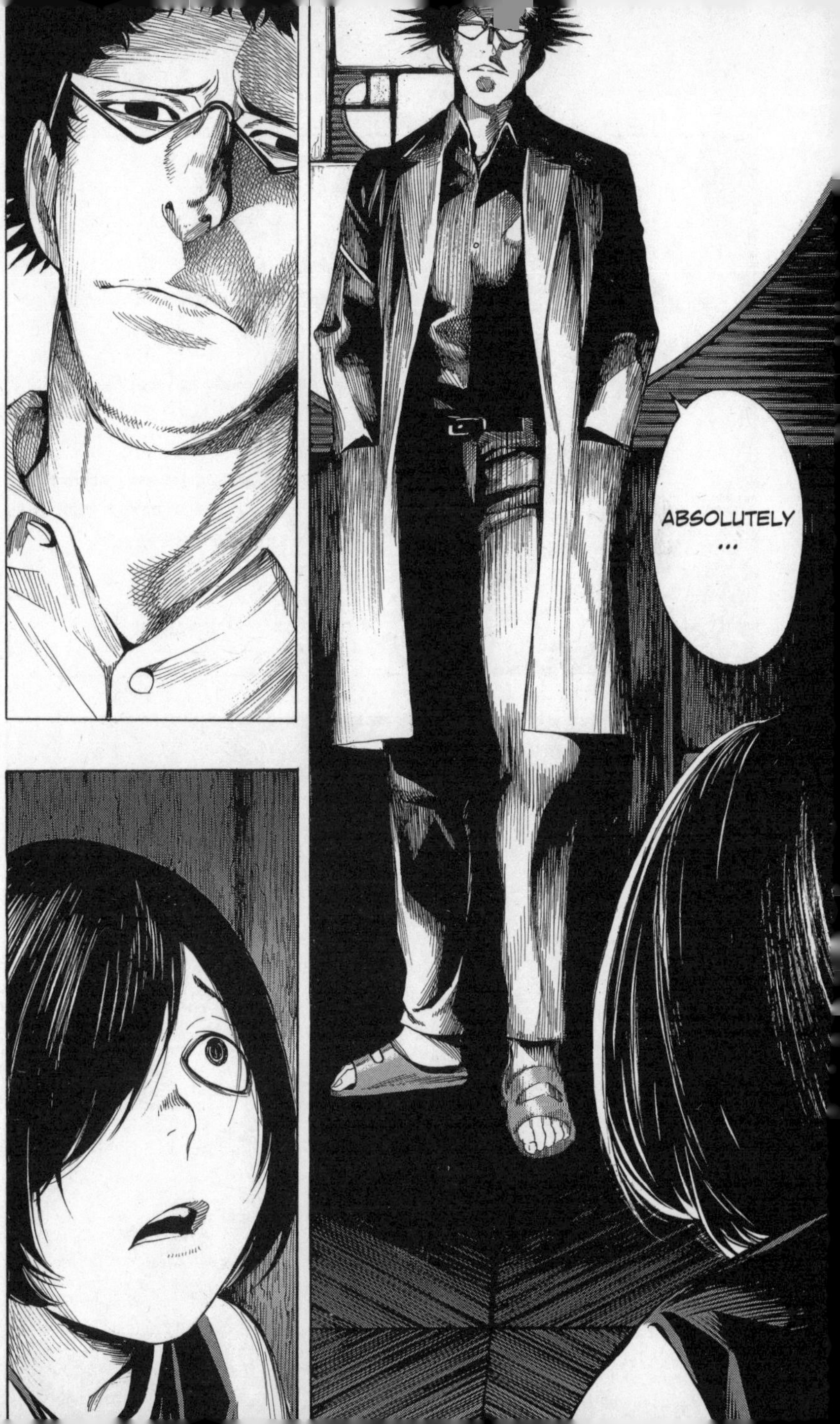
ABSOLUTELY ...

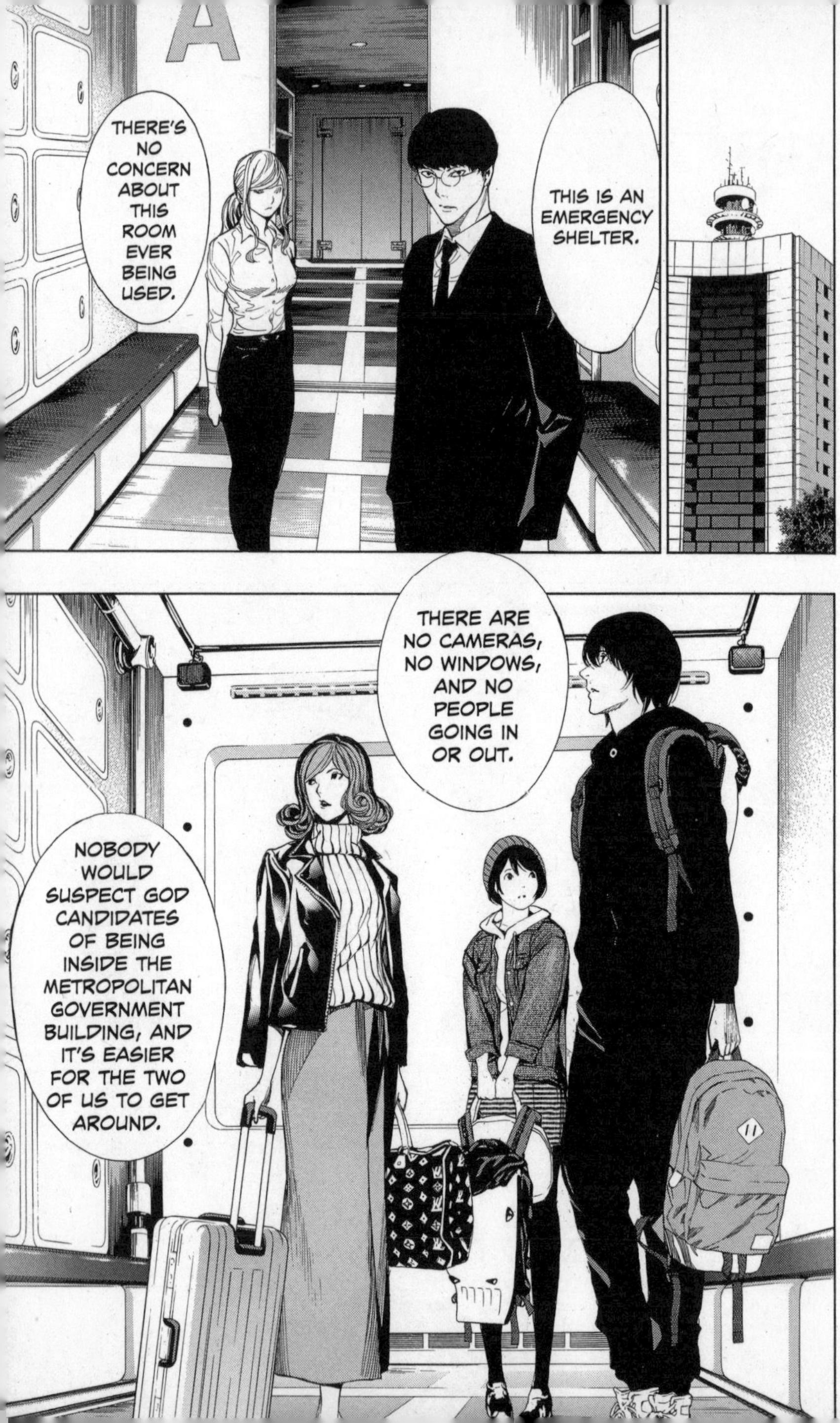
THIS IS AN EMERGENCY SHELTER.
THERE'S NO CONCERN ABOUT THIS ROOM EVER BEING USED.
THERE ARE NO CAMERAS, NO WINDOWS, AND NO PEOPLE GOING IN OR OUT.
NOBODY WOULD SUSPECT GOD CANDIDATES OF BEING INSIDE THE METROPOLITAN GOVERNMENT BUILDING, AND IT'S EASIER FOR THE TWO OF US TO GET AROUND.

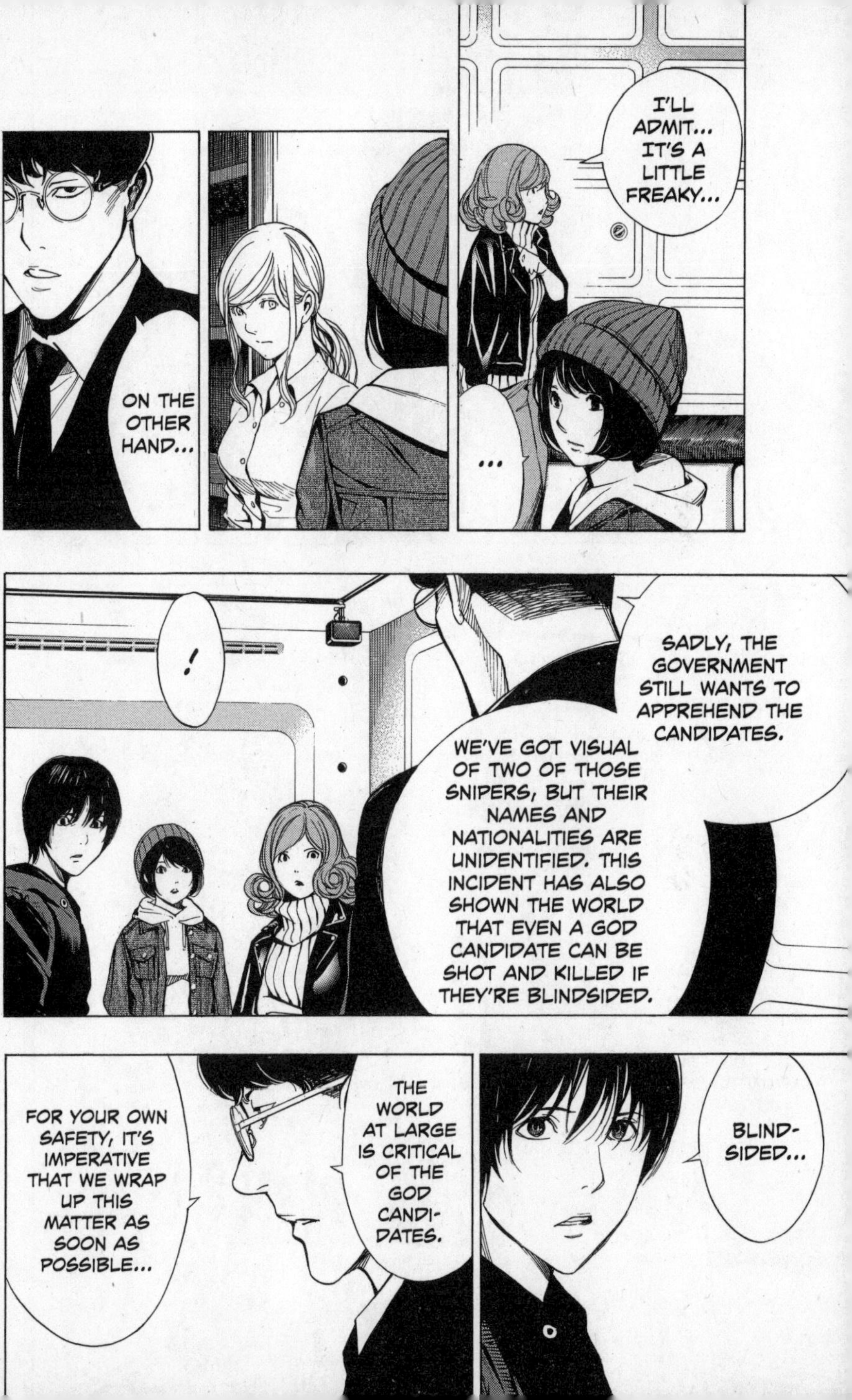
I'LL ADMIT... IT'S A LITTLE FREAKY...
...
ON THE OTHER HAND...
SADLY, THE GOVERNMENT STILL WANTS TO APPREHEND THE CANDIDATES.
WE'VE GOT VISUAL OF TWO OF THOSE SNIPERS, BUT THEIR NAMES AND NATIONALITIES ARE UNIDENTIFIED. THIS INCIDENT HAS ALSO SHOWN THE WORLD THAT EVEN A GOD CANDIDATE CAN BE SHOT AND KILLED IF THEY'RE BLINDSIDED.
!
BLIND-SIDED...
THE WORLD AT LARGE IS CRITICAL OF THE GOD CANDI-DATES.
FOR YOUR OWN SAFETY, IT'S IMPERATIVE THAT WE WRAP UP THIS MATTER AS SOON AS POSSIBLE...

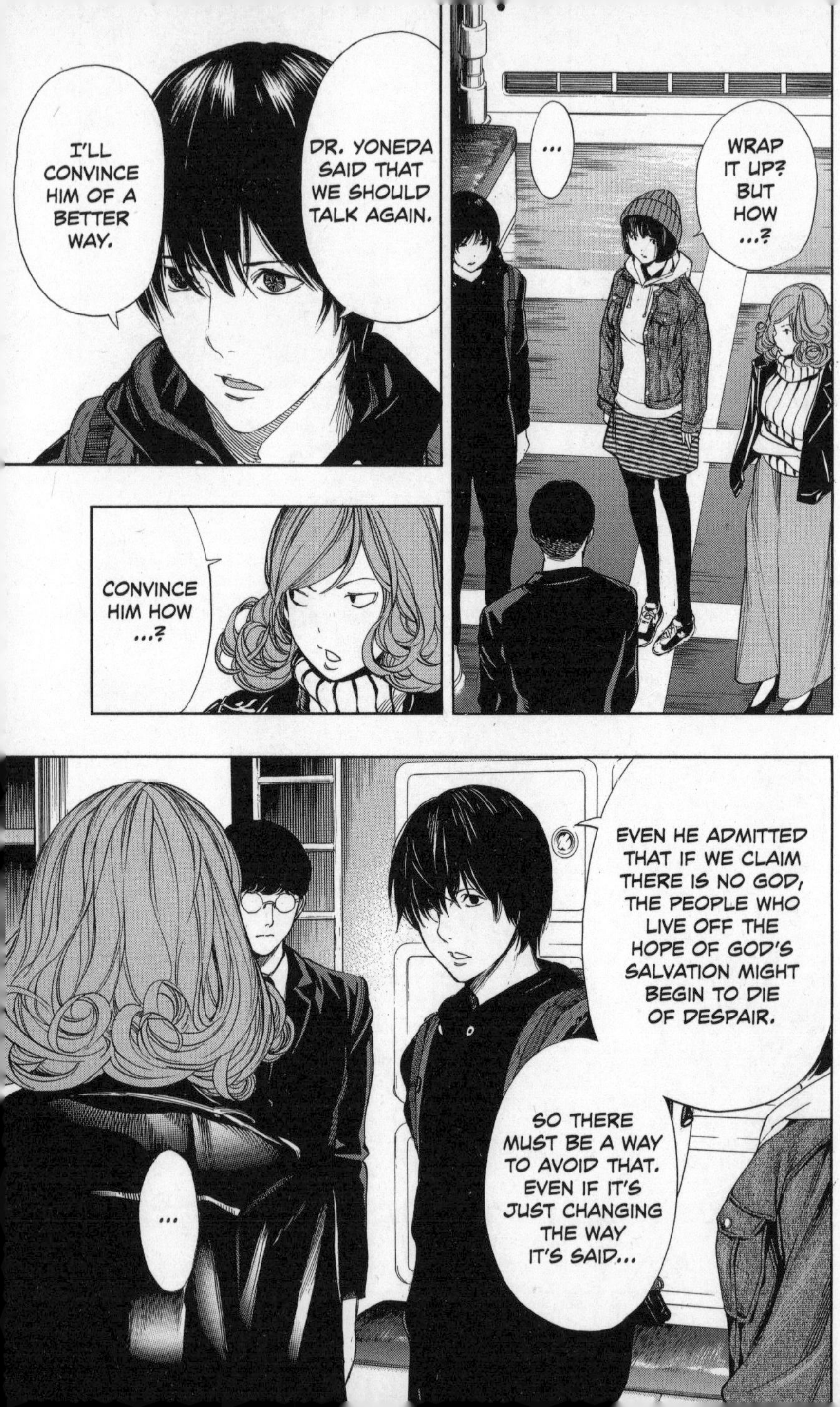
WRAP IT UP? BUT HOW ...?
...
DR. YONEDA SAID THAT WE SHOULD TALK AGAIN.
I'LL CONVINCE HIM OF A BETTER WAY.
CONVINCE HIM HOW ...?
EVEN HE ADMITTED THAT IF WE CLAIM THERE IS NO GOD, THE PEOPLE WHO LIVE OFF THE HOPE OF GOD'S SALVATION MIGHT BEGIN TO DIE OF DESPAIR.
SO THERE MUST BE A WAY TO AVOID THAT. EVEN IF IT'S JUST CHANGING THE WAY IT'S SAID...
...

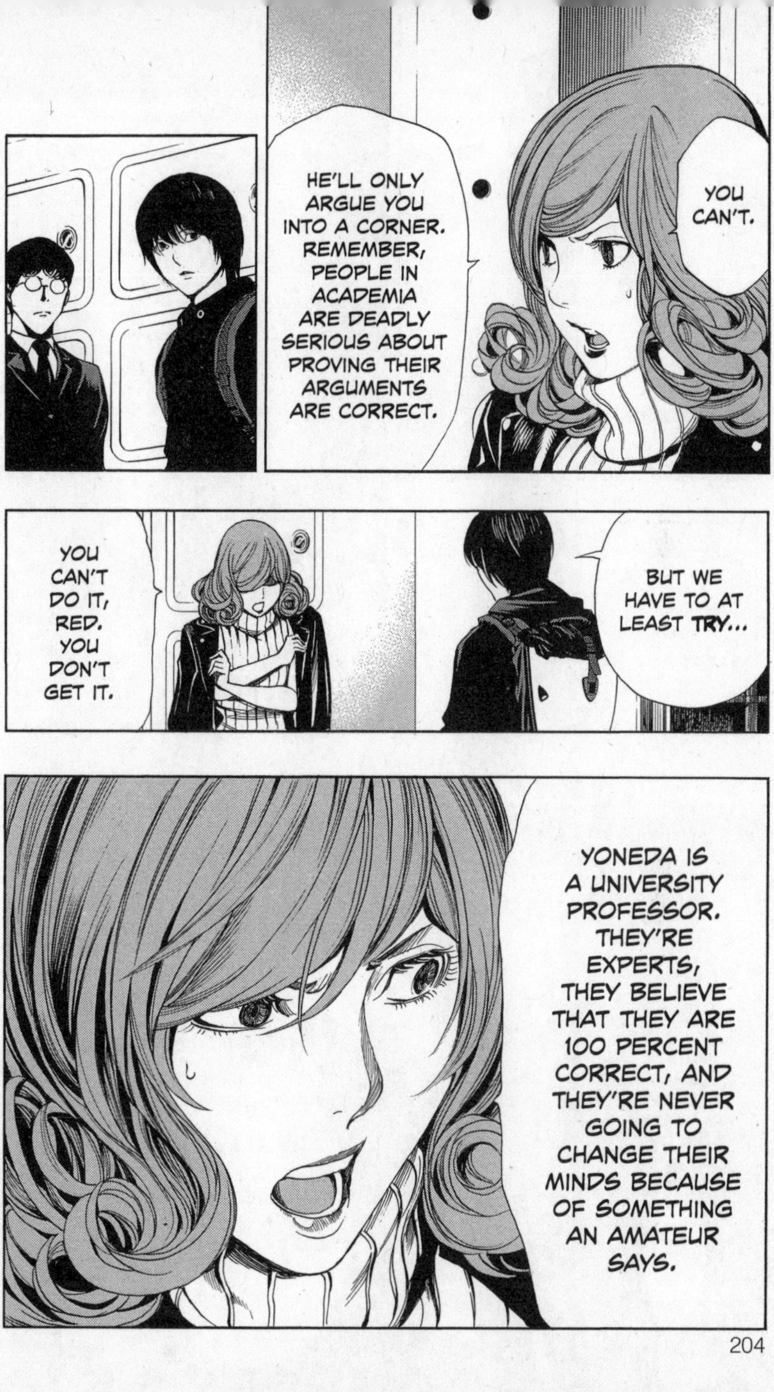
YOU CAN'T.
HE'LL ONLY ARGUE YOU INTO A CORNER. REMEMBER, PEOPLE IN ACADEMIA ARE DEADLY SERIOUS ABOUT PROVING THEIR ARGUMENTS ARE CORRECT.
BUT WE HAVE TO AT LEAST **TRY**...
YOU CAN'T DO IT, RED. YOU DON'T GET IT.
YONEDA IS A UNIVERSITY PROFESSOR. THEY'RE EXPERTS, THEY BELIEVE THAT THEY ARE 100 PERCENT CORRECT, AND THEY'RE NEVER GOING TO CHANGE THEIR MINDS BECAUSE OF SOMETHING AN AMATEUR SAYS.

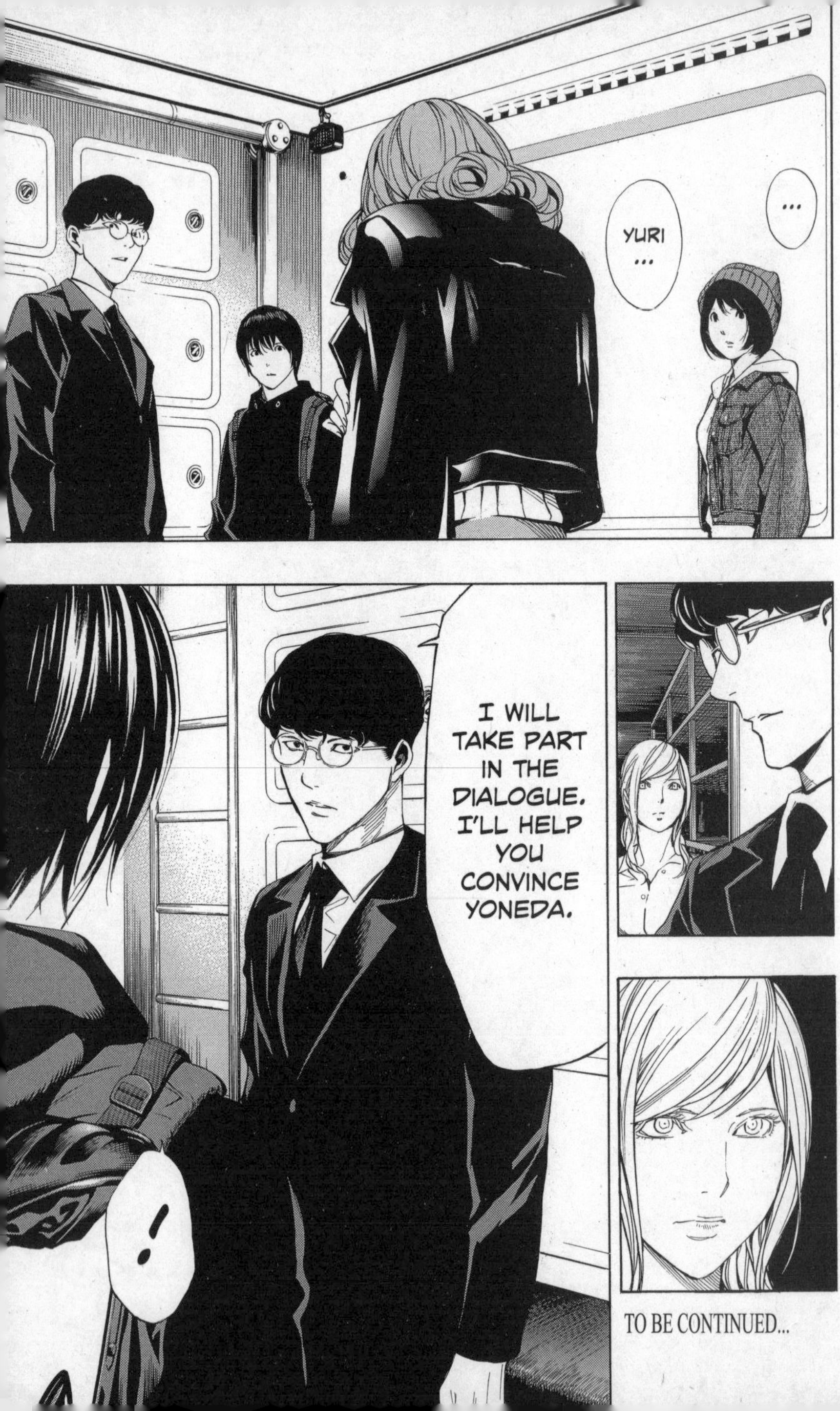
...
YURI ...
I WILL TAKE PART IN THE DIALOGUE. I'LL HELP YOU CONVINCE YONEDA.
!
TO BE CONTINUED...

T s u g u mi **Oh** b **a**

Born in Tokyo, Tsugumi Ohba is the author
of the hit series *Death Note* and *Bakuman*.

Ta **k** e s **h** i Oba **ta**

Takeshi Obata was born in 1969 in Niigata,
Japan, and first achieved international
recognition as the artist of the wildly popular
Shonen Jump title *Hikaru no Go*, which won the
2003 Tezuka Osamu Cultural Prize: Shinsei
"New Hope" Award and the 2000 Shogakukan
Manga Award. He went on to illustrate the smash
hit *Death Note* as well as the hugely successful
manga *Bakuman*. and *All You Need Is Kill*.

PLATINVM END

VOLUME 11
SHONEN JUMP Manga Edition

STORY **Tsugumi Ohba**

ART **Takeshi Obata**

TRANSLATION Stephen Paul
TOUCH-UP ART & LETTERING James Gaubatz
DESIGN Shawn Carrico
EDITOR Alexis Kirsch

ORIGINAL COVER DESIGN Narumi Noriko

Printed in the U.S.A.

Published by VIZ Media, LLC
P.O. Box 77010
San Francisco, CA 94107

10 9 8 7 6 5 4 3 2 1
First printing, April 2020

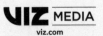

viz.com

shonenjump.com

YOU'RE READING THE **WRONG WAY!**

PLATINUM END reads from right to left, starting in the upper-right corner. Japanese is read from right to left, meaning that action, sound effects and word-balloon order are completely reversed from English order.

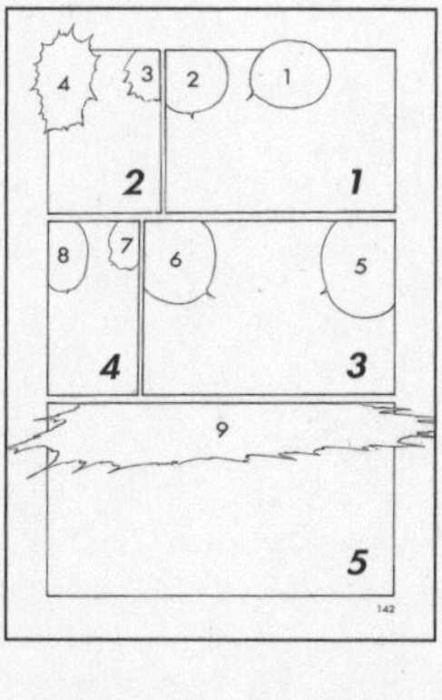
1
2
3
4
1
2
5
6
7
8
3
4
9
5
142

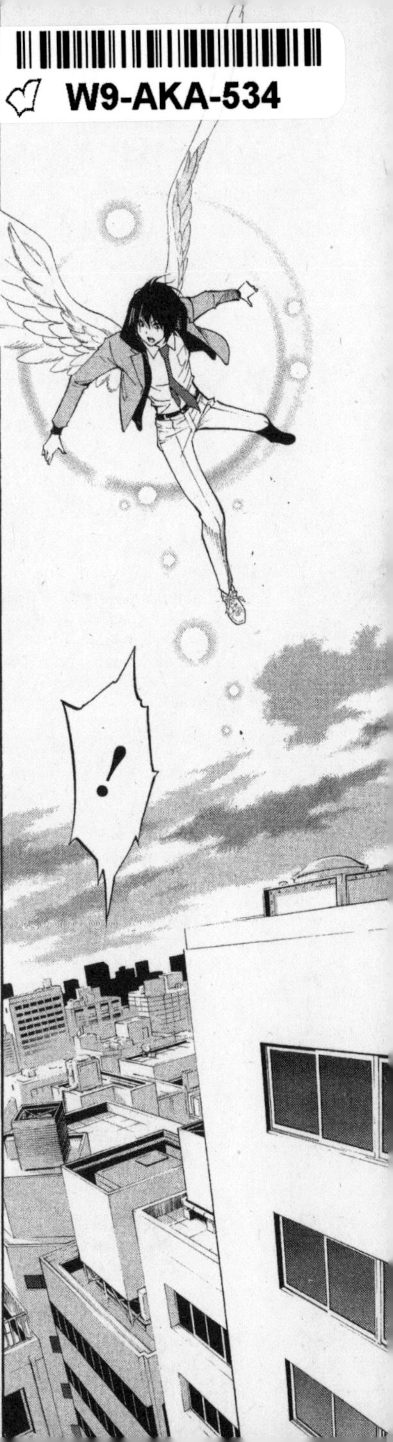
!